2010年同等学力人员申请硕士学位
英语水平全国统一考试

Paper One 试卷一（90 minutes）

Part I Dialogue Communication（10 minutes, 10 points）

Section A Dialogue Completion

Directions: *In this section, you will read 5 short incomplete dialogues between two speakers, each followed by 4 choices marked A, B, C and D. Choose the answer that best suits the situation to complete the dialogue. Then mark the corresponding letter with a single bar across the square brackets on your machine-scoring* **Answer Sheet.**

1. A: Can you take over for me here for a little while? I have a friend coming to see me.
   B: I'd like to, but _____. Ask Peter, he is not so occupied at this moment.
   A. how can I do it   B. that's alright
   C. I have my hands full   D. that's impossible

2. A: To get an outside line, just dial 0 and the phone number. Or we can place a call for you, if you want.
   B: No, thanks a lot. _____
   A. Just put me through.   B. I'll try it myself.
   C. I'd rather not.   D. I'll appreciate your help.

3. A: Now, it's just work, work, work. I work hard all day, every day.
   B: Oh, come on. _____ You're making a good salary now.
   A. Don't complain.   B. Sorry to hear about it.
   C. Anything I can do for you?   D. What's your plan?

4. A: Pamela, can you come to a meeting on Friday?
   B: _____ Let me check my schedule. When are you having it?
   A. No big deal.   B. I'm not sure.
   C. Can I?   D. Sure thing!

5. A: I'm really getting fed up with the salespersons who keep calling.
   B: _____
   A. I hope it's nothing serious.   B. They are so stupid!
   C. So am I. It's so annoying.   D. You are right. Forget it.

Section B Dialogue Comprehension

Directions: *In this section, you will read 5 short conversations between a man and a woman. At the end of each conversation there is a question followed by 4 choices marked A, B, C and D. Choose the best answer to the question from the 4 choices by marking the corresponding letter with a single bar across the square brackets on your machine-scoring **Answer Sheet**.*

6. Man: I've figured it all out. It looks like it will take us about 5 hours to drive from here to Chicago.

   Woman: It'd be more relaxing to take the train. But I guess we should watch our expenses.

   Question: What does the woman imply?

   A. She likes to drive when she travels.

   B. She doesn't want to go to Chicago.

   C. She doesn't know the cost of the train trip.

   D. It's cheaper to go to Chicago by car.

7. Man: How about the examination last week?

   Woman: If I'd got more time, I could have made it.

   Question: What does the woman imply?

   A. She was asked to take another examination.

   B. She failed the examination last week.

   C. She did quite well in the examination.

   D. She didn't take the examination last week.

8. Man: Harvard or the State University, have you decided yet?

   Woman: Well, I'd rather be a big fish in a small pond.

   Question: Which university is the woman likely to choose?

   A. The State University. B. Harvard.

   C. Neither. D. She hasn't decided yet.

9. Man: I've just found a great location to open a new shop.

   Woman: But you haven't researched the market. Don't you think this is putting the cart before the horse?

   Question: What does the woman mean?

   A. The man shouldn't make the decision so quickly.

   B. It's too risky to choose such a location.

   C. The man is doing things in the wrong order.

   D. It's possible for him to make a better choice.

10. Woman: My results are a bit flattering because I've had quite a lot of luck.

    Man: Nonsense, you're head and shoulders above the others in your group.

    Question: What does the man think is the reason for the woman's success?

    A. She's really lucky. B. She's far better than the others.

    C. She's got the others' support. D. She's been working hard.

Part II Vocabulary (20 minutes, 10 points)

Section A

Directions: *In this section, there are 10 sentences, each with one word or phrase underlined. Choose the one from the 4 choices marked A, B, C and D that best keeps the meaning of the sentence. Then mark the corresponding letter with a single bar across the square brackets on your machine-scoring* **Answer Sheet**.

11. Betty was offended because she felt that her friends had ignored her purposefully at the party.
    A. desperately   B. definitely   C. deliberately   D. decisively

12. There has been enough playing around, so let's get down to business.
    A. make a deal   B. begin our work
    C. reach an agreement   D. change our plan

13. How is it possible for our human body to convert yesterday's lunch into today's muscle?
    A. alter   B. develop   C. modify   D. turn

14. It is important for families to observe their traditions even as their children get older.
    A. notice   B. watch   C. follow   D. celebrate

15. It is difficult to comprehend, but everything you have ever seen, smelt, heard or felt is merely your brain's interpretation of incoming stimuli.
    A. explanation   B. evaluation
    C. recognition   D. interruption

16. Life is more important than the pressures and stresses that we place on ourselves over work and other commitments.
    A. appointments   B. arrangements
    C. obligations   D. devotions

17. If you continue to indulge in computer games like this, your future will be at stake.
    A. in danger   B. without question   C. on guard   D. at large

18. Romantic novels, as opposed to realistic ones, tend to present idealized versions of life, often with a happy ending.
    A. in contrast to   B. in regard to   C. in terms of   D. in light of

19. Most people would agree that, although our age far surpasses all previous ages in knowledge, there has been no correlative increase in wisdom.
    A. improves   B. precedes   C. imposes   D. exceeds

20. Many students today display a disturbing willingness to choose institutions and careers on the basis of earning potential.
    A. offensive   B. depressive   C. troublesome   D. tiresome

Section B

Directions: *In this section, there are 10 incomplete sentences. For each sentence there are 4 choices* marked A, B, C and D. Choose the one that best completes the sentence. Then mark the corresponding letter with a single bar across the square brackets on your machine-scoring **Answer Sheet**.

21. My oldest son had just finished an _____ holiday stay prior to moving to a new state, a new job, and the next chapter in his life.
    A. enlarged　　　B. expanded　　　C. extended　　　D. increased

22. Blacks and American Indians _____ less than 10% of students in the top 30 business schools, while they are about 28% of the U.S. population.
    A. make up　　　B. take up　　　C. reach out　　　D. turn out

23. With demand continuing to rise in _____ economies such as China and India, energy traders believe that oil futures are a good bet.
    A. employing　　　B. emerging　　　C. embracing　　　D. emitting

24. Laws and regulations in each country have to be made _____ the constitution of the country.
    A. in honor of　　　B. in memory of　　　C. in return for　　　D. in line with

25. The jury's _____ was that the accused was guilty.
    A. verdict　　　B. sentence　　　C. trial　　　D. debate

26. In English learning, a _____ cycle occurs when a student makes more errors after being scolded.
    A. vertical　　　B. vicious　　　C. vivid　　　D. vigorous

27. Isn't it _____ when you learn something you've never known before?
    A. cool　　　B. crazy　　　C. cold　　　D. cute

28. There are several factors _____ the rapid growth of sales promotion, particularly in consumer markets.
    A. resorting to　　　B. appealing to　　　C. applying to　　　D. contributing to

29. The Internet has been developing at a speed _____ people's expectations in the past two decades.
    A. over　　　B. of　　　C. under　　　D. beyond

30. It is obvious that the sports games are no longer amateur affairs; they have become professionally _____.
    A. laid off　　　B. laid out　　　C. put off　　　D. put out

Part III　Reading Comprehension (45 minutes, 30 points)

Directions: There are 5 passages in this part. Each passage is followed by 6 questions or unfinished statements. For each of them there are 4 choices marked A, B, C and D. Choose the best one and mark the corresponding letter with a single bar across the square brackets on your machine-scoring **Answer Sheet**.

Passage One

Loneliness has been linked to depression and other health problems. Now, a study says it can also spread. A friend of a lonely person was 52% more likely to develop feelings of loneliness. And a friend of that friend was 25% more likely to do the same.

Earlier findings showed that happiness, fatness and the ability to stop smoking can also grow like infections within social groups. The findings all come from a major health study in the American town of Framingham, Massachusetts.

The study began in 1948 to investigate the causes of heart disease. Since then, more tests have been added, including measures of loneliness and depression.

The new findings involved more than 5,000 people in the second generation of the Framingham Heart Study. The researchers examined friendship histories and reports of loneliness. The results established a pattern that spread as people reported fewer close friends.

For example, loneliness can affect relationships between next-door neighbors. The loneliness spreads as neighbors who were close friends now spend less time together. The study also found that loneliness spreads more easily among women than men.

Researchers from the University of Chicago, Harvard and the University of California, San Diego, did the study. The findings appeared last month in the *Journal of Personality and Social Psychology*.

The average person is said to experience feelings of loneliness about 48 days a year. The study found that having a lonely friend can add about 17 days. But every additional friend can decrease loneliness by about 5%, or two and a half days.

Lonely people become less and less trusting of others. This makes it more and more difficult for them to make friends—and more likely that society will reject them.

John Cacioppo at the University of Chicago led the study. He says it is important to recognize and deal with loneliness. He says people who have been pushed to the edges of society should receive help to repair their social networks.

The aim should be to aggressively create what he calls a "protective barrier" against loneliness. This barrier, he says, can keep the whole network from coming apart.

31. Besides loneliness, which of the following can also spread among people?

    A. Friendship.   B. Happiness.   C. Depression.   D. Smoking.

32. The Framingham Heart Study starting from 1948 _____.

    A. expanded its research topics

    B. involved 5,000 patients of depression

    C. identified loneliness as one key factor for heart disease

    D. examined the relationship between loneliness and depression

33. Which of the following is true about the spread of loneliness?

    A. It leads to a gradual loss of friends.

    B. It is a common phenomenon among women.

    C. It is often found in the neighborhood.

    D. It ruins the relationships between close friends.

34. Having a lonely friend, you are more likely to _____.
    A. strengthen your friendship   B. develop new friendship
    C. increase the sense of loneliness   D. reduce the sense of loneliness

35. According to John Cacioppo at the University of Chicago, loneliness can _____.
    A. result in aggressiveness   B. cause people to be overprotective
    C. infect social networks   D. push people to the verge of poverty

36. What is the main idea of the passage?
    A. Loneliness can spread.   B. Loneliness is linked to depression.
    C. Lonely people tend to grow fat.   D. Lonely people need more friends.

Passage Two

California has a new program called the Digital Textbook Initiative. "Starting this fall with high school math and science, we will be the first state in the nation to provide schools with a state-approved list of digital textbooks." That was Governor Arnold Schwarzenegger in June, talking about his effort to get schools to use materials available free online. He listed reasons why he thinks digital textbooks make sense.

California approves traditional textbooks in six-year cycles. Digital ones can offer the latest information. They lighten the load of school bags. They save paper and trees, and make learning more fun and interactive. And above all, he said, they help schools with their finances.

The state has had to make severe cuts in school spending because of deep financial problems. More than six million students attend California public schools.

Earlier this year, California invited content developers to offer digital math and science materials for high schools. These had to meet at least 90% of the state's learning requirements. Specially trained teachers examined 16 textbooks and approved ten of them.

Six of the ten were published by the CK12 Foundation, a nonprofit group that had been developing digital science and math books for about two years. The foundation paid teachers and other education professionals to write and edit them. The money came from a group financed by the Khosla family.

California cannot require schools to use the digital textbooks. Individual school districts will have to decide for themselves.

Susan Martimo, a California Department of Education official, says she does not expect widespread use right away. Her best guess is that some schools with a lot of technology will be the first to use them, but only in addition to their traditional books.

School administrators point out that the texts may be free online, but students need a way to access them. Not everyone has a computer or electronic reader. Schools could print out copies, but that would not help the environment. Also, there is the cost to train teachers to use digital textbooks effectively.

37. The Digital Textbook Initiative _____.
    A. will probably take effect in six years   B. covers all the high school subjects
    C. has been approved by all states   D. is advocated by California state governor

38. The main reason for promoting digital textbooks is to _____.
    A. help save money   B. benefit the environment
    C. provide interesting materials D. reduce students' heavy burden

39. The digital textbooks were approved by _____.
    A. trained teachers   B. content developers
    C. Khosla family   D. CK12 Foundation

40. What is true of CK12 Foundation?
    A. It produced 16 digital textbooks.
    B. It paid teachers to write digital textbooks.
    C. It is financed by California state government.
    D. It makes money through developing digital textbooks.

41. According to Susan Martimo, digital textbooks _____.
    A. are not likely to have a widespread use
    B. will soon replace traditional ones
    C. will first be adopted by well-equipped schools
    D. are certain to be approved by school districts

42. It can be inferred from the last paragraph that _____.
    A. schools are reluctant to print out copies
    B. the use of digital textbooks is not really free
    C. students need to pay for computers
    D. trained teachers to use the textbooks is not efficient

Passage Three

Doctors in Britain are warning of an obesity time bomb, when children who are already overweight grow up. So, what should we do? Exercise more? Eat less? Or both? The government feels it has to take responsibility for this expanding problem.

The cheerful Mr. Pickwick, the hero of the novel by Charles Dickens, is seen in illustrations as someone who is plump(胖乎乎的)—and happy. In 18th century paintings beauty is equated with rounded bodies and soft curves. But nowadays being overweight is seen as indicating neither a cheerful character nor beauty but an increased risk of heart disease and stroke.

So what do you do? Diet? Not according to England's chief medical officer, Sir Liam Donaldson. He says that physical activity is the key for reducing the risks of obesity, cancer and heart disease. And the Health Secretary John Reid even said that being inactive is as serious a risk factor in heart disease as smoking.

So, having bought some cross trainers, how much exercise should you do? According to Sir Liam Donaldson, at least 30 minutes of moderate activity five days a week. Is going to the gym the answer? Luckily for those who find treadmills(跑步机) tedious, the Health Development Agency believes that physical activity that fits into people's lives may be more effective. They suggest taking the stairs rather than the lift, walking up escalators, playing active games with your children, dancing or gardening. And according to a sports psychologist, Professor Biddle, gyms "are not making the nation fit", and may even cause harm.

There's new scientific evidence that too much exercise may actually be bad for you. Scientists at the University of Ulster have found that unaccustomed exercise releases dangerous free radicals that can adversely affect normal function in unfit people. The only people who should push their bodies to that level of exercise on a regular basis are trained athletes.

So, should we forget about gyms and follow some experts' advice to increase exercise in our daily life? After all, getting off the bus a stop early and walking the rest of the way can't do any harm! One final thought. How come past generations lacked gym facilities but were leaner and fitter than people today?

43. This passage is mainly about _____.
   A. how to keep fit and avoid fatness
   B. increasing risks for overweight people
   C. the dangers of exercise in the gym
   D. the benefit of a balanced diet

44. What does "this expanding problem" (Para. 1) refer to?
   A. The slow growing up of overweight children.
   B. The obesity time bomb warned of by doctors.
   C. Too little exercise and too much diet.
   D. Neglect of the health issue by the government.

45. Why does the author mention Mr. Pickwick in Charles Dickens' novel?
   A. He was portrayed in an 18th century painting.
   B. He is the hero of a world famous novel.
   C. He suffered from heart disease and stroke.
   D. He is the image of being plump and happy.

46. According to Sir Liam Donaldson, what is the best way to avoid obesity?
   A. Being on diet.
   B. Giving up smoking.
   C. Being as inactive as possible.
   D. Doing physical activities.

47. Which of the following is NOT recommended by the Health Development Agency?
   A. Walking up escalators, dancing or gardening.
   B. Going to the gym to walk on treadmills.
   C. Taking the stairs rather than the lift.
   D. Playing active games with your children.

48. It can be inferred from the last paragraph that _____.
   A. too much exercise may actually be bad for health
   B. experts' advice cannot be always followed
   C. past generations longed for gym facilities we have today
   D. moderate daily-life exercise can make us leaner and fitter

Passage Four

A metaphor is a poetic device that deals with comparison. It compares similar qualities of two dissimilar objects. With a simple metaphor, one object becomes the other: Love is a rose. Although this does not sound like a particularly rich image, a metaphor can communicate so much about a particular image that poets use them more than any other type of figurative language. The reason for this is that poets compose their poetry to express what they are experiencing emotionally at that moment. Consequently, what the poet imagines love to be may or may not be our perception of love. Therefore, the poet's job is to enable us to experience it, to feel it the same way as the poet does.

Let's analyze this remarkably unsophisticated metaphor concerning love and the rose to see what it offers. Because the poet uses a comparison with a rose, first we must examine the characteristics of that flower. A rose is spectacular in its beauty, its petals(花瓣) are nicely soft, and its smell is pleasing. It's possible to say that a rose is actually a feast to the senses of sight, touch, and smell. The rose's appearance seems to border on perfection, each petal seemingly symmetrical in form. Isn't this the way one's love should be? A loved one should be a delight to one's senses and seem perfect. However, there is another dimension added to the comparison by using a rose. Roses have thorns. The poet wants to convey the idea that roses can be pricky. So can love, the metaphor tells us. When one reaches out with absolute trust to touch the object of his or her affection, ouch, a thorn can cause great harm! "Be careful," the metaphor warns: Love is a feast to the senses, but it can overwhelm us, and it can also hurt us and cause acute suffering. This is the poet's perception of love—an admonition(劝诫). What is the point? Just this: It took almost 14 sentences to clarify what a simple metaphor communicates in only four words! That is the artistry and the joy of the simple metaphor.

49. According to the passage, what is a metaphor?

　　A. A comparison between two different objects with similar features.

　　B. A contrast between two different things to create a vivid image.

　　C. A description of two similar objects in a poetic way.

　　D. A literary device specially employed in poetry writing.

50. The main idea of this passage is that _____.

　　A. rose is a good image in poetry　　B. love is sweet and pleasing

　　C. metaphor is ambiguous　　D. metaphor is a great poetic device

51. It can be inferred from the passage that a metaphor is _____.

　　A. difficult to understand　　B. rich in meaning

　　C. not precise enough　　D. like a flower

52. As is meant by the author, thorns of a rose _____.

　　A. protect the rose from harm

　　B. symbolize reduced love

　　C. add a new element to the image of love

　　D. represent objects of one's affection

53. The meaning of the love-is-a-rose metaphor is that _____.

    A. love is a true joy

    B. true love comes once in a lifetime

    C. love does not last long

    D. love is both good and bad experiences

54. According to the passage, poetry is intended to _____.

    A. release anger   B. entertain the readers

    C. express poets' ideas   D. reward the senses

Passage Five

Some 23 million additional U.S. residents are expected to become more regular users of the U.S. health care system in the next several years, thanks to the passage of health care reform. Digitizing medical data has been promoted as one way to help the already burdened system manage the surge in patients. But putting people's health information in databases and online is going to do more than simply reduce redundancies. It is already shifting the very way we seek and receive health care.

"The social dynamics of care are changing," says John Gomez, vice president of Eclipsys, a medical information technology company. Most patients might not yet be willing to share their latest CT scan images over Facebook, he notes, but many parents post their babies' ultrasound images, and countless patients nowadays use social networking sites to share information about conditions, treatments and doctors.

With greater access to individualized health information—whether that is through a formal electronic medical record, a self-created personal health record or a quick instant-messaging session with a physician—the traditional roles of doctors and patients are undergoing a rapid transition.

"For as long as we've known, health care has been 'I go to the physician, and they tell me what to do, and I do it,'" says Nitu Kashyap, a physician and research fellow at the Yale Center for Medical Informatics. Soon more patients will be arriving at a hospital or doctor's office having reviewed their own record, latest test results and recommended articles about their health concerns. And even more individuals will be able to skip that visit altogether, instead sending a text message or e-mail to their care provider or consulting a personal health record or smart-phone application to answer their questions.

These changes will be strengthened by the nationwide shift to electronic medical records, which has already begun. Although the majority of U.S. hospitals and doctors' offices are still struggling to start the change over, many patients already have electronic medical records—and some even have partial access to them. The My Chart program, in use at Cleveland Clinic, the University of Texas Southwestern Medical Center at Dallas and other facilities, is a Web portal(门户) through which patients can see basic medical information as well as some test results.

Medical data is getting a new digital life, and it is jump-starting a "fundamental change in how care is provided," Gomez says.

55. Which of the following is the best title for this passage?

    A. The Future of Your Medical Data

B. Challenges Against Doctors and Hospitals

C. Benefits of the U.S. Health Care Reform

D. How to Access and Share Your Health Information

56. Putting patient information in databases and online _____.

    A. enables more Americans to join the health care system

    B. contributes to the passage of health care reform

    C. increases the burden of the U.S. health care system

    D. changes how people seek and receive health care

57. According to John Gomez, many patients use social networking sites to _____.

    A. change their social interactions

    B. post their latest CT scan images

    C. share information about their health care

    D. show their babies' recent pictures

58. Which of the following is NOT changing the traditional roles of doctors and patients?

    A. A formal electronic medical record.

    B. An easier access to information online.

    C. A self-created personal health record.

    D. A quick instant-messaging session with a doctor.

59. According to Nitu Kashyap, more patients in the future will _____.

    A. refuse to follow their doctors' advice

    B. be more dependent on their doctors

    C. leave out their visit to doctors' offices and hospitals

    D. have their health conditions examined through e-mail

60. It is stated in the passage that _____.

    A. nationwide digitalization of medical data will begin soon

    B. most of U.S. hospitals and doctors are against the shift

    C. patients are worried about the security of their health information

    D. patients are starting to make use of their electronic medical records

Parts IV Cloze (15 minutes, 15 points)

Directions: *In this part, there is a passage with 15 blanks. For each blank there are 4 choices marked A, B, C and D. Choose the best answer for each blank and mark the corresponding letter with a single bar across the square brackets on your machine-scoring **Answer Sheet**.*

Are you single but too busy to search for love? Then you need to try the latest dating phenomenon that is sweeping __61__ the UK—speed dating.

Speed dating __62__ men and women meeting in a room and finding out as much as they can about possible __63__ in three minutes. It's proving very __64__ with Britain's young people who find that they haven't got the time to meet that special one.

At a speed dating event you are given three minutes to talk, __65__, with a member of the opposite sex. Then a bell is __66__ and you move to another person and start chatting again. By the end of the evening you will have spoken with up to twenty men or women!

If, by the end of a conversation, you __67__ the person or would like to see them again, you write it __68__ on a card. Then, if the other person also fancies you, the organisers will contact you with their details.

But is three minutes long enough to make an impression and __69__ if you want to see someone again? Research suggests that __70__ can be felt within the first thirty seconds of meeting someone, and that is __71__ speed dating is all about, knowing quickly if you are going to like someone.

And what about romance? Is it possible to make a good __72__ in such a short time? __73__, people say you can't hurry love. However, Britain will soon have its first marriage from a speed date.

So, if you are on a __74__ to find Mr. or Miss Right, what have you got to lose? __75__, you still go home on your own. But at best, the person of your dreams could be just three minutes away.

61. A. off   B. across   C. over   D. through
62. A. requires   B. inquires   C. revolves   D. involves
63. A. partners   B. spouses   C. friends   D. counterparts
64. A. practical   B. popular   C. favorable   D. normal
65. A. all in one   B. one after one   C. one on one   D. one and all
66. A. knocked   B. shaken   C. swung   D. rung
67. A. attract   B. enjoy   C. chase   D. fancy
68. A. down   B. off   C. up   D. back
69. A. work on   B. work out   C. work at   D. work up
70. A. emotion   B. sentiment   C. chemistry   D. attachment
71. A. how   B. what   C. all   D. where
72. A. conclusion   B. reflection   C. guess   D. judgment
73. A. In all   B. After all   C. Of all   D. And all
74. A. tour   B. route   C. direction   D. mission
75. A. At last   B. At first   C. At worst   D. At end

Paper Two 试卷二 (60 minutes)

Part I Translation (30 minutes, 20 points)

Section A

Directions: *Translate the following passage into Chinese. Write your translation on the **Answer Sheet**.*

An ecosystem is a group of animals and plants living in a specific region and interacting with one another and with their physical environment. Ecosystems include physical and chemical components, such as soils, water, and nutrients that support the organisms living there. These organisms may range from large animals to microscopic bacteria. Ecosystems also can be thought of as the interactions among all organisms in a given area; for instance, one species may serve as food for another. People are part of the ecosystems where they live and work. Human activities can harm or destroy local ecosystems unless actions such as land development for housing or businesses are carefully planned to conserve and sustain the ecology of the area.

Section B

Directions: *Translate the following passage into English. Write your translation on the **Answer Sheet**.*

全球化作为一种新的经济和社会发展趋势,给中国带来了机遇,也带来了挑战。一方面,中国正成为世界制造业中心并在国际舞台上发挥着日益重要的作用;另一方面,我们也面临着如何在全球化进程中既要发展经济,又能传承优秀文化传统的问题。

Part II   Writing (30 minutes, 15 points)

Directions: *In this part, you are allowed 30 minutes to write a composition of no less than 150 words. Your composition should be based on the following two questions after you have read the story given in Chinese. Please remember to write your composition clearly on the **Composition Sheet**.*

1. What do you think about the story?
2. What do you learn from it?

第二稿

英国史学家卡莱尔经过多年的伏案,写成了《法国大革命史》的全部文稿。那时候没有电脑,一切都得用手来完成,而且难得有"备份"。卡莱尔写完后的第一件事,就是将它交给最信任的好友米尔去完善。

然而,就在第二天,手稿被米尔家的女佣当作废纸丢进了火炉!而且,更糟糕的是,为了保持书房的整洁,卡莱尔每写完一章,随手就把原来的笔记、手稿撕碎。可以想象卡莱尔当时的心情,但他很快就平静下来,反而安慰伤心的米尔:"没关系,就当我将作文交给老师批阅,老师说'这篇不行,重写一次吧,你可以写得更好!'"

卡莱尔再起炉灶,重写这部巨著。如今人们读到的《法国大革命史》,就是他的第二稿。这一稿的质量,无论在文字上还是在内涵上,都达到了卡莱尔写作生涯的巅峰。

2010年同等学力人员申请硕士学位英语水平全国统一考试

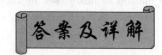

Paper One 试卷一

Part I Dialogue Communication

Section A

1. [正确答案] C

    [句子翻译] A:你能替我一会儿吗？我的朋友来看我了。

    B:我很乐意，但是我现在很忙。你可以问问彼得，他这会儿不是很忙。

    [考点剖析] A项和D项虽然表示拒绝，但不符合英语表达习惯；B项在逻辑上与题中的but相矛盾。

2. [正确答案] B

    [句子翻译] A:如果打外线，您可以先拨0，然后拨电话号码。或者如果您愿意的话，我们可以帮您拨打。

    B:不用了，谢谢。我可以自己来。

    [考点剖析] A项的意思是接受帮助，与题意不符；C、D项不符合英语中"拒绝"的表达习惯。

3. [正确答案] A

    [句子翻译] A:现在每天除了工作、工作还是工作。我每天都得努力工作一整天。

    B:少来了！不要抱怨了，你现在的薪水很不错。

    [考点剖析] B项是在听到他人不幸的消息时说的话；C项是为他人提供帮助的用语；D项与语境不相符。

4. [正确答案] B

    [句子翻译] A:帕梅拉，周五你能来参加聚会吗？

    B:我不太确定。我看看日程表吧。聚会是在什么时候？

    [考点剖析] A项"没什么大不了的"，不符合语境；C项不符合英文的表达习惯；D项的意思明显与原文相矛盾。

5. [正确答案] C

    [句子翻译] A:我真是受够了推销员一直打电话！

    B:我也是，太烦人了！

    [考点剖析] 只有C项是对说话人观点的赞同。

Section B

6. [正确答案] D

    [句子翻译] 男士:我已经都算过了，从这里开车去芝加哥大概需要5个小时。女士:坐火车

· 14 ·

应该会更轻松些。但是我认为我们还要考虑下费用。

[考点剖析] 由上下文转折可知,乘火车虽舒适,但他们也要考虑费用,由此可知驾车去芝加哥应该比较便宜。

7. [正确答案] B

   [句子翻译] 男士:上周的考试怎么样? 女士:如果时间再多些,我就能通过考试了。

   [考点剖析] 此题是对虚拟语气的考查,也就是实际的语义是相反的。所以,女士的意思是她并没有通过考试。

8. [正确答案] A

   [句子翻译] 男士:哈佛还是州立大学,你做好决定了吗? 女士:我宁愿做小池塘里的大鱼。

   [考点剖析] 女士的话就相当于"宁为鸡头不做凤尾"。解答本题需要了解这两所学校的差别。

9. [正确答案] C

   [句子翻译] 男士:我刚发现了一个开新店的好地方。女士:但是你还没有研究过市场。难道你不认为这是本末倒置吗?

   [考点剖析] put the cart before the horse 是"本末倒置"的意思,也就是说男士将问题的重心放偏了。

10. [正确答案] B

    [句子翻译] 女士:我的成绩有点超过我的想象,我只是有点运气罢了。男士:胡说,你已经在你们组中处于领先地位了。

    [考点剖析] head and shoulders above the others 是指"头和肩都超过其他人了",也就是"领先别人很多"的意思。

Part Ⅱ   Vocabulary

Section A

11. [正确答案] C

    [考点类型] 副词

    [考点剖析] 题干中的 purposefully 意为"故意地;蓄意地"。desperately"绝望地,拼命地"; definitely"明确地,一定地"; deliberately"故意地"; decisively"决然地,果断地"。

12. [正确答案] B

    [考点类型] 动词短语

    [考点剖析] 题干中的 get down to business 意为"开始做正事"。make a deal"达成交易"; begin our work"开始工作"; reach an agreement"达成协议"; change our plan"改变计划"。

13. [正确答案] D

    [考点类型] 动词

    [考点剖析] 题干中的 convert 意为"转变,转化"。alter"改变,更改"; develop"发展"; modify"修改,更改"; turn"使变成"。

14. [正确答案] C

    [考点类型] 动词

[考点剖析] 题干中的 observe 意为"遵守,遵循"。notice"注意";watch"注意";follow"遵循";celebrate"庆祝"。

15. [正确答案] A
    [考点类型] 名词
    [考点剖析] 题干中的 interpretation 意为"解释,说明"。explanation"解释";evaluation"估价,评价";recognition"认识,识别";interruption"中断,打断"。

16. [正确答案] C
    [考点类型] 名词
    [考点剖析] 题干中的 commitments 意为"承担的义务;不得不做的事情"。appointments"约会";arrangements"安排;约定";obligations"义务,责任";devotions"奉献,忠诚"。

17. [正确答案] A
    [考点类型] 介词短语
    [考点剖析] 题干中的 at stake 意为"处于危险中;在紧要关头"。in danger"在危险中";without question"毫无疑问";on guard"站岗;警惕";at large"在逃;整个地"。

18. [正确答案] A
    [考点类型] 介词短语
    [考点剖析] 题干中的 as opposed to 意为"相对于"。in contrast to"与……形成对照";in regard to"关于";in terms of"就……而言";in light of"按照,根据"。

19. [正确答案] D
    [考点类型] 动词
    [考点剖析] 题干中的 surpasses 意为"超过,优于"。improves"提高";precedes"走在……前面,先于";imposes"强迫,强加";exceeds"超过,超越"。

20. [正确答案] C
    [考点类型] 形容词
    [考点剖析] 题干中的 disturbing 意为"令人不安的"。offensive"讨厌的";depressive"郁闷的";troublesome"令人不安的";tiresome"令人生厌的"。

Section B

21. [正确答案] C
    [考点类型] 近义词辨析
    [考点剖析] enlarged"(物件尺寸)扩大的";expanded"(范围)扩张的";extended"(时空上)延展的";increased"(某事物数量或强度)增长的"。

22. [正确答案] B
    [考点类型] 固定搭配
    [考点剖析] make up"编造,补足";take up"占,占据";reach out"延伸,扩展";turn out"关掉,结果是"。

23. [正确答案] B
    [考点类型] 形近词辨析
    [考点剖析] employing"利用,雇用";emerging"新兴的,出现的";embracing"拥抱,包含";e-

mitting"发出,放出"。

24. [正确答案] D
    [考点类型] 固定搭配
    [考点剖析] in honor of"为了向……表示敬意"; in memory of "为了纪念……"; in return for "作为(对……的)回报"; in line with"跟……一致,符合"。

25. [正确答案] A
    [考点类型] 近义词辨析
    [考点剖析] verdict"(陪审团的)裁决,裁定"; sentence"宣判,判决"; trial"审判,审理"; debate"争论,争吵"。

26. [正确答案] B
    [考点类型] 形近词辨析
    [考点剖析] vertical"垂直的,竖的"; vicious"恶性的;邪恶的"; vivid"鲜明的"; vigorous"精力充沛的"。

27. [正确答案] A
    [考点类型] 逻辑关系
    [考点剖析] cool"酷,很棒"; crazy"疯狂的"; cold"寒冷的"; cute"可爱的"。

28. [正确答案] D
    [考点类型] 逻辑关系
    [考点剖析] resorting to"诉诸,采取"; appealing to"向……请求;对……有吸引力"; applying to"适用于,应用于"; contributing to"有助于"。

29. [正确答案] D
    [考点类型] 介词辨析
    [考点剖析] over"(数量上)超过"; of"……的"; under"在……之下"; beyond"超出"。

30. [正确答案] B
    [考点类型] 固定搭配
    [考点剖析] laid off"停止工作(活动)"; laid out"陈设,展开"; put off"延期"; put out"扑灭,出版,发行"。

Part Ⅲ Reading Comprehension

Passage One

孤独已经与抑郁以及其他健康问题联系在一起了。如今,一项研究表明孤独也能传播。一个孤独的人的朋友有超过52%的可能产生孤独感,而那位朋友的朋友有超过25%的可能产生孤独感。

早期研究结果表明:快乐、肥胖以及戒烟能力在社交圈中都能像传染病一样传播。这些调查结果都出自一项在马萨诸塞州的弗雷明翰这个美国小镇的重大健康研究。

这项研究始于1948年,旨在调查心脏病发病的原因。此后,研究中增添了更多测试,包括孤独和抑郁。

这项新发现涉及了五千多人,这些人是弗雷明翰心脏研究的第二代研究对象。研究者调查了他们的交友记录和孤独病例报告。研究结果确立了传播模式,即孤独在那些密友很少的人传播。

　　例如，孤独会影响邻里关系。若邻居曾是好友，如今却很少串门，孤独便会蔓延。研究还发现，孤独在女性之间比在男性之间更容易传播。

　　来自芝加哥大学、哈佛大学和加利福尼亚大学圣地亚哥分校的研究人员共同进行了这项研究。研究结果刊登在上个月的《人格与社会心理学杂志》上。

　　据说平均每个人每年大约有 48 天会感到孤独。研究发现，有一个孤独的朋友会增加约 17 天的孤独感。但是每增加一个朋友能减轻大约 5%的孤单感，或约 2 天半的孤独感。

　　孤独的人会越来越不相信别人，这导致他们交朋友变得越来越困难——同时遭遇社会排挤的可能性也会更高。

　　这项研究的负责人——芝加哥大学的约翰·卡乔波称识别并处理好孤独十分重要。他还表示应当帮助那些曾经被推向社会边缘的人们修复他们的社交网络。

　　研究的目标应该是积极建立他所宣称的"防护屏障"以对抗孤独。他说这种屏障能够避免人们的整个网络崩溃。

31. [正确答案] B
　　[考点类型] 细节题
　　[题目翻译] 除了孤独之外，还有以下哪项可以在人与人之间传播？
　　　　A. 友谊。
　　　　B. 快乐。
　　　　C. 抑郁。
　　　　D. 吸烟。
　　[考点剖析] 从文中第二段第一句话中就能直接找到答案。而 D 项是个迷惑项，原文是指戒烟能力，不是吸烟。

32. [正确答案] A
　　[考点类型] 细节题
　　[题目翻译] 始于 1948 年的弗雷明翰心脏研究_____。
　　　　A. 扩展了它的研究主题
　　　　B. 涉及了 5 000 名抑郁症患者
　　　　C. 认为孤独是患心脏病的一个关键因素
　　　　D. 调查孤独与抑郁之间的关联
　　[考点剖析] 文中第三段体现了 A 项的含义。原文是说第二代研究对象涉及了五千多人，B 项属于以偏概全；C 项和 D 项在文中没有体现。

33. [正确答案] A
　　[考点类型] 细节题
　　[题目翻译] 下列有关孤独会传播的说法，哪一项是正确的？
　　　　A. 它会导致朋友逐渐减少。
　　　　B. 它在女性之间很普遍。
　　　　C. 它在邻里之间很常见。
　　　　D. 它会破坏亲密朋友之间的关系。
　　[考点剖析] 文中倒数第三段表明孤独的人会越来越不相信别人，这导致他们交朋友变得越

来越困难,从而推知 A 项正确。B 项,文中原意是孤独在女性之间比在男性之间更容易传播;C 项,原文是指孤独会影响邻里关系;D 项在文中没有具体体现。

34. [正确答案] C
    [考点类型] 细节题
    [题目翻译] 有一个孤独的朋友,你很可能会 _____。
        A. 增进友谊
        B. 结交新朋友
        C. 增加孤独感
        D. 减少孤独感
    [考点剖析] A、B 项在文中没有体现;D 项与原文描述相反;从倒数第四段可以得出 C 项正确。

35. [正确答案] C
    [考点类型] 推理题
    [题目翻译] 根据芝加哥大学的约翰·卡乔波的观点可知,孤独能够 _____。
        A. 导致攻击行为
        B. 引起人们过度的自我保护
        C. 影响社交网络
        D. 将人们推向贫困的边缘
    [考点剖析] 文中最后两段表明了约翰·卡乔波的观点,由此可以推断出孤独和社交网络的关系。其他选项在文中没有涉及。

36. [正确答案] A
    [考点类型] 主旨题
    [题目翻译] 本文的主要观点是什么?
        A. 孤独能够传播。
        B. 孤独与抑郁有关。
        C. 孤独的人容易变胖。
        D. 孤独的人需要更多的朋友。
    [考点剖析] 纵观全文可知,文章主要是在讲述经过研究发现孤独能够传播,并影响人们的社交网络。B、D 项是片面的信息,C 项在文中没有涉及。

Passage Two

　　加利福尼亚州有一个名为"电子教科书倡议"的新项目。"从今年秋季的高中数学和科学开始,我们将是全美第一个为学校提供国家批准的电子教科书的州。"该州州长阿诺德·施瓦辛格在六月份说道。这次讲话说的是他正在力图使学校用上免费的网络教学材料。他列出了他认为电子教科书是有意义的原因。

　　加利福尼亚州批准学校每六年要换一次传统教科书。电子版可以给学生提供最新的信息,减轻书包的重量,节省纸张和木材,并且使学习更加有趣且更具互动性。他说,最重要的是,它们有助于学校节约资金。

这个州由于深层次财政问题不得不大幅缩减学校开支。有超过600万名的学生进入加利福尼亚州的公立学校学习。

今年早些时候,加利福尼亚州邀请了内容开发人员为高中提供数学和科学的电子教材。这些教材的内容至少要达到该州要求学习内容的90%。受过专门训练的教师审核了16本教材,其中10本通过了这次审核。

这10本书中有6本是由CK12基金会出版的,这一非营利组织已经开发了大约两年的科学和数学的电子教科书。基金会向撰写并编辑这些教材的教师和其他教育专家支付薪酬,而这些钱来自一个由科斯拉家族资助的组织。

加利福尼亚州不能要求学校使用电子教科书,个别学区须自行决定。

加利福尼亚州教育局的一位官员——苏珊·马蒂莫说,她并不期待这些教科书会立即得到广泛使用。她认为最好的情况是一些有雄厚技术实力的学校将会首先使用电子教科书,但是这一情况仅仅存在于使用传统教科书之余。

学校行政人员指出这些课文或许在网上是免费的,但是学生们需要一种获取这些课文的途径。不是每个人都有电脑或电子阅读器。学校可以打印出副本,但是这并不能改善学生的学习环境。还有,培训教师有效使用电子教科书也是需要花钱的。

37. [正确答案] D

  [考点类型] 细节题

  [题目翻译]"电子教科书倡议"_____。

    A. 将有可能在6年内生效

    B. 将涵盖所有高中学科

    C. 已经被所有的州批准

    D. 是由加利福尼亚州州长倡导

  [考点剖析] D项在文中第一段就有体现;A项,文中没有明确说明何时使用电子教科书;从文中Earlier this year, California invited content developers to offer digital math and science materials for high schools 可以推知 B 项不正确;C 项在文中没有体现。

38. [正确答案] A

  [考点类型] 细节题

  [题目翻译] 倡导使用电子教科书的主要原因是为了_____。

    A. 帮助节省资金

    B. 有益于环境

    C. 提供有趣的资料

    D. 减轻学生沉重的负担

  [考点剖析] 由第二段最后一句话 And above all, he said, they help schools with their finances 得知这个倡议是为了减轻学校的财政负担,A项正确。其他选项不是主要原因。

39. [正确答案] A

  [考点类型] 细节题

  [题目翻译] 电子教科书由 _____ 审核通过。

    A. 受过专门训练的教师

B. 内容开发人员
C. 科斯拉家族
D. CK12 基金会

[考点剖析] 文中第四段 Specially trained teachers examined 16 textbooks and approved ten of them 明确指出这些电子教科书是由受过专门训练的教师审核批准的。

40. [正确答案] B
    [考点类型] 细节题
    [题目翻译] 以下哪项是关于 CK12 基金会的正确描述？
        A. 它出版了 16 本电子教科书。
        B. 它向撰写电子教科书的老师支付薪酬。
        C. 它由加利福尼亚州政府资助。
        D. 它通过开发电子教科书营利。
    [考点剖析] 从文中第五段可以看出，这个组织出版了通过审核的 10 本书中的 6 本，并且是一个非营利性且由科斯拉家族资助的一个组织。由此推出 A、C、D 项均不正确。而从 The foundation paid teachers and other education professionals to write and edit them 中可以看出 B 项正确。

41. [正确答案] C
    [考点类型] 细节题
    [题目翻译] 根据苏珊·马蒂莫的观点，电子教科书 _____。
        A. 可能不会得到很广泛的使用
        B. 很快会取代传统教科书
        C. 将首先被设施比较先进的学校所采用
        D. 一定会被学区认可
    [考点剖析] 文中官员的原意是说她不期待电子教科书会立即得到广泛使用，而未强调能不能得到广泛使用，所以 A 项不正确。B、D 项的说法都比较绝对，故排除。

42. [正确答案] B
    [考点类型] 推理题
    [题目翻译] 从文中最后一段可以推断出 _____。
        A. 学校不愿意把教科书副本打印出来
        B. 电子教科书不能在真正意义上达到免费使用
        C. 学生需要支付电脑费用
        D. 培训教师使用这种教科书不是很有效率
    [考点剖析] A 项与原文意思不相符，原文是说学校可以打印副本，但是对改变学生的学习环境无益；C 项概括不全面；D 项是对原文最后一句话的曲解。

Passage Three

英国的医生警告说，当超重的孩子们长大成人时，他们的身体内会存在一颗定时炸弹——肥胖症。那么我们该怎么做呢？多锻炼？少吃饭？还是两者一起做？政府感到必须在这个越来越严重的问题上负起责任。

快乐的匹克威克先生——查尔斯·狄更斯小说中的主人公——就被看作是一个肥胖且幸福的人的例证。在18世纪的绘画中,圆滚的身材和柔软的曲线就意味着美。但在今天,超重既不等同于开朗的性格,也不是美的象征,而是预示着增加罹患心脏病和中风的风险。

那你该怎么办呢?控制饮食?根据英国首席医学官员利亚姆·唐纳森爵士的意见,该答案是不可取的。他说,降低肥胖症、癌症和心脏病患病风险的关键是体育活动。卫生部长约翰·里德甚至说,怠惰和吸烟一样,都是引发心脏病的危险因素。

如此说来,如果你已经买了健身器械,你应该做多少训练呢?据利亚姆·唐纳德爵士的观点,每天至少应适度活动30分钟,每周五天。去健身房行吗?那些认为跑步机很乏味的人应该感到幸运,因为健康发展机构认为适合人的生活的体育活动可能更有效一些。他们建议人们走楼梯而不要乘电梯,在乘坐自动扶梯时走上去,同孩子一起做游戏,跳跳舞或做些园艺工作。运动心理学家比德尔教授说,健身房"没有让全国人民健康起来",甚至还可能对人造成了伤害。

新的科学证据表明:过量的锻炼实际上对人有害。阿尔斯特大学的科学家发现,不规律的锻炼会释放有害的自由基,这些自由基会反过来影响不健康的人的正常功能。只有训练有素的运动员才应该让身体进行那种程度的有规律的锻炼。

那么,我们是否应该忘了健身房,听从专家的意见,在日常生活中增加锻炼量呢?毕竟,从公交车上早下一站走完剩余的路也没什么坏处。最后一个问题:过去的几代人缺乏健身设施,但他们怎么反而比今天的人更瘦、更健康呢?

43. [正确答案] A

  [考点类型] 主旨题

  [题目翻译] 文章主要是关于_____。
  A. 如何保持身体健康并且防止肥胖
  B. 超重人群所面临的增加的风险
  C. 在健身房进行锻炼的危险
  D. 平衡饮食的好处

  [考点剖析] 第一段通过医生发出的警告引出文章主题——肥胖是超重儿童体内的一颗定时炸弹,下文讨论如何有效地保持身体健康并且预防肥胖。所以 A 项正是文章的大意。而其他选项均无法回答题目所问,均排除。

44. [正确答案] B

  [考点类型] 词汇题

  [题目翻译] 第一段提到的"这一日益严重的问题"指的是什么?
  A. 超重儿童成长缓慢。
  B. 医生所发出的有关肥胖是定时炸弹的警告。
  C. 过少的运动与过度饮食。
  D. 政府忽视的健康问题。

  [考点剖析] 解题关键是要找到"这一日益严重的问题"指代的是什么。文章第一段第一句话就是答案所在。

45. [正确答案] D

  [考点类型] 细节题

  [题目翻译] 作者为什么要提到查尔斯·狄更斯小说中的主人公——匹克威克先生?

A. 他是18世纪绘画中的绘画形象。
B. 他是世界名著中的英雄人物。
C. 他患有心脏病并且中风了。
D. 他是肥胖且幸福的人的象征。

[考点剖析] D项与文章第二段第一句话一致。其他三项都没在原文中体现。

46. [正确答案] D

   [考点类型] 细节题

   [题目翻译] 根据利亚姆·唐纳森爵士的意见,哪一个是预防肥胖的最佳方式?

   A. 节食。
   B. 戒烟。
   C. 尽可能地懒散。
   D. 锻炼身体。

   [考点剖析] 从文章第三段 He says that physical activity is the key for reducing the risks of obesity, cancer and heart disease 可以判断出本题正确答案为 D 项。

47. [正确答案] B

   [考点类型] 细节题

   [题目翻译] 下列哪一项不是由健康发展机构提出的建议?

   A. 在乘坐自动扶梯时走上去,跳跳舞或做些园艺工作。
   B. 去健身房在跑步机上运动。
   C. 走楼梯不要乘电梯。
   D. 同孩子做游戏。

   [考点剖析] 从文章第四段第五句 They suggest taking the stairs rather than the lift, walking up escalators, playing active games with your children, dancing or gardening 可以找到 A、C、D 三项。

48. [正确答案] D

   [考点类型] 推理题

   [题目翻译] 从文章最后一段可以推断出 _____。

   A. 过量的运动实际上可能对健康不利
   B. 不必一直按专家的建议去做
   C. 过去的几代人渴望我们现在所拥有的健身设施
   D. 适量的日常锻炼能使我们更加苗条、健康

   [考点剖析] A项在最后一段中没有体现,而 B、C 项不是作者要表达的思想。

Passage Four

作为一种涉及比喻的诗歌手法,暗喻用于比较两种具有相似性的不同物体。用一个简单的暗喻,一个对象就可以转变成其他事物,比如:爱是一朵玫瑰。虽然这听起来不像是一个特别丰富的意象,但暗喻可以传达一个特定形象的很多信息,以至于相比于其他类型的修辞语言,诗人更常使用它。原因是诗人创作诗歌来表达自己在某个时刻的情感。因此,诗人所想象的爱可能是也可能不是我们所感知的爱。所以,诗人的任务就是使我们能对他们当时的情感感同身受。

让我们分析一下这个关于爱情和玫瑰的非常朴实的暗喻意味着什么吧。既然诗人用玫瑰作比,所以我们首先来看看这种花所具备的特点:玫瑰花的美是令人赞叹的,它的花瓣柔软,气味芳香。可以说,欣赏玫瑰确实是视觉、触觉和嗅觉的一场盛宴。而且玫瑰的外形几近完美,每朵花瓣的形状都那么对称。这不正是一个人爱的方式吗?一个坠入爱河的人在情感上一定是愉悦的、几近完美的。然而,在用玫瑰作比的时候,还有另外一种含义:玫瑰是带刺的。诗人想要表达的是玫瑰也是会扎手的。这个暗喻告诉我们,爱情也是一样的。当一个人对钟情的他或她敞开心扉,完全接受他或她的爱时,玫瑰的刺就会有巨大的杀伤力!"小心!"这个暗喻告诫我们的是,爱情是感情的盛宴,但是它能让我们沉浸其中,也会伤害我们,让我们痛彻心扉。这就是诗人对爱情的感知——一种劝诫。重点是什么?那就是原本需要用近14个句子才能讲述清楚的事情,如果用暗喻的话,四个字就够了!这就是简明暗喻的艺术性和乐趣。

49. [正确答案] A

   [考点类型] 细节题

   [题目翻译] 根据文章所说,什么是暗喻?

       A. 两个不同物体相似特性的比较。

       B. 两个不同事物通过比较创造鲜明的意象。

       C. 以诗歌方式对两个相似物体的描述。

       D. 一种专门用于诗歌创作的文学创作方法。

   [考点剖析] 文章开篇前两句话对 metaphor 做了含义的界定。可以通过 similar 和 dissimilar 两个词所修饰的事物判断出答案是 A 项。

50. [正确答案] D

   [考点类型] 主旨题

   [题目翻译] 这篇短文的主旨是_____。

       A. 玫瑰是诗歌中一种好的意象

       B. 爱情是甜美的、令人愉悦的

       C. 暗喻是隐晦模糊的

       D. 暗喻是一种很重要的诗歌修辞手法

   [考点剖析] 文章第一段第四、五句表明诗人在写作时经常会使用暗喻的修辞手法,因为它看似简单,却最能传达诗人在某个时刻想表达的情感。

51. [正确答案] B

   [考点类型] 细节题

   [题目翻译] 从文中可以推断出暗喻_____。

       A. 很难理解

       B. 有丰富的内涵

       C. 不够准确

       D. 像一朵花

   [考点剖析] 根据文章第一段第四句可以得知,暗喻有丰富的内涵。

52. [正确答案] C

   [考点类型] 细节题

   [题目翻译] 根据作者的意思,玫瑰的刺_____。

A. 保护玫瑰免受伤害
B. 代表减少的爱
C. 给爱情这一意象增加了新的元素
D. 代表某人喜欢的对象

[考点剖析] 根据 Roses have thorns 这句话前后的两个句子可以推断出,玫瑰既可以代表美好的爱情,又有令人受伤的一面。这个暗喻告诉我们:爱情不只有美好的一面。

53. [正确答案] D
[考点类型] 细节题
[题目翻译] "爱是一朵玫瑰"这一暗喻的意义是_____。
A. 爱情是真正的快乐
B. 真爱在生命中只出现一次
C. 爱情不会持续很久
D. 爱情是好坏兼备的经历

[考点剖析] 此题可以根据上题的解析得出正确答案,也可以根据原文第二段 Love is a feast to the senses, but it can overwhelm us…中作者要表达的意思得出答案。

54. [正确答案] C
[考点类型] 细节题
[题目翻译] 根据文章可知,诗歌是用来_____的。
A. 释放愤怒
B. 愉悦读者
C. 表达诗人想法
D. 回报感情

[考点剖析] 根据文中第一段中间部分 The reason for this is that poets compose their poetry to express what they are experiencing emotionally at that moment 可知,正确答案为 C 项。

Passage Five

由于医疗改革的通过,又将有约 2 300 万名的美国居民在未来数年有望成为美国医疗保健系统的固定用户。人们提倡医疗数据数字化,以帮助不堪重负的系统管理激增的患者人数。然而把人们的健康信息录入在线数据库并分享到网络上要做的不仅仅是减少冗余。我们寻求和接受医疗保健的方式已经发生了变化。

"社会的保健服务状态正在发生变化。"医疗信息技术公司 Eclipsys 的副总裁约翰·戈麦斯说道。他指出,大多数病人可能并不愿意在脸书上分享他们最新的 CT 扫描图像,但许多父母却愿意上传他们孩子的超声波图像。如今无数父母都用社交网站分享身体状况、治疗方法和医生等信息。

随着人们能够获得更多个性化的健康信息——无论是通过正式的电子医疗记录,还是自创的个人健康记录或是与医生快速即时的通信——传统的医生和患者角色都经历着迅速的转变。

"就像我们知道的那样,医疗保健一直是'我去看医生,他们告诉我怎么做,我就怎么做。'"耶鲁大学医学信息中心的一位医生和研究员尼图·迦叶波说道。不久,更多的病人会到已经看过他们病史记录、最新的检测结果和相关文献的医院或医生办公室看病。甚至更多的人将会跳过看医生这一环节,取而代之的是给他们的医疗服务提供者发送文字信息或电子邮件,或查阅个人健康记录,或利用智能手机的应用程序来回答他们的问题。

　　这些变化将会随着已经开始的全国电子医疗记录的转变而加强。虽然大多数美国医院和医生办公室仍然在努力推进这一变革,但是许多病人已经有了电子医疗记录,有些人甚至有访问这些记录的部分权限。My Chart 方案是一个网络门户,已经被克利夫兰诊所、得克萨斯大学达拉斯西南医学中心和其他机构试用。患者可以通过这个门户看到基本医疗信息,以及一些化验结果。

　　医学数据正变成一种新的数字生活,它正在迅速启动"提供医疗服务方式的根本改变",戈麦斯说道。

55. [正确答案] A
　　 [考点类型] 主旨题
　　 [题目翻译] 下列哪项是这篇文章最恰当的题目?
　　　　　　　A. 你的医疗数据的未来
　　　　　　　B. 对医生和医院的挑战
　　　　　　　C. 美国医疗改革的好处
　　　　　　　D. 怎样访问和分享你的健康信息
　　 [考点剖析] 通过对整篇文章的把握,可以知道文章主要讨论的是医疗数据数字化的相关问题,所以"你的医疗数据的未来"为最佳标题。

56. [正确答案] D
　　 [考点类型] 细节题
　　 [题目翻译] 把病人的信息放进数据库并分享到网络上 _____。
　　　　　　　A. 能够使更多的美国人加入医疗保健系统
　　　　　　　B. 有助于医疗改革的进程
　　　　　　　C. 增加美国医疗保健系统的负担
　　　　　　　D. 改变人们寻求和接受医疗保健的方式
　　 [考点剖析] 通过第一段最后一句话…shifting the very way we seek and receive health care 可知,D 项是对原文的同义改写。

57. [正确答案] C
　　 [考点类型] 细节题
　　 [题目翻译] 根据约翰·戈麦斯的观点可知,很多病人利用社交网站 _____。
　　　　　　　A. 改变他们的社会活动
　　　　　　　B. 发布他们最新的 CT 扫描图像
　　　　　　　C. 分享他们的医疗保健信息
　　　　　　　D. 展示他们孩子的近照
　　 [考点剖析] 根据第二段可知,病人会利用社交网站来分享他们的医疗保健信息。

58. [正确答案] B
　　 [考点类型] 细节题
　　 [题目翻译] 下面哪项没有改变医生和病人的传统角色?
　　　　　　　A. 一个正式的电子医疗记录。
　　　　　　　B. 一个更容易在网上获取信息的方式。

C. 一个自创的个人健康记录。

D. 与医生快速即时的一次通信。

[考点剖析] 根据文中第三段,可以排除 A、C、D 项。

59. [正确答案] C

[考点类型] 细节题

[题目翻译] 根据尼图·迦叶波的观点可知,未来会有更多的病人_____。

A. 拒绝遵循医生的建议

B. 更加依赖他们的医生

C. 省略去医院或医生办公室的步骤

D. 通过电子邮件来诊断他们的健康状况

[考点剖析] 根据第四段…to skip that visit…可知正确答案为 C 项。A 项太过绝对;B 项在文中没有提及;D 项,文中是指通过电子邮件向医生咨询,而非通过电子邮件进行诊断。

60. [正确答案] D

[考点类型] 细节题

[题目翻译] 文中说到_____。

A. 全国的医疗数据数字化将会很快开始

B. 大部分美国医院和医生都反对这种转变

C. 病人很担心他们健康信息的安全性

D. 病人开始使用他们的电子医疗记录

[考点剖析] 此题可定位到文章第五段,第五段第二句提到 many patients already have electronic medical records,故 D 项正确。

Part Ⅳ Cloze

你是单身却因为太忙而没时间寻求爱情吗?那么你可以尝试席卷英国的最新约会形式——速配。

速配是指男女在一个房间里会面,并在 3 分钟内尽可能多地了解与你存在可能性的伴侣。实践证明,这是一个非常受英国年轻人欢迎的形式,因为他们发现自己没有时间遇见那个特别的人。

速配时你可以一对一地与异性交谈 3 分钟。然后,钟声响起,你走向另一个人,与他开始聊天。到了晚上结束时,你会与多达 20 个男子或女子交谈过!

如果到谈话结束时,你喜欢某些人或想再次见到他们,你可以把他们的名字写到一张卡片上。然后,如果那个人也中意你,主办单位将告知你他们的详细资料。

但 3 分钟是否足以让人留下印象并且让你决定是否要跟某人再次见面?研究表明,两个人之间强烈的吸引力能在你见到某人的 30 秒钟内就感觉到,这就是速配——让你很快知道你是否会喜欢某人。

浪漫又是怎么回事?你是否有可能在如此短的时间内做出正确的判断?毕竟,人们会说你不能如此匆忙地对待爱情。然而,一个英国人会因速配而很快开始第一次婚姻。

所以,如果你的任务是找到你的另一半,你又会有什么损失呢?最坏的结果只不过是你依旧一个人回家。但最好的结果是,你梦中的人可能距离你只有 3 分钟之遥。

61. [正确答案] B

    [解析过程] sweeping across "扫过,席卷"。此句的意思是"席卷英国的最新约会形式"。

62. [正确答案] D

    [解析过程] involves"涉及,包括",在这里最符合语境。本句是指涉及的人和形式,但并不是硬性规定,故 requires"要求"、inquires"询问"和 revolves"转动"都不符合语境。

63. [正确答案] A

    [解析过程] partners "伴侣"。这里是指"在3分钟内尽可能多地了解与你存在可能性的伴侣"。counterparts"相对应的人或物",强调同等级别的对应。

64. [正确答案] B

    [解析过程] It's proving very popular with sb. "经证明,这对某人来说是非常受欢迎的"。因为文章开篇已经提出 sweeping across the UK,根据前后文对照原则,B 项更符合语境。

65. [正确答案] C

    [解析过程] one on one"一对一,单对单",在这里是插入语,表示"……一对一地与异性交谈3分钟"。

66. [正确答案] D

    [解析过程] "… a bell is rung"是被动语态结构,正常的动宾结构应为 ring a bell。

67. [正确答案] D

    [解析过程] fancy"(一时地)喜欢"。本句的意思是"如果到谈话结束时,你喜欢某些人或想再次见到他们……"。另外,通过本段第二句话 Then, if the other person also fancies you,…也可知道该空应填入 fancy。

68. [正确答案] A

    [解析过程] write down "写下,记录下"。本句的意思是"……写到一张卡片上"。

69. [正确答案] B

    [解析过程] work out "解决,做出,产生结果"。本句指"3分钟是否足以让人留下印象并且让你决定是否要跟某人再次见面"。work on "致力于……"; work at "在……工作,从事于……"; work up "逐步发展到……"。均不符语境。

70. [正确答案] C

    [解析过程] emotion"感情"; sentiment"(哀伤的)情绪"; chemistry"强烈吸引力(尤其是两性之间)"; attachment"(亲人间的)依恋"。因此,这里选 C 项更符合语境。

71. [正确答案] B

    [解析过程] 根据语法,这里缺少 about 的宾语。所以只有 B 项既是连词又能在从句中充当成分。

72. [正确答案] D

    [解析过程] make a good judgment"做出正确判断"。本句话的意思是:"你是否有可能在如此短的时间内做出正确的判断?"

73. [正确答案] B

    [解析过程] After all"毕竟"。本句话的意思是"毕竟,人们会说你不能如此匆忙地对待爱情"。

2010年同等学力人员申请硕士学位英语水平全国统一考试答案及详解

74. [正确答案] D

 [解析过程] on a mission to do…"从事……任务,做……事"。本句的意思是"……任务是找到你的另一半"。

75. [正确答案] C

 [解析过程] At last"最终";At first"首先";At worst"最坏";At end"在末端"。At worst 与 But 后的 at best 形成对比,因此选 C 项。

Paper Two 试卷二

Part Ⅰ Translation

Section A

1. An ecosystem is a group of animals and plants living in a specific region and interacting with one another and with their physical environment.

 [结构分析] 这是一个现在分词作定语的结构,living 和 interacting 作后置定语,共同修饰 a group of animals and plants,相当于一个定语从句。后半句中共有两个连词 and,均表示并列。第一个 and 连接两个分词结构:living 和 interacting;第二个 and 连接两个介词短语:with one another 和 with their physical environment,这两个介词短语共同和 interacting 搭配。

 [词义推敲] ecosystem"生态系统"。

 [参考译文] 生态系统是指共同生活在一个特定区域内的动植物之间以及这些动植物与其生存环境之间相互作用而形成的一个整体。

2. Ecosystems include physical and chemical components, such as soils, water, and nutrients that support the organisms living there.

 [结构分析] 本句考查对 that 引导的定语从句的理解,其先行词为 nutrients(营养物质)。本句也出现了列举,但是结构比较简单。

 [词义推敲] component"成分,组成部分";organism"有机物,生物"。

 [参考译文] 生态系统包括物理和化学成分,如土壤、水以及维持生物生存的营养物质。

3. These organisms may range from large animals to microscopic bacteria.

 [结构分析] 本句是个简单句,range from… to…"范围从……到……"。

 [词义推敲] microscopic"微小的,细微的";bacteria"细菌"。

 [参考译文] 生物可以是大型的动物,也可以是微小的细菌。

4. Ecosystems also can be thought of as the interactions among all organisms in a given area; for instance, one species may serve as food for another.

 [结构分析] 本句重在理解几个短语搭配。think of A as B"把 A 看作 B";among all organisms in a given area:由 among 和 in 两个介词引导的状语共同修饰 interactions,分别表示范围和地点。在翻译的时候,可以把这种英文的状语翻译成为中文的定语。

· 29 ·

[词义推敲] interaction"相互作用,配合"; species "物种"; serve as "充当,担任"。

[参考译文] 生态系统也可以被看作是在某一特定区域内所有生物间的相互作用,比如说一种生物可能是另一种生物的食物。

5. People are part of the ecosystems where they live and work.

[结构分析] 句子的后半部分是由 where 引导的定语从句,修饰 ecosystems。

[词义推敲] 无生词。

[参考译文] 人类也是他们生活和工作所处的生态系统的一部分。

6. Human activities can harm or destroy local ecosystems unless actions such as land development for housing or businesses are carefully planned to conserve and sustain the ecology of the area.

[结构分析] 本句整体上是个主从复合句。主句:Human activities can harm or destroy local ecosystems;从句:unless actions such as land development for housing or businesses are carefully planned to conserve and sustain the ecology of the area。unless 引导的是条件状语从句;actions 是从句的主语,are carefully planned 是从句的谓语,to conserve and sustain the ecology of the area 是从句的目的状语。

[词义推敲] harm "伤害"; conserve "保护,保藏"; sustain "维持"。

[参考译文] 除非人类在为住房或商业需求进行土地开发活动时做好精心计划以保护和维持本地区的生态环境,否则人类活动就会损害或破坏当地的生态系统。

Section B

1. 全球化作为一种新的经济和社会发展趋势,给中国带来了机遇,也带来了挑战。

[结构分析] 第一个逗号前面的部分是主语部分,其余的是谓语部分。这里面的主语部分是由一个复杂的结构充当的。在翻译的时候,可以抓住中心词"全球化",把"作为……"放在状语的位置,这样就能有效地用英语来表达原有意思了。

[词义推敲] 全球化"globalization";机遇与挑战"opportunities and challenges"。

[参考译文] As a new economic and social trend, globalization has brought China opportunities and challenges as well.

2. 一方面,中国正成为世界制造业中心并在国际舞台上发挥着日益重要的作用。

[结构分析] 一个"并"字就能体现出这句话的并列关系,那么相应的译文也要用并列句呈现出来。这句话的关键是文中句子是否能够找出相对应的英文表达。

[词义推敲] 制造业中心"manufacturing center";国际舞台"the international arena"。

[参考译文] On the one hand, China is on the road to become the world's manufacturing center, and plays an increasingly significant role in the international arena.

3. 另一方面,我们也面临着如何在全球化进程中既要发展经济,又能传承优秀文化传统的问题。

[结构分析] 这句话的关键点是"既要……又能……"这一结构。

[词义推敲] 传承优秀文化传统"pass down the outstanding cultural traditions"。

[参考译文] On the other hand, we are faced with the problem as to how to pass down the outstanding cultural traditions while we develop our economy in the process of globalization.

Part Ⅱ Writing

本次考试的作文属于材料型作文,并且给出了主要内容的限制。因此,我们需要根据题目要求去写一篇议论文。第一段,概括材料所陈述的主要内容;第二段和第三段,点明材料暗含的寓意,可以结合自身谈谈体验;第四段,总结全文。

The short paragraph above tells us a real story about the history of the well-known writing *French Revolution History*. The author Carlyle, a great historian, suffered from frustration and lost his script of *French Revolution History* in the course of writing, which could have broken him down. However, the great historian was not beaten by the suffering but found his confidence back and started his composition from the beginning. At last, he finished his great writing with an unyielding will.

The course of creation of the composition shows us that an unyielding will is the key to success. Reviewing the whole story, what helped the author get to success was mainly his perseverance. He did not give up his goal even when suffering from a great strike, which made me remember a thing happening upon me.

Once I wanted to join the football team in my school but was refused by them because of my poor performance. Then I never gave up my dream and kept practising my skills, although it was a tough period. At last I made it and got the permission to the team.

Actually the two stories share the same meaning that an unyielding will is the most important element on the way to success.

第一段:对材料所给的内容进行归纳和概括,提炼出主要内容。

第二段:点明材料隐含的寓意,总结出坚强不屈的意志是取得成功的关键。

第三段:以自己的亲身经历为例,进一步支持上段的观点。

第四段:一句话作为全文的总结及结束语,再次点明材料反映的寓意,点明主题。

文章主题明确,论据充分,全文逻辑思维比较清晰。文章句型变换灵活,比如 The course of creation of the composition shows us that an unyielding will is the key to success 以及 Reviewing the whole story, what helped the author get to success was mainly his perseverance 两个句子用了宾语从句和 what 引导的名词性从句等句型,可供大家学习。

2011年同等学力人员申请硕士学位英语水平全国统一考试

Paper One 试卷一 (90 minutes)

Part I Dialogue Communication (10 minutes, 10 points)

Section A Dialogue Completion

Directions: *In this section, you will read 5 short incomplete dialogues between two speakers, each followed by 4 choices marked A, B, C and D. Choose the answer that best suits the situation to complete the dialogue. Then mark the corresponding letter with a single bar across the square brackets on your machine-scoring Answer Sheet.*

1. A: David said he bought a new BMW for £5,000!
   B: _____ Sounds pretty cheap to me!
   A: Well, that's what he said.
   A. Are you sure?   B. Come to think of it.
   C. Do you think so?   D. Is he crazy?

2. A: We just came back from Phoenix. And we had the best vacation in years.
   B: _____ I'm glad to hear it.
   A. Oh, my goodness!   B. How was it?
   C. Oh, there you go again. D. Good for you.

3. A: I just can't stand this class any more!
   B: _____ It's required, and you have to sit in it in order to graduate.
   A. Well, why not just drop out of it?   B. Why, you can say that again!
   C. Well, you might as well get used to it. D. Why, I couldn't agree more!

4. A: I don't know about you, but I thought that film was terrific.
   B: _____ The action was great, and so was the music.
   A. Just the same.   B. I was with you there.
   C. More or less.   D. I sure do.

5. A: Dan gave me a free ride home, but I paid for the gas.
   B: You know what they say, _____
   A. there's no free lunch.   B. don't bite off more than you can chew.
   C. one good turn deserves another.   D. it's who you know that counts.

Section B Dialogue Comprehension

Directions: *In this section, you will read 5 short conversations between a man and a woman. At the end of each conversation there is a question followed by 4 choices marked A, B, C and D. Choose the best answer to the question from the 4 choices by marking the corresponding letter with a single bar across the square brackets on your machine-scoring* **Answer Sheet.**

6. Woman: I'd rather not talk about it. Just don't ask.

   Man: Come on. I think you need to let off some steam.

   Question: What does the man advise the woman to do?

   A. To talk to him about the problem.

   B. To keep the secret.

   C. To reduce the workload.

   D. To have a good rest.

7. Woman: Julie's dress looks funny. That style went out last year.

   Man: Oh, come on, as long as it looks good on her.

   Question: What does the man try to emphasize?

   A. Julie's dress is not outdated.   B. Julie's dress does not suit her.

   C. Julie should follow the fashion.   D. Julie looks fine in that dress.

8. Man: What kind of snacks do you prefer?

   Woman: Oh, I've got a sweet tooth, you know.

   Question: What does the woman probably like?

   A. Sandwich.   B. Hot dogs.   C. Ice cream.   D. Potato chips.

9. Woman: I'm tired of driving all the way to work and back every day. If only cars could drive themselves!

   Man: Well, some car manufacturers are working on them. I guess you'll soon buy one if you can afford it.

   Question: What does the man imply?

   A. The woman will be able to buy an intelligent car.

   B. Cars that drive themselves may be very expensive.

   C. He is working with a car producer on intelligent cars.

   D. Driving to work is really a headache.

10. Man: Annie, how does it not even cross your mind that you might want a future with someone?

    Woman: It's simple. I don't mind being married to my career.

    Question: What's Annie's attitude towards her future?

    A. She will stay with someone unmarried.

    B. She will live a simple life.

    C. She will quit her job to get married.

    D. She will fully focus on her job.

Part II Vocabulary (20 minutes, 10 points)

Section A

Directions: *In this section, there are 10 sentences, each with one word or phrase underlined. Choose the one from the 4 choices marked A, B, C and D that best keeps the meaning of the sentence. Then mark the corresponding letter with a single bar across the square brackets on your machine-scoring **Answer Sheet**.*

11. The news reports completely overlooked the more profound political implications of the events.
    A. neglected   B. foresaw   C. explored   D. assessed

12. Teachers and nurses who deal with children are obliged to report cases of suspected child abuse to authorities.
    A. reminded   B. expected   C. compelled   D. requested

13. Your grade will be based in large part on the originality of your ideas.
    A. creativity   B. popularity   C. feasibility   D. flexibility

14. We suspect there is a quite deliberate attempt to sabotage the elections and undermine the electoral commission.
    A. conscious   B. desperate   C. clumsy   D. intentional

15. So strange were the circumstances of my story that I can scarcely believe myself to have been a party to them.
    A. just   B. hardly   C. almost   D. definitely

16. Smoke particles and other air pollutants are often trapped in the atmosphere, thus forming dirty fog.
    A. constrained   B. caught   C. concealed   D. concentrated

17. Employees in chemical factories are entitled to receive extra pay for doing hazardous work.
    A. poisonous   B. difficult   C. dangerous   D. harmful

18. Curt Carlson, the wealthiest man in Minnesota, owned a hotel and travel company with sales reaching in the neighborhood of $9 billion.
    A. precisely   B. merely   C. substantially D. approximately

19. The tendency of the human body to reject foreign matter is the main obstacle to successful organ transplantation.
    A. factor   B. constituent   C. barrier   D. break

20. Whenever you need Tom, he is always there whether it be an ear or a helping hand, so you can always lean on him.
    A. count on   B. benefit from C. stand for   D. stick to

Section B

Directions: *In this section, there are 10 incomplete sentences. For each sentence there are 4 choices marked A, B, C and D. Choose the one that best completes the sentence. Then mark the corresponding letter with a single bar across the square brackets on your machine-scoring **Answer Sheet**.*

21. It _____ without saying that consumers would be happier if prices were lower.

    A. takes   B. appears   C. makes   D. goes

22. The world economic recession put an _____ end to the steel market upturn that began in 2002.

    A. irregular   B. illegal   C. abrupt   D. absurd

23. I'm _____ about how you discovered my website, and I'm very glad if you enjoy it.

    A. mysterious   B. furious   C. serious   D. curious

24. The Labor Party's electoral strategy, based on a(n) _____ with other smaller parties, has proved successful.

    A. acquaintance   B. integration   C. alliance   D. intimacy

25. The new aircraft will be _____ to a test of temperatures of -65℃ and 120℃.

    A. suspended   B. suppressed

    C. summoned   D. subjected

26. The money I got from teaching on the side was a useful _____ to my ordinary income.

    A. profit   B. supplement   C. subsidy   D. replacement

27. Chinese people are now enjoying better dental health, as shown by the declining _____ of tooth decay.

    A. treatment   B. incidence   C. consequence   D. misfortune

28. Many countries have conservation programs to prevent certain _____ of fish from becoming extinct.

    A. species   B. sources   C. numbers   D. members

29. Susan never took any cookery courses; she learned cooking by _____ useful tips from TV cookery programs.

    A. picking up   B. bringing up   C. putting up   D. pulling up

30. The President _____ his deputy to act for him while he was abroad.

    A. promoted   B. substituted   C. authorized   D. displaced

Part III Reading Comprehension (45 minutes, 30 points)

Directions: *There are 5 passages in this part. Each passage is followed by 6 questions or unfinished statements. For each of them there are 4 choices marked A, B, C and D. Choose the best one and mark the corresponding letter with a single bar across the square brackets on your machine-scoring* **Answer Sheet.**

Passage One

Until last spring, Nia Parker and the other kids in her neighborhood commuted to school on Bus 59. But as fuel prices rose, the school district needed to find a way to cut its transportation costs. So the school's busing company redrew its route map, eliminating Nia's bus altogether. Now Nia and her neighbors travel the half mile to school via a "walking school bus"—a group of kids, supervised by an adult or two, who make the walk together.

Like the rest of us, school districts are feeling pinched by rising fuel costs—and finding new ways to adapt. The price of diesel fuel has gone up 34 percent in the past two years. For the typical American school district, bus bills total 5 percent of the budget. As administrators look to trim, busing is an inviting target, since it doesn't affect classroom instruction (or test scores). More than one third of American school administrators have eliminated bus stops or routes in order to stay within budget.

Many parents are delighted to see their kids walking to school, partly because many did so themselves: according to a 1969 survey, nearly half of school kids walked or biked to school, compared with only 16 percent in 2001. Modern parents have been unwilling to let kids walk to school for fear of traffic, crime or simple bullying, but with organized adult supervision, those concerns have diminished.

Schools and busing companies are finding other ways to save. In rural areas where busing is a must, some schools have even chosen four-day school weeks. Busing companies instruct drivers to eliminate extra stops from routes and to turn off the engine while idling. They are also using computer software to determine the most fuel-efficient routes, which aren't always the shortest ones.

There could be downsides, however, to the busing cutbacks. If every formerly bused student begins walking to school, it's an environmental win—but if too many of their parents decide to drive them instead, the overall carbon footprint can grow. Replacing buses with many more parent-driven cars can also increase safety risks: A 2002 report concluded students are 13 times safer on a school bus than in a passenger car, since buses have fewer accidents and withstand them better due to their size. And some students complain about the long morning hikes, particularly when the route contains a really big hill.

31. The "walking school bus" _____.
   A. does not consume fuel
   B. aims to keep children fit
   C. seldom causes traffic jams
   D. is popular with school kids

32. In America the responsibility for busing kids to school lies with _____.
   A. individual schools
   B. school districts
   C. teachers
   D. parents

33. As regards walking to school, modern parents seem much concerned with the _____.
   A. time spent on the way
   B. changes in the route
   C. kids' physical strength
   D. safety of their children

34. To save money, some schools choose to _____.
   A. take the shortest routes
   B. shorten the school week
   C. give drivers better training
   D. use fuel efficient buses

35. Busing cutbacks may eventually lead to _____.
   A. fiercer competition among bus companies
   B. more students taking public transportation
   C. an increase in carbon dioxide emissions
   D. a decrease in the safety of school buses

36. Which of the following best describes the author's attitude towards busing cutbacks?

   A. Favorable.　　　　B. Critical.　　　　C. Objective.　　　　D. Indifferent.

Passage Two

People are living longer than ever, but for some reason, women are living longer than men. A baby boy born in the United States in 2003 can expect to live to be about 73, a baby girl, about 79. This is indeed a wide gap, and no one really knows why it exists. The greater longevity (长寿) of women, however, has been known for centuries. It was, for example, described in the seventeenth century. However, the difference was smaller then—the gap is growing.

A number of reasons have been proposed to account for the differences. The gap is greatest in industrialized societies, so it has been suggested that women are less susceptible to work strains that may raise the risk of heart disease and alcoholism. Sociologists also tell us that women are encouraged to be less adventurous than men (and this may be why they are more careful drivers, involved in fewer accidents).

Even smoking has been implicated in the age discrepancy. It was once suggested that working women are more likely to smoke and as more women entered the work force, the age gap would begin to close, because smoking is related to earlier deaths. Now, however, we see more women smoking and they still tend to live longer although their lung cancer rate is climbing sharply.

One puzzling aspect of the problem is that women do not appear to be as healthy as men. That is, they report far more illnesses. But when a man reports an illness, it is more likely to be serious.

Some researchers have suggested that men may die earlier because their health is more strongly related to their emotions. For example, men tend to die sooner after losing a spouse than women do. Men even seem to be more weakened by loss of a job. (Both of these are linked with a marked decrease in the effectiveness of the immune system.) Among men, death follows retirement with an alarming promptness.

Perhaps we are searching for the answers too close to the surface of the problem. Perhaps the answers lie deeper in our biological heritage. After all, the phenomenon is not isolated to humans. Females have the <u>edge</u> among virtually all mammalian (哺乳动物的) species, in that they generally live longer. Furthermore, in many of these species the differences begin at the moment of conception; there are more male miscarriages (流产). In humans, after birth, more baby boys than baby girls die.

37. What can we learn from the first two paragraphs?

   A. Men's lifespan remains almost unchanged.

   B. Researchers have found the causes of the age gap.

   C. The more advanced a society, the greater the age gap.

   D. The age gap was noticed only recently.

38. As is suggested in Paragraph 2, the two factors relevant to women's longer lifespan are _____.

   A. diseases and road accidents

B. industrialization and work strains

C. their immunity to heart disease and refusal of alcohol

D. their endurance of work strains and reluctance for adventure

39. According to Paragraph 3, which of the following statements is true?

    A. The great number of male smokers contributes to the age gap.

    B. The growing number of smoking women will narrow the age gap.

    C. Female workers are more likely to smoke than male workers.

    D. Smoking does not seem to affect women's longevity.

40. Which of the following phenomena makes researchers puzzled?

    A. Men's health is more closely related to their emotions.

    B. Though more liable to illnesses, women still live longer.

    C. Men show worse symptoms than women when they fall ill.

    D. Quite a number of men die soon after their retirement.

41. The word "edge" in Paragraph 6 means "_____".

    A. margin   B. side   C. advantage   D. quality

42. What is the main idea of the passage?

    A. The greater longevity of women remains a mystery.

    B. That women are healthier than men well explains their longevity.

    C. People are living longer as a result of industrialization.

    D. Women are less emotionally affected by difficulties in life.

Passage Three

Many are aware of the tremendous waste of energy in our environment, but fail to take advantage of straightforward opportunities to conserve that energy. For example, everyone knows that lights should be switched off when no one is in an office. Similarly, when employees are not using a meeting room, there is no need to regulate temperature.

Fortunately, one need not rely on human intervention to conserve energy. With the help of smart sensing and network technology, energy conservation processes such as turning off lights and adjusting temperature can be readily automated. Ultimately, this technology will enable consumers and plant managers to better identify wasteful energy use and institute procedures that lead to smarter and more efficient homes, buildings and industrial plants.

Until now, wires and cables for power and connectivity have limited the widespread adoption of sensor(传感器) networks by making them difficult and expensive to install and maintain. Battery-powered wireless networks can simplify installation and reduce cost. But their high power consumption and the corresponding need for regular battery replacement has made wireless networks difficult and costly to maintain. Nobody wants to replace hundreds or thousands of window sensor batteries in a large building on a regular basis.

The promise of wireless sensor networks can only be fully realized when the wiring for both the data communication and the power supply is eliminated. Doing so requires a true battery-free wireless solution, one that can utilize energy harvested directly from the environment. To facilitate the widespread deployment of wireless sensor networks, GreenPeak has developed an ultra-low-power communication technology that can utilize environmental energy sources such as light, motion and vibration. This technology, employing on-board power management circuits and computer software to monitor energy harvesters and make the best use of harvested energy, enables sensors to operate reliably in a battery-free environment.

Wireless sensor networks deployed in our offices and homes will have an enormous impact on our daily lives, helping to build a smarter world in which energy is recycled and fully utilized. These wireless platforms, equipped with advanced sensing capability, will enable us to better control our lives, homes and environment, creating a truly connected world that enables people worldwide to live in a more comfortable, safer, and cleaner environment.

43. By "human intervention" (Paragraph 2), the author refers to _____.
    A. the reduction of great energy waste in the environment
    B. the grasping of straightforward opportunities available
    C. acts like turning off lights when no one is in the room
    D. the adoption of smart sensing and network technology

44. Batteries are not an ideal energy source for sensor networks because they _____.
    A. have to be replaced from time to time
    B. contain metals that pollute the environment
    C. require automatic recharging
    D. are difficult and costly to maintain

45. Battery-free wireless sensor networks are made possible by the fact that _____.
    A. there is energy in the environment to be utilized
    B. the cost of using them has been drastically reduced
    C. modern data communication consumes little energy
    D. their maintenance has been greatly simplified

46. According to the passage, GreenPeak _____.
    A. is the first company to install wireless sensor networks
    B. promotes the application of wireless sensor networks
    C. supplies batteries operating on harvested energy
    D. benefits handsomely from communication technology

47. The focus of Paragraph 4 is on the _____.
    A. replacement of batteries in harvesters
    B. monitoring of energy harvested from the environment
    C. elimination of batteries in sensor networks
    D. impact of sensor networks on power supply

48. Wireless sensor networks promise to _____.

   A. bring businesses high profits

   B. further develop the sensing technology

   C. turn motion into a major source of energy

   D. improve the daily lives of people worldwide

Passage Four

If you haven't heard or seen anything about Road Rage in the last few months, you've probably been avoiding the media. There have been countless stories about the new and scary phenomenon, considered a type of aggressive driving. You have most likely encountered aggressive driving and/or Road Rage recently if you drive at all.

While drunk driving remains a critical problem, the facts about aggressive driving are surely as disturbing. For instance, according to the National Highway Transportation Safety Association, 41,907 people died on the highway last year. Of those fatalities, the agency estimates that about two-thirds were caused at least in part by aggressive driving behaviors.

Why is this phenomenon occurring more than ever now, and why is it something that seemed almost nonexistent a few short years ago? Experts have several theories, and all are probably partially correct. One suggestion is sheer overcrowding. In the last decade, the number of cars on the roads has increased by more than 11 percent, and the number of miles driven has increased by 35 percent. However, the number of new road miles has only increased by 1 percent. That means more cars in the same amount of space; and the problem is magnified in urban areas. Also, people have less time and more things to do. With people working and trying to fit extra chores(琐事) and activities into the day, stress levels have never been higher. Stress creates anxiety, which leads to short tempers. These factors, when combined in certain situations, can spell Road Rage.

You may think you are the last person who would drive aggressively, but you might be surprised. For instance, have you ever yelled out loud at a slower driver, sounded the horn long and hard at another car, or sped up to keep another driver from passing? If you recognize yourself in any of these situations, watch out!

Whether you are getting angry at other drivers, or another driver is visibly upset with you, there are things you can do to avoid any major confrontation. If you are susceptible to Road Rage, the key is to discharge your emotion in a healthy way. If you are the target of another driver's rage, do everything possible to get away from the other driver safely, including avoiding eye contact and getting out of their way.

49. The first sentence in Paragraph 1 implies that _____.

   A. people not interested in the media know little about recent happenings

   B. Road Rage has received much media coverage in the last few months

   C. one may be raged by media reports and wants to avoid them

   D. the media coined the term "Road Rage" only a few months ago

50. According to the National Highway Transportation Safety Association, last year _____.

  A. drunk driving remained the No. 1 killer on the highways

  B. more people were killed by aggressive driving than by drunk driving

  C. two thirds of drivers were killed by aggressive driving

  D. 41, 907 people feel victim to aggressive driving

51. Which of the following is NOT mentioned as a cause of aggressive driving?

  A. Increasing number of cars.   B. Drivers' stress and anxiety.

  C. Overcrowded roads.   D. Rush hour traffic.

52. The word "spell" in Paragraph 3 means "_____".

  A. speak   B. cause   C. describe   D. spare

53. Which of the following characterizes aggressive driving?

  A. Talking while driving.   B. Driving fast.

  C. Yelling at another driver.   D. Sounding the horn when passing.

54. The last paragraph is intended to _____.

  A. tell people how to cope with Road Rage

  B. inform people how aggressive drivers could be

  C. tell people how to control themselves when angry

  D. warn people against eye contact with another driver

Passage Five

  In the early 20th century, a horse named Clever Hans was believed capable of counting and other impressive mental tasks. After years of great performance, psychologists discovered that though Hans was certainly clever, he was not clever in the way everyone expected. The horse was cleverly picking up on tiny, unintentional bodily and facial signals given out not only by his trainer, but also by the audience. Aware of the "Clever Hans" effect, Lisa Lit at the University of California and her colleagues wondered whether the beliefs of professional dog handlers might similarly affect the outcomes of searches for drugs and explosives. Remarkably, Dr. Lit found, they do.

  Dr. Lit asked 18 professional dog handlers and their dogs to complete brief searches. Before the searches, the handlers were informed that some of the search areas might contain up to three target scents, and also that in two cases those scents would be marked by pieces of red paper. What the handlers were not told was that none of the search areas contained scents of either drugs or explosives. Any "detections" made by the teams thus had to be false.

  The findings reveal that of 144 searches, only 21 were clean (no alerts). All the others raised one alert or more. In total, the teams raised 225 alerts. While the sheer number of false alerts struck Dr. Lit as fascinating, it was where they took place that was of greatest interest.

  When handlers could see a red piece of paper, allegedly marking a location of interest, they were much more likely to say that their dogs signaled an alert. The human handlers were not only distracted on almost every occasion by the stimulus aimed at them, but also transmitted that distraction to their animals—who responded accordingly. To mix metaphors, the dogs were crying "wolf" at the unconscious signal of their handlers.

How much that matters in the real world is unclear. But it might. If a handler, for example, unconsciously "profiled" people being sniffed by a drug, or explosive-detecting dog at an airport, false positives could abound. That is not only bad for innocent travelers, but might distract the team from catching the guilty.

55. What did psychologists find out about Clever Hans?
   A. He was as clever as people claimed. B. He was really good at counting.
   C. He could understand human language. D. He merely responded to human signals.

56. Lisa Lit and her colleagues _____.
   A. questioned the "Clever Hans" effect B. discovered the "Clever Hans" effect
   C. confirmed the "Clever Hans" effect D. rejected the "Clever Hans" effect

57. The dog handlers learned before the searches that _____.
   A. each search area contained three target scents
   B. there was actually no target scent in the search area
   C. some target scents may be labeled with a special mark
   D. their dogs were expected to find the scents of red paper

58. What was most significant about the experiment, according to Dr. Lit?
   A. The location of the false alerts. B. The regularity of the false alerts.
   C. The number of the false alerts. D. The timing of the false alerts.

59. It can be concluded from the experiment that _____.
   A. dog handlers are more likely to be distracted than their dogs
   B. dogs may act in response to their handlers' bodily signals
   C. the cooperation between dogs and their handlers is key to success
   D. well-trained dogs can better understand their handlers' signals

60. The author thinks that Dr. Lit's findings _____.
   A. should raise our concern in real life B. may not be useful in real situations
   C. should be backed up by further evidence D. will be widely applied in the near future

Part IV Cloze (15 minutes, 15 points)

Directions: *In this part, there is a passage with 15 blanks. For each blank there are 4 choices marked A, B, C and D. Choose the best answer for each blank and mark the corresponding letter with a single bar across the square brackets on your machine-scoring **Answer Sheet**.*

Zoos have become an important site for the preservation and protection of wildlife resources, __61__ those species that are endangered. __62__, many zoos displayed live animals for public entertainment. Presently some zoos have become scientific and educational __63__ that have contributed to the understanding and conservation of wild animal populations. __64__ the challenges facing modern zoos are the cost of upgrading old facilities, the struggle to obtain __65__ operating funds, and the need to attract more visitors to new and entertaining exhibits.

Many __66__ zoos in American cities have undergone renovation(翻新) during the last decades of the twentieth century. Among the recent trends in zoo __67__ is the construction of new enclosures that resemble natural habitats（栖息地）. The replacement of traditional steel bars and concrete floors __68__ appropriately designed surroundings improves visitor appreciation of the animals. Such renovations may __69__ stress on animals and allow them to interact with one another more naturally.

Several major zoos conduct captive propagation programs. A captive propagation program includes the breeding of __70__ zoo or wild animals to obtain offspring. Usually for release to __71__ or for transfer to other zoos. Captive breeding is one method of __72__ some species from extinction.

Zoos have expanded and improved public education programs also, with education departments that develop programs __73__ zoo exhibits. Public activities include in-school programs, zoo tours, special events, and websites. The Zoological Society of New York, for example, conducted a major project with a Western African government to monitor an elephant herd __74__ it moved throughout its range.

The importance of zoos will increase as natural habitats are diminishing. Through their efforts __75__ conservation, education, and environmental advocacy, zoos will continue to play a critical role in wildlife preservation throughout the world.

61. A. superficially	B. especially	C. importantly	D. supposedly
62. A. By that time	B. By the time	C. At one time	D. At that time
63. A. institutions	B. associations	C. foundations	D. corporations
64. A. Along	B. Toward	C. Among	D. Through
65. A. limited	B. professional	C. sufficient	D. excessive
66. A. newer	B. older	C. former	D. later
67. A. management	B. improvement	C. achievement	D. assessment
68. A. under	B. for	C. into	D. with
69. A. reduce	B. cause	C. increase	D. avoid
70. A. selected	B. sustained	C. promising	D. surviving
71. A. natural	B. the natural	C. wild	D. the wild
72. A. restraining	B. saving	C. sheltering	D. exempting
73. A. attributed to	B. opposed to	C. referred to	D. related to
74. A. as	B. as if	C. so	D. so that
75. A. in search of	B. in honor of	C. in support of	D. in charge of

Paper Two 试卷二 (60 minutes)

Part I Translation (30 minutes, 20 points)

Section A

Directions: *Translate the following passage into Chinese. Write your translation on the **Answer Sheet**.*

Over the years, we tend to think that nuclear technologies and the necessary know-how to ensure nuclear safety have been developed to a level that possibilities for any major nuclear accidents are almost non-existent and if it does happen, it will be controlled in the capable hands of nuclear engineers. However, reality has proved again that you just can't be too careful to handle nuclear energy. We don't know for sure yet what will be left behind Japan's nuclear crisis, but it will be certain that it is time to re-examine our nuclear practices and many more efforts need to be made to ensure nuclear safety in the future.

Section B

Directions: *Translate the following passage into English. Write your translation on the **Answer Sheet**.*

中国有着5 000年的文化传统,历经劫难,而生生不息。我们一定要充分发扬祖国的文化传统。同时我们也懂得,要学习和借鉴世界先进的文明。只有这样,才能使祖国的文化得到进一步发展,也就是我常说的,只有开放包容,才能使祖国强大。

Part II Writing (30 minutes, 15 points)

Directions: *In this part, you are to write within 30 minutes a composition of no less than 150 words under the title of "**How to Handle Stress**". The clues given below are for your reference only, NOT the outline you should follow. Please remember to write your composition clearly on the **Composition Sheet**.*

1. Common sources of stress.
2. Healthy ways to reduce stress.
3. How do you overcome stressful situations.

2011年同等学力人员申请硕士学位英语水平全国统一考试

Paper One 试卷一

Part I Dialogue Communication

Section A

1. [正确答案] A

    [句子翻译] A:大卫说他花5 000英镑买了一辆全新的宝马!
    B:你确定?对我来说真便宜!
    A:他就是这么说的。

    [考点剖析] 通过空格之后的句意以及句末的叹号可推测,回答者在表达惊讶语气。此题易在A项和C项之间徘徊,A项是对事实的确认,C项是对观点的确认,显然对方是在陈述一个事实。

2. [正确答案] D

    [句子翻译] A:我们刚从凤凰城回来。这次度假是近几年来玩得最好的一次。
    B:很不错。听到你这么说我很高兴。

    [考点剖析] 对方在陈述一件快乐的事,回答者应表达祝贺。这一点从空格之后的句意也可推断出来。四个选项中只有D项有这一功能。注意C项,在口语中常用于表达回答者的不耐烦的语气,意为"噢,你又来了(又说/做这事了)"。

3. [正确答案] C

    [句子翻译] A:我再也受不了这门课了!
    B:好了,你最好习惯它。这门课是必修的,你得好好完成它才能毕业。

    [考点剖析] 对方语气显然很烦躁,加之空格后回答者在陈述必须好好上课的理由,因此可以推断空格处应是回答者向对方表示安慰。A、B、D项都无法和后文形成顺承关系。尤其注意B项,You can say that again是个常用表达,意为"你说得太对了"。

4. [正确答案] B

    [句子翻译] A:我不知道你怎么想,但我觉得那部电影非常棒。
    B:我同意。那部电影不仅演员演得很好,而且配乐也很美。

    [考点剖析] 从空格之后的句意可推断,回答者表示对说话人观点的赞同。B项中的I was with you there是一个常用于表达赞同的句子。注意A项,一般不用于表示赞同,

· 14 ·

而是用来形容两物或者两事一模一样。而D项用于对方提出一个以"Do"开头的一般疑问句的情况,用在此处不符合语法。

5. [正确答案] A

   [句子翻译] A:丹免费把我载回了家,但我付了油钱。
   B:你知道的,人们常说天下没有免费的午餐。

   [考点剖析] 此题四个选项都是习语,需了解每个选项的意思。A项"天下没有免费的午餐";B项"贪多嚼不烂";C项"善有善报";D项"认识的人才最重要"。

Section B

6. [正确答案] A

   [句子翻译] 女士:我不愿就此多谈,别问我。男士:说说吧。我想你需要发泄一下情绪。

   [考点剖析] 此题关键在于理解回答者let off some steam是什么意思,结合语境,再从字面上理解,很容易看出是鼓励对方发泄情绪、说出这件事的意思。因此,从四个选项中可以看出A项的意思最为相似。

7. [正确答案] D

   [句子翻译] 女士:朱莉的裙子看起来真搞笑,那个款式去年就过时了。男士:别这样说,只要她穿着好看就行。

   [考点剖析] 此题关键在于理解as long as(只要),这句话说明男士也觉得裙子不太好看,但因为穿的人是"她",所以表达了赞美。这句话说明男士说话的重点在"她"身上,而不是裙子上,所以排除A、B项。而因男士表达了赞美,觉得"她"穿着好看,并没有建议"她"应该紧跟潮流,所以也排除C项。

8. [正确答案] C

   [句子翻译] 男士:你喜欢吃哪种点心?女士:噢,我最爱甜食,你知道的。

   [考点剖析] sweet tooth常用于形容人喜欢吃甜食,理解了这一点还不够,还需区分四个选项各属于哪一种点心。A项"三明治"、B项"热狗"和D项"薯条"都是西餐中常见的咸味食物,只有C项"冰淇淋"属于甜食。

9. [正确答案] B

   [句子翻译] 女士:我受够了每天开车上下班。要是汽车能自动驾驶,那该多好啊!男士:嗯,一些汽车厂商正在研发这种汽车。如果你能买得起的话,我想你很快就可以买到一辆这样的汽车了。

   [考点剖析] 此题容易在A、B项之间徘徊。从男士最后一句话的if可知,女士要想买到车,是需要条件的——有足够的钱。可是A项十分肯定地说女士可以在将来买一辆智能车,没有提到任何条件,因此不能选。而从这一条件中可以推测,女士很难拥有足够的钱买这种车,暗示这种智能汽车将会很昂贵。

10. [正确答案] D

    [句子翻译] 男士:安妮,你为什么从来没有和某人共度一生的想法呢?女士:答案很简单,我并不介意和我的事业"结婚"。

[考点剖析]安妮想与事业"结婚"的想法透露了她对现有工作的喜爱与重视。因此 D 项最符合她的意思。

Part Ⅱ Vocabulary

Section A

11. [正确答案] A

    [考点类型] 动词

    [考点剖析] 题干中的 overlooked 意为"忽略,未注意到"。neglected"忽略";foresaw"预见";explored"开发";assessed"评估"。

12. [正确答案] D

    [考点类型] 动词

    [考点剖析] 题干中的 obliged 意为"(以法律、义务等)强迫,迫使"。reminded"提醒";expected"盼望";compelled"强制,使必须";requested"(正式或礼貌地)要求"。

13. [正确答案] A

    [考点类型] 名词

    [考点剖析] 题干中的 originality 意为"独创性,创意,独特构思"。creativity"创造性";popularity"普及";feasibility"可行性";flexibility"灵活性"。

14. [正确答案] D

    [考点类型] 形容词

    [考点剖析] 题干中的 deliberate 意为"故意的,蓄意的,存心的"。conscious"意识到的";desperate"不顾一切的";clumsy"笨拙的";intentional"有意的"。

15. [正确答案] B

    [考点类型] 副词

    [考点剖析] 题干中的 scarcely 意为"几乎不,勉强"。just"仅";hardly"几乎不";almost"几乎";definitely"肯定地"。

16. [正确答案] B

    [考点类型] 动词

    [考点剖析] 题干中的 trapped 意为"使困住"。constrained"强迫";caught"陷入";concealed"隐藏";concentrated"集中"。

17. [正确答案] D

    [考点类型] 形容词

    [考点剖析] 题干中的 hazardous 意为"危险的,有害的"。poisonous"有毒的";difficult"困难的";dangerous"危险的";harmful"有害的"。

18. [正确答案] D

    [考点类型] 副词

    [考点剖析] 题干中的 in the neighborhood of 意为"近于,大约"。precisely"精确地";merely"仅仅";substantially"大体上";approximately"大约"。

2011年同等学力人员申请硕士学位英语水平全国统一考试答案及详解

19. [正确答案] C

    [考点类型] 名词

    [考点剖析] 题干中的 obstacle 意为"障碍,阻碍,绊脚石"。factor"因素";constituent"成分";barrier"障碍";break"中断"。

20. [正确答案] A

    [考点类型] 动词短语

    [考点剖析] 题干中的 lean on 意为"依靠,依赖(……的帮助和支持)"。count on"依靠";benefit from"从……受益";stand for"代表,支持";stick to"坚持"。

Section B

21. [正确答案] D

    [考点类型] 固定搭配

    [考点剖析] takes"取走";appears"出现";makes"使……";goes without saying"不言而喻"。

22. [正确答案] C

    [考点类型] 形近词辨析

    [考点剖析] irregular"不规则的";illegal"非法的";abrupt"突然的";absurd"荒谬的"。

23. [正确答案] D

    [考点类型] 形近词辨析

    [考点剖析] mysterious"神秘的";furious"激烈的";serious"严肃的";curious"好奇的"。

24. [正确答案] C

    [考点类型] 逻辑关系

    [考点剖析] acquaintance"相识";integration"整合";alliance"联盟";intimacy"亲密"。

25. [正确答案] D

    [考点类型] 形近词辨析

    [考点剖析] suspended"延缓";suppressed"抑制";summoned"召唤";subjected"经受"。

26. [正确答案] B

    [考点类型] 逻辑关系

    [考点剖析] profit"利润";supplement"补充";subsidy"津贴";replacement"替换"。

27. [正确答案] B

    [考点类型] 逻辑关系

    [考点剖析] treatment"治疗";incidence"事件,发生率";consequence"结果";misfortune"不幸"。

28. [正确答案] A

    [考点类型] 逻辑关系

    [考点剖析] species"物种";sources"来源";numbers"数量";members"成员"。

· 17 ·

29. [正确答案] A

　　[考点类型] 固定搭配

　　[考点剖析] picking up"学会,获得";bringing up"提出";putting up"举起";pulling up"拔起"。

30. [正确答案] C

　　[考点类型] 逻辑关系

　　[考点剖析] promoted"提拔,促进";substituted"代替";authorized"授权";displaced"置换"。

Part Ⅲ　Reading Comprehension

Passage One

　　直到去年春天,妮娅·帕克和其邻居家的孩子都是坐59号校园巴士上学。但因为燃油涨价,所以学区必须找到降低交通成本的方法。于是学校巴士公司重画了路线图,取消了妮娅所住地区的校车。现在,妮娅和她的邻居们通过"步行校车"走半英里去上学,"步行校车"指的是一群孩子由一两个成人护送,步行上学。

　　学区负责人也和我们一样,因燃油成本上涨而烦恼,并且正在寻找新的解决方法。在过去的两年中,柴油的价格已经上升了34%。对美国典型的学区来说,巴士费用总额占预算的5%。当管理者将注意力放在降低成本上时,校车接送便成了他们考虑到的目标,因为它不影响课堂教学(或测试分数)。超过三分之一的美国学校管理者为了控制预算而取消了巴士站或接送路线。

　　许多家长很高兴看到自己的孩子走路上学,部分原因是他们中的许多人也曾走路上学。根据1969年的一项调查显示,几乎一半学生走路或骑车上学,而2001年这一数据只有16%。现代父母不愿意让孩子走路上学,因为害怕交通意外、犯罪或怕孩子受欺负,但有成人护送,这些担心就可以减少一些。

　　学校和巴士公司正寻找其他方法省钱。在那些校车必不可少的乡村地区,一些学校甚至选择每周只上四天课。巴士公司指导司机,让他们取消接送路线中的额外停站,并且在汽车空转时关掉发动机。他们也应用计算机软件来确定最高效节能的接送路线,而这些路线通常不一定为最短路线。

　　然而,减少巴士数量可能带来负面效应。如果每个以前坐校车上学的学生开始步行上学,那将会对环境有利。但如果太多的父母决定自己开车送孩子上学以代替校车,那么二氧化碳的排放量将会增长,同时还会增加安全风险。一份2002年的报告得出结论:学生坐校车比坐私家车安全13倍,因为校车事故更少,且校车的车身结构更能经得起事故。当然也有一些学生抱怨早上上学要走很长的路,特别是路上要经过很高的山坡。

31. [正确答案] A

　　[考点类型] 推理题

　　[题目翻译] "步行校车"_____。

　　　　A. 不消耗燃料

　　　　B. 目标是使孩子们保持身体健康

　　　　C. 很少引起交通阻塞

　　　　D. 很受学生欢迎

[考点剖析] 由文章第一段的最后一句话中关于步行校车的解释"一群孩子由一两个成人护送,步行上学"可推断正确答案为 A 项。

32. [正确答案] B
    [考点类型] 推理题
    [题目翻译] 在美国,用校车接送孩子的责任由_____承担。
    A. 私人学校　　　　B. 学区
    C. 老师　　　　　　D. 父母
    [考点剖析] 由文章第二段我们得知,学区负责人由于燃油成本上涨感到压力而采取了减少预算等措施,由此可推断正确答案为 B 项。

33. [正确答案] D
    [考点类型] 细节题
    [题目翻译] 对于步行上学,现代父母似乎更关注_____。
    A. 路上花费的时间
    B. 路线的变化
    C. 孩子们的体力
    D. 孩子们的安全
    [考点剖析] 由文章第三段的最后一句我们得知,现代父母不愿意让孩子走路上学是因为害怕交通意外、犯罪或孩子被欺负,故本题答案为 D 项。

34. [正确答案] B
    [考点类型] 细节题
    [题目翻译] 为了省钱,一些学校选择_____。
    A. 走最短的路线
    B. 缩短每周上学的时间
    C. 更好地培训司机
    D. 使用节能的巴士
    [考点剖析] 由文章第四段的第二句我们得知,一些学校选择每周只上四天学,故本题答案为 B 项。

35. [正确答案] C
    [考点类型] 细节题
    [题目翻译] 减少巴士数量最终可能导致_____。
    A. 巴士公司间更激烈的竞争
    B. 更多的学生乘坐公共交通工具
    C. 二氧化碳的排放量增加
    D. 校车的安全性降低
    [考点剖析] 由文章第五段的第二句我们得知,如果太多的父母决定开车送孩子上学,那么这将会导致二氧化碳的排放量增加,所以选择 C 项。

36. [正确答案] C
   [考点类型] 主旨题
   [题目翻译] 下列哪项最能概括作者对降低校车数量的态度？
      A. 赞成的。   B. 批评的。
      C. 客观的。   D. 漠不关心的。
   [考点剖析] 从文章各段作者多角度的叙述可知，作者未作任何判断，也并未提出自己的看法，所以是客观的描述，因此选择C项。

Passage Two

人类寿命比以往更长，但由于某种原因，女性比男性更长寿。一名2003年出生的美国男婴预计可活到73岁，而女婴可活到79岁。这的确是一个很大的差距，然而没人真正明白为什么会产生这种现象。几个世纪以来，女性更长寿一直是众所周知的，例如，17世纪已有记载。然而，当时的差距比较小，现在差距正在扩大。

若干原因已被提出来解释这种差距。在工业化社会中，这种差距最大。因此，人们认为，这种差距是由于女性较少受工作压力影响的原因，因为工作压力会增大罹患心脏病和酗酒的风险。同时，社会学家告诉我们，相比男性，女性很少被鼓励冒险（而这可能是她们更小心驾车、较少发生车祸的原因）。

吸烟也与年龄差距有关。过去人们曾认为职业女性更有可能吸烟，并且随着更多女性加入劳动大军，男女寿命差距将开始缩小，因为吸烟会导致人们过早死亡。然而，现在我们看到更多女性吸烟，尽管她们的肺癌患病率急剧上升，但是她们的寿命仍然较长。

令人困惑的是，女性似乎并不像男性那么健康，也就是说，她们所患的疾病更多。但男性一旦生病，将可能更严重。

一些研究者认为，因为男性的健康更多与情绪有关，所以男性可能死得更早。例如，相比女性，男性丧偶后更易死亡。失去工作时男性甚至似乎更脆弱（这两种情况都与免疫力的显著下降有关）。男性的死亡紧随退休而来，时间之短令人惊恐。

可能我们寻找答案时过于关注问题表面，而答案可能深藏在我们的生物遗传中。毕竟，这种现象并不单独存在于人类当中。在绝大多数哺乳动物中，雌性都拥有这种优势，所以她们通常都活得更久。此外，很多物种在怀孕阶段，这种差距就已经显现：流产更多的是雄性。而人类出生后，男孩比女孩死亡更多。

37. [正确答案] C
   [考点类型] 推理题
   [题目翻译] 从前两段，我们可以得知什么？
      A. 男性的寿命几乎保持不变。
      B. 研究者发现了年龄差距的原因。
      C. 社会越先进，年龄差距越大。
      D. 年龄差距最近才被注意到。
   [考点剖析] 由文章第一段的最后一句我们得知，年龄的差距在以前比较小，而现在差距正

在扩大,由此推断本题答案为 C 项。另外,第二段第二句也论证了这一选项。

38. [正确答案] D
    [考点类型] 推理题
    [题目翻译] 第二段提到女性寿命较长的两个因素是 _____。
              A. 疾病和交通事故
              B. 工业化和工作压力
              C. 她们对心脏疾病的免疫和拒绝喝酒
              D. 她们较高的工作抗压能力与较低的冒险欲
    [考点剖析] 根据文章第二段第二、三句我们得知,女性较少受工作压力的影响,而且相比男性,女性很少被鼓励冒险,由此可推断本题答案为 D 项。

39. [正确答案] D
    [考点类型] 细节题
    [题目翻译] 根据第三段,下列哪项陈述正确?
              A. 大量的男性烟民对年龄差距造成影响。
              B. 越来越多的女性烟民将缩短男女之间的年龄差距。
              C. 女性工作者比男性工作者更有可能吸烟。
              D. 吸烟似乎不影响女性长寿。
    [考点剖析] 根据文章第三段的最后一句"尽管她们的肺癌患病率急剧上升,但是她们的寿命仍然较长"可知本题答案为 D 项。

40. [正确答案] B
    [考点类型] 细节题
    [题目翻译] 下列哪种现象使研究者感到困惑?
              A. 男性的健康与他们的情绪关系更密切。
              B. 尽管女性更容易得病,但她们的寿命仍然更长。
              C. 男性得病时会表现出比女性更重的症状。
              D. 相当多的男性在退休不久后就死去了。
    [考点剖析] 文章第四段提到"令人困惑的是,女性似乎并不像男性那么健康,她们所患的疾病更多。但是男性一旦生病,将可能更严重"。故答案为 B 项。

41. [正确答案] C
    [考点类型] 词汇题
    [题目翻译] 第六段中的 edge 意为"_____"。
              A. 利润   B. 方面   C. 优势   D. 质量
    [考点剖析] 文章第六段第四句的大意为"在绝大多数哺乳动物中,雌性通常活得更长"。这里应该是指雌性寿命更长这一优势普遍存在,故 C 项正确。

42. [正确答案] A
    [考点类型] 主旨题
    [题目翻译] 本文的主旨是什么?
              A. 女性更长寿仍然是个谜。

B. 女性比男性健康的现象很好地解释了她们长寿的原因。
C. 由于工业化的原因,人们越来越长寿。
D. 女性的情绪更少受生活困难的影响。

[考点剖析] 由文章最后一段的首句可推测出我们仍然在寻找女性长寿的答案,故本题答案为 A 项。

Passage Three

许多人都意识到了我们环境中巨大的能源浪费,但并未利用一些简单的方式来节约那些能源。例如,每个人都知道,当办公室里没人的时候,应该把灯关掉。同样,当员工们都没有使用会议室的时候,室温并不需要调节。

幸好,节能不需要依赖人类介入。有了智能感应和网络技术的帮助,诸如关灯和调节温度这样的节能过程可自动完成。最终,这项科技将会使消费者和生产经理更好地辨别能源的浪费行为,并且使用这些程序可以使住宅、大厦和工厂变得更加智能和高效。

到目前为止,因为提供能源和起连通作用的线路和电缆具有安装和维护成本高和难度大的特点,所以限制了传感器网络的广泛应用。由电池驱动的无线网络可以简化安装程序,并且降低成本。但由于无线网络系统耗能高,并且需要频繁更换电池,所以这些系统的维护变得困难且昂贵。没人愿意对一整栋大楼中成百上千个传感器的电池进行定期更换。

要完全实现无线传感网络的愿景,必须同时实现数据传输和能源供应的无线化。要做到这一点,需要制定一个真正的无须电池驱动的无线解决方案。这一方案可以直接利用从环境中获取的能源。为了促进无线传感网络的大规模应用,GreenPeak 公司已经开发了一种超低功耗的传输技术,它所用的能源就是直接从环境中获取的,比如从光、移动和振动中获取的能量。这种技术应用了板载电源管理电路和电脑软件来监控能源获取过程,并最大限度地利用所获取的能源,使传感器在无电池驱动的环境中可靠运作。

办公室和住宅中配置的无线传感网络将会对我们的日常生活产生巨大的影响,它能让能源循环并被最大化地使用,以帮助我们建立一个更加智能的世界。这些具有先进的传感功能的无线平台,将会使我们更好地掌控我们的生活、家庭和环境,并且创造出一个真正紧密联系的世界,让全世界的人们都拥有一个更加舒适、安全和清洁的生活环境。

43. [正确答案] C

[考点类型] 词汇题

[题目翻译] 作者在第二段中提到的"人类介入"指的是_____。

A. 减少环境中巨大的能源浪费
B. 把握直接可用的机会
C. 房间无人时关灯这一类的举动
D. 采用智能感应和网络技术

[考点剖析] 虽然问题出现在第二段,但答案出现在第一段里面。第一段中将人走关灯作为人们知道如何节省能源的例子。然后第二段的 Fortunately 表示转折,该句的意思是"幸好节能不需要人类介入"。"人类介入"就是指人走关灯这类举动。因此选 C 项。

2011年同等学力人员申请硕士学位英语水平全国统一考试答案及详解

44. [正确答案] D

[考点类型] 细节题

[题目翻译] 对感应网络系统来说,电池并不是理想的能量来源,这是因为它们_____。

A. 必须时常更换

B. 含有一些会污染环境的金属物质

C. 需要自动充电

D. 维护起来困难且昂贵

[考点剖析] 关于电池的信息出现在第三段,从第三段中可以找到直接信息。该段提到因为无线网络系统耗能高,又经常需要替换电池,所以这些系统的维护变得困难且昂贵。由此可知D项正确。A项虽然涉及有效信息,但是不全面。

45. [正确答案] A

[考点类型] 细节题

[题目翻译] 无须电池驱动的无线传感网络变为现实的前提是_____。

A. 环境中有能被利用的能量

B. 使用它们的成本已被大大降低

C. 现代数据传输只耗费很少的能量

D. 它们的维护已被极大地简化

[考点剖析] 第四段中提到,无线传感网络的使用需要一个无须电池驱动的无线解决方案,并且指出这一方案可以直接利用从环境中获得的能源。因此选A项。

46. [正确答案] B

[考点类型] 推理题

[题目翻译] 根据本文内容可知,GreenPeak公司_____。

A. 是第一家安装无线传感网络的公司

B. 推动无线传感网络的应用

C. 供应靠捕获能源进行工作的电池

D. 通过通信技术获取了丰厚的利益

[考点剖析] 本题答案在第四段的后半部分。该段提到GreenPeak公司发展了一种能够利用环境中的能源的科技,而这种科技可以促进无线传感网络的使用。因此选B项。

47. [正确答案] B

[考点类型] 细节题

[题目翻译] 第四段的重点是_____。

A. 获取过程中电池的更换

B. 监控从环境中获取的能源

C. 在传感网络中不使用电池

D. 传感网络系统对能量供应的影响

[考点剖析] 题目问的是第四段的重点,而第四段主要说到 GreenPeak 公司的科技能监控能源获取过程,并最大限度地利用从环境中获取的能源。因此选 B 项。

48. [正确答案] D
    [考点类型] 细节题
    [题目翻译] 无线传感网络有希望_____。
       A. 为企业带来高利润
       B. 使传感技术得到更好的发展
       C. 使移动成为能量的主要来源
       D. 改善全世界人们的日常生活
    [考点剖析] 最后一段说到无线传感网络的使用会对人们的生活、环境和家庭产生很大的影响。因此选 D 项。

Passage Four

如果你在过去的几个月中从没听过或看过任何有关"路怒症"的消息,那么你可能没有关注媒体。这种新兴而又可怕的现象是一种冲动的驾驶行为,且已经有了不少事例。如果你开车的话,你最近大概已经遇到过类似的冲动驾驶或者"路怒症"了。

目前,醉驾行为依然是一个严重的问题,而冲动驾驶的烦人程度并不亚于它。举个例子,根据美国高速公路交通安全协会的报告可知,去年有 41 907 人死于高速公路事故。据该机构估算,大约有三分之二的事故原因与冲动驾驶行为有部分关系。

为什么现在这类现象比以前发生得更多了呢?在几年之前,这类事故好像并不存在,这又是为什么呢?专家们有几个理论来解释这一现象,而且都可能是部分正确的。有一个解释就是"单纯的过度拥堵"。在过去的 10 年里,公路上的汽车数量增长了超过 11%,而行驶里程数也增长了 35%。然而,新的公路里程却只增长了 1%。这便意味着,在同样的空间里有更多的汽车,这种现象在城市中更加明显。而且人们的时间变得越来越少,要做的事情却越来越多。而对于上班族,他们每天还要应对额外的琐事和活动,因此压力达到了峰值。而压力能产生焦虑感,这便引发了人们的暴脾气。这些因素一旦作用于某些特定场景,就会导致"路怒症"。

你可能在想,你绝不可能成为冲动驾驶的人,但事实也许会让你大吃一惊。比如,你是否对着一个开车很慢的司机叫嚷过?或者对着另一辆车用力地长按喇叭?又或者为防止别人超车而不断加速?如果你发现自己已有过如上的任一情形,那么一定要注意!

不管你对其他司机发火还是别的司机明显地冲你撒气,你都可以用一些办法来避免你们之间的正面冲突。如果你是"路怒症"的"易感人群",那么最好的办法便是用健康的方式来发泄你的情绪。如果你是另外一名司机的泄愤对象,那么尽量采取一些安全的措施来避开他,包括避免直接对视以及驶离他的路线等。

49. [正确答案] B
    [考点类型] 推理题
    [题目翻译] 第一段的第一句暗示_____。
       A. 对媒体不感兴趣的人对最近发生的事了解很少

B. "路怒症"在过去的几个月中已经得到了媒体的很多报道

C. 人们可能会被媒体报道激怒,从而排斥这些报道

D. 媒体在几个月前才创造出"路怒症"这个词

[考点剖析] 题干重点词语是 implies"暗示"。第一句话是说如果你最近几个月没看过或听说过"路怒症"的话,那你可能并没有关注媒体,言外之意是媒体对此类问题进行了大量报道。C、D 项为无关选项,A 项是干扰选项,但是 A 项是第一句话的同义改写,并不是暗示。所以选 B 项。

50. [正确答案] B

[考点类型] 细节题

[题目翻译] 根据美国高速公路交通安全协会的报告可知,去年_____。

A. 醉驾仍然稳居"高速公路杀手"第一名

B. 死于冲动驾驶的人数比死于醉驾的人数要多

C. 三分之二的司机死于冲动驾驶

D. 41 907 人感觉自己是冲动驾驶的受害者

[考点剖析] 第二段第三句给出了一个数据"三分之二",也就是"三分之二的交通事故是跟冲动驾驶有部分关系的",明显多于一半,所以 A 项不对。原文是说三分之二的交通事故是跟冲动驾驶有部分关系的,C 项不对,D 项也不对。文中是说有 41 907 人死于交通事故,而这些事故的大部分原因与冲动驾驶有关,所以选 B 项。

51. [正确答案] D

[考点类型] 细节题

[题目翻译] 下列哪一项不是文章所提及的导致冲动驾驶的原因?

A. 日益增加的汽车数量。

B. 司机的压力和焦虑感。

C. 过度拥挤的道路。

D. 上下班高峰期的交通状况。

[考点剖析] 第三段提到,车的数量增多,路上的车辆变多,以及人因压力变大而产生焦虑情绪都可能导致冲动驾驶。所以 A、B、C 项都是对的,而 D 项文中并没有提到,故选 D 项。

52. [正确答案] B

[考点类型] 词汇题

[题目翻译] 第三段中 spell 一词的意思是"_____"。

A. 说话   B. 导致

C. 描述   D. 抽出

[考点剖析] "spell"出现在第三段句末,整句话 These factors, when combined in certain situations, can spell Road Rage 出现在作者分析了导致冲动驾驶的因素之后,是得出结论的句子,所以可推断该句子的意思是这些因素导致了(引起了)"路怒症"。可见最接近 spell 的选项是 B 项。

53. [正确答案] C
    [考点类型] 细节题
    [题目翻译] 下列哪一种行为是冲动驾驶的特点？
        A. 边开车边聊天。 B. 提高车速。
        C. 对另外一名司机大吼大叫。 D. 经过时鸣喇叭。
    [考点剖析] 第四段中，作者提醒读者可能要进入冲动驾驶状态的征兆，比如对其他司机大吼等。题目问的是冲动驾驶的特点，因此明显应该选 C 项。

54. [正确答案] A
    [考点类型] 主旨题
    [题目翻译] 最后一段是为了_____。
        A. 告诉人们如何应对"路怒症"
        B. 提醒人们冲动的驾驶员是什么样的
        C. 告诉人们发怒时应该如何控制自己
        D. 警告人们不要与其他司机直接对视
    [考点剖析] 最后一段一直传达的中心思想是当你可能要进入冲动驾驶的状态或者成为"路怒症"的目标时，你该如何摆脱冲动驾驶的状况，并且作者给读者提出了建议。由此可知应该选择 A 项。B 项文中未提及，C、D 项都只涵盖了部分信息。

Passage Five

20世纪初期，人们认为一匹叫"聪明汉斯"的马具备了数数字和从事其他令人印象深刻的脑力劳动的能力。它数年的精彩表现使心理学家发现，尽管汉斯确实聪明，但是它其实不像人们预想的那样聪明。此马可以学会驯马师和观众无意间做出的一些细微的肢体动作及面部表情。加利福尼亚大学的莉莎·利特和她的同事们在意识到了这种"聪明汉斯"效应之后，她们想知道专业驯狗师的看法是否也同样会影响毒品和爆炸物品的搜索结果。利特博士发现答案是肯定的。

利特博士让18位专业驯狗师和他们的狗完成简单的搜索任务。在搜索开始前，驯狗师被告知某些搜索区域可能有三种目标气味，而且有两种目标气味会用红纸进行标记。但是，驯狗师未被告知的是搜索区内根本没有毒品或炸药的气味。因此，这个队伍所给出的任何"方位"都是错的。

这些发现表明，144次搜索中只有21次是安全的（没有警报的）。其他所有的搜索都触动了一个或多个警报，这个队伍总共触动了225次警报。尽管错误警报的数量让利特博士感到震惊，但是这些错误警报的发生地点却是最有趣的。

当驯狗师看到一张红纸并据此标记了一处感兴趣的位置时，他们很可能会说是他们的狗发出了警报。几乎在所有的场合，人类驯兽师不仅会因为那些针对他们的刺激而分心，而且也会把这种分心传递给他们的动物，这些动物也会相应地作出反应。含糊地说，狗是在对主人的无意识的信号发出假警报。

在现实世界中，这会起到多大的作用不得而知。但是这确实是可能存在的。例如，当驯狗师在机场无意识地怀疑某人是嫌疑人时,受其影响,毒品和炸药探测犬在闻这类人时,误报可能会发生。这不仅对无辜的旅行者不利,而且会使警队的注意力离开真正的犯罪分子。

55. [正确答案] D

　　[考点类型] 细节题

　　[题目翻译] 关于"聪明汉斯",心理学家们发现了什么?

　　　　A. 它跟人们说的一样聪明。

　　　　B. 它很擅长数数字。

　　　　C. 它能理解人类的语言。

　　　　D. 它只是对人类给出的信号作出反应。

　　[考点剖析] 定位至文章第一段第二句、第三句,可知心理学家发现"聪明汉斯"并不像人们预想的那样聪明,它能学会的只是人们做出的一些肢体动作及面部表情。因此本题答案为 D 项。

56. [正确答案] C

　　[考点类型] 细节题

　　[题目翻译] 莉莎·利特和她的同事们_____。

　　　　A. 质疑了"聪明汉斯"效应

　　　　B. 发现了"聪明汉斯"效应

　　　　C. 证实了"聪明汉斯"效应

　　　　D. 反对了"聪明汉斯"效应

　　[考点剖析] 定位至文章第一段最后两句,可知是莉莎·利特和她的同事们意识到这一现象后,又通过实验证实了它。因此本题答案为 C 项。

57. [正确答案] C

　　[考点类型] 细节题

　　[题目翻译] 驯狗师在搜索工作进行之前了解到_____。

　　　　A. 每个搜索区域包含 3 种目标气味

　　　　B. 搜索区域内并没有目标气味

　　　　C. 有的目标气味可能有特殊的标记

　　　　D. 人们希望他们的狗找到用红纸标记的气味

　　[考点剖析] 定位至文章第二段第二句,可知驯狗师被告知一些气味是用红纸标记出来的。因此本题答案为 C 项。

58. [正确答案] A

　　[考点类型] 细节题

　　[题目翻译] 对利特博士来说这个实验最重要的是什么?

　　　　A. 错误警报的位置。

　　　　B. 错误警报的规律性。

　　　　C. 错误警报的数量。

　　　　D. 错误警报的时间。

[考点剖析] 定位至文章第三段最后一句,可知最重要的是错误警报的位置。因此本题答案为 A 项。

59. [正确答案] B

    [考点类型] 推理题

    [题目翻译] 由这个实验可得出_____。

    A. 驯狗师比狗更容易受干扰

    B. 狗会对驯狗师的肢体信号作出反应

    C. 狗和驯狗师之间的合作是成功的关键

    D. 训练良好的狗能更好地理解驯狗师的信号

    [考点剖析] 定位至文章倒数第二段第二句,从中可知这些狗会对驯狗师的身体信号作出相应的反应。因此本题答案为 B 项。

60. [正确答案] A

    [考点类型] 细节题

    [题目翻译] 作者认为利特博士的发现_____。

    A. 在现实生活中应引起关注

    B. 在现实情况中可能没有用

    C. 应进行进一步求证

    D. 在不久的将来会被广泛应用

    [考点剖析] 定位至文章最后一段,可知作者认为误报可能发生,这不仅对无辜的旅行者不利,而且会让真正的犯罪分子逃跑,作者表示了一种担忧。故本题答案为 A 项。

Part Ⅳ Cloze

　　动物园已经成为保护野生动物资源的重要场地,尤其是对那些濒临灭绝的物种而言。从前,很多动物园展出活体动物的目的是娱乐大众。目前,一些动物园已成为了解和保护野生动物的科学教育机构。现代动物园面临的众多挑战包括更新陈旧设施的成本费用、如何获取充足的运转资金以及吸引更多游客前来观看新奇且有趣的展品。

　　在美国,一些比较旧的动物园在 20 世纪最后的几十年里已经做了翻新。近期对动物园的改良工作主要是增添类似自然栖息地的新围场。传统的铁栏杆和混凝土地板已经被精心设计的栖息地所替代,这有助于改善游客观看动物的体验。这样的改变有助于减少动物的压力,并且使它们相互能更自然方便地交流。

　　一些较大规模的动物园开展了圈养动物繁殖项目。该项目使动物园动物或野生动物在喂养状态下繁殖后代,用这种方式获取的后代通常会被放生野外或者转养到其他动物园。圈养繁殖项目是使野生物种免于灭绝的方式之一。

　　动物园也扩大和改进了公共教育项目,教育部门也开展了与动物展出相关的项目。公共活动包括学校的内部教育项目、动物园参观、专项活动以及网站等方式。例如,纽约动物学会与西非政府共同开展了针对象群的迁移进行观察的重大项目。

　　动物园的重要性将随着自然栖息地的减少而增加。通过对动物保护、公众教育和环境保护的支持,动物园在全世界范围内的野生动物保护方面将继续发挥至关重要的作用。

2011年同等学力人员申请硕士学位英语水平全国统一考试答案及详解

61. [正确答案] B
    [解析过程] superficially"浅薄地";especially"尤其,特别";importantly"重要地";supposedly"据认为,据推测"。

62. [正确答案] C
    [解析过程] By that time"到那时为止";By the time"到……时候为止";At one time"一度,从前";At that time"在那时"。后面有presently,可以推断出此处是从前与目前状况的一个对比。

63. [正确答案] A
    [解析过程] institutions"机构";associations"协会,社团";foundations"建立,设立,创办";corporations"公司"。

64. [正确答案] C
    [解析过程] Along"沿着,循着,顺着";Toward"向,朝";Among"在……中";Through"通过"。三者或三者以上的选择用among。

65. [正确答案] C
    [解析过程] limited"有限的";professional"职业的,专业的";sufficient"足够的,充足的";excessive"过度的,过分的"。文中表示的是"充足的运转资金",所以根据语境选择C项。

66. [正确答案] B
    [解析过程] newer"较新的";older"较旧的";former"在前的,以前的";later"较晚的,后来的"。

67. [正确答案] B
    [解析过程] management"管理,经营";improvement"改善,改良";achievement"成就,成绩";assessment"评价,评定"。

68. [正确答案] D
    [解析过程] under"在……之下";for"为了";into"向,朝";with"伴随,带有"。将with代入文中,符合语境。

69. [正确答案] A
    [解析过程] reduce"减少,减小";cause"导致";increase"增加,增大";avoid"避开,避免"。

70. [正确答案] A
    [解析过程] selected"选择的,挑选的";sustained"持续不变的,持久的";promising"有希望的,有前途的";surviving"继续存在的,未死的,依然健在的"。

71. [正确答案] D
    [解析过程] natural"自然的,天然的";the natural"有天赋的人;擅长做某事的人";wild"野生的,未驯化的";the wild"户外"。

72. [正确答案] B
    [解析过程] restraining"抑制,遏制";saving"挽救,搭救";sheltering"掩蔽;庇护";exempting"使免除"。save sth. from sth."保护某物以避免……"为固定搭配且符合语境。

73. ［正确答案］D

　　［解析过程］attributed to "把某事归因于……"; opposed to "反对"; referred to "提及"; related to "与……相关"。

74. ［正确答案］A

　　［解析过程］as "当……的时候"; as if "似乎"; so "所以"; so that "以便"。

75. ［正确答案］C

　　［解析过程］in search of "寻找"; in honor of "为了向……表示敬意"; in support of "支持"; in charge of "负责"。

Paper Two　　试卷二

Part I　Translation

Section A

1. Over the years, we tend to think that nuclear technologies and the necessary know-how to ensure nuclear safety have been developed to a level that possibilities for any major nuclear accidents are almost non-existent and if it does happen, it will be controlled in the capable hands of nuclear engineers.

   ［结构分析］这是一个比较复杂的复合句，主句是 we tend to think that…，此处 that 引导一个宾语从句，该宾语从句的主句是 nuclear technologies and the necessary know-how to ensure nuclear safety have been developed。而 level 后的 that 引导了一个包含并列结构的同位语从句，并列结构中的第二个句子包含一个由 if 引导的条件状语从句。

   ［词义推敲］nuclear technology "原子能技术，核技术"; know-how "诀窍，实际知识，专门技能"; ensure "保证"; non-existent "不存在的"; capable "有能力的"。

   ［参考译文］这些年来，我们习惯性地认为原子能技术和必要的保证核安全的实践经验已经发展到了一个水平，即一切重大的核事故几乎都不存在，哪怕其真的发生，也会被有能力的核工程师们控制影响。

2. However, reality has proved again that you just can't be too careful to handle nuclear energy.

   ［结构分析］这是一个复合句，主句是 reality has proved that…，此处 that 引导了一个宾语从句。

   ［词义推敲］can't be too… to… 意为"再……也不为过"（注意，too… to… 短语常为"太……而不能"的意思，与本句中 can't be too… to… 的意思有明显区别）; handle "处理"。

   ［参考译文］然而，事实再一次证明处理核能源再小心都不为过。

3. We don't know for sure yet what will be left behind Japan's nuclear crisis, but it will be certain that it is time to re-examine our nuclear practices and many more efforts need to be made to ensure nuclear safety in the future.

[结构分析] 这是一个以 but 为标志的表示转折关系的并列结构,前半部分还带有一个 what 引导的宾语从句,后半句的第一个 it 作形式主语,后面的 that 引导主语从句。

[词义推敲] re-examine"重新审视";ensure"保证,确保"。

[参考译文] 我们现在还不确定日本的核灾难会留下什么影响,但现在一定是我们重新审查原子能实践的时候了。为确保将来的核安全,我们还需付出更多努力。

Section B

1. 中国有着5 000年的文化传统,历经劫难,而生生不息。我们一定要充分发扬祖国的文化传统。

    [结构分析] 汉语句子的逻辑关系表面上看很不清晰,需要对整个意群进行理解。本句可被看作两部分,从"我们"之前隔开。前半部分描述事实,后半部分得出结论。

    [词义推敲] 文化传统"cultural tradition";历经"undergo";劫难"hardship";生生不息"maintains its vitality generation after generation";发扬"advance/promote"。

    [参考译文] China has 5,000 years of cultural tradition. Having undergone various hardships, the country still maintains its vitality generation after generation. It is imperative for us to fully advance our motherland's cultural heritage.

2. 同时我们也懂得,要学习和借鉴世界先进的文明。

    [结构分析] 这个句子结构比较简单,原句的后半句可以用不定式的非谓语动词结构表达。

    [词义推敲] 同时"at the same time";学习"learn from";借鉴"draw upon";先进的文明"advanced civilization"。

    [参考译文] At the same time, we understand the importance to learn from and draw upon advanced civilizations of the world.

3. 只有这样,才能使祖国的文化得到进一步发展,也就是我常说的,只有开放包容,才能使祖国强大。

    [结构分析] 这个句子前半部分是个强调句式,可以对应英语的强调句型。而后面的"也就是我常说的",可以用英语的从句结构指代前文,并引出之后的"只有开放包容,才能使祖国强大",而这个句子同样也是强调句。

    [词义推敲] 进一步发展"make further development";开放包容"open and tolerant";只有……才……"only... can..."。

    [参考译文] Only in this way can the culture of our motherland make further development. That is what I always say—only by keeping open and tolerant can we make our motherland stronger.

Part II Writing

这是一篇议论文,并且给出了题目。我们可以根据提纲列出的三点思路去写作。第一段,开场白,简要介绍压力的来源;第二段,提出观点,建议如何减压,可以适当地结合压力的来源来思考减压措施;第三段,总结减压措施,与自己的实际做法相结合,再做适当引申,结束全文。

How to Handle Stress

Nowadays, more and more people have been under various stresses and there has been an increase in stress-related diseases among employees and students. This phenomenon has aroused immediate concern and widespread discussion among the general public. From my perspective, the sources of stresses can be from our work, family and also from the society, and learning how to deal with stresses has far-reaching significance to our mental and physical health.

As a matter of fact, some solutions to reduce stresses can be illustrated below. The first one that comes to my mind readily is to share our stresses with others. It can be enormously helpful because we may feel quite relaxed after talking to others and things will even turn better if we get any valuable suggestions from them. What's more, making time for fun such as listening to music and watching movies may be good medicine. Additionally, it is also a great way to reduce anxiety by doing a large number of physical activities.

From what has been discussed above, I strongly believe that we should know how to reduce enormous stress because it poses a general threat to mental and physical health. As a common employee, I often feel severe stress at work. In those cases, I always tried to talk with my close friends to hear their advice or just listen to my favorite music. Only by having both mental and physical health can we hope to do our jobs well in the future.

第一段：简要介绍了人们面临压力的现状，以及这一现象造成的影响。之后，分析了压力的来源，并提出观点——学会正确减压对人很有好处，为下文介绍减压措施做了铺垫。

第二段：用一句话简单开头之后，分别介绍了三种减压方法：与他人分享心情、做放松的事以及做运动。衔接自然，方法也较为合理。

第三段：重申自己的观点——学会减压非常重要，并且结合自己普通职员的身份，介绍了个人常用的倾诉和听音乐的减压方法；然后加以引申，指出只有身心健康才能做好工作，结束全文。

文章结构清晰有条理，完全覆盖了题目的三点内容；并且运用了不少较出彩的句型或词语，如"has far-reaching significance to""As a matter of fact""It can be enormously helpful""poses a general threat"等。如能将这些表达自然运用，一定会为你的作文增色不少。

2012年同等学力人员申请硕士学位
英语水平全国统一考试

Paper One 试卷一 (90 minutes)

Part I Dialogue Communication (10 minutes, 10 points)

Section A Dialogue Completion

Directions: *In this section, you will read 5 short incomplete dialogues between two speakers, each followed by 4 choices marked A, B, C and D. Choose the answer that best suits the situation to complete the dialogue. Then mark the corresponding letter with a single bar across the square brackets on your machine-scoring* **Answer Sheet**.

1. A: Frank, where are the cookies? Don't tell me you ate them all!
   B: _____ They were so good.
   A. Yes, forget it.
   B. Yes, I couldn't help it.
   C. No, I'm sorry.
   D. No, don't be mad.

2. A: The train is delayed again.
   B: _____ How long do we have to wait?
   A. What a pity!
   B. How annoying!
   C. I'm sorry to hear that.
   D. So far so good.

3. A: When Lisa saw me at the mall, she didn't even say hello to me.
   B: I can't understand why _____. I thought you were good friends.
   A. you greeted her first
   B. she was also there at the time
   C. she gave you the cold shoulder
   D. you should have cared

4. A: I used to make delicious pies, but this one tastes terrible.
   B: I think you're really _____.
   A. out of date

B. out of touch

C. out of hand

D. out of practice

5. A: Dr. Smith, what's wrong with my father?

   B: Well, _____ , considering his advanced age.

   A. he's in pretty good shape

   B. don't ask me such a question

   C. I have no idea

   D. I have nothing to say for the moment

Section B Dialogue Comprehension

Directions: *In this section, you will read 5 short conversations between a man and a woman. At the end of each conversation there is a question followed by 4 choices marked A, B, C and D. Choose the best answer to the question from the 4 choices by marking the corresponding letter with a single bar across the square brackets on your machine-scoring **Answer Sheet**.*

6. Woman: Bob, if you weed the garden, I'll do the dishes.

   Man: It's a deal.

   Question: What does the man mean?

   A. He agrees to the proposal.

   B. He rejects the idea.

   C. He thinks it's unfair.

   D. He stands to gain.

7. Woman: Can I go skiing with you and your friends this weekend?

   Man: The more, the merrier.

   Question: What does the man mean?

   A. There are already too many people.

   B. He can't promise the woman now.

   C. The woman is welcome to join them.

   D. The woman can come next time.

8. Man: This suitcase costs me 200 dollars.

   Woman: 200 dollars for a piece of junk like that? That's a rip-off!

   Question: What does the woman mean?

   A. It's a bit expensive.

   B. It's a real bargain.

   C. It's not worth the price.

   D. It's unexpected.

9. Woman: The house seems in a bad shape.

   Man: Yes, we've decided to rebuild it from scratch.

   Question: What would the man probably do to the house?

   A. He would scratch the paint off its surface.

   B. He would tear it down first.

   C. He would make some repairs.

   D. He would rebuild it by himself.

10. Ted: I ate four hamburgers, Mom.

    Mother: Well, you've made a pig of yourself.

    Question: What do we learn from the conversation?

    A. Pigs love hamburgers too.

    B. Ted looks overweight.

    C. The hamburgers were delicious.

    D. Ted ate too many hamburgers.

Part II Vocabulary (20 minutes, 10 points)

Section A

Directions: *In this section, there are 10 sentences, each with one word or phrase underlined. Choose the one from the 4 choices marked A, B, C and D that best keeps the meaning of the sentence. Then mark the corresponding letter with a single bar across the square brackets on your machine-scoring **Answer Sheet**.*

11. In his closing remarks, the chairman expressed his thanks to all those who had contributed to the success of the conference.

    A. comments   B. speech   C. criticism   D. lecture

12. Both Tom and his brother take after their father not only in appearance but also in character.

    A. resemble   B. assimilate   C. follow   D. reflect

13. The hurricane was incredibly devastating and left thousands homeless.

    A. forceful   B. mighty   C. destructive   D. dangerous

14. Readers are required to comply with the rules of the library and mind their manners.

    A. evaluate   B. memorize   C. protect   D. observe

15. Economic factors aside, the imbalanced distribution of educational resources also affects fairness of education.

    A. unjust   B. impartial   C. uneven   D. improper

16. Watching me pulling the calf awkwardly to the barn, the Irish milkmaid fought hard to hold back her laughter.

    A. check   B. keep   C. stop   D. retain

17. The government has called an independent inquiry into the incident.

    A. requirement   B. examination   C. analysis   D. investigation

18. A great number of houses would have to be removed to make way for the new amusement park.

    A. take the place of   B. give space for   C. build up   D. work out

19. Drug use accounts for approximately three-quarter of all reported cases of HIV in the country.

    A. possibly   B. roughly   C. generally   D. specifically

20. For their own safety, household pets should be confined to their own yard.

    A. tamed   B. regained   C. restricted   D. contained

Section B

Directions: *In this section. there are 10 incomplete sentences. For each sentence there are 4 choices marked A, B, C and D. Choose the one that best completes the sentence. Then mark the corresponding letter with a single bar across the square brackets on your machine-scoring* **Answer Sheet**.

21. By a strange _____, both candidates have come up with the same solution to the problem.

    A. coincidence   B. encounter   C. chance   D. overlap

22. The discussion was so prolonged and exhausting that _____ the speaker stopped for refreshments.

    A. at large   B. at intervals   C. at ease   D. at random

23. Mr Tunick filed suit against the New York police department after city officials _____ his request.

    A. turned down   B. turned in   C. turned off   D. turned out

24. The fireman had a _____ escape when a staircase collapsed beneath his feet.

    A. close   B. narrow   C. hard   D. near

25. Many painters, rock singers, and street dancers have distinct hair styles, _____ to their group.

    A. particular   B. essential   C. special   D. peculiar

26. That he brought the company big profits wouldn't _____ putting the company's money into his own pockets.

    A. justify   B. clarify   C. testify   D. amplify

27. We're _____ 50 new staff this year as business grows.

    A. taking over   B. taking in   C. taking on   D. taking up

28. Is the theory of evolution in direct _____ with religious teachings, or does it leave room for debate?

    A. comparison   B. distinction   C. disturbance   D. contradiction

29. Libraries are an investment for the future and should not be allowed to fall into _____.

    A. dissolution   B. decay   C. decline   D. depression

30. A transplant operation is successful only if doctors can prevent the body from rejecting the _____ organ.

    A. borrowed   B. strange   C. novel   D. foreign

Part III Reading Comprehension (45 minutes, 30 points)

Directions: *There are 5 passages in this part. Each passage is followed by 6 questions or unfinished statements. For each of them there are 4 choices marked A, B, C and D. Choose the best one and mark the corresponding letter with a single bar across the square brackets on your machine-scoring* **Answer Sheet**.

Passage One

A 10-year-old boy decided to study judo (柔道) despite the fact that he had lost his left arm in a terrible car accident. The boy began lessons with an old Japanese judo master, and he was doing well. But he couldn't understand why, after three months of training, the master had taught him only one move.

"Sir," the boy finally said, "shouldn't I be learning more moves?"

"This is the only move you know, but this is the only move you'll ever need to know," the master replied.

Not quite understanding, but believing in his teacher, the boy kept training.

Several months later, the master took the boy to his first tournament (锦标赛).

Surprising himself, the boy easily won his first two matches. The third match proved to be more difficult, but after some time, his opponent became impatient and charged; the boy skillfully used his one move to win the match. Still amazed by his success, the boy was now in the finals.

This time, his opponent was bigger, stronger, and more experienced. For a while, the boy appeared to be overmatched. Concerned that the boy might get hurt, the referee called a time-out. He was about to stop the match when the judo master intervened.

"No," the judo master insisted. "Let him continue."

Soon after the match resumed, his opponent made a critical mistake: he dropped his guard. Instantly, the boy used his move to pin him. The boy had won the match and the tournament. He was the champion.

On the way home, the boy and his judo master reviewed every move in each and every match. Then the boy summoned the courage to ask what was really on his mind.

"Sir, how did I win the tournament with only one move?"

"You won for two reasons," the master answered.

"First, you've almost mastered one of the most difficult throws in all of judo. Second, the only known defense for that move is for your opponent to grab your left arm."

31. Why did the boy want to learn judo?

   A. He wanted to get over the accident.

   B. He wanted to make up for his disability.

   C. He wanted to exercise his right arm.

   D. The reason was not mentioned in the passage.

32. When a referee calls a "time-out," _____.

　　A. the time has run out　　　　　B. the game stops for a short time

　　C. either side can claim victory　　D. the game ends in a tie

33. Why did the master insist on continuing the match?

　　A. He didn't want to give the opponent an advantage.

　　B. The boy was confident of winning.

　　C. He had confidence in the boy's skill.

　　D. All he cared about was winning the final.

34. What probably caused the defeat of the boy's opponent in the final?

　　A. Over-confidence.　　　　　　B. Impatience.

　　C. Inexperience.　　　　　　　　D. Exhaustion.

35. Why did the master teach the boy only that one move?

　　A. The boy could not do other moves with only one arm.

　　B. It was the only move the master knew well.

　　C. It was the move his opponent would not be good at.

　　D. His opponent would be helpless once he made that move.

36. What does the passage mainly tell us?

　　A. One can turn a weakness into an advantage.

　　B. It is very difficult to have a good teacher.

　　C. Even a disabled person can win a match.

　　D. Practice makes perfect.

Passage Two

　　My five-year-old daughter knew exactly what she wanted for Christmas of 1977, and told me so. Yes, she still would like the pink-and-green plastic umbrella, books, long nightgown, slippers—fine. But really, there was only one thing that mattered: a Barbie Townhouse, with all the accessories.

　　This was a surprise. Rebecca was not a Barbie girl, preferred stuffed animals to dolls, and wasn't drawn to play in a structured environment. Always a make-up-the-rules, design-my-own-world, do-it-my-way kid. Maybe, I thought, the point wasn't Barbie but the house, which she could claim for herself, since we'd already moved five times during her brief life.

　　Next day, I stopped at the mall. The huge Barbie Townhouse box was there: "3 Floors of High-Styled Fun! Elevator Can Stop on All Floors!" Some Assembly Required. Uh-oh. My track record for assembling things was miserable. Brooklyn-born, I was raised in apartment buildings in a family that didn't build things. A few years earlier, I'd spent one week assembling a six-foot-tall jungle gym from a kit containing so many parts. I spent the first four hours sorting and the last two hours trying to figure out why there were so many pieces. The day after I finished building it, as if to remind me of my limitations, a tornado (龙卷风) touched down close enough to scatter the jungle gym across an acre of field.

I assembled the Barbie Townhouse on Christmas Eve. Making it level, keeping the columns from looking like they'd melted and been refrozen, and getting that elevator to work were almost more than I could manage. And building it in curse-free silence so my daughter would continue sleeping—if, in fact, she was sleeping—added a layer of challenge. By dawn I was done.

Shortly thereafter, my daughter walked into the living room. Her surprise may not be real, but her delight was utterly genuine and moves me to this day, 34 years later. Rebecca had spurred me to do something I didn't think I could do. It was for her, and—like so much of the privilege of being her father—it brought me further outside myself and let me overcome doubts about my capacities.

37. In the author's eyes, his little daughter was _____.
    A. obedient   B. unstable   C. original   D. stubborn

38. The author thought that his daughter's choice of the Barbie Townhouse _____.
    A. was natural for a five-year-old girl
    B. was influenced by her life experience
    C. reflected the change in her taste
    D. brought her back to normal

39. For the author, assembling things _____.
    A. was largely in his blood   B. was a challenge he enjoyed
    C. was always his weak point   D. was part of his family education

40. Assembling the Barbie Townhouse _____.
    A. brought out the author's potentials
    B. turned out to be easier than expected
    C. actually drove the author crazy
    D. was a bad memory for the author

41. In the last paragraph the author mainly expressed _____.
    A. his pride in being a father
    B. his gratitude to his daughter
    C. his concern about his capability
    D. his delight in helping his daughter

42. What can be learned about the relationship between the author and his daughter?
    A. They are on good terms with each other.
    B. They barely speak to each other.
    C. They are polite but cold to each other.
    D. They keep secrets from each other.

Passage Three

It is all very well to blame traffic jam, the cost of petrol and the fast pace of modern life, but manners on the roads are becoming <u>deplorable</u>. Everybody knows that the nicest men become monsters behind the wheel. It is all very well, again, to have a tiger in the tank, but to have one in the driver's seat is another matter. You might tolerate the odd road-hog(占道者), but nowadays the well-mannered motorist is the exception to the rule. Perhaps the situation calls for a "Be Kind to Other Drivers" campaign, otherwise it may get completely out of hand.

Road courtesy is not only good manners, but good sense too. It takes the most good-tempered of drivers to resist the temptation to hit back when subjected to uncivilized behavior. A friendly nod or a wave of acknowledgment in response to an act of courtesy helps to create an atmosphere of goodwill and tolerance so necessary in modern traffic conditions. But such acknowledgments of courtesy are all too rare today. Many drivers nowadays don't even seem able to recognize courtesy when they see it.

Contrary to general opinion, young drivers have better manners than their seniors. But this is short-lived in the world of modern driving where many drivers neither expect nor give any mercy. This may be encouraged on the battlefield but is out of place on the roads.

Lorry drivers say they have almost abandoned the practice of signaling cars to overtake when the road is clear, because many of the cars took too long to pass. They couldn't be bothered to select a lower gear. The car drivers, after overtaking, slowed down again and hogged the road. Again, a motoring magazine has recently drawn attention to the increasing number of drivers who never wait for gaps. "They manufacture them by force, using their direction indicators as a threat rather than a warning." Punch-ups(打群架) are quite common. It can't be long before we hear of pistols and knives being used.

Driving is essentially a state of mind. However technically skilled a driver may be, he can't be an advanced motorist if he is always arrogant and aggressive.

43. The author is most concerned about _____.

    A. traffic jam					B. road manners
    C. fast pace of life			D. high cost of petrol

44. The word "deplorable" (Para. 1) most probably means "_____".

    A. more serious					B. more tempting
    C. disturbing					D. noticeable

45. What is the main idea of Paragraph 2?

    A. Many drivers tend to fight back against rude behaviors.
    B. A little courtesy may help ease the tensions on the road.
    C. Goodwill and tolerance may help relieve traffic jam.
    D. Many drivers nowadays lack a good sense of courtesy.

46. It can be learned from Paragraph 3 that _____.

    A. young drivers are more aggressive
    B. young drivers would soon lose their good manners
    C. elder drivers are more cautious
    D. elder drivers should improve their driving skills

47. An example of good manners on the roads is _____.

A. signaling cars to overtake
B. manufacturing a gap
C. selecting a lower gear
D. using the direction indicator

48. According to the author, a good driver should _____.
    A. be technically skilled
    B. have a good state of mind
    C. be sympathetic with others
    D. take good care of his vehicle

Passage Four

On how the world has changed over the last 50 years, not all of it has been good. As you are looking for organic food information, you have obviously become aware that a better alternative exists and you are taking a critical look at the source and production practices of the companies producing the world's food supplies.

The purpose of organic food information is to give you an understanding of what is going into your food. You will see that there are many benefits to organic food that you didn't know before. The basis behind knowing about organic food information is the fact that farmers are resorting to using artificial fertilizers and pesticides(杀虫剂) to control disease and insect attack in order to produce more crops to satisfy growing demand. These artificial fertilizers leave something poisonous in and on the fruit and vegetables we consume which in turn is absorbed and stored by our bodies.

Even the quality of food has gone down in recent years. Today's fruits have nowhere near the Vitamin C levels they did at one time. However, with organic food information you learn that organic food has fifty percent more nutrients, minerals and vitamins than any other form of produce that has been grown under intensive farming. If you are eating non-organic produce you will have to eat more fruit in order to make up for this deficiency. But then the dangerous cycle continues since you will be eating more chemicals that are worse for your health than they are good for you.

Another aspect of organic food information is the production of meat and poultry(家禽). Most only consider produce when it comes to organic food information disregarding the antibiotics and hormones that are given to both cattle and poultry that are being force fed. Ask yourself what happens to all these antibiotics and hormones when the animal is killed, the remaining of these antibiotics and growth hormones reside in the meat which are then consumed, digested and stored in human bodies. There is no way that an animal that isn't kept in healthy conditions can produce healthy food for humans to eat.

You have nothing to lose by trying organic product, not only will it be healthy for you but you will also be able to eat produce and meat the way they are supposed to be. You will likely be so impressed with the taste of organic fruit that you will never return to the mass-produced fruit again. While cost and availability can be a big issue for some, you can do a bit of research online and find a local store that stocks organic produce for a reasonable price.

49. It is stated in Paragraph 1 that organic food _____.
    A. is considered as a better choice
    B. is mostly supplied by world-famous companies

C. has become popular over the last 50 years

D. reflects the change of production practices

50. Farmers use artificial fertilizers and pesticides to _____.

    A. satisfy people's critical demand   B. develop better farming technology

    C. get a higher crop yield   D. keep people in better health

51. According to Paragraph 3, organic food _____.

    A. has gone down in quality   B. has more nutrients

    C. can replace mass-produced food   D. lacks Vitamin C

52. What does the author say about meat and poultry?

    A. Organic meat and poultry is hardly available.

    B. A great amount of meat is consumed every year.

    C. Merciless killing of the animals lowers their quality.

    D. They may contain antibiotics and growth hormones.

53. In the last paragraph, people are advised to _____.

    A. eat traditional produce and meat

    B. return to mass-produced fruits

    C. do the cost and availability research

    D. try organic product for better health and taste

54. This passage is mainly about _____.

    A. the benefits of organic food information

    B. the challenges facing the world food industry

    C. changes in food production practices

    D. a growing demand for high quality food

Passage Five

    Drinking wastewater? The idea may sound distasteful, but new federally funded research says more Americans are doing so—whether they know or not—and this reuse will be increasingly necessary as the U.S. population expands.

    Treated wastewater poses no greater health risks than existing water supplies and, in some cases, may be even safer to drink, according to a report released by the National Research Council. "We believe water reuse is an option to deal with growing water scarcity, especially in coastal areas," says Jorg Drewes, an engineering professor at the Colorado School of Mines. "This can be done reliably without putting the public at risk," he says, citing technological advances. He says it's a waste not to reuse the nation's wastewater, because almost all of it is treated before discharge. This water includes storm runoff (径流) as well as used water from homes, businesses and factories.

    In many places, the report says, the public does not realize it's drinking water that was treated after being discharged as wastewater somewhere upstream. For example, wastewater discharged into the Trinity

River from Dallas/Fort Worth flows south into Lake Livingston, the source for Houston's drinking water.

Despite the growing importance of this reuse, the report says there's been no systemic analysis of its extent nationwide since a 1980 study by the U.S. Environmental Protection Agency(EPA). Alan Roberson of the American Water Works Association says wastewater reuse is common, so the council's report is important but not surprising. Roberson expects this recycling will continue to increase, especially for irrigation and industrial needs. He says it will take longer to establish potable(适于饮用的) uses because of public nervousness about drinking wastewater, however treated.

"We have to do something to address water scarcity," says Olga Naidenko, a senior scientist at the non-profit Environmental Working Group. "Less than 10% of potable water is used for drinking, cooking, showering or dishwashing. We flush it down the toilet, literally." Technologies exist to safely treat the water, she says, although some are expensive.

The report says water reuse projects tend to cost more than most water conservation options but less than seawater desalination(脱盐)and other supply alternatives. It calls on the EPA to develop rules that set safe national standards.

55. As can be learned from Paragraph 1, drinking wastewater _____.
    A. is to become a growing necessity   B. is well received by the Americans
    C. has caused heated public debates   D. has become the dominant option

56. Which of the following statements would Jorg Drewes agree to?
    A. Water reuse may eventually put the public at risk.
    B. Water reuse is preferable to wasting water.
    C. Water reuse is far from a solution to water shortage.
    D. Water reuse is possible only after greater tech advances.

57. Lake Livingston is mentioned to show that the public _____.
    A. accepts the fact of drinking wastewater calmly
    B. is concerned about the safety of the drinking water
    C. does not believe that wastewater is safe to drink
    D. is not aware of the nature of their drinking water

58. According to Alan Roberson, _____.
    A. it is not safe to drink wastewater
    B. the report has surprised the public
    C. the report helps build up public confidence
    D. the public has yet to accept drinking wastewater

59. Olga Naidenko's remarks emphasize _____.
    A. the recent progress   B. the existing problems
    C. the new perspective   D. the potential risks

60. What does the report suggest to the EPA?

A. Weighing different water conservation options.
B. Exploring new technologies to treat wastewater.
C. Setting up national standards for water reuse.
D. Monitoring water supplies at a national level.

Part Ⅳ Cloze (15 minutes, 15 points)

Directions: *In this part, there is a passage with 15 blanks. For each blank there are 4 choices marked A, B, C and D. Choose the best answer for each blank and mark the corresponding letter with a single bar across the square brackets on your machine-scoring* **Answer Sheet**.

Why do kids hate Brussels sprouts(芽甘蓝)? Because Brussels sprouts are bitter, and kids generally don't like bitter tastes. But it's not their __61__. Researchers say that a dislike for bitter and sour is a survival instinct, since most toxic substances __62__ that way too. On the other hand, sweetness typically indicates that something is __63__ to eat, so children are born with a __64__ for sweet.

What we like to eat changes over time. As we age, we realize that __65__ something tastes bitter or sour, it won't kill us, and we learn to __66__ it. When we're older, we __67__ some of our smell sensitivity. Humans need smell to experience flavor, which is different from taste. With our senses diminished, we'll probably begin __68__ sugar and salt to our food to heighten the flavor. __69__, there's a theory that the reason many especially "big"-tasting wines in recent years have won awards is that wine critics are getting older and finding subtle flavors __70__ to sense.

If someone is __71__ to detect flavors at all, he may have a taste __72__, which can be caused by a tongue injury or brain damage. Or it could be a problem with __73__. The channel that separates the mouth from the nose allows us to smell behind our nose and is __74__ enjoying most complex flavors. That's why food seems __75__ when we have a stuffy nose—except chicken noodle soup. It's so salty.

61. A. fault   B. choice   C. habit   D. regret
62. A. feel   B. look   C. sound   D. taste
63. A. strange   B. necessary   C. safe   D. ready
64. A. capacity   B. preference   C. awareness   D. consideration
65. A. now that   B. in case   C. if only   D. even though
66. A. enjoy   B. improve   C. treat   D. alter
67. A. form   B. lose   C. reduce   D. gain
68. A. putting   B. balancing   C. adding   D. limiting
69. A. In essence   B. In conclusion   C. In fact   D. In short
70. A. softer   B. nicer   C. worse   D. harder
71. A. unlikely   B. unable   C. impossible   D. improbable
72. A. disorder   B. symptom   C. therapy   D. illusion
73. A. mood   B. taste   C. flavor   D. smell

74. A. subject to   B. liable to   C. crucial for   D. beneficial for
75. A. delicious   B. flavorless   C. bitter   D. smelly

Paper Two 试卷二 (60 minutes)

Part I Translation (30 minutes, 20 points)

Section A

Directions: *Translate the following paragraph into Chinese. Write your translation on the **Answer Sheet**.*

In many ways the Internet has had a very positive effect on society. It has improved communication, simplified handling tasks, offered a huge convenience, enabled faster processing, and provided more options, all of which frees more time to do other things. Yet, interestingly enough, the Internet has in some ways had negative effects. The quality of communication has declined and people are impatient because they have become accustomed to instant satisfaction, and using the Internet also takes up a lot of time.

Section B

Directions: *Translate the following passage into English. Write your translation on the **Answer Sheet**.*

乔布斯(Steve Jobs)去世后备受敬仰,原因之一是他创造了科技产品的美感。乔布斯认为无论是汽车还是电脑,人们都愿意购买一些比同类产品更为美观的东西。在乔布斯的领导下,从产品外形、材料到使用感受等各个方面,苹果都带来了无与伦比的体验,让人们的生活变得更美丽。

Part II Writing (30 minutes, 15 points)

Directions: *In this part, you are to write within 30 minutes a composition of no less than 150 words under the title of "**My Favorite Way of Keeping Fit**". Some clues are given below in Chinese. Please remember to write your composition clearly on the **Composition Sheet**.*

保持健康有多种做法……,我最喜欢的做法是……。

2012年同等学力人员申请硕士学位英语水平全国统一考试

Paper One 试卷一

Part I Dialogue Communication

Section A

1. [正确答案] B
   [句子翻译] A:弗兰克,饼干哪儿去啦?别说你全吃了!
              B:是的,我没忍住。太好吃了。
   [考点剖析] A项"是的,忘了吧";B项"是的,我没忍住";C项"没有,对不起";D项"没有,别生气了"。

2. [正确答案] B
   [句子翻译] A:火车又晚点了。
              B:好烦人!我们要等多久?
   [考点剖析] A项"太遗憾了";B项"好烦人";C项"听到这个消息,我很遗憾";D项"到目前为止,还不错"。

3. [正确答案] C
   [句子翻译] A:莉莎在购物中心看到了我,但她甚至不跟我打招呼。
              B:我不明白她为什么对你很冷淡,我以为你们是好朋友。
   [考点剖析] A项"你先打招呼";B项"她当时也在场";C项"她对你很冷淡";D项"你本应该在意"。

4. [正确答案] D
   [句子翻译] A:我以前做的派很好吃的,但这个味道不好。
              B:我想你是很久没做,生疏了。
   [考点剖析] A项"过时了";B项"好久没联系了";C项"脱手了";D项"生疏了"。

5. [正确答案] A
   [句子翻译] A:史密斯医生,我爸爸怎么了?
              B:嗯,考虑到他年纪大了,身体还算相当不错。
   [考点剖析] A项"他身体还算相当不错";B项"别问我这个问题";C项"我不知道";D项"现在我没什么好说的"。

Section B

6. [正确答案] A

   [句子翻译] 女士:鲍勃,如果你给花园除草,我就来洗碗。男士:一言为定。

   [考点剖析] 此题的关键是理解 It's a deal 的含义。A 项"他同意这个建议";B 项"他拒绝这个主意";C 项"他认为这不公平";D 项"他会获利"。只有 A 项符合逻辑。

7. [正确答案] C

   [句子翻译] 女士:周末我能和你还有你的朋友去滑雪吗? 男士:人越多越好。

   [考点剖析] 此题的关键是理解 The more, the merrier 的含义。A 项"人已经太多了";B 项"他现在没法答应她";C 项"男士欢迎她的加入";D 项"她可以下次参加"。只有 C 项符合逻辑。

8. [正确答案] C

   [句子翻译] 男士:这个手提箱花了我 200 美元。女士:200 美元买个这样的垃圾? 太不值了!

   [考点剖析] 此题的关键是理解 That's a rip-off 的含义。A 项"手提箱有点贵";B 项"手提箱的价格真实惠";C 项"它不值这个价";D 项"这太出乎意料了"。只有 C 项符合逻辑。

9. [正确答案] B

   [句子翻译] 女士:这房子好像情况不好。男士:是的,我们打算从头开始重建。

   [考点剖析] A 项"他将把表面的漆刮掉";B 项"他首先要拆掉它";C 项"他会对这座房子做一些修缮";D 项"他会自己重建"。只有 B 项符合逻辑。

10. [正确答案] D

    [句子翻译] 泰德:妈妈,我吃了 4 个汉堡。妈妈:好吧,你吃得太多了。

    [考点剖析] 此题的关键是理解 made a pig of yourself 的含义。A 项"猪也喜欢吃汉堡";B 项"泰德看起来过胖";C 项"汉堡很好吃";D 项"泰德吃了太多汉堡"。只有 D 项符合逻辑。

Part Ⅱ Vocabulary

Section A

11. [正确答案] B

    [考点类型] 名词

    [考点剖析] 题干中的 remarks 意为"讲话"。comments"评论";speech"演讲";criticism"批评";lecture"讲课"。

12. [正确答案] A

    [考点类型] 动词

    [考点剖析] 题干中的 take after 意为"与……相像"。resemble"类似";assimilate"吸收";follow"跟随";reflect"反射"。

13. [正确答案] C
    [考点类型] 形容词
    [考点剖析] 题干中的 devastating 意为"毁灭性的"。forceful "有说服力的"；mighty "强有力的"；destructive "破坏的"；dangerous "危险的"。

14. [正确答案] D
    [考点类型] 动词
    [考点剖析] 题干中的 comply with 意为"遵守"。evaluate "评估"；memorize "记忆"；protect "保护"；observe "遵守"。

15. [正确答案] C
    [考点类型] 形容词
    [考点剖析] 题干中的 imbalanced 意为"不平衡的"。unjust "不公平的"；impartial "公平的"；uneven "不均匀的"；improper "不正确的"。

16. [正确答案] C
    [考点类型] 动词
    [考点剖析] 题干中的 hold back 意为"控制住，抑制"。check "检查"；keep "保持"；stop "停止"；retain "保留"。

17. [正确答案] D
    [考点类型] 名词
    [考点剖析] 题干中的 inquiry 意为"调查"。requirement "要求"；examination "考试"；analysis "分析"；investigation "调查"。

18. [正确答案] B
    [考点类型] 动词短语
    [考点剖析] 题干中的 make way for 意为"给……让路"。take the place of "代替"；give space for "给……让出空间"；build up "加强"；work out "解决"。

19. [正确答案] B
    [考点类型] 副词
    [考点剖析] 题干中的 approximately 意为"大约"。possibly "可能"；roughly "大约"；generally "一般地"；specifically "明确地"。

20. [正确答案] C
    [考点类型] 动词
    [考点剖析] 题干中的 confined 意为"限制"。tamed "驯服"；regained "重新获得"；restricted "限制"；contained "包含"。

Section B

21. [正确答案] A
    [考点类型] 固定搭配
    [考点剖析] by a strange coincidence "太凑巧了"是固定搭配；encounter "遭遇"；chance "机会"；overlap "重叠"。

2012年同等学力人员申请硕士学位英语水平全国统一考试答案及详解

22. [正确答案] B

   [考点类型] 逻辑关系

   [考点剖析] at large"一般地";at intervals"不时";at ease"安逸";at random"随意"。

23. [正确答案] A

   [考点类型] 固定搭配

   [考点剖析] turn down request"拒绝要求"是固定搭配;turned in"上交";turned off"关闭";turned out"出席"。

24. [正确答案] B

   [考点类型] 固定搭配

   [考点剖析] close"紧密的";have a narrow escape"幸免于难"是固定搭配;hard"困难的";near"接近"。

25. [正确答案] D

   [考点类型] 近义词辨析

   [考点剖析] particular"独有的";essential"必要的";special"专门的";peculiar"独特的"。

26. [正确答案] A

   [考点类型] 逻辑关系

   [考点剖析] justify"证明合法";clarify"阐明";testify"作证";amplify"放大"。

27. [正确答案] C

   [考点类型] 固定搭配

   [考点剖析] taking over "接管";taking in"理解";taking on"雇用";taking up"开始从事"。

28. [正确答案] D

   [考点类型] 固定搭配

   [考点剖析] comparison"对比";distinction"区别";disturbance"干扰";in contradiction with "与……相矛盾"是固定搭配。

29. [正确答案] C

   [考点类型] 逻辑关系

   [考点剖析] dissolution"分解";decay"腐烂";decline "衰落";depression"不景气"。

30. [正确答案] D

   [考点类型] 固定搭配

   [考点剖析] borrowed "借来的"; strange"奇怪的";novel "新奇的";foreign organ"异质器官"是固定搭配。

Part Ⅲ　Reading Comprehension

Passage One

一个十岁的小男孩在一场严重的车祸中失去了左臂,尽管如此,他仍然决心学习柔道。他的老师是一位日本柔道老教练,小男孩跟着老师学得也很棒。但他不明白为什么,在三个月的训练中,教练只教他一个招式。

· 17 ·

英语 历年真题·点石成金

男孩终于说道:"老师,我可以再学更多招式吗?"

教练说:"这是你知道的唯一招式,而且这也是你唯一需要知道的招式。"

男孩并不是特别理解,但是他相信他的老师并继续训练。

几个月过后,教练带领男孩参加他的第一场锦标赛。

令男孩惊讶的是,他很轻松地赢得了前两场比赛。第三场比赛难一些,但是不久后,他的对手变得焦躁不安并冲向男孩,男孩娴熟地用他的那个招式赢得了比赛。带着对成功的惊讶,男孩进入了决赛。

这次,他的对手高大、强壮且经验丰富。一时间,男孩好像被打败了。裁判考虑到男孩可能会受伤,因此吹了暂停哨,准备暂停比赛。这时,男孩的教练拦住了他。

"不,"教练坚持说,"让他继续"。

比赛重新开始后不久,他的对手犯了个非常严重的错误,他弄掉了自己的防护装置。男孩立即用他的那个招式将其压住。最终男孩赢得了那场比赛和整个锦标赛,他是冠军。

回家的路上,男孩和他的教练回顾着每场比赛的每一个招式,然后男孩鼓起勇气问了那个一直萦绕在他脑海中的问题。

"老师,我怎么能只用一个招式就赢得了锦标赛呢?"

教练答道:"有两个原因。"

"首先,你掌握了柔道所有击打招式中最难的一招。第二,对手要破解这一招,只有抓住了你的左臂才能办到。"

31. [正确答案] D

　　[考点类型] 细节题

　　[题目翻译] 这个男孩为什么想学柔道?

　　　　　　A. 他想克服车祸(给他带来的影响)。

　　　　　　B. 他想弥补他的残疾。

　　　　　　C. 他想锻炼他的右臂。

　　　　　　D. 文章没有提到原因。

　　[考点剖析] 此篇文章并没有提到他为什么要学柔道,所以选择 D 项。

32. [正确答案] B

　　[考点类型] 细节题

　　[题目翻译] 裁判员吹"暂停"哨表示_____。

　　　　　　A. 时间到了

　　　　　　B. 比赛暂停一段时间

　　　　　　C. 任何一方都可声称胜利

　　　　　　D. 比赛结果不分胜负

　　[考点剖析] C 项和 D 项容易排除。文中的 He was about to stop the match when the judo master intervened. "No," the judo master insisted. "Let him continue." 显示比赛会继续,而不是终止,所以选择 B 项。

33. [正确答案] C

[考点类型] 推理题

[题目翻译] 为什么他的教练要求比赛继续？

A. 他不想让对手占优势。

B. 男孩有信心赢得比赛。

C. 他对男孩的技能有信心。

D. 他关注的只是最终赢得比赛。

[考点剖析] 从文章最后一段可推断出只有 C 项符合原文意思，其他选项文章均未提及。

34. [正确答案] A

[考点类型] 推理题

[题目翻译] 决赛中对手可能因为什么输掉了比赛？

A. 过分自信。

B. 没有耐心。

C. 缺乏经验。

D. 筋疲力尽。

[考点剖析] 文章第七段提到他的对手高大、强壮且经验丰富，所以 C、D 项可以排除。第九段提到他的对手犯了个严重的错误，于是男孩迅速反击，所以他的对手是对他自己的技能过分地自信，文中并没有提到他的耐心问题。

35. [正确答案] D

[考点类型] 细节题

[题目翻译] 为什么他的教练自始至终只教他一个招式？

A. 男孩只有一个手臂，不能做其他招式。

B. 教练只熟知这一个招式。

C. 这是他的对手不擅长的招式。

D. 他只要做这个招式，他的对手就无法反击。

[考点剖析] 文章最后提到了教练给他解释他能赢得比赛的原因：①他掌握了柔道中最难的一个招式，②做这个招式，对手只有抓住他的左臂（而他在一场车祸中失去了自己的左臂，所以他的对手根本抓不住他的左臂）才能破解。因此选 D 项。

36. [正确答案] A

[考点类型] 主旨题

[题目翻译] 文章主要告诉我们什么？

A. 人可以变弱势为优势。

B. 很难有个好老师。

C. 即使是残疾人，也可赢得比赛。

D. 熟能生巧。

[考点剖析] 文章讲的是一个小男孩因为车祸失掉了左臂，但他还是决定开始学柔道。他的教练只教他一个招式，使其规避劣势、发挥优势，所以他最终赢得了比赛。

Passage Two

1977年,我五岁的女儿非常清楚她想要什么圣诞节礼物,并且告诉了我。是的,她仍然喜欢粉绿色搭配的塑料小伞、书、长睡衣、拖鞋——这些都很好。但只有一个东西让我感到为难:带着很多装饰物的芭比小别墅。

这确实是令人惊讶的,因为丽贝卡不是个会喜欢芭比的女孩,她喜欢填充动物胜过娃娃,且不会在特定的规定好规则的环境中玩耍。她是一个总是喜欢自己制定规则、自我设计、我行我素的女孩。我想,也许关键不在芭比,而在于房子,一个她能够宣布属于自己的房子。要知道,在她短暂的生活中,我们已搬了五次家。

第二天,我在购物商场停下来,看到了一个很大的装有芭比小屋的盒子,上面写着:高达三层的高层趣味别墅! 电梯可以停在任意一层! 部分零件需要自行组装。噢,有生以来,我组装东西的回忆都是痛苦的。我生长在布鲁克林一个公寓式的房子里,家人没有自己建造过东西。几年前,我花了一周时间将一个含有众多零件的配套元件组装成了一个六英尺高的攀爬架。在开始的四个小时我将它们分类,然后用最后两小时试图搞清楚它们为什么有这么多部件。在我完成它的第二天,龙卷风袭来,将我的攀爬架吹散了一地,似乎是在提醒我,我的能力有限。

圣诞前夕,我组装了芭比小别墅。我让小屋保持平衡,使柱子尽量看起来不像是经热熔冷却后固定的。但使电梯运行起来几乎超过了我的能力。为了让我的女儿安然入睡,如果她确实睡着了,我就必须在完全寂静的环境中完成它,这可增加了我的挑战难度。黎明的时候我完成了。

没过一会儿,她走到起居室,或许她并不是真的感到惊讶,但她确实是开心的,她那份开心在34年后的今天仍然触动着我。丽贝卡激励我做成了我认为自己做不成的事情。为了她,就像一种作为父亲的特权一样,让我超越了自己,打破了对自己能力的怀疑。

37. [正确答案] C

    [考点类型] 细节题

    [题目翻译] 在作者眼中,他的女儿是_____。

        A. 顺从的

        B. 好动的

        C. 有独创性的

        D. 固执的

    [考点剖析] 文章第二段提到他的女儿喜欢自己制定规则、自我设计、我行我素,所以选C项。

38. [正确答案] B

    [考点类型] 细节题

    [题目翻译] 作者认为他的女儿选择了芭比小别墅_____。

        A. 对一个五岁的小女孩来说很正常

        B. 是受她生活经历的影响

        C. 反映了她品位的变化

        D. 使她回归了正常

    [考点剖析] 第二段最后一句提到关键不是芭比而是房子。因为在她短暂的生活中,他们已经搬了五次家,这样的生活经历对她影响较大,所以选B项。

39. [正确答案] C
    [考点类型] 细节题
    [题目翻译] 对作者来说,组装物件_____。
        A. 是他与生俱来的能力
        B. 是他享受的一项挑战
        C. 一直以来都是他的弱项
        D. 是他家庭教育的一部分
    [考点剖析] 原文第三段第五句提到作者过去组装东西的回忆都是痛苦的。以 assembling things 为核心词到原文精准定位可知答案为 C 项。

40. [正确答案] A
    [考点类型] 细节题
    [题目翻译] 组装芭比小别墅_____。
        A. 激发了作者的潜力
        B. 结果比作者想象的要简单
        C. 实际上令作者很抓狂
        D. 对作者来说是个不好的回忆
    [考点剖析] 综合文章后三段可看出作者以前的组装技能很糟糕,但他女儿激发了他的潜力,让他成功地组装好了别墅,所以选 A 项。

41. [正确答案] B
    [考点类型] 推理题
    [题目翻译] 最后一段中作者主要表达了_____。
        A. 作为一个父亲的骄傲
        B. 他对女儿的感激
        C. 他对自己能力的担心
        D. 自己为帮了女儿而感到高兴
    [考点剖析] 原文最后一句说到为了女儿,作者做到了他以为做不到的事,作者表达了对女儿的感激。结合文中重点词汇,以及字里行间作者的语气,综合考虑得出正确答案为 B 项。

42. [正确答案] A
    [考点类型] 主旨题
    [题目翻译] 我们能了解到作者与女儿的关系是怎样的?
        A. 他们相处得非常好。
        B. 他们互相不怎么说话。
        C. 他们之间很讲礼貌但对彼此很冷淡。
        D. 他们对彼此留有很多秘密。
    [考点剖析] 原文提到了作者曾经对组装东西很不擅长,后面又提到了为女儿组装芭比玩具屋,因此可直接得出 A 项正确。结合整篇文章可排除其他选项。

Passage Three

　　我们可以抱怨交通拥挤、油价高、现代生活节奏快,但现在道路上的行为规范问题也越来越糟糕。大家都知道,即使最好的人开车后也能变成恶人。坦克里有一只老虎还不算是最糟糕的,但是要是驾驶座上有老虎的话那就完全是另一回事了。过去也许你会容忍奇怪的占道者,但现在有礼貌的司机已经算例外人物了。或许现在的情况需要一场名为"对其他司机友好"的运动,否则后果会完全不堪设想。

　　道路上的礼节不仅仅是一种好的行为习惯,还是一种明智的做法。道路礼节需要好脾气的司机抵制报复不文明行为的诱惑。一个善意的点头或者对文明行为赞同地挥挥手都能营造出和谐、宽容的气氛,这在现今的交通情况下是不可或缺的。但是现在赞同这种想法的人越来越少了。如今很多司机看见那些行为,甚至还不能辨别那些就是行车礼节。

　　与大众观点相反的是,年轻司机比年长司机开车更注重礼节。但是如今太多司机既不期待按礼节行事,也不对这种行为给予同情,所以年轻司机的这些好习惯也变得非常"短命"。这种行为在战场上可以受到鼓励,但是在公路上是不合适的。

　　大货车司机们都说,当路面车少的时候,他们基本都会放弃亮灯超车的规则,因为要超车的话基本都要开很远才能做到。汽车司机都不愿意挂低挡,并且这些司机超了车之后就会再次减速,在前面挡道。而且,一家汽车杂志最近也开始留意到越来越多的司机不在意车距。"他们依靠暴力来制造车距,把转向灯当威胁用而不是当警示灯用。"打群架的情况也变得很常见,动刀开枪的情况想必也不远了。

　　驾驶从根本上说是一种精神状态。如果一个人总是很傲慢又好斗,就算他驾驶技术再高也不是个好司机。

43. [正确答案] B

　　[考点类型] 细节题

　　[题目翻译] 作者最关注的是_____。

　　　　A. 交通拥挤

　　　　B. 公路上的行为规范

　　　　C. 快节奏生活

　　　　D. 高油价

　　[考点剖析] 原文中多处出现了 road courtesy 这一关键词,还提到了很多行车不文明行为,细读首尾句,可找出所说主题,因此 B 项正确。

44. [正确答案] C

　　[考点类型] 词汇题

　　[题目翻译] 第一段中的 deplorable 这个词最可能的意思是"_____"。

　　　　A. 更严重的

　　　　B. 更吸引人的

　　　　C. 引起烦恼的

　　　　D. 显著的

[考点剖析] A 项与 C 项为易混淆选项,因此将两个单词带进原文,观察是否合适,继而选择。原文第一段说到了驾驶汽车不良行为的消极方面,而且 B 项与 D 项基本是同义词,因此都不选。原文第一句中是以 manners 和前面几个方面比较,说明以前 manners 并没有任何影响,但现在不一样了。再结合选项,serious 用来修饰 manners 显然不合适,因此 C 项正确。

45. [正确答案] D

[考点类型] 细节题

[题目翻译] 第二段的大意是什么?

A.很多司机都抗议粗鲁行为。

B.一些好的礼节会缓解路上的紧张气氛。

C.善意和耐性可以缓解交通堵塞。

D.现在很多司机缺少礼节意识。

[考点剖析] 原文第二段一直在讲 courtesy,因此从 B 项与 D 项里选,本段末句转折部分提到了 D 项,而 B 项在文中未提及。本题以选项核心词排除无关选项,然后以转折语境为依据,得出作者的观点。

46. [正确答案] B

[考点类型] 推理题

[题目翻译] 从第三段能看出_____。

A.年轻司机比较好斗

B.年轻司机很快也会不讲礼节了

C.年长司机更加小心

D.年长的司机应该提升驾驶技术

[考点剖析] 原文第三段第二句提到了 short-lived 这个词,说年轻司机的礼节是"短命"的,因此 B 项符合原文意思。

47. [正确答案] A

[考点类型] 细节题

[题目翻译] 路上的一种好习惯是_____。

A.超车时发信号示意

B.控制车距

C.选择低挡

D.用转向灯

[考点剖析] 原文倒数第二段提到了司机超车时需要亮灯的这一惯例,因此 A 项为正确选项。

48. [正确答案] B

[考点类型] 细节题

[题目翻译] 按照作者的意思,一个好司机应该_____。

A. 驾驶技术好

B. 有好的驾驶状态

C. 同情其他人

D. 照顾好他的车

[考点剖析] 文章末段第一句提到驾驶从根本上说是一种精神状态，故 B 项正确。

Passage Four

纵观50年来世界的发展变化，并不是一切都朝着好的方向发展。当你查找有机食品信息的时候，你会很明显地发现一种更好的选择存在，而且你自己也在用批判的眼光审视着食品的来源，以及那些为全世界供给食物的厂家的生产实践。

查找有机食品信息的目的，是让大家了解食物当中都有什么。你会发现有机食品有很多你以前不知道的好处。要想了解有机食品，首先要知道一个事实，即农民们为了多产作物以满足日益增长的需求，而不得以用人造化肥和杀虫剂来防治病虫害。这些人造化肥会在我们吃的水果和蔬菜的表面以及内部留下毒素，而这些东西也被我们摄入并存储在体内了。

最近几年的食品质量甚至也下降了，如今的水果再也达不到以前那种维生素 C 的含量等级。然而，通过有机食品信息，你会发现和其他在集约化农业下种植出来的农产品相比，有机食品含有高出 50% 的营养、矿物质和维生素。如果你吃非有机农产品，你就要吃更多的水果，来补充缺少的这些营养物质。但是之后，你吃着更多对你健康弊大于利的化学物质，于是恶性循环便又继续了。

有机食品信息的另一类是肉类和家禽的生产。一提到有机食品信息，大多数人只会关注农产品，却忽视了给豢养的牛和家禽使用抗生素和激素这一事实。试想一下，当动物被杀死后将会发生什么：这些残留在动物体内的抗生素和生长激素将会被人类食用、消化，然后存在人类体内。在不健康环境下养出来的动物是不可能产出健康的食物给人类食用的。

尝试一下有机产品，你不会有任何损失，它不仅健康而且还能让你吃到纯天然的农产品和肉类。你可能会非常喜欢有机水果的味道，然后就再也不想吃那些大批量生产的水果了。有些地方价格可能会高一些，也可能没有有机食品可售。你可以做一些网上调查，来找找本地哪家店的有机食品有存货，同时价钱又比较公道。

49. [正确答案] A

[考点类型] 细节题

[题目翻译] 第一段里指出了有机食品_____。

A. 被当成一种更好的选择

B. 基本是由国际知名厂商提供

C. 在最近五十年变得流行

D. 反映了生产实践的变化

[考点剖析] 第一段中提到"当你查找有机食品信息的时候，你会很明显地发现一种更好的选择存在"，因此 A 项为正确选项。

50. [正确答案] C

[考点类型] 细节题

[题目翻译] 农民使用人造肥料和杀虫剂来_____。

　　A. 满足人们严苛的要求

　　B. 发展更好的农业科技

　　C. 提高产量

　　D. 使人们更健康

[考点剖析] 原文第二段第三句说到了农民使用人造肥料和杀虫剂是为了提高产量,因此C项正确。

51. [正确答案] B

[考点类型] 细节题

[题目翻译] 从第三段中能看出,有机食品_____。

　　A. 质量下降了

　　B. 有更多营养

　　C. 可以替代大规模生产的食物

　　D. 缺少维生素C

[考点剖析] 原文第三段第三句说到"有机食物含有高出50%的营养、矿物质和维生素",故B项正确。同类事物的不同特点混杂在一起,细节定位要精准,分清各自关系。要明确对应食品质量、水果、有机食品的各项是什么内容。

52. [正确答案] D

[考点类型] 细节题

[题目翻译] 作者是怎么说肉类和家禽的?

　　A. 有机肉类和家禽很难获得。

　　B. 每年都能消耗很多肉食品。

　　C. 残忍地杀害动物降低了肉的质量。

　　D. 它们可能含有抗生素和生长激素。

[考点剖析] 以肉和家禽定位,找到原文第四段,结尾部分可以清楚地找到D项的内容。

53. [正确答案] D

[考点类型] 细节题

[题目翻译] 在最后一段中,作者建议人们_____。

　　A. 吃传统的农产品和肉

　　B. 吃大批量产的水果

　　C. 做个花费和可用量的调查

　　D. 为了更健康和更美味,可以试试有机食品

[考点剖析] 细读原文末段,理解作者意思,归纳段意,选出答案为D项。

54. [正确答案] A

[考点类型] 主旨题

[题目翻译] 这篇文章主要讲了_____。
A. 有机食品信息的好处
B. 全球食品行业面临的挑战
C. 食品生产实践的变化
D. 高质量食品需求的日益增长

[考点剖析] 全文通篇都在强调有机食品,再结合主旨大意,可以选出答案为A项。

Passage Five

喝废水?也许这个想法听起来会使人不快,但是一项由联邦政府资助的调查显示,越来越多的美国人正在这样做,无论他们是否知道。随着美国人口的增加,这样的重复利用变得越来越有必要。

国家研究委员会发布的一篇报道显示,经过处理的废水的健康风险并不会比目前所供应的水更大,并且在某些情况下,它甚至更安全。科罗拉多矿业大学的工程教授乔治·德鲁说:"我们相信,废水再利用是应对水资源短缺的一个选择,特别是在沿海地区。这样的做法是可靠的,并且不会使公众处于危险中。"他提到了科技进步。他说不重复利用国家的废水是一种浪费,因为几乎所有的水在排放前都是经过处理的。这些水包括暴雨径流以及家用、商用和工厂废水。

据报道,很多地方的公众并没有意识到他们喝的水是上游排出的废水经过处理而来。例如,废水从达拉斯、沃斯堡市被排到三一河,向南流向休斯敦的水源地利文斯顿湖。

尽管这种重复利用变得越来越重要,但报道称,自美国环境保护署1980年开展的一项研究以来,全国范围内还没有针对废水利用的情况展开过系统分析。美国自来水厂协会的艾伦·罗伯森说,废水利用是普遍的,因此,该委员会的报道很重要但并不令人意外。罗伯森期望这样的循环会增加,特别是在灌溉和工业需求方面。他说,由于公众对饮用废水的紧张情绪,所以无论怎样处理废水,让公众将经过处理的废水作为饮用水还需要更长的时间。

美国非营利环境工作组的资深科学家奥尔加·奈登科说:"我们需要做一些事情来应对水资源的缺乏。低于10%的可用水被用来饮用、做饭、洗澡或洗盘子。实际上,我们多用这些水来冲厕所。"她说,现有技术能够很安全地将废水处理掉,但是一些设备很贵。

该报告表示,废水再利用工程的花费要比节约水资源的花费更多,但是少于海水淡化和其他选择。这个工程需要环境保护署确定废水安全饮用的国家标准。

55.[正确答案] A

[考点类型] 细节题

[题目翻译] 从第一段中能够得出,饮用废水_____。
A. 这一需求正在增长
B. 受到美国人的欢迎
C. 引起了大众的热议
D. 已经成为首选

[考点剖析] 饮用废水已经越来越有必要了。这点可以从原文第一段最后一句可知,即由于

美国人口的增加,水的再利用变得越来越必要了,因此选 A 项。

56. [正确答案] B

[考点类型] 细节题

[题目翻译] 乔治·德鲁最可能赞同以下哪种观点?

A. 废水再利用会让公众陷入危险。

B. 废水再利用比浪费水要好。

C. 废水再利用很难解决水资源匮乏问题。

D. 废水再利用只有在科技更加进步后才能实现。

[考点剖析] 乔治·德鲁在第二段倒数第二句中说不重复利用国家的废水也是一种浪费。可以直接得出 B 项正确,即再次利用废水比浪费水好。

57. [正确答案] D

[考点类型] 细节题

[题目翻译] 文中提到利文斯顿湖是为了表明公众_____。

A. 淡然地接受了饮用废水的事实

B. 在关注饮用水的安全性

C. 觉得废水喝起来不安全

D. 还不知道他们在饮用废水的事实

[考点剖析] 第三段提到,根据报道,公众并没有意识到他们喝的水是上游经过处理的废水。选项中的 is not aware of the nature…和文中的 does not realize 意思是相同的。

58. [正确答案] D

[考点类型] 细节题

[题目翻译] 艾伦·罗伯森指出_____。

A. 喝废水不安全

B. 这篇报道让公众震惊

C. 这篇报道树立了公众的信心

D. 公众还没接受饮用废水

[考点剖析] 第四段最后一句提到他认为让公众将经过处理的废水作为饮用水还需要更长的时间, 因为公众对喝废水还是十分紧张的,因此选 D 项。

59. [正确答案] B

[考点类型] 推理题

[题目翻译] 奥尔加·奈登科的话强调了_____。

A. 最近的进步

B. 现存的问题

C. 最新的想法

D. 潜在的风险

[考点剖析] 她在第五段第一句指出我们应该采取一些实际的行动来应对缺水问题,后面她

继续解释饮用水的使用存在的问题。所以她主要论述的是存在的问题,只有 B 项符合题意。

60. [正确答案] C

[考点剖析] 细节题

[题目翻译] 报道建议环境保护署(EPA)做什么?

A. 权衡不同的节约用水方式。

B. 探索处理废水的高新科技。

C. 确立国家级的废水利用标准。

D. 监控国家级水供给。

[考点剖析] 最后一段最后一句说环境保护署(EPA)应该确定废水安全饮用的国家标准,故 C 项"确立国家级的废水利用标准"正确。

Part IV Cloze

为什么孩子们不喜欢吃布鲁塞尔芽甘蓝?因为它比较苦,而孩子们通常不喜欢苦味。但那并不是他们的错。研究者发现不喜欢苦味和酸味是人的生存本能,因为大多数有毒物质尝起来也是那个味道。另一方面,甜的东西尝起来通常会让人觉得安全,因此孩子们天生偏爱吃糖果。

我们所喜欢吃的东西是随时间不断变化的。当我们年龄增长时,我们会发现即使有些东西尝起来苦或酸,但它并不会对我们的生命造成威胁,所以,我们会学着去享受它。当我们年老时,我们的嗅觉敏感度就降低了。人们需要用嗅觉感知味觉,它与尝是不一样的。随着我们的味觉下降,我们可能会开始给我们的食物添加糖和盐,来加重口味。事实上,有个理论说,近年来"重"口味的葡萄酒赢得奖项的原因是,酒评家变老了,所以较难感觉到细微的口感。

如果一个人完全不能辨别味道,他可能是味觉紊乱,那可能是由于舌头受伤或脑损伤导致的,也可能是嗅觉问题。鼻子和嘴巴分开的管道使我们能闻到鼻子后面的味道,这对享受复杂的口味有非常重要的作用。这就是为什么当我们的鼻子堵塞时,食物也会没有味道——除了鸡汤面,因为它实在太咸了。

61. [正确答案] A

[解析过程] 后面说的是不喜欢苦的食物是天性,所以前面只有 A 项最恰当。fault"错误";choice"选择";habit"习惯";regret"后悔"。

62. [正确答案] D

[解析过程] 文中前面提到芽甘蓝时谈论的都是味道。feel"感觉";look"看起来";sound"听起来";taste"尝起来",D 项符合语境。

63. [正确答案] C

[解析过程] 与前面有毒的食品通常是苦的对比,甜味的说明没毒,也就是安全的,选 safe。strange"奇怪";necessary"必需的";safe"安全的";ready"准备好的"。

64. [正确答案] B

[解析过程] 所以孩子们生来对甜的食物是有偏好的。这句话是从上面的理由论述中自然得出的结论。capacity"能力";preference"偏好,喜好";awareness"意识";consideration"思考"。因此正确选项为 B 项。

65. [正确答案] D

[解析过程] 从前半句一些东西是苦的,到后半句说它不会杀死我们(说明没毒),结合第一段的论点可以看出这之间是转折,只能选 D 项"即使"。now that"既然";in case "万一";if only"如果";even though"即使"。

66. [正确答案] A

[解析过程] 我们开始去享受苦或酸的食物。和前一句相连,我们渐渐发现即使苦或酸的食物也没有毒,所以是学着享受。enjoy"享受";improve"改进";treat"对待";alter "转化"。

67. [正确答案] B

[解析过程] 当我们年老时,我们丧失一部分的嗅觉。与后面的内容相符,故选 B 项。form "形成";lose"丢失";reduce"减少",通常是指数量上的减少;gain"增加",与题意相反。

68. [正确答案] C

[解析过程] 我们的味觉在下降,所以需要加入糖或盐提味。后面的 heighten 与 add 相呼应。putting"放置";balancing"平衡";adding"添加";limiting"限制"。

69. [正确答案] C

[解析过程] 事实上,有后面的一种理论。In essence"本质上";In conclusion"结论是";后面接的不是一个对上面的总结,而是一个事实,故正确选项应为 In fact"事实上";In short"简而言之"不符合语境。

70. [正确答案] D

[解析过程] 重口味的葡萄酒得奖的原因是酒评家的年龄大了,并且比较难感觉到细微的口感。softer"更柔软";nicer"更好";worse"更坏";harder"更难"。

71. [正确答案] B

[解析过程] 根据整句话的意思,可以推出由于舌头受伤或大脑损伤可导致有些人不能辨别味道。Be unable to do 不能做某事。unlikely"不太可能";unable"不能",指能力;impossible"不可能",指一件事的可能性;improbable"不适合"。

72. [正确答案] A

[解析过程] 这个空的位置要填一个表示味觉丧失的词,是由后面的舌头和大脑损伤造成的某种问题,只有 A 项"紊乱",符合语境。disorder"紊乱";symptom"症状";therapy"疗法";illusion"幻觉"。

73. [正确答案] D

[解析过程] 这句话后面解释的是从鼻子到嘴之间管道的作用,可以看出是 D 项"嗅觉"。mood"心情";taste"味道";flavor"口味";smell"嗅觉"。

74. [正确答案] C

[解析过程] 通过后面一句的说明可以推断出这条管道对享受复杂的口味有非常重要的作用,正确答案为 C 项。subject to"使遭受";liable to"易受";crucial for"重要";beneficial for"有好处"。

75. [正确答案] B

[解析过程] 这条管道很重要,这就是为什么我们在鼻子堵塞的时候会闻不到味道,故选 B 项。delicious"美味的";flavorless"没有味道的";bitter"苦的";smelly"有臭味的"。

Paper Two   试卷二

Part Ⅰ   Translation

Section A

1. In many ways the Internet has had a very positive effect on society.

   [结构分析] 这是一个简单句,翻译时要注意句子顺序。

   [词义推敲] way 有很多种含义,在这里结合句子整个意思,应该译为"方面"。

   [参考译文] 因特网在很多方面对社会有非常积极的影响。

2. It has improved communication, simplified handling tasks, offered a huge convenience, enabled faster processing, and provided more options, all of which frees more time to do other things.

   [结构分析] 这是一个长句但并不是难句,要能看出完成时的并列结构,以及最后的非限制性定语从句。

   [词义推敲] 名词+ing 可以用来表达比原意更为广泛的含义,例如 reason—reasoning 表达"成因",function—functioning 表达"行使功能(名词)",因此 handling 在这里是"处理"的意思。

   [参考译文] 它增进了人们之间的交流,简化了处理事情的方法,给人们提供了巨大的便捷,使得处理过程更快速以及提供了更多的选择,所有这些都节省出了更多的时间来做其他事情。

3. Yet, interestingly enough, the Internet has in some ways had negative effects.

   [结构分析] 这是一个简单句,现在完成时的结构。

   [词义推敲] interestingly enough 这个短语结合前后句可以译为"有趣的是",以使整个句子更加连贯;way 还是和第一句里的一样,表示"方面"。

   [参考译文] 然而,有趣的是,因特网在某些方面却有负面的影响。

4. The quality of communication has declined and people are impatient because they have become accustomed to instant satisfaction, and using the Internet also takes up a lot of time.

   [结构分析] 第一个 and 表并列,然后 because 引导原因状语从句,第二个 and 后的并列分句是以动名词作主语。

   [词义推敲] decline 有"削弱,减少"的意思,结合前面的 quality,这里应该是质量下降的意思,后面的短语 accustom to 和 take up 的含义要清楚。

   [参考译文] 人们交流的质量下降了,也变得没有耐心,因为他们习惯了即时的满足,而且网络还占据了人们大量的时间。

Section B

1. 乔布斯(Steve Jobs)去世后备受敬仰,原因之一是他创造了科技产品的美感。

   [结构分析] 句子出现了"原因之一"这样的表达,because 引导的原因状语从句不宜使用,one of the reasons 这样的表达比较不容易出错,同时一个长句说不清就可以拆分成两个分句,然后用一些必要连接词来使句子连贯。

   [词义推敲] "敬仰"可以选择 respect,admire,homage 等,"美感"可以选择 beauty,grace,aesthetic perception 之类的表达,"科技产品"要知道用 technical 或 technological products,最后,"去世"尽量不要用 died,最好用 passed away。

   [参考译文] People pay great homage to Steve Jobs after he has passed away, one of the reasons is that he has created the aesthetic perception for technological products.

2. 乔布斯认为无论是汽车还是电脑,人们都愿意购买一些比同类产品更为美观的东西。

   [结构分析] "无论"出现了,还是选择 No matter 作为开头最合适,后面还需要用到比较级 more... than...的结构。

   [词义推敲] "美观"可以用 look better,with better appearance 等表达,但要注意整个句子的语法不要出错。再加上比较级,用 more beautiful than 的结构更容易。"同类产品"可以用 products in the same category/counterparts 之类的结构表达。"愿意购买"可以用多种词语表达。

   [参考译文] No matter whether cars or computers, according to Steve Jobs, consumers are willing to buy those products which look more beautiful than their counterparts.

3. 在乔布斯的领导下,从产品外形、材料到使用感受等各个方面,苹果都带来了无与伦比的体验,让人们的生活变得更美丽。

   [结构分析] 在某人的领导下可以用 with 或 under someone's leadership 来表达。后半句也可以使用逗号加 which 引导的非限制性定语从句。最后注意英语的特点,主谓宾尽量往前放,其他修饰限制表达放在后面,让句子不要头重脚轻。

   [词义推敲] "使用感受"可以用 feeling of usage,utility feedback, usage comment 等表达;"无与伦比"这种四字成语要注意,只要表达出成语本身含义即可,unrivaled,incomparable,unique 之类的表达都可以。

   [参考译文] With the leadership of Steve Jobs, Apple has brought about the unrivaled experiences and beautified people's daily lives in all respects from the appearance and materials of products to the feeling of usage.

Part II Writing

本文属于命题作文,提供了写作的思路。写好这类作文要注意:审题准确,逻辑清晰,理由充分,合情合理,还要注意首尾照应。大致可以分为三段来写:第一段可以按照提示的中文意思,明确文章主题:保持健康有多种方式,但是我最喜欢的是哪种方式。第二段,具体说明理由,支持自己的观点,一般要写3个以上的理由。最后一段,呼应首段。

My Favorite Way of Keeping Fit

Nowadays it has to be admitted that the whole society is faced with the "health issue". According to a recent survey conducted on the Internet, 42 in a hundred people are likely to suffer from vital diseases after retirement. This phenomenon has led to considerable thoughts and considerations about the issue of health among the general public. For my perspective, I believe that proper diet and exercise are the upmost importance to health.

First, proper diet will undoubtedly become the prior one. Mounting fruits and vegetables are supposed to be listed in daily menu for their plenty of fibers and little fat. As a remarkable proverb says, " An apple a day keeps the doctor away." Second, those food that contain too much fat and sugar, such as candies, butter, pork and chocolate, should be kept under the strict limit line. And excessive coffee is harmful too. Third, exercise comes up closely. Regular exercise burns extra energy and builds proper shapes. For instance, people with habit of jogging everyday are much healthier than those without it.

From what has been discussed above, I believe that these aspects should be given due attention now. On one hand, people should always bear these in mind for their own good; On the other hand, more advanced health information shall be open to the public. Only in this way can we keep good health and enjoy a pleasant life.

这篇文章很灵活地运用了常见的作文模板,并进行了相应替换。

第一段:借用社会调查引出保健话题,然后明确自己的主题和观点。

第二段:用三个理由有力地支持了自己的观点。而且用词准确、细致,句型灵活多样。比如:prior, be supposed to, harmful 等高频词汇,可以像范文中一样,在作文中灵活运用。这是帮助考生的作文在众多作文中脱颖而出的亮点。

第三段:首尾呼应,发出积极号召,升华主题。

这样,文章在布局、遣词造句、主题升华等多方面的亮点,提升了作文的层次!

2013年同等学力人员申请硕士学位
英语水平全国统一考试

Paper One 试卷一 (100 minutes)

Part Ⅰ Oral Communication (15 minutes, 10 points)

Section A

Directions: In this section there are two incomplete dialogues and each dialogue has three blanks and three choices A, B and C, taken from the dialogue. Fill in each of the blanks with one of the choices to complete the dialogue and mark your answer on the **Answer Sheet**.

Dialogue One

A. It sounds like a flu.
B. I also advise resting for a couple of days.
C. Boy, when it rains, it pours.

Doctor: What has been bothering you?
Patient: I have a stuffy nose and a sore throat. Plus, I've been coughing a lot. __1__
Doctor: Any stomach pains?
Patient: Actually, yes. My stomach's been upset for a few days.
Doctor: __2__ It's been going around lately.
Patient: Anything I can do for it?
Doctor: I'll prescribe some medicines for you to take. __3__
Patient: Does that mean I shouldn't go to work?
Doctor: Only when you feel up to it. You should stay home for at least a day or two.

Dialogue Two

A. So, what are you going to do with the money?
B. You have lots of money.
C. How much do I owe you?

Joshua: Dad. Allowance day. Can I have my allowance?
Father: Oh. I forgot about that.
Joshua: You always forget.

Father: I guess I do. 4

Joshua: Just $13.

Father: Well, I'm not sure if I have that much.

Joshua: Go to the bank. 5

Father: Lots of money, uh? Uh, well, I think the bank is closed.

Joshua: Then, what about your secret money jar under your bed?

Father: Oh, I guess I could do that. 6

Joshua: I'm going to put some in savings, give some to the poor people, and use the rest to buy books.

Father: Well, that sounds great, Joshua.

Section B

Directions: *In this section there is one incomplete interview which has four blanks and four choices A, B, C and D, taken from the interview. Fill in each of the blanks with one of the choices to complete the interview and mark your answer on the **Answer Sheet**.*

A. Nationalities stay in their own areas,

B. People don't queue like they do here in England.

C. What I liked best was that I could work and still lead a normal life.

D. Some supermarkets are open twenty-four hours a day.

Interviewer: How long did you live in the States?

Interviewee: I was there for two years, in New York, and I enjoyed it tremendously. 7 I mean, the shops are open till 10:00 p.m.

Interviewer: All shops?

Interviewee: Yes, everything. Food shops, chemists, and department stores. 8 And on public holidays, only the banks are shut.

Interviewer: I see, emn... Do you think New York is as multinational as London?

Interviewee: Oh, that's for sure. But it's not as mixed. 9 like there's Russian section, the German section and China Town. But I think the major difference between these two cities was the height of the place. Everything was up in the Big Apple. We lived on the thirty-fifth floor. And of course everything is faster and the New Yorkers are much ruder.

Interviewer: Oh! In what way?

Interviewee: Well, pushing in the street, fights about getting on the bus. 10 And of course the taxi drivers! New York taxi drivers must be the rudest in the world!

Part II Vocabulary (10 minutes, 10 points)

Directions: *In this part there are ten sentences, each with one word or phrase underlined. Choose the one from the four choices marked A, B, C and D that best keeps the meaning of the sentences. Mark your answer on the **Answer Sheet**.*

11. I read the newspaper every day so that I can stay informed about current events.
    A. important   B. international   C. latest   D. cultural
12. After seven days in the desert, the explorer was relieved when he eventually found water.
    A. predictably   B. finally   C. luckily   D. accidentally
13. When we gave the children ice cream, they immediately ceased crying.
    A. started   B. continued   C. resumed   D. stopped
14. The science teacher demonstrated the process of turning solid gold into liquid.
    A. showed   B. elaborated   C. devised   D. simplified
15. John's application for admission to graduate studies in the School of Education has been approved.
    A. entrance   B. acceptance   C. experience   D. allowance
16. Most college students in the United States live away from home.
    A. apart   B. down   C. elsewhere   D. along
17. The pursuit of maximum profit often drives manufacturers to turn out things that can do harm to people's health.
    A. preserve   B. promote   C. process   D. produce
18. Many different parts make up an airplane: the engine(s), the wings, the tail, and so on.
    A. compose   B. decorate   C. construct   D. derive
19. You make it sound as if I did it on purpose.
    A. carefully   B. unwillingly   C. incredibly   D. deliberately
20. He could never have foreseen that one day his books would sell in millions.
    A. understood   B. explained   C. expected   D. believed

Part III Reading Comprehension (45 minutes, 25 points)

 Section A

Directions: *In this section there are four passages followed by questions or unfinished statements, each with four suggested answers A, B, C and D. Choose the best answer and mark your answer on the Answer Sheet.*

Passage One

Five or six years ago, I attended a lecture on the science of attention. A philosopher who conducts research in the medical school was talking about attention blindness, the basic feature of the human brain that, when we concentrate intensely on one task, causes us to miss just about everything else. Because we can't see what we can't see, our lecturer was determined to catch us in the act. He had us watch a video of six people tossing basketballs back and forth, three in white shirts and three in black, and our task was to keep track only of the tosses among the people in white. The tape rolled, and everyone began counting.

Everyone except me. I'm dyslexic(有阅读障碍的), and the moment I saw that grainy tape with the confusing basketball tossers, I knew I wouldn't be able to keep track of their movements, so I let my mind wander. My curiosity was aroused, though, when about 30 seconds into the tape, a gorilla(大猩猩) came in among the players. She (we later learned a female student was in the gorilla suit) stared at the camera, thumped her chest, and then strode away while they continued passing the balls.

When the tape stopped, the philosopher asked how many people had counted at least a dozen basketball tosses. Hands went up all over. He then asked who had counted 13, 14, and congratulated those who'd scored the perfect 15. Then he asked, "And who saw the gorilla?"

I raised my hand and was surprised to discover I was the only person at my table and one of only three or four in the large room to do so. He'd set us up, trapping us in our own attention blindness. Yes, there had been a trick, but he wasn't the one who had played it on us. By concentrating so hard on counting, we had managed to miss the gorilla in the midst.

21. This passage describes _____.
    A. a basketball match   B. an experiment
    C. a philosopher   D. a gorilla

22. "Attention blindness" refers to _____.
    A. the fact that one can't see what one can't see
    B. seeing one thing while missing all else
    C. keeping track of just about everything
    D. the condition of being blind to details

23. "Catch us in the act" (Para. 1) is closest in meaning to "find us _____".
    A. doing something improper
    B. sleeping during the lecture
    C. counting the basketball tosses
    D. failing to notice something within sight

24. How many people in the room saw the gorilla in the video?
    A. 1.   B. 3 or 4.   C. 13 or 14.   D. 15.

25. Whom does "he" (last paragraph) refer to?
    A. The author.   B. The gorilla.   C. The lecturer.   D. The student.

Passage Two

There are few sadder sights than piles of fan letters, lovingly decorated with hand drawings, suffering in a bin. The sparkly envelopes were addressed to Taylor Swift, a pop star much beloved by teenage and pre-teen girls.

"Dear Taylor," reads one discarded message, "I love you so much!! You are the best!! And you are really beautiful and cute!! I'm really enjoying your songs."

This, along with hundreds of other similar letters sent from around the world, was discovered in a Nashville recycling disposal unit by a local woman. Swift's management was quick to reassure her admirers that they had been thrown out accidentally. The response may come as a disappointment to any devotee who imagines, as they compose their letters, that Swift makes time to view each one personally.

Dealing with piles of fan mail is, however, an administrative burden for most celebrities. While some celebrities do like to go through their mail personally, the majority simply do not have time. "But the fate of their correspondence is something most committed fans will not wish and dwell on," says Lynn Zubernis, an expert in the psychology of fandom at West Chester University.

"There's this little bit of every fan that thinks theirs will be the one that stands out—it's not an expectation, but a hope that theirs will be seen by the celebrity."

While the relationship between the fan and the celebrity may exist only in the mind of the former, it stems from a deeply-rooted human need for community and belonging, Zubernis believes. As a result, even receiving a mass-produced letter of acknowledgement and a photo stamped with a reproduced signature can be a powerful experience.

"People have a tremendous need to connect with the person they are idolising (偶像化)," she says. "They can't ring them up and say, 'Can we have coffee?' It's not about the autograph (签名). It's about the moment of connection."

26. Which of the following statements is true?

    A. The letters in the bin were exaggerating.

    B. Some letters to Swift were thrown away unread.

    C. A woman discovered the letters and discarded them.

    D. Poorly decorated letters were left unread.

27. Swift's management claimed that _____.

    A. Swift had read each one of the letters

    B. fans could trust them with their letters

    C. they were quick in response to the incident

    D. they didn't intend to throw away the letters

28. Most celebrities _____.

    A. are too busy to read fan mail

    B. are afraid of receiving fan mail

    C. try their best to read fan mail themselves

    D. care about the fate of fan mail

29. According to Zubernis, fans want their letters to be read because they _____.

    A. hope to show their hand drawings

    B. want the celebrities to see their talent

    C. desire to get connected with the stars

    D. dream of getting a photo of the stars

30. Which of the following will fans cherish the most?

    A. The feeling of being related to their stars.

    B. The sense of being similar to their stars.

    C. The time spent with their stars.

    D. The autograph of their stars.

Passage Three

Facelift (紧肤术) followed by a week on a beach in Thailand? Hip surgery with a side of shopping in Singapore? Over the last 10 years, Asia's rise on the medical tourism scene has been quick. Eastern nations dominate the global scene. Now Bali wants a slice of the action.

The Indonesian island recently opened its first facility specifically targeting medical tourists with packages and services, Bali International Medical Centre(BIMC) Nusa Dua. BIMC already has an international hospital in Kuta, which opened in 1998.

The new internationally managed facility offers surgical and non-surgical cosmetic procedures and dental care.

Unlike most of the region's hospitals, BIMC is designed to feel more like a spa or resort (度假村) than a medical facility.

The 50-bed hospital has a 24-hour medical emergency entrance and hotel-like lobby at the front of the building servicing the hospital's medicals, and dental centers.

If you're a celebrity who doesn't want everyone to know you're here for a bit of lipo (吸脂术), no worries. There's a private entrance that leads to the Cosmetic Centre, which offers views of a golf course.

BIMC has even teamed up with the nearby Courtyard by Marriott Bali, which provides specific after-care services like tailor-made meals and wellness programs for patients.

Latest technology and cool interiors are a start, but breaking into a regional industry that already has some of the world's top international hospitals will be tough, says Josef Woodman, CEO of U.S.-based medical travel consumer guide Patients Beyond Borders (PBB).

"As a newcomer, Bali faces stiff competition from nearby international healthcare providers. To compete, Bali will need to demonstrate a quality level of care and promote its services to the region and the world. On the positive side, Bali is blessed as one of the region's safest, most popular tourist destinations, with a built-in potential to attract medical travelers."

"The Indonesian island couldn't have picked a better time to get into the game," says PBB. "The world population is aging and becoming wealthier at rates that surpass the availability of quality health care resources," says the company's research.

31. What does "medical tourism" (Para. 1) probably mean?
   A. Treating a disease during a trip.
   B. Attracting patients with package tours.
   C. Cosmetic treatment and a tour in one.
   D. Turning hospitals into tourist attractions.

32. How does BIMC differ from regular hospitals?
   A. It offers cosmetic surgery.
   B. It has better environment and services.
   C. It accepts international patients.
   D. It has more beds and longer service hours.

33. BIMC wishes to attract celebrities with its _____.
   A. privacy measures   B. first-class design
   C. free golf course   D. tailor-made meals

34. According to Woodman, BIMC _____.
    A. threatens its regional competitors
    B. will soon take the lead in the industry
    C. needs further improvement
    D. faces both challenges and opportunities

35. What can be concluded from the last paragraph?
    A. The population is developing faster than medical resources.
    B. Healthcare is hardly available for the aging population.
    C. The world is in need of more quality medical care.
    D. The world population is becoming older and richer.

Passage Four

For many of us, asking for help is a difficult concept. We may feel as if we are admitting a weakness that the world would not have known about, had we not asked for help.

Ironically, it's been my experience that people who are able to deliver well-positioned requests for help are seen as very strong individuals. When they demonstrate the humility (谦卑) to ask for help, they earn the respect of others. People who receive a heartfelt request for help are usually honored by the request. In turn, we are strengthened by the very help that is provided.

One of my clients (we'll call her Kira) recently made a shift in how she was interacting with her boss. When asked to prepare presentations, she assumed that she was expected to go away, develop the content, deliver it at the required meeting and then wait for feedback from her boss. Her boss was highly regarded for the impact of his presentations, while Kira often felt that her presentations were lacking. When she took a hard look at how this approach was working for her, Kira recognized that she had not yet made use of her boss's support. She could learn far more about creating attractive presentations by walking through a draft with her boss—focusing on the content plus her delivery—and obtaining feedback earlier in the process rather than at the back end. So she made the request for his support.

The outcome? Her boss was delighted to coach Kira and was enthusiastic about the opportunity to put into use his own strength by teaching presentation skills more effectively to her. By taking the time to work together on preparation for a number of Kira's key presentations, she benefited from her boss's thought process and was able to distinguish the critical components to enhance her own presentations. Kira's presentations now have punch!

Some of us are uncomfortable asking for help because we believe that our request places burdens on the other person. Ironically, we may be missing an opportunity to show others how we value and respect them. People who know you and think well of you are often highly motivated to help. Furthermore, the more specific you can be about what you need from them, the easier it is for them to assist you.

36. Many people are unwilling to ask for help because they _____.
    A. are confident of themselves   B. do not trust other people
    C. are ashamed of doing so   D. do not think it necessary

37. Which of the following may the author agree with?
    A. Asking for help means admitting weaknesses.
    B. Helping others is helping oneself.
    C. Well-positioned requests for help are welcomed.
    D. Weak people often need more help.
38. Kira's request for help _____.
    A. turned out rewarding   B. was turned down
    C. led to her promotion   D. benefited her boss in return
39. "Kira's presentations now have punch" means her presentations are _____.
    A. forceful   B. controversial
    C. well received   D. highly motivating
40. The purpose of the passage is to _____.
    A. illustrate how to ask for help
    B. show the importance of mutual help
    C. call for attention to others' requests
    D. encourage people to ask for help

Section B

Directions: *In this section, you are required to read one quoted blog and the comments on it. The blog and comments are followed by questions or unfinished statements, each with four suggested answers A, B, C and D. Choose the best answer and mark your answer on the* **Answer Sheet**.

A fascinating new study reveals that Americans are more likely to call their children "intelligent", while European parents focus on happiness and balance.

Here's what one parent had to say about the intelligence of her 3-year-old, which was apparent to her from the very first moments of her life:

"I have this vivid memory, when she was born, of them taking her to clean her off... And she was looking all around... She was alert from the very first second... I took her out when she was six weeks old to a shopping mall to have her picture taken—people would stop me and say, 'What an alert baby.' One guy stopped me and said, 'Lady, she was an intelligent baby.'"

Not only are Americans far more likely to focus on their children's intelligence and cognitive skills, they are also far less likely to describe them as "happy" or "easy" children to parent.

"The U. S.'s unhealthy interest in cognitive development in the early years overlooks so much else," the researchers told us.

Comment 1

Probably indicates more about differences in cultural attitudes towards humility and boasting than about parenting styles. Here in the Netherlands if someone called their child "intelligent", I'd be rolling my eyes, both because it's probably biased and overstated and because it's just a rotten thing to draw attention to; as if it's all about whose child is "better". Life isn't that much of a damn contest to us.

Comment 2

Agreed! That would apply in Sweden too. Parenting is more focused on the child's well-being than social competition (there may be pressures here too, but it is not socially acceptable to express those things).

Comment 3

I agree and I live in the U. S. Parents' opinions of their children's intellect are definitely biased and overstated. It is the most annoying thing to listen to. Being "advanced" at a young age has little if anything to do with their ability to learn as they get older and EVERY child is a genius if you give them a chance and an ear to listen to them. The happier the kid is, the smarter they will be. Happiness and healthy is the key.

41. The passage is mainly concerned with cultural differences in _____.
    A. bringing up one's children
    B. describing one's children
    C. social contests
    D. choosing a place to live in

42. The word "alert" (Para. 3) is closest in meaning to "_____".
    A. intelligent   B. easy-going
    C. quick at noticing things D. happy

43. According to **Comment 1**, in the Netherlands, calling one's own child "intelligent" is _____.
    A. boasting   B. acceptable
    C. encouraging   D. reasonable

44. What nationality is the writer of **Comment 2**?
    A. Dutch.   B. American.   C. Swedish.   D. French.

45. All of the following are true of **Comment 3** EXCEPT that _____.
    A. it agrees with all the other comments
    B. being happy and healthy is important
    C. being intelligent at a young age makes no sense
    D. children's intellect varies from person to person

Part Ⅳ　Cloze (10 minutes, 10 points)

Directions: *In this part, there is a passage with ten blanks. For each blank there are four choices marked A, B, C and D. Choose the best answer for each blank and mark your answer on the **Answer Sheet**.*

Riding a bike is good exercise and great fun. But what do you do with a bike after you outgrow it? Nicole Basil, 12, has a terrific answer to this question. When she was 8 years old, she __46__ Pedal Power. It is a charity that collects bikes that kids have outgrown and donates them to Chicago public schools.

Since 2008, Nicole has collected and donated more than 1,000 bikes. __47__ the bicycles, Pedal Power supplied riders with 400 helmets (头盔) last year. "It is important to ride __48__ on a bike, and helmets are a big part of that," Nicole says. The Wilmette Bicycle & Sport Shop helps to __49__ that all donated bikes are safe to ride. Each bike receives a five-minute __50__ by the shop's employees.

The bikes are given to students who have good grades and perfect attendance. Nicole says: "Some kids aren't as lucky as others, __51__ they still do well in school. I think they should be __52__ for that." Nicole has received e-mails and phone calls from parents and teachers that say test __53__ are improving. "Bikes can take you far," she says. "Good grades can take you even __54__."

Barton Dassinger is the principal of Cesar E. Chavez school in Chicago. Students in his school have received bikes. "It's been a great way to __55__ students to do their best," Dassinger says. "They work hard to make it happen."

46. A. joined	B. created	C. helped	D. reformed
47. A. In addition to	B. In honor of	C. In line with	D. In exchange for
48. A. safely	B. happily	C. freely	D. quickly
49. A. insist	B. accept	C. remember	D. ensure
50. A. look-out	B. drop-out	C. check-up	D. line-up
51. A. and	B. so	C. but	D. or
52. A. remembered	B. rewarded	C. repaid	D. recommended
53. A. papers	B. scores	C. conditions	D. methods
54. A. higher	B. better	C. further	D. greater
55. A. require	B. exploit	C. entitle	D. motivate

Part V   Text Completion (20 minutes, 20 points)

Directions: *In this part, there are three incomplete texts with 20 questions (Ranging from 56 to 75). Above each text there are three or four phrases to be completed. First, use the choices provided in the box to complete the phrases. Second, use the completed phrases to fill in the blanks of the text. Note you should blacken the letters that indicate your answers on the **Answer Sheet**.*

Text One

A. optimistic about
B. a need
C. a third

Phrases:
  A. they felt __56__ for
  B. most were __57__ the future for women
  C. less than __58__ of them

In a recent survey, 55% of 3,000 Japanese women polled said they weren't being treated equally with men at work, and __59__ said they expected women's lives to improve over the next two decades.

Yet, only 26% of the women said __60__ a strong and organized women's movement. In a similar survey of American women, a much smaller 29% believed they were treated unfairly at work, __61__, and 37% said a women's movement was needed.

Text Two

```
A. up to
B. collections
C. library
```

Phrases:

A. introduce you to our __62__ facilities

B. check out __63__ five books

C. houses our humanities and map __64__

Welcome to the university library. This tour will __65__. First of all, the library's collection of books, reference materials, and other resources are found on levels one to four of this building. Level one __66__. On level two, you will find our circulation desk, current periodicals and journals, and our copy facilities. Our science and engineering sections can be found on level three. Finally, group study rooms and the multimedia center are located on level four. Undergraduate students can __67__ for two weeks. Graduate students can check out fifteen books for two months. Books can be renewed up to two times.

Text Three

```
A. to understand them
B. to think about
C. not accent elimination
D. give them the most trouble
```

Phrases:

A. identify which specific areas of pronunciation __68__

B. give you some things __69__

C. make it difficult for native speakers __70__

D. focus on accent reduction, __71__

Many ESL learners are concerned about eliminating their accents, but before you run out and spend hundreds of dollars on the latest pronunciation course, let me __72__.

First, the main goal of any pronunciation course should be to __73__, which is virtually impossible. Rather, students should work on reducing areas of their pronunciation that affect comprehensibility, that is, areas of their accents that __74__. Second, with this goal in mind, students need to be able to __75__. Of course, there are universal areas of pronunciation that affect specific language groups, and reading up on these commonalities will help you.

Paper Two 试卷二 (50 minutes)

Part VI Translation (20 minutes, 10 points)

Directions: *Translate the following passage into Chinese. Write your answer on the **Answer Sheet**.*

Being unhappy is like an infectious disease. It causes people to shrink away from the sufferer. He soon finds himself alone and miserable. There is, however, a cure so simple as to seem, at first glance, ridiculous: if you don't feel happy, pretend to be!

It works. Before long you will find that instead of pushing people away, you attract them. You discover how deeply rewarding it is to be the center of wider and wider circles of good will.

Then the make-believe becomes a reality. Being happy, once it is realized as a duty and established as a habit, opens doors into unimaginable gardens filled with grateful friends.

Part VII Writing (30 minutes, 15 points)

Directions: *Write a composition of at least 150 words about the topic:* ***The Possibility of Using the Mobile Phone to Study English*** (*or any other subject*). *You should write according to the outline given below. Write your composition on the **Answer Sheet**.*

1. 我认为手机(不)可以用来学习英语或其他知识。
2. 理由是……
3. 结论。

2013年同等学力人员申请硕士学位英语水平全国统一考试

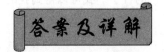

Paper One 试卷一

Part I Oral Communication

Section A

对话一

    A. 听起来像是流感。

    B. 我建议你休息几天。

    C. 哎,真是祸不单行。

医生:你怎么了?(什么困扰着你?)

病人:我鼻塞,嗓子疼,而且一直在咳嗽。__1__

医生:肚子疼吗?

病人:是的,我的肚子不舒服好几天了。

医生:__2__ 它最近很流行。

病人:我该怎么做呢?

医生:我会给你开点药。__3__

病人:那是否意味着我不应该去工作了?

医生:等你觉得能去上班了再去。你至少应该在家休息一到两天。

1. [正确答案] C

   [考点剖析] 医生说"你怎么了",病人说"我鼻塞,嗓子疼,而且一直在咳嗽",说明病人身体不适的症状有很多,C项符合对话所表达的含义。

2. [正确答案] A

   [考点剖析] 医生对病人的病情得出一个结论,后文医生说"它最近很流行",根据语境并结合各选项的意思可知,应选A项。

3. [正确答案] B

   [考点剖析] 医生说"我会给你开点药",病人说"那是否意味着我不应该去工作了",根据语境并结合各选项的意思可知,应选B项。

对话二

    A. 那你打算怎么用这笔钱呢？

    B. 你有很多钱。

    C. 我欠你多少钱呢？

    约书亚：爸爸，今天是给零花钱的日子。我可以得到我的零花钱吗？

    父亲：我把这事忘记了。

    约书亚：您总是忘记。

    父亲：我也觉得是这样。__4__

    约书亚：只是 13 美元而已。

    父亲：好吧，但我不确定我是否有那么多钱。

    约书亚：到银行取啊。__5__

    父亲：很多钱？哦……但是我觉得银行关门了。

    约书亚：那你床底下的小金库呢？

    父亲：哦，我想是可以用那些钱的。__6__

    约书亚：我打算存起来一部分，捐献给穷人一部分，剩下的用来买书。

    父亲：哦，听起来非常好，约书亚。

4. [正确答案] C

    [考点剖析] 本题解题关键在于下面的回答——"只是 13 美元而已"，问题应该是就此而提问，询问钱的数量。C 项"我欠你多少钱呢？"符合语境。

5. [正确答案] B

    [考点剖析] 本题解题关键在于父亲的回答——"很多钱？"，由此可知 B 项"你有很多钱"符合语境。

6. [正确答案] A

    [考点剖析] 本题解题关键依然在约书亚的回答"我打算存起来一部分，捐献给穷人一部分，剩下的用来买书"，由此可知，此处是在问钱的用途，A 项符合语境。

Section B

    A. 各个国家有各自的区域，

    B. 人们不会像在英国那样排队。

    C. 我最喜欢的是我在工作的同时仍然能过着正常的生活。

    D. 有些超市 24 小时营业。

    采访人：你在美国住了多长时间？

    受访人：我在纽约待了 2 年，而且我非常喜欢那儿的生活。__7__ 我的意思是商店会营业到晚上 10 点。

采访人:所有的商店吗?

受访人:是的,所有的。食品店、药店和百货商店。__8__ 而且在公共假日的时候,只有银行会关门。

采访人:嗯,我明白了。你认为纽约像伦敦一样是个多民族的城市吗?

受访人:那是肯定的。但是它没有伦敦那么混杂。__9__ 例如,那里有俄罗斯区、德国区和唐人街。但是我认为这两个城市主要的不同点在于地方的高度。在纽约这个"大苹果"(对纽约的别称)上,一切都处在高处。我们居住在三十五层。当然,这里的一切节奏都比较快,而且纽约人更粗鲁些。

受访人:哦,粗鲁表现在哪些方面?

采访人:比如在街上推搡,争吵着上公交车。__10__ 当然,出租车司机也是。纽约的出租车司机一定是世界上最粗鲁的人!

7. [正确答案] C

　　[考点剖析] 采访人问"你在美国住了多长时间?",受访人说"我在纽约待了2年,而且我非常喜欢那儿……"。enjoy 和 like 是同义词,C 项的 liked best 是进一步解释前面喜欢的内容。而空后面的句子 I mean…是对 C 项内容的解释。根据语境并结合各选项的意思可知,C 项"我最喜欢的是我在工作的同时仍然能过着正常的生活"为正确选项。

8. [正确答案] D

　　[考点剖析] 采访人问"所有的商店吗",受访人说"是的,所有的。食品店、药店和百货商店……"。D 项"有些超市 24 小时营业"刚好是上句话的具体例证。根据语境并结合各选项的意思可知,应选 D 项。

9. [正确答案] A

　　[考点剖析] 本题的解题关键在空后面的内容。like 是举例的标志,那么前面空格要填写的句子应该是对后面具体例子的一个抽象概括;后文说到,那里有俄罗斯区、德国区等不同的区域,A 项的意思刚好和后文相吻合,而且也是对前句话"它没有伦敦那么混杂"的具体解释。

10. [正确答案] B

　　[考点剖析] 受访人在这里依然在解释纽约和伦敦不一样的方面——排队。B 项的隐含意思是在英国人们会排队,而在纽约则不会。根据语境并结合各选项的意思可知 B 项为正确选项。

Part Ⅱ　Vocabulary

11. [正确答案] C

　　[考点类型] 形容词

　　[考点剖析] 题干中的 current 意为"最新的,流行的"。important"重要的";international"国际化的";latest"最新的,最近的";cultural"文化的"。只有 C 项与题干中画线单词的含义相近。

12. [正确答案] B

    [考点类型] 副词

    [考点剖析] 题干中的 eventually 意为"最后,终于"。predictably"可预见地,不出所料地";finally"最终,终于";luckily"幸运地";accidentally"偶然地,意外地"。只有 B 项与题干中画线单词的含义相近。

13. [正确答案] D

    [考点类型] 动词

    [考点剖析] 题干中的 ceased 意为"停止,终止"。started"开始";continued"继续";resumed"重新开始,恢复,重新取得";stopped"停止"。只有 D 项与题干中画线单词的含义相近。

14. [正确答案] A

    [考点类型] 动词

    [考点剖析] 题干中的 demonstrated 意为"证明,展示"。showed"展示,演示";elaborated"详尽说明";devised"设计";simplified"简化"。只有 A 项与题干中画线单词的含义相近。

15. [正确答案] B

    [考点类型] 名词

    [考点剖析] 题干中的 admission 意为"准许进入;承认"。entrance"入口,进入方式";acceptance"接受";experience"经验,经历";allowance"津贴"。只有 B 项与题干中画线单词的含义相近。

16. [正确答案] A

    [考点类型] 副词

    [考点剖析] 题干中的 away 意为"远离,在远处"。apart"相隔,相距";down"向下";elsewhere"在别处";along"沿着"。只有 A 项与题干中画线单词的含义相近。

17. [正确答案] D

    [考点类型] 动词

    [考点剖析] 题干中的 turn out 意为"生产,制造"。preserve"保护";promote"提升,促进";process"加工,处理";produce"生产,制造"。只有 D 项与题干中画线单词的含义相近。

18. [正确答案] A

    [考点类型] 动词

    [考点剖析] 题干中的 make up 意为"组成;构成"。compose"组成";decorate"装饰,点缀";construct"建造";derive"源于,导出"。只有 A 项与题干中画线单词的含义相近。

19. [正确答案] D

    [考点类型] 副词

    [考点剖析] 题干中的 on purpose 意为"故意地"。carefully"认真地";unwillingly"不愿意地";incredibly"难以置信地";deliberately"故意地"。只有 D 项与题干中画线单词的含义相近。

20. [正确答案] C

[考点类型] 动词

[考点剖析] 题干中的 foreseen 意为"预见"。understood"理解，明白"；explained"解释"；expected"预料"；believed"相信"。只有 C 项与题干中画线单词的含义相近。

Part Ⅲ　Reading Comprehension

Section A

Passage One

五六年前，我参加了一个关于注意力科学的讲座。一位在医学院进行研究的哲学家正在谈论注意力盲区，这是人脑的基本特征——当我们全神贯注于一项任务时，我们会忽略其他一切事情。因为我们注意不到我们不会去看的东西，所以我们的讲师决定用实际行动来让我们体会这个观点。他让我们看一段 6 个人来回投篮球的视频，其中三人穿着白衬衫，而另外三人穿着黑衬衫。我们的任务是只记录穿白衬衫的人的投球情况。录像开始播放，所有人都开始计数。

这些人中不包括我，因为我有阅读障碍，一看到模糊不清的录像带中那一群令人困惑的篮球投手，我就知道我跟不上他们的节奏，所以我开始漫不经心起来。但是，当录像带播放到大约 30 秒时，一只大猩猩来到球员当中，我的好奇心被激发起来了。她盯着相机，拍打着胸部，然后大步离开，此时球员仍在传球（我们后来知道这是一位穿着大猩猩服装的女学生）。

当录像带停止播放后，哲学家问有多少人统计出投球数至少在 12 次以上，大家都把手举了起来。然后他问谁的统计数字是 13 和 14，并祝贺那些统计数字为 15 的人。然后他问："谁看见大猩猩了吗？"

我举起了我的手，并惊讶地发现我是我所在桌子上唯一一个举手的人，也是这个大房间内仅有的三四个举手人之一。他给我们设了一个圈套，诱使我们陷入自己的注意力盲区。是的，这是一个把戏，但他不是那个对我们要把戏的人。由于我们将注意力集中在计数上，所以就会错过出现在其中的大猩猩。

21. [正确答案] B

[考点类型] 主旨题

[题目翻译] 这篇文章描写了_____。

A. 一场篮球比赛

B. 一项实验

C. 一位哲学家

D. 一只大猩猩

[考点剖析] 主旨题需要把各段落大意进行串联和总结，通读全文可知，本篇旨在向我们讲述一个哲学家所做的实验：当我们全神贯注于一项任务时，我们会忽略其他一切事情。所以答案为 B 项，其他选项都属于个别细节，不能全面地概括文章内容。

22. [正确答案] B

　　[考点类型] 推理题

　　[题目翻译] "注意力盲区"指的是_____。

　　　　　　A. 这样一个事实：我们注意不到我们不会去看的东西

　　　　　　B. 只看到一件事情，而忽略或者错过其他一切事情

　　　　　　C. 一直注意所有的事情

　　　　　　D. 忽略细节的条件

　　[考点剖析] 推理词汇或短语的意思时，要注意理解该词汇或者短语在原文出现的语境、语句含义。第一段第二句 the basic feature of the human brain that, when we concentrate intensely on one task, causes us to miss just about everything else 刚好是对 attention blindness 的具体解释，该部分的语句含义也就是正确答案所在：这是人脑的基本特征——当我们全神贯注于一项任务时，我们会忽略其他一切事情。所以答案为 B 项。

23. [正确答案] D

　　[考点类型] 词汇题

　　[题目翻译] 与 catch us in the act(第一段)含义最相近的是："发觉我们_____"。

　　　　　　A. 在做一件不恰当的事情

　　　　　　B. 在听讲座的时候睡觉

　　　　　　C. 在数篮球投球数

　　　　　　D. 没能注意到视野中的一些事情

　　[考点剖析] 在做此类题型的时候，要注意理解该词汇或者短语在原文出现的语境、语句含义。Because we can't see what we can't see, our lecturer was determined to catch us in the act 是对前句话的承接。根据前面语境可知，当我们全神贯注于一项任务时，我们会忽略其他一切事情。我们注意不到我们不会去看的东西，所以我们的讲师决定用实际行动来解释这一现象。讲师是要通过实验来让我们发现自己没能注意到视野中的一些事情。所以答案为 D 项。

24. [正确答案] B

　　[考点类型] 细节题

　　[题目翻译] 房间里有多少人看到了视频中出现的大猩猩？

　　　　　　A. 1 个。

　　　　　　B. 3 或 4 个。

　　　　　　C. 13 或 14 个。

　　　　　　D. 15 个。

　　[考点剖析] 倒数第二段最后一句讲师提出了"谁看见大猩猩了吗"这一问题。最后一段第一句指出"我举起了我的手，并惊讶地发现我是我所在桌子上唯一一个举手的人，也是这个大房间内仅有的三四个举手人之一"。可知答案为 B 项。

25. [正确答案] C
    [考点类型] 推理题
    [题目翻译] he(最后一段)指的是谁?
              A.作者。
              B.大猩猩。
              C.讲师。
              D.学生。
    [考点剖析] 分析画线单词所在句可知,此处的he指的是前面给我们设置陷阱的讲师。所以答案为C项。

Passage Two

没有一幕比看见一堆粉丝精心设计的手绘信件被丢进垃圾桶更让人悲伤的了。这些引人注目的信件是寄给泰勒·斯威夫特的,她是一位深受十几岁甚至更年轻的女孩喜爱的流行歌星。

一封被丢弃的信中这样写道:"亲爱的泰勒,我非常爱你!!你是最棒的!!你是如此漂亮、如此可爱!!我真的很喜欢你的歌!!"

这封信连同其他数百封来自世界各地的类似的信件被一个当地妇女在纳什维尔回收处理单位发现。斯威夫特的管理人员迅速安抚她的粉丝,称信件是被不小心扔掉的。粉丝们对这种行为感到十分失望,因为他们在写信的时候期待斯威夫特能抽时间亲自阅读每封信件。

然而,对于大多数名人来说,处理成堆的粉丝邮件是一种负担。虽然一些名人确实喜欢亲自看邮件,但大多数名人根本没有时间。西切斯特大学影迷心理学专家林恩·祖贝尼斯说:"大多数忠实粉丝不愿意细想他们寄出的信件命运如何。"

"每一名粉丝都认为自己的信件能够与众不同——这不是期待,而是一种希望,希望自己的信能够被偶像看见。"

祖贝尼斯认为,虽然粉丝和名人之间的关系可能只存在于粉丝心里,但是这源于人类对社会和归属感的迫切需要。因此,即使收到一封批量打印的感谢信和一张带有复制签名的照片也是一种振奋人心的体验。

她说:"人们有一种强烈的需要,把自己与偶像联系起来;他们不能给自己的偶像打电话说:'我们可以喝杯咖啡吗?'这不是签名的问题,而是自己与偶像有关联时的感觉。"

26. [正确答案] B
    [考点类型] 细节题
    [题目翻译] 下面选项中哪种表述是正确的?
              A.垃圾箱中的信件非常夸张。
              B.有些邮寄给斯威夫特的信件没被阅读就被丢掉了。
              C.一个女人发现并且丢掉了这些信件。
              D.设计简陋的信件没被阅读。
    [考点剖析] 根据前三段内容可知,粉丝寄给斯威夫特的很多精心设计的手绘信件没被阅读就被扔掉了。A项原文并未涉及,C项和D项故意曲解原文含义,所以答案为B项。

27. [正确答案] D
    [考点类型] 细节题
    [题目翻译] 斯威夫特的管理人员声称_____。
        A. 斯威夫特已经阅读了每封信件
        B. 粉丝可以放心地把信件交给他们
        C. 针对这件事他们迅速地作出了回应
        D. 他们不是故意把信件丢掉的
    [考点剖析] 根据题干定位到第三段第二句 Swift's management was quick to… accidentally，D 项中的 didn't intend 和该句最后一个单词 accidentally 是同义替换。所以答案为 D 项。

28. [正确答案] A
    [考点类型] 细节题
    [题目翻译] 大多数名人_____。
        A. 太忙而无法阅读粉丝的邮件
        B. 害怕收到粉丝的邮件
        C. 尽最大可能亲自阅读粉丝的邮件
        D. 很关心粉丝邮件的命运
    [考点剖析] 根据题干定位到原文第四段第二句 majority simply do not have time，可知虽然一些名人确实喜欢亲自看邮件，但大多数名人根本没有时间。所以答案为 A 项。

29. [正确答案] C
    [考点类型] 细节题
    [题目翻译] 根据祖贝尼斯的观点，粉丝们想要他们的信件被偶像阅读是由于他们_____。
        A. 想要展现他们的手工绘画
        B. 想要偶像看到他们的才能
        C. 盼望能与偶像取得联系
        D. 梦想得到一张偶像的照片
    [考点剖析] 根据最后一段内容可知，粉丝想要自己的信被偶像看到是因为他们想与明星有联系。所以答案为 C 项。

30. [正确答案] A
    [考点类型] 推理题
    [题目翻译] 下列选项中哪个是粉丝最为珍惜的？
        A. 自己与偶像有所关联的感觉。
        B. 与偶像相似的那种感受。
        C. 与偶像共度的时光。
        D. 偶像的亲笔签名。
    [考点剖析] 根据最后一段内容可知，粉丝不太可能与偶像约会，自然不会有与偶像共度的时光，所以，粉丝最珍惜的是自己与偶像有所关联的感觉。所以答案为 A 项。

Passage Three

在紧肤术之后来一次泰国海滨一周游？在髋部手术后在新加坡进行一次购物？在过去的10年里，亚洲医疗旅游业迅速兴起。东方国家主导全球舞台。现在巴厘岛也想做出行动。

印尼最近开放了它首家拥有专门针对医疗游客而设置的包装与服务的机构——巴厘岛国际医疗中心(BIMC)努沙杜瓦。早在1998年，BIMC已在库塔开设了一家国际医院。

这家全新的国际管理机构提供手术和非手术整形术以及牙科保健服务。

不同于大多数地区医院的是，BIMC的设计使人们感觉它更像是温泉浴场或度假村而不是医疗机构。

这家配备有50张床的医院拥有24小时急诊入口，大楼前部是酒店式的大堂，为医院的医疗和牙科中心提供服务。

如果你是一个名人，不希望大家知道你在这里接受吸脂术，不用担心，医院里有一个私人入口可以带你进入整容中心，在那里你还可以观看高尔夫比赛。

BIMC还与附近的巴厘岛万豪酒店合作为病人提供诸如特制食物和健康计划这样的后续特殊服务。

最新技术和一流就医环境是一个开始，但是要进入一个已经拥有一些世界顶级国际医院的区域产业将很艰难，美国基础医疗旅游消费者指南《患者无国界》的首席执行官约瑟夫·伍德曼说道。

"作为一个新手，巴厘岛将面临来自附近的国际医疗保健机构的激烈竞争。为了竞争，巴厘岛将需要证明自己的护理水平并向区域和世界推广其服务。从积极的方面来看，巴厘岛作为该区域最安全、最受欢迎的旅游目的地之一，具有吸引医疗游客的内在潜力。"

"印尼没有比现在更恰当的时间来迈入这个领域。"PBB公司说道。该公司的研究表明：世界人口老龄化和财富增加的速度超过了提供优质医疗资源的能力。

31. ［正确答案］C

　　［考点类型］词汇题

　　［题目翻译］第一段中的medical tourism可能是什么意思？

　　　　　　　A. 在旅行的时候治疗疾病。

　　　　　　　B. 用包办旅游来吸引病人。

　　　　　　　C. 集美容整形和旅游于一体。

　　　　　　　D. 把医院转型为旅游景点。

　　［考点剖析］根据第一段内容可知，medical tourism指的是医疗旅游，即集医疗与旅游于一体。所以答案为C项。

32. ［正确答案］B

　　［考点类型］细节题

　　［题目翻译］BIMC与其他常规医院有何不同？

　　　　　　　A. 它能提供整容手术。

　　　　　　　B. 它有更好的环境和服务。

C. 它能接收国际病人。

D. 它有更多的病床和更长的服务时间。

[考点剖析] 根据题干可以定位到第四段,该段提到,不同于大多数地区医院的是,BIMC 的设计使人们感觉它更像是温泉浴场或度假村而不是医疗机构。这些都是在说医院的环境和服务。所以答案为 B 项。D 项是迷惑选项,原文中并未对病床数量和服务时间进行比较。

33. [正确答案] A

[考点类型] 细节题

[题目翻译] BIMC 希望通过_____来吸引名人。

A. 隐私措施

B. 顶级的设计

C. 免费的高尔夫球场

D. 特制的食物

[考点剖析] 文中提到"名人"的地方在第六段:如果你是一个名人,不希望大家知道你在这里接受吸脂术,不用担心,医院里有一个私人入口可以带你进入整容中心,在那里你还可以观看高尔夫比赛。由此看出,BIMC 用保护隐私的方式吸引名人。所以答案为 A 项。

34. [正确答案] D

[考点类型] 推理题

[题目翻译] 根据伍德曼的说法,BIMC _____。

A. 威胁到该区的竞争者

B. 很快就会引领这个行业

C. 需要进一步提高

D. 挑战和机遇并存

[考点剖析] 文中第八段 but breaking into a regional industry… will be tough 说明 BIMC 进入这个行业是艰难的,也就是说存在挑战;而第九段 On the positive side… the region's safest, most popular tourist destinations… to attract medical travelers 又说 BIMC 具有优势,换言之,它也拥有机会。由此推知,BIMC 的挑战和机遇是并存的。所以答案为 D 项。

35. [正确答案] C

[考点类型] 推理题

[题目翻译] 从最后一段我们可以得出什么结论?

A. 人口比医疗资源增长得更快。

B. 老龄化人口很难获得医疗护理。

C. 世界需要更优质的医疗护理。

D. 世界人口更趋老龄化且更富有。

[考点剖析] 根据最后一段可知,世界人口老龄化和财富增加的速度超过了提供优质医疗资源的能力。所以答案为 C 项。

Passage Four

对我们大多数人而言,寻求帮助是一个困难的观念。我们可能会觉得这是在承认自己的一个弱点;相反,如果我们不寻求别人的帮助,全世界都不会知道这个弱点。

具有讽刺意味的是,我曾有过这样一种亲身的感受——那些能够恰当地请求别人给予帮助的人被视为非常强大的人。当他们谦卑地寻求别人的帮助时,他们也获得了他人的尊重。被求助的人通常都很荣幸能收到别人的衷心求助。反过来说,我们恰恰是因为所提供的帮助而使自己变得强大。

我的一个客户(我们叫她基拉),最近改变了她与她老板的互动方式。当她被要求准备演讲时,她认为她该做的就是走开,去准备演讲的内容,并在指定的会议上进行演讲,然后等待老板的反馈。她的老板因其出色的演讲影响力而受人尊重,而基拉经常觉得她的演讲有很多不足之处。当她仔细思考自己如何用老板的方法来提高自己的演讲能力时,基拉意识到,她尚未向老板寻求帮助。通过和老板排演一下讲稿,她可以学到更多关于写出有吸引力演讲的知识——注重内容和演讲方式——她应该在早期而不是在最后得到反馈。所以她请求老板帮助她。

结果呢? 基拉的老板很高兴教她,并且非常乐意把自己擅长的演讲技能倾囊相授予她。通过花时间和老板一起准备演讲过程中的一些关键陈述,基拉从她老板的思维过程中受益颇多,并能够辨别关键部分来提高自己的演讲水平。基拉的演讲现在很棒!

对于向别人寻求帮助,我们中有些人会感到不舒服,因为我们认为,我们的请求会给别人带来负担。具有讽刺意味的是,我们可能会错过一个向别人展示我们对他们的重视和尊重的机会。理解你和赞赏你的人经常会积极地帮助你。此外,你越具体地知道你需要从他们那里得到什么帮助,他们就越容易帮助到你。

36. [正确答案] C

[考点类型] 细节题

[题目翻译] 很多人不愿意寻求帮助是因为他们_____。

  A. 对他们自己很有信心

  B. 不相信别人

  C. 对向他人寻求帮助感到羞愧

  D. 认为没有必要

[考点剖析] 根据第一段内容可知,对我们大多数人而言,寻求帮助是一个困难的观念。我们可能会觉得这是在承认自己的一个弱点;相反,如果我们不寻求别人的帮助,全世界可能都不知道这个弱点。所以答案为 C 项。

37. [正确答案] C

[考点类型] 推理题

[题目翻译] 作者可能同意下列哪个说法?

A.向他人求助意味着承认自己的弱点。
B.帮助他人就是帮助自己。
C.恰当请求别人的帮助是受欢迎的。
D.有弱点的人通常需要更多帮助。

[考点剖析] 根据第二段内容可知,那些能够恰当地请求别人给予帮助的人被视为非常强大的人。当他们谦卑地寻求别人的帮助时,他们也获得了他人的尊重。被求助的人通常都很荣幸能收到别人的衷心求助。反过来说,我们恰恰因为所提供的帮助而使自己变得强大。文章的后面用基拉的事例为此论点提供支持,所以答案为C项。

38. [正确答案] A

[考点类型] 细节题

[题目翻译] 基拉的求助_____。
A.结果证明是有回报的 B.被拒绝了
C.让她得到晋升 D.反过来她的老板也受益

[考点剖析] 根据第四段后两句…she benefited from her boss's… and was able to distinguish… to enhance… have punch 可知,通过花时间和老板一起准备演讲过程中的一些关键陈述,基拉从她老板的思维过程中受益颇多,并能够辨别关键部分来提高自己的演讲水平。基拉的演讲现在很棒!这说明基拉的这次寻求帮助是有回报的。所以答案为A项。

39. [正确答案] A

[考点类型] 词汇题

[题目翻译] Kira's presentations now have punch 的意思是她的演讲_____。
A.有力度的 B.有争议的
C.受欢迎的 D.鼓舞人心的

[考点剖析] 本题关键在于理解 punch 一词,它的意思是"一拳,用拳猛击",而且语境的含义在说基拉的演讲能力获得很大提高,由此推断,此处应指基拉的演讲很有力度。所以答案为A项。

40. [正确答案] D

[考点类型] 主旨题

[题目翻译] 本文的目的是_____。
A.举例说明如何寻求帮助
B.展示互相帮助的重要性
C.呼吁关注他人的请求
D.鼓励人们向他人求助

[考点剖析] 通读全文内容可知,文章举例证明了寻求帮助对求助者和施助者都有很大的好处,因此鼓励人们适时寻求别人的帮助。所以答案为D项。

Section B

一项引人注目的新研究表明:美国人更倾向于夸自己的孩子"聪明",而欧洲的父母却注重快乐和平衡。

下面是一位母亲如何描述其3岁孩子的智商的,很明显这是在其生命的最初时刻给出的评价:

"我对此记忆犹新,当她出生时,他们把她抱出来清洗干净……她四处张望……她刚出生就很机灵……当她六周大时,我抱她去一个购物中心拍照——人们会拦住我并对我说:'好机灵的孩子啊!'一个男孩拦住我说:'女士,她是个聪明的孩子。'"

美国人不仅更可能多地侧重孩子的智商和认知能力,而且他们还很少用"快乐"或"乖巧"等字眼来描述孩子。

研究者告诉我们:"美国对孩子早期认知能力发展的不健康的关注导致他们忽视了太多其他的东西。"

评论1

这可能更多地表明了不同国家在谦卑和自夸方面文化态度的差异,而不是育儿风格的差异。在荷兰,如果有人说他们的孩子"聪明",我会翻白眼,一是因为它可能存在偏见和夸张,二是因为这只是为了引人注意而说的糟糕的措辞;好像这是在比较谁的孩子"更好"。我们生活中没有那么多该死的竞赛。

评论2

同意!瑞典也是这样。育儿更注重孩子的健康而不是社会竞争(这里可能也有压力,但是表达那些事情的做法是不被社会接受的)。

评论3

我同意,我住在美国。父母对孩子智商的看法绝对存有偏见和夸大。这是听起来最让人恼火的事情。随着年龄的增长,小时候的优秀表现和长大后的学习能力几乎没有关系。如果你给孩子机会并倾听他们的心声,那么每个孩子都是天才。孩子越快乐,就会越聪明。快乐和健康才是关键。

41. [正确答案] B
    [考点类型] 主旨题
    [题目翻译] 文章主要是关注_____方面的文化差异。
    A. 抚养孩子   B. 描述孩子
    C. 社会竞赛   D. 选择一个居住地
    [考点剖析] 主旨题首先要整合文章各段落的内容。文章首句和评论1~3的第一句都在讲不同国家在描述孩子用词方面存在很大差异,而不是育儿风格的差异。所以答案为B项。

42. [正确答案] C
    [考点类型] 词汇题
    [题目翻译] 第三段 alert 一词的含义最接近于"_____"。
    A. 聪明的   B. 随和的
    C. 反应快的   D. 快乐的

[考点剖析] alert意为"机警的,机灵的"。所以答案为C项。

43. [正确答案] A
    [考点类型] 细节题
    [题目翻译] 根据评论1,在荷兰,用"聪明"描述自己的孩子是_____。
    A.夸张的 B.可接受的
    C.令人鼓舞的 D.合理的
    [考点剖析] 根据题干定位到评论1中第二句,"在荷兰,如果有人说他们的孩子'聪明',我会翻白眼,一是因为它可能存在偏见和夸张,二是因为这只是为了引人注意而说的糟糕的措辞;好像这是在比谁的孩子'更好'"。所以答案为A项。

44. [正确答案] C
    [考点类型] 细节题
    [题目翻译] 评论2的作者是哪国人?
    A.荷兰人。 B.美国人。
    C.瑞典人。 D.法国人。
    [考点剖析] 根据评论2中第一句可知,评论2的作者可能是一个瑞典人"Swedish"。所以答案为C项。

45. [正确答案] D
    [考点类型] 推理题
    [题目翻译] 下列关于评论3的选项都是正确的,除了_____。
    A.同意其他评论
    B.快乐和健康很重要
    C.在小的时候聪明没有什么意义
    D.孩子的智商因人而异
    [考点剖析] 根据评论3的内容可知,A、B、C三项均正确,而D项"孩子的智商因人而异"不正确,这与文章中EVERY child is a genius if you give them a chance and an ear to listen to them"如果你给孩子机会并倾听他们的心声,那么每个孩子都是天才"的表述相互矛盾。所以答案为D项。

Part Ⅳ Cloze

骑自行车不但是一项很好的锻炼,而且也十分有趣。但是当你因年龄增长而骑不了原来的自行车时你会怎么办呢?12岁的妮科尔·巴兹尔对此给出了一个极好的答案。她在8岁时,加入了"踏板的力量",这是一个慈善机构,主要收集孩子们骑不了的自行车并把它们捐赠给芝加哥公立学校。

自2008年以来,妮科尔收集并捐献了1 000多辆自行车。除自行车外,去年"踏板的力量"还为骑自行车者提供了400个头盔。"安全骑车很重要,其中头盔是安全骑车的重要组成部分。"妮科尔说。威尔梅特自行车运动商店会帮助确保所有捐献的自行车都能安全骑行。每辆自行车都会接受店员5分钟的检查。

自行车被分给那些成绩好而且出勤率高的学生。妮科尔说:"一些孩子不像其他孩子那样幸运,但是他们在学校的表现也很优秀。我认为他们应该为此得到奖励。"妮科尔收到很多来自家长和老师的邮件和电话,说孩子的考试分数在提高。她说:"自行车可以带你去向远方,好的成绩能使你走得更远。"

巴顿·达辛格是芝加哥塞萨尔·E.查韦斯学校的校长。他学校的学生已经收到了自行车。达辛格说:"这是一个激励孩子不断进步的好方法。他们在努力学习以获得自行车。"

46. [正确答案] A
    [解析过程] 此处是讲妮科尔在8岁时加入了"踏板的力量"这个慈善机构。joined"参加"符合题意。

47. [正确答案] A
    [解析过程] 根据下文的"去年'踏板的力量'还给骑自行车者提供了400个头盔"可知,此处是"除了……之外"之意。

48. [正确答案] A
    [解析过程] 此处是讲安全骑车很重要,其中头盔是安全骑车的重要组成部分。safely"安全地"符合题意。

49. [正确答案] D
    [解析过程] 此处是讲确保所有捐献的自行车都可以安全骑行。ensure"确保"符合题意。

50. [正确答案] C
    [解析过程] 此处是讲每辆自行车都会接受店员5分钟的检查。check-up"检查"符合语境。

51. [正确答案] C
    [解析过程] 此处是讲一些孩子不像其他孩子那样幸运,他们在学校的表现也很优秀。分析可知,前后两句之间存在转折关系。

52. [正确答案] B
    [解析过程] 此处是讲我认为他们应该为此得到奖赏。rewarded"奖赏"符合题意。

53. [正确答案] B
    [解析过程] 此处是讲妮科尔收到很多来自家长和老师说明孩子考试分数在提高的电子邮件和电话。scores"分数"符合题意。

54. [正确答案] C
    [解析过程] 根据前面的Bikes can take you far可知,此处应填further。

55. [正确答案] D
    [解析过程] 此处是讲激励孩子不断进步,他们在努力学习以获得自行车。motivate"激励"符合题意。

Part V Text Completion

Text One

在最近的一项调查中,投票的3 000名日本女性中有55%的人表示她们在工作中受到与男性不平等的待遇;她们中有不到三分之一的人表示期待女性的生活能在未来20年内得到改善。但是只有26%的女性认为她们需要一个强大且有组织的女性运动。在一项针对美国女性的与此类似的调查中,低于29%的人认为她们在工作中受到不公平待遇,大部分人对女性的未来持乐观积极态度,37%的人认为需要女性运动。

56. [正确答案] B

    [解析过程] 根据空格前的 felt 和空格后的介词 for 并结合各选项含义可知,空格处应填入 a need,a need for 表示"需要……"。

57. [正确答案] A

    [解析过程] 根据空格前的系动词 were 和后面的名词 future 并结合各选项含义可知,空格处应填入 optimistic about,optimistic about 表示"对……乐观"。

58. [正确答案] C

    [解析过程] 根据空格前的 less than 可知,空格处应填入数字。a third 符合题意。

59. [正确答案] C

    [解析过程] 根据语境可知,空格处应是一个主句的主语部分,且和前面一句形成并列关系;再结合各选项含义可知,C 项 less than a third of them 代入空格处能构成合理搭配。

60. [正确答案] A

    [解析过程] 本句仍然和前面两句形成并列关系,所以句型也是相似的。本句缺少的是宾语从句的主语和谓语,又根据语境可知,下文是针对美国女性的类似的调查,且下文提到"37% 的人认为需要女性运动",故 A 项正确。

61. [正确答案] B

    [解析过程] 从语法角度来讲,这里缺少了一个完整的句子,而根据语境可知,上文提到日本女性对未来的态度,故这里需要填入美国女性对未来的态度。

Text Two

欢迎来到大学图书馆。此行我将向您介绍我们的图书馆设施。首先,图书馆的一到四层放置的是收藏的图书、参考书及其他资料。第一层存放的是人文和地图方面的藏书。在第二层,有图书借还台、当前的期刊和我们的复印设备。我们的理科和工程藏书区域在第三层。最后,讨论室和多媒体中心位于第四层。本科生两周内最多可借阅 5 本书。研究生两月内可借阅 15 本书。图书可续借两次。

62. [正确答案] C

    [解析过程] 根据空格前的 our 和空格后的 facilities,可知需要填一个名词与"设施"进行搭配。结合各选项,空格处应填入 library。

63. [正确答案] A

    [解析过程] 根据空格后的 five books 可知,空格处应填入一个与数字相搭配的词或短语,up to 符合题意。

64. [正确答案] B

    [解析过程] 根据空格前的 humanities and map,再结合各选项可知,此处应该是在介绍这些方面的藏书。空格处应填入 collections。

65. [正确答案] A

    [解析过程] 根据语境可知,短文在介绍图书馆,所以答案是 A 项。

66. [正确答案] C

2013年同等学力人员申请硕士学位英语水平全国统一考试答案及详解

  [解析过程] 根据后文的语境可知，应该是逐层介绍图书馆的藏书，空格处应填入具体的藏书类型，所以答案是 C 项。

67. [正确答案] B

  [解析过程] 根据本句和后句的语境可知，这里在介绍不同学生借书的规定。空格所在句是在讲本科生两周内能借的书量，B 项代入原文能构成合理搭配。

Text Three

  很多非母语英语课程学习者都关心如何去除自己的口音，但是在你急于花几百美金去上发音课之前，让我告诉你一些注意事项。

  首先，任何发音课程的主要目标应该是减少口音而不是消除口音，因为后者是很难实现的。相反，学生应该努力减少能影响语言理解的音区，即让本土人很难理解的部分。第二，有了这个目标，学生需要能够辨别给他们带来发音问题的具体音区。当然，有能影响特定人群的普遍音区，研读这些共同性会对你有所帮助。

68. [正确答案] D

  [解析过程] 从语法角度分析句子结构可知，空格处应填入从句的谓语动词。只有 D 项 give them the most trouble 符合题意。

69. [正确答案] B

  [解析过程] 根据空格前的 give 可知，空格处应填入不定式，而 some things 作不定式的宾语，to think about 符合题意。再结合第 72 题的语境，在短文第一段引出话题进行思考也是符合语境的。

70. [正确答案] A

  [解析过程] 根据 "make it + 形容词 + for sb. to do sth." 可知，to understand them 符合要求，且结合下文第 74 题语境 "影响语言理解的音区"，可知答案是 A 项。

71. [正确答案] C

  [解析过程] 根据空格前的 accent reduction 可知，not accent elimination 能与之形成对比，即 "注重……而不是……"。再结合第 73 题语境 "语音课程的主要目标"，可知答案是 C 项。

72. [正确答案] B

  [解析过程] 根据语境和 B 项的含义可知，该句放在首段引出短文要表达的中心。

73. [正确答案] D

  [解析过程] 根据语境可知，空格所在句句意应该是提出发音课程的主要目标是什么，在 D 项的前半句有交代，且空格后面的定语从句说的是一件不能做到的事，刚好符合 D 项后半句含义。

74. [正确答案] C

  [解析过程] 空格要把定语从句补充完整来限定先行词 area of their accents，根据语境可知，空格所在句是对前一句 "相反，学生应该努力减少影响语言理解的音区" 的进一

· 29 ·

步解释,故 C 项正确。

75. [正确答案] A

[解析过程] 根据语境可知,空格所在句句意应该是要告诉学生正确的做法,且下面的语境也是在描述给发音者带来麻烦的一些共性的问题,故 A 项正确。

Paper Two 试卷二

Part VI Translation

1. Being unhappy is like an infectious disease.

   [结构分析] 这是一个系表结构的简单句。

   [词义推敲] infectious"传染的"。

   [参考译文] 闷闷不乐就像一种传染病。

2. It causes people to shrink away from the sufferer.

   [结构分析] 这是一个简单句,即固定句型 It causes sb. to do sth. "使某人……"。

   [词义推敲] shrink"收缩,缩小"; sufferer"患者,受害者"; shrink away from sb./sth. "远离某人/某物"。

   [参考译文] 它会让周围的人对其避而远之。

3. He soon finds himself alone and miserable.

   [结构分析] 这是一个简单句:find oneself + *adj.* "发现自己处于某种状态"。

   [词义推敲] miserable"悲惨的,痛苦的"。

   [参考译文] 得这种"病"的人很快就会发现自己很孤单、很痛苦。

4. There is, however, a cure so simple as to seem, at first glance, ridiculous: if you don't feel happy, pretend to be!

   [结构分析] 这句结构有些复杂。if 引导状语从句,主句是 There be 句型, so simple…ridiculous 为 a cure 的后置定语,而 if you don't feel happy, pretend to be 作 cure 的同位语,进一步解释治疗的方法是什么。

   [词义推敲] ridiculous"可笑的,荒谬的"; pretend to be"假装做某事"。

   [参考译文] 然而,这种病症有一种很简单的治疗方法,乍看起来很可笑,那就是:如果你感觉不快乐,那就假装快乐吧!

5. It works. Before long you will find that instead of pushing people away, you attract them.

   [结构分析] 第二句是一个主从复合句,主句是 you will find that…,这里的 that 引导一个宾语从句,宾语从句的主语是 you。

   [词义推敲] Before long"不久以后"。

   [参考译文] 这个方法很有效。不久你就会发现你不但不会令人反感,反而会吸引他人。

6. You discover how deeply rewarding it is to be the center of wider and wider circles of good will.

   [结构分析] 这是一个主从复合句,how 引导的宾语从句作 discover 的宾语。

[词义推敲] rewarding "值得的;有报酬的"。

[参考译文] 你会发现,成为广结善缘的中心人物是一件多么值得的事。

7. Then the make-believe becomes a reality.

[结构分析] 这是一个简单句。

[词义推敲] make-believe "假装;假扮"(在这里作名词理解成"假装的事")。

[参考译文] 这样,原本假装的快乐就变成真正的快乐了。

8. Being happy, once it is realized as a duty and established as a habit, opens doors into unimaginable gardens filled with grateful friends.

[结构分析] 这是一个主从复合句,从句是 once 引导的状语从句,主句中 being happy 作主语,opens 是主句的谓语。filled with grateful friends 作 gardens 的后置定语。

[词义推敲] established "建立,确立"(在这里理解为"养成",和"习惯"进行搭配);unimaginable "难以想象的"。

[参考译文] 一旦使快乐成为一种责任并且成为一种习惯的时候,它就会打开不可思议的神秘"花园"之门,那里云集心怀善意的朋友们。

Part Ⅶ Writing

这是一篇议论文,且给出了提纲。我们可以根据提纲列出的三点思路去展开。第一段,提出观点,手机(不)可以用来学习英语或者其他知识。第二段,对上段的观点给出论据,说明原因,一般写3个。第三段,对全篇进行总结,呼应首段观点。

Nowadays, more and more people have begun to learn with cellphones. This phenomenon has aroused immediate concern and widespread discussion among the general public. From my perspective, learning with cellphones is of utmost ability and far-reaching significance for our modern people.

As a matter of fact, some aspects of its possibility can be illustrated below. The first one that comes to my mind readily is that cellphone can save massive informations which may be equal to hundreds of books according to the size of hardware. That's also the reason why almost all young people are busy with cellphones in the subway. What's more, in recent years, cellphones are all accessible to the webs. Everything useful can be downloaded directly into the phones. Besides, cellphone is the lightest tool with so many contents inside. This will be more obvious with the development of technology.

From what has been under discussion above, I strongly believe that learning with cellphone is possible and benefits modern people as a whole. Therefore, we should pay much attention to the function of those tools, especially those useful softwares and websites. Only in this way can we make full use of phones and be more knowledgeable.

这篇范文很巧妙地运用了常见的作文写作模板,并在相应之处做了灵活替换,所以文章思路和结构都显得比较清晰,给人印象很不错。我们来看一下内容:

第一段:用模板例句套用合理,指出用手机学习的现象很普遍,并且已引起公众的关注。在段落最后提出自己的观点。

第二段:用三个理由支持上段提出的观点,说明手机作为学习工具使用的优点。

第三段:再次强调首段提出的观点,与之相互呼应,并指出有用的学习软件和网页会更有利于我们的学习。

论述有理有据,思路简单、清晰,模板运用灵活、合理,这些是作文考试中拿到理想分数的有力保障。

2014年同等学力人员申请硕士学位英语水平全国统一考试

Paper One 试卷一（100 minutes）

Part I Oral Communication （15 minutes, 10 points）

Section A

Directions: In this section there are two incomplete dialogues and each dialogue has three blanks and three choices A, B and C, taken from the dialogue. Fill in each of the blanks with one of the choices to complete the dialogue and mark your answer on the **Answer Sheet**.

Dialogue one

A. I thought you said there were three men
B. They had been in there for about 5 minutes
C. It's the other man I'm talking about

Burney: There were two men, I think. No, three. They ran into the bank and the one with the gun, the tall one, he runs up to the window, and starts shouting something, I don't know, "Give me all your money" and the other one...
Police officer: __1__ ?
Burney: No, there were two men and a girl. __2__ , the one carrying the suitcase, well, he goes up to the other guy.
Police officer: The one with the gun?
Burney: Yes, and he opens the suitcase and the cashier, well, she—well, all the other people behind the window—they hand over piles of money and the two men put it into the suitcase and they run out. It was 1:35. __3__ .

Dialogue Two

A. People today don't like that
B. I like a good story
C. They still make movies like that

Speaker A: I like watching old movies and I think they are the best.
Speaker B: I agree with you, even though they're in black and white. I think a good story is more

important than color.

Speaker A: And there was no violence in old movies.

Speaker B: No, there wasn't. 4 .

Speaker A: They like lots of action.

Speaker B: 5 .

Speaker A: I like to see actors who are like real people.

Speaker B: Like real people with real problems.

Speaker A: 6 .

Speaker B: Yes, but they never make much money.

Section B

Directions: *In this section there is one incomplete interview which has four blanks and four choices A, B, C and D, taken from the interview. Fill in each of the blanks with one of the choices to complete the interview and mark your answer on the **Answer Sheet**.*

A. I do a lot of research on the Internet too

B. I do a lot of my shopping on the net now

C. Of course they mail their friends endlessly

D. I document everything

Interviewer: Ms. Chen, can you tell us which pieces of technology are important to you?

Interviewee: Three things: my Sharp laptop; my iPhone 5; and my Olympus digital camera. 7 : the kids, art, buildings, clothes, scenes that catch my eye as I walk past.

Interviewer: What do you use your computer for?

Interviewee: Well, I send emails all the time. But I do a lot of my design work on screen now and I can send my ideas straight to directors and producers. 8 —there are some fantastic sites around now.

Interviewer: Who uses the computer at home?

Interviewee: The kids use the computer all the time at home. 9 —and on top of that they're always texting on their mobile phones! They play computer games when they think I or their father aren't looking! They don't like doing homework, of course, but there are some really good revision sites on the Internet. 10 —15 minutes for a whole supermarket "visit"! That feels really good.

Part II Vocabulary (10 minutes, 10 points)

Directions: *In this part there are ten sentences, each with one word or phrase underlined. Choose the one from the four choices marked A, B, C and D that best keeps the meaning of the sentence. Mark your answer on the **Answer Sheet**.*

11. Conditions for the growth of this plant are <u>optimum</u> in early summer.

    A. most acceptable   B. most expressive

    C. most favorite   D. most desirable

12. She often says her greatest happiness consists in helping the disadvantaged children.
    A. is proportionate to
    B. is composed of
    C. lies in
    D. relies on

13. Now and in the future, we will live as free people, not in fear and never at the mercy of any foreign powers.
    A. for the sake of
    B. at the cost of
    C. in the interest of
    D. under the control of

14. Public acceptance of rabbit as an economical source of protein depends on how aggressively producers market it.
    A. vigorously
    B. rigorously
    C. efficiently
    D. effectively

15. Many New England communities do not permit the construction of a "modernist" building, lest it alter their overall architectural integrity.
    A. in order that
    B. for fear that
    C. in case that
    D. in spite that

16. Essentially, a theory is an abstract, symbolic representation of what is conceived to be reality.
    A. impression
    B. imagination
    C. expression
    D. presentation

17. Television commercials have been under constant scrutiny for the last few years.
    A. reflection
    B. examination
    C. attack
    D. pressure

18. The mayor has spent a handsome amount of time in his last term working to bring down the tax rate.
    A. plenty
    B. sufficient
    C. moderate
    D. considerable

19. His poor performance may be attributed to the lack of motivation.
    A. focused on
    B. caused by
    C. viewed as
    D. taken for

20. The new cut in interest rate is meant to promote domestic investment.
    A. obtain
    B. encourage
    C. publicize
    D. advertise

Part III Reading Comprehension (45 minutes, 25 points)

Section A

Directions: *In this section, there are four passages followed by questions or unfinished statements, each with four suggested answers A, B, C and D. Choose the best answer and mark your answer on the **Answer Sheet**.*

Passage One

Last week, I read a story about a 34-year-old British woman who is extremely afraid of metal forks.

She's been using plastic ones for 17 years because the sound of a fork rubbing against a plate gives her a panic attack.

Strange, right? But she's not alone. While popular phobias (恐惧症) about snakes and spiders might get all of the attention, there are a wide variety of not-so-obvious horrors that make people nervous.

While some phobias might seem a bit silly, they can cause serious emotional distress. My co-worker Magda is terrified of pigeons, a phobia that is taking over her life. She won't walk in certain parts of the city and runs screaming from the subway when one of these "rats with wings" finds its way onto the platform. Another friend is disgusted with cheese. Once I saw her run away from a slice of it. So where does an irrational fear of cheese come from?

Are phobias something we inherit from our genes or do we acquire these unusual anxieties overtime?

Ever since I can remember I have been unreasonably frightened of elevators. There was no terrible childhood experience and I am fine with confined spaces, but something about elevators makes me nervous. And so, when my boyfriend and I found ourselves trapped in an elevator last year—because these sorts of things always happen eventually—I was anticipating the worst.

While he gave me a suggestive eyebrow raise and proposed we "take advantage of the situation", I began screaming uncontrollably. I was far from turned on by the whole facing my worst nightmare thing.

However, after the fear subsided (消退) I realized that, yes, this was my greatest fear come true, and yet—it wasn't all that bad. Nervous and inconvenient maybe, but terrifying? Not so much.

Liberating yourself from a deep-seated phobia can be a long and difficult process, but sometimes it can be as simple as confronting it head on.

21. The 34-year-old British woman is extremely afraid of metal forks because _____.

    A. she couldn't bear their sound on plate

    B. she is afraid that they may hurt her

    C. she has never used them before

    D. she has been injured by them before

22. The phrase "rats with wings" (Para. 3) refers to _____.

    A. devils   B. exotic rats   C. pigeons   D. strange birds

23. The author's fear of elevators is the result of _____.

    A. her dislike of being in closed spaces

    B. her terrible experience

    C. her phobia for no reason

    D. her nervousness of being alone

24. After the fear subsided, the author realized that _____.

    A. an elevator ride could be exciting

    B. it was not as horrible as she had thought

    C. her boyfriend's help was important

    D. she could have had a good time with her boyfriend

25. The purpose for the author to share her experience is to _____.

    A. introduce what strange fears people have

B. explain why people have strange fears

C. illustrate conquering a fear can be difficult

D. encourage people to overcome their fears

Passage Two

The American public's obsession with dieting has led to one of the most dangerous health misconceptions of all times. Many television ads, movies, magazine articles, and diet-food product labels would have consumers believe that carbohydrates (碳水化合物) are bad for the human body and that those who eat them will quickly become overweight. We are advised to avoid foods such as potatoes, rice and white bread and opt for meats and vegetables instead. Some companies promote this idea to encourage consumers to buy their "carb-free" food products. But the truth is, the human body needs carbohydrates to function properly, and a body that relies on carbohydrates but is exhausted of this dietary element is not in good shape after all.

Most foods that we consume on a daily basis like potatoes and rice are loaded with carbohydrates. Contrary to popular belief, carbohydrates have many health benefits: some fight diseases such as high blood pressure and heart disease, and others help to prevent cancer and stroke. Cutting these foods out of your diet may deprive your body of the many health benefits of carbohydrates.

One of the best benefits of carbohydrates is their ability to help to maintain the health of our organs, tissues, and cells. Scientific studies have shown that one type of carbohydrate called fiber reduces the risk of heart disease. Carbohydrates also contain antioxidants (抗氧化剂), which protect the body's cells from harmful particles with the potential to cause cancer.

This does not mean that the human body can survive on a diet composed entirely of carbohydrates. We also need certain percentages of proteins and fats to maintain healthy bodies. But carbohydrates certainly should not be avoided altogether. In fact, the food pyramid, the recommended basis of a healthy diet, shows that a person should consume six to eleven servings of breads and grains, as well as three to four servings each of fruits and vegetables—all carbohydrate-containing foods. It is easy to see why cutting carbohydrates out of a person's diet is not a good idea.

The only way to know what is truly healthy for your own body is to talk to a nutritionist or dietician, who can help you choose foods that are right for you as well as guide you toward a proper exercise program for weight loss, or muscle gain. These professionals will never tell you to cut out carbohydrates entirely! The bottom line: listen to the experts, not the advertisers!

26. As is used in Paragraph 1, the word "exhausted" most possibly means _____.

    A. startled   B. starving   C. derived   D. deprived

27. According to the author, advertisers who sell "carb-free" products _____.

    A. value consumers' well-being   B. are not telling the truth
    C. offer healthy options   D. are responsible for obesity

28. Which of the following is NOT one of the health benefits of carbohydrates?

    A. Prevention of stroke.   B. Prevention of cancer.

C. Prevention of fiber reduction.   D. Prevention of heart disease.

29. It can be inferred from the passage that a healthy diet _____.

   A. is low in carbohydrates and high in proteins and fats

   B. contains equal amounts of carbohydrates and proteins

   C. needs enough proteins but no fat for us to maintain energy

   D. is balanced between carbohydrates, and proteins and fats

30. The main purpose of the passage is to _____.

   A. describe the variety of carbohydrates

   B. explain how to live a healthy life

   C. promote more physical exercise

   D. advocate a healthy diet

Passage Three

Of all the lessons taught by the financial crisis, the most personal has been that Americans aren't so good at money-management. We take out home loans we can't afford. We run up sky-high credit-card debt. We don't save nearly enough for retirement.

In response, supporters of financial-literacy education are moving with renewed enthusiasm. School districts in states such as New Jersey and Illinois are adding money-management courses to their curriculums. The Treasury and Education departments are sending lesson plans to high schools and encouraging students to compete in the National Financial Capability Challenge that begins in March.

Students with top scores on that exam will receive certificates—but chances for long-term benefits are slim. As it turns out, there is little evidence that traditional efforts to boost financial know-how help students make better decisions outside the classroom. Even as the financial-literacy movement has gained steam over the past decade, scores have been falling on tests that measure how well students learn about things such as budgeting, credit cards, insurance and investments. A recent survey of college students conducted for the JumpStart Coalition for Personal Financial Literacy found that students who'd had a personal-finance or money-management course in high school scored no better than those who hadn't.

"We need to figure out how to do this the right way," says Lewis Mandell, a professor at the University of Washington who after 15 years of studying financial-literacy programs has come to the conclusion that current methods don't work. A growing number of researchers and educators agree that a more radical approach is needed. They advocate starting financial education a lot earlier than high school, putting real money and spending decisions into kids' hands and talking openly about the emotions and social influences tied to how we spend.

Other initiatives are tackling such real-world issues as the commercial and social pressures that affect purchasing decisions. Why exactly do you want those expensive brand-name shoes so badly? "It takes confidence to take a stand and to think differently," says Jeroo Billimoria, founder of Aflatoun, a nonprofit whose curriculum, used in more than 30 countries, aims to help kids get a leg up in their financial lives. "This goes beyond money and savings."

31. The financial-literacy education is intended to _____.
   A. renew Americans' enthusiasm about money-management
   B. increase Americans' awareness of the financial crisis
   C. help Americans to overcome the financial crisis
   D. enable Americans to manage money wisely

32. According to the author, the National Financial Capability Challenge will be _____.
   A. ineffective   B. rewarding
   C. costly   D. well-received

33. By saying that "the financial-literacy movement has gained steam" (Para. 3), the author means that the movement _____.
   A. has received much criticism
   B. has been regarded as imaginative
   C. has been more and more popular
   D. has gone through financial difficulties

34. Lewis Mandell suggests that we should figure out how to _____.
   A. manage money in a more efficient way
   B. carry out financial-literacy education properly
   C. improve the social awareness of financial education
   D. help students score better in money-management courses

35. Jeroo Billimoria is most likely to agree that commercial and social pressures make one's purchasing decisions _____.
   A. acceptable   B. difficult
   C. feasible   D. unwise

Passage Four

Cheating is nothing new. But today, educators and administrators are finding that instances of academic dishonesty on the part of students have become more frequent—and are less likely to be punished—than in the past. Cheating appears to have gained acceptance among good and poor students alike.

Why is student cheating on the rise? No one really knows. Some blame the trend on a general loosening of moral values among today's youth. Others have attributed increased cheating to the fact that today's youth are far more pragmatic (实用主义的) than their more idealistic predecessors. Whereas in the late sixties and early seventies, students were filled with visions about changing the world, today's students feel great pressure to conform and succeed. In interviews with students at high schools and colleges around the country, both young men and women said that cheating had become easy. Some suggested they did it out of spite for teachers they did not respect. Others looked at it as a game. Only if they were caught, some said, would they feel guilty. "People are competitive," said a second-year college student named Anna, from Chicago. There's an underlying fear. If you don't do well, your life is going to be ruined. The pressure is not only from parents and friends but from oneself. To achieve. To succeed. It's almost as though we have to outdo other people to achieve our own goals.

Edward Wynne, a magazine editor, blames the rise in academic dishonesty on the schools. He claims that administrators and teachers have been too hesitant to take action. Dwight Huber, chairman of the English department at Amarillo, sees the matter differently, blaming the rise in cheating on the way students are evaluated. "I would cheat if I felt I was being cheated," Mr. Huber said. He feels that as long as teachers give short-answer tests rather than essay questions and rate students by the number of facts they can memorize rather than by how well they can put information together, students will try to beat the system. "The concept of cheating is based on the false assumption that the system is legitimate and there is something wrong with the individuals who are doing it," he said. "That's too easy an answer. We've got to start looking at the system."

36. Educators are finding that students who cheat _____.
    A. have poor academic records
    B. are more likely to be punished than before
    C. tend to be dishonest in later years
    D. are not only those academically weak

37. According to the passage, which of the following statements is true?
    A. Students do not cheat on essay tests.
    B. Students' cheating has deep social roots.
    C. Punishment is an effective method to stop cheating.
    D. Reform in the testing system will eliminate cheating.

38. Which of the following points of view would Mr. Huber agree with?
    A. Parents must take responsibility for the rise in cheating.
    B. Punishment for cheaters should be severe in this country.
    C. Students who cheat should be expelled from school.
    D. Cheating would be reduced through an educational reform.

39. The expression "the individuals" (the last paragraph) refers to _____.
    A. teachers   B. parents
    C. students who cheat   D. school administrators

40. The passage mainly discusses _____.
    A. people's tolerance of students' cheating
    B. the decline of moral standards of today's youth
    C. factors leading to academic dishonesty
    D. ways to eliminate academic dishonesty

Section B

Directions: *In this section, you are required to read one quoted blog and the comments on it. The blog and comments are followed by questions or unfinished statements, each with four suggested answers A, B, C and D. Choose the best answer and mark your answer on the **Answer Sheet**.*

One of the central principles of raising kids in America is that parents should be actively involved in their children's education: meeting with teachers, volunteering at school, helping with homework, and doing a hundred other things that few working parents have time for. These obligations are so baked into American values that few parents stop to ask whether they're worth the effort.

Until this January, few researchers did, either. In the largest-ever study of how parental involvement affects academic achievement, Keith Robinson and Angel L. Harris, two sociology professors at Duke, found that mostly it doesn't. The researchers combed through nearly three decades' worth of surveys of American parents and tracked 63 different measures of parental participation in kids' academic lives, from helping them with homework, to talking with them about college plans. In an attempt to show whether the kids of more-involved parents improved over time, the researchers indexed these measures to children's academic performance, including test scores in reading and math.

What they found surprised them. Most measurable forms of parental involvement seem to yield few academic dividends for kids, or even to backfire (适得其反)—regardless of a parent's race, class, or level of education.

Do you review your daughter's homework every night? Robinson and Harris's data show that this won't help her score higher on standardized tests. Once kids enter middle school, parental help with homework can actually bring test scores down, an effect Robinson says could be caused by the fact that many parents may have forgotten, or never truly understood, the material their children learn in school.

While Robinson and Harris largely disproved that assumption, they did find a handful of habits that make a difference, such as reading aloud to young kids (fewer than half of whom are read to daily) and talking with teenagers about college plans. But these interventions don't take place at school or in the presence of teachers, where policy makers have the most influence—they take place at home.

Comment 1

Basically the choice is whether one wants to let kids to be kids. Persistent parental involvement and constantly communicating to the kids on what the parents want consciously or unconsciously would help the kids grow up or think like the parents sooner than otherwise.

Comment 2

It also depends on the kid. Emotional and social maturity have a lot to do with success in college and in life. Some kids may have the brains and are bored by high school, but that doesn't mean they are ready for college or the work place.

Comment 3

The article doesn't clearly define "helping", but I understood it as actually assisting children in the exercises (e.g. helping them to solve a math problem) and/or reviewing their work for accuracy rather than simply making sure they've completed their work. I think the latter is more helpful than the former. I would also certainly hope that no study would discourage parents from monitoring their children's performance!

41. The word "they" (Para. 1) refers to _____.

  A. principles   B. studies   C. obligations   D. values

42. What is main conclusion of the Robinson and Harris's study?

  A. Parental involvement may not necessarily benefit children.

B. The kids of more-involved parents improve over time.

   C. Schools should communicate with parents regularly.

   D. Parental involvement works better with low-achievers.

43. **Comment 1** suggests that _____.

   A. kids should be kids after all

   B. parents should leave their children alone

   C. persistent parental involvement is a must

   D. parents may influence children's thinking

44. The writer of **Comment 2** would probably agree that _____.

   A. getting ready for college is an emotional process

   B. high intelligence does not guarantee success

   C. high school is often boring in the U.S.

   D. social maturity is sufficient to achieve success in life

45. Which of the following parental helps will the writer of **Comment 3** consider proper?

   A. Monitoring kids' class performance.

   B. Reviewing kids' homework for accuracy.

   C. Making sure kids have finished their work.

   D. Assisting kids in their exercises.

Part IV   Cloze (10 minutes, 10 points)

Directions: *In this part, there is a passage with ten blanks. For each blank there are four choices marked A, B, C and D. Choose the best answer for each blank and mark your answer on the **Answer Sheet**.*

Ironically, a study finds that we're awful gift-givers precisely because we spend too much time trying to be considerate. We imagine our friends __46__ a gift that is impressive, expensive, and sentimental. We imagine the look of happiness and surprise on their faces and the warmth we feel __47__. But there's something that the most sentimental gift-givers tend not to think too much about: __48__ the gift is practical in the first place.

__49__, practicality seems like an enemy of great gift giving. Beautiful jewelry, lovely watches, perfect rugs, finely crafted kitchen hardware: These things __50__ great gifts because they communicate something beyond practicality. They communicate that the giver cares.

But do the receivers care? Often, no. "Gift receivers would be __51__ if givers gave them exactly what they requested __52__ attempting to be 'thoughtful and considerate' by buying gifts they did not explicitly request" to surprise them, the researchers write. Their clever paper asks givers and receivers to __53__ gifts from two perspectives: desirability (e.g. the cost of a coffee maker) and feasibility (e.g. the __54__ of the coffee maker). Across several experiments, they find that givers consistently give gifts based on desirability and receivers __55__ favor gifts based on feasibility.

46. A. opened   B. have opened   C. opening   D. to open

47. A. in return	B. in place	C. in turn	D. in person
48. A. How	B. Why	C. When	D. Whether
49. A. In many cases	B. In many ways	C. To sum up	D. To be sure
50. A. take up	B. make for	C. lead to	D. work out
51. A. surprised	B. happy	C. more surprised	D. happier
52. A. but for	B. as to	C. rather than	D. regardless of
53. A. measure	B. select	C. classify	D. decide
54. A. ease	B. cost	C. quality	D. look
55. A. continuously	B. nevertheless	C. whereas	D. unexpectedly

Part V Text Completion (20 minutes, 20 points)

Directions: *In this part, there are three incomplete texts with 20 questions (ranging from 56 to 75). Above each text there are three or four phrases to be completed. First, use the choices provided in the box to complete the phrases. Second, use the completed phrases to fill in the blanks of the text. Mark your answer on the **Answer Sheet**.*

Text One

> A. so
> B. watching TV
> C. hire them

Phrases:

A. and understandably __56__

B. that the companies that __57__ want money

C. that could be spent __58__

Children are a special target of advertisers, __59__. Young people are shopping and spending more than ever before. Researchers suggest that children who are highly involved in consumer culture are more prone to childhood depression and anxiety and have worse relationships with their parents. They said: "You cannot totally protect your kids from advertising because it is everywhere. So you can explain to your kids that advertisers have an agenda and __60__. They don't have our best interests in mind."

They also suggest that family should watch very little television. You can fill the time __61__ with other activities, such as reading and playing games together.

Text Two

> A. beyond
> B. sending
> C. as well as

Phrases:

A. __62__ the wages of average families

B. __63__ the reach of most Americans

C. __64__ young people to college

A research group in California has released a "national report card on higher education." The report says the price of college has increased more than four hundred percent since 1982. Costs have climbed much faster than other prices— __65__ . The group warns that a continuation of these trends would put higher education __66__ . And it would mean greater debt for those who do go to college. The report also expresses concern that the United States is losing its leadership in __67__ .

Text Three

A. imitate
B. between
C. otherwise
D. accelerate

Phrases:

A. from __68__ its feathers

B. would be difficult to __69__

C. it __70__ could

D. enabling the bird to __71__

The emperor penguin traps air in its feathers. Not only does this insulate the bird against extreme cold but it also enables it to move two or three times faster than __72__ . How? Marine biologists have suggested that it does so by releasing tiny air bubbles __73__ . As these bubbles are released, they reduce friction on the surface of the penguin's wings, __74__ .

Interestingly, engineers have been studying ways to make ships go faster by using bubbles to reduce friction against their hulls (船身). However, researchers acknowledge that further investigation is challenging because "the complexity of penguin's wings __75__ ."

Paper Two 试卷二 (50 minutes)

Part VI Translation (20 minutes, 10 points)

Directions: *Translate the following passage into Chinese. Write your answer on the **Answer Sheet**.*

The social costs of unemployment go far beyond the welfare and unemployment payments made by the government. Unemployment increases the chances of divorce, child abuse, and alcoholism, a new federal survey shows. Some experts say the problem is only temporary—that new technology will eventually create as many jobs as it destroys. But futurologist Hymen Seymour says the astonishing efficiency of the new technology means there will be a simple net reduction in the amount of human labor that needs to be done. "We should treat this as an opportunity to give people more leisure. It may not be easy, but society will have to reach a new agreement on the division and distribution of labor," Seymour says.

Part VII Writing (30 minutes, 15 points)

Directions: *Write a composition in no less than 150 words on the topic: **A Way to Success**. Read the following article in Chinese, then write according to the outline given below. Write your composition on the **Answer Sheet**.*

大学毕业时,小刘决定不找工作。他默默地从事起了网络翻译工作。当时几乎没有人看好他,大家认为,大学刚毕业,最好找一个好单位,学点本领、积累点经验,然后才能有好出路。

5年过去了,虽然我们很多人毕业时都信誓旦旦地说,一旦在单位里学到本领,积累够经验,就出去打拼一番属于自己的事业,但大多数人在单位这个避风港里,已经失去了面对大风浪和新环境的勇气,辞职创业逐渐成了空谈。可小刘已经开了公司,成了一名成功的企业主。

在一次同学会上,小刘说出了他的"秘密"。他说:"成功往往取决于你敢不敢往人少的地方走,这可能会有风险,但因为没人或很少有人走过,留给你的可能是硕果累累。走别人开辟的老路,虽然看起来很安全,但因为走的人太多,财富与资源大多已被人占有。即使幸运地发现了一小部分,也必然会被蜂拥而至的人群争抢与瓜分。"

1. 根据以上文章写一篇读后感;
2. 你如何看待小刘的成功之道;
3. 关于成功你有什么经验和建议?

2014年同等学力人员申请硕士学位英语水平全国统一考试

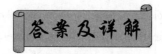

Paper One 试卷一

Part I Oral Communication

Section A

对话一

A. 我还以为你说有三个男人
B. 他们在那里待了大约5分钟
C. 我现在说的是另外一个男人

伯尼：我觉得有两个男人。不，是三个。他们冲进银行，其中一个高个子带着枪，跑到柜台玻璃前，开始喊着"给我所有的钱"之类的，我不知道，而且，另外一个……
警察：__1__？
伯尼：不，有两个男人和一个女孩。__2__，拿着箱子的那个，他走向另外一个家伙。
警察：带着枪那个？
伯尼：是的。他打开箱子，那个女收银员，以及玻璃窗后的其他所有人——他们把成堆的钱递过来，那两个男人把钱装进箱子后，跑出去了。时间大约是1:35。__3__。

1. [正确答案] A
   [考点剖析] 在空格上一句，伯尼说 the other one，一般是说两者中的另外一个，而且，空格后一句，伯尼的回答"不，有两个男人和一个女孩"，显然是对人数的相关回答。由此推出空格处对这两处承上启下，因此 A 项是正确答案。

2. [正确答案] C
   [考点剖析] 根据语境，这里在对一个人进行具体描述，因此 C 项正确，而 B 项是在描述时间，明显不符合语境。

3. [正确答案] B
   [考点剖析] 空格前面出现了时间，且根据语境也能很明显地把答案锁定在 B 项，指抢劫犯在银行待了5分钟。

对话二

A. 如今人们不喜欢那样的了
B. 我喜欢好的故事情节

C. 他们仍然在制作那样的电影

讲话人A:我喜欢看老电影,我觉得老电影是最好的电影。
讲话人B:我也觉得是这样,即使它们是黑白的。我觉得一个好的故事情节比色彩更重要。
讲话人A:而且老电影里也没有暴力情节。
讲话人B:是啊,没有。__4__。
讲话人A:他们喜欢电影带有很多动作情节。
讲话人B:__5__。
讲话人A:我喜欢看演得真实的演员。
讲话人B:就像真实的人物带着真实的问题。
讲话人A:__6__。
讲话人B:是的,但是他们一直都没赚到很多钱。

4. [正确答案] A
   [考点剖析] 空格后一句,第一个说话人说"他们喜欢……","他们"必然指代前面出现过的人物,选项里只有A项出现了People这个具体人物,再通过语境验证,意思上也是通顺的。

5. [正确答案] B
   [考点剖析] 本题空格前后两句都是双方在发表自己的看法,由此推出空格处也应该是这个内容。所以选择B项,以表达个人观点。

6. [正确答案] C
   [考点剖析] 空格下面的回答内容,是对上文进行肯定,又说他们一直都没赚到很多钱。由此推出上一句即空格处应该出现they所对应的内容。

Section B

A. 我也在网上做很多调查
B. 我现在经常在网上购物
C. 当然,他们没完没了地给朋友发邮件
D. 我记录了每一件事

采访人:陈女士,能告诉我们对您来讲哪些技术产品会比较重要吗?
受访人:三种东西:我的夏普笔记本电脑、苹果5,还有我的奥林巴斯数码相机。__7__:有孩子们、艺术、建筑、衣服以及我路过时吸引我眼球的景色。
采访人:您的电脑都用来做什么呢?
受访人:嗯,我一直用它发电子邮件。但是现在我会在屏幕上做很多设计工作,而且我能把我的创意直接发给导演和制片人。__8__——现在周围有一些出色的网站。
采访人:在家里的时候谁使用电脑呢?
受访人:在家里,孩子总是使用电脑。__9__——此外,他们一直用自己的移动电话发信息。当他们认为我或者他们的父亲没看见的时候,就在电脑上玩游戏。当然,他们不喜欢做作业,但网上确实有一些很好的帮助复习功课的网站。__10__——15分钟"游览"整个超市！这感觉真的很不错！

7. [正确答案] D

   [考点剖析] 查看题目所在句的上下文。上文受访人说："三种东西：我的夏普笔记本电脑、苹果5，还有我的奥林巴斯数码相机。"下文说："有孩子们、艺术、建筑、衣服以及我路过时吸引我眼球的景色。"空格处要填写的内容应该是对后文的一个概括，冒号后是对这个句子的具体内容的介绍。D项"我记录了每一件事"，符合语境，为正确答案。

8. [正确答案] A

   [考点剖析] 查看题目所在句的上文。采访人说："您的电脑都用来做什么呢？"受访人说："我一直用它发电子邮件。但是现在我会在屏幕上做很多设计工作，而且我能把我的创意直接发给导演和制片人。"A项"我也在网上做很多调查"，与后文说到的"有一些出色的网站"相照应。根据语境并结合各选项的意思可知A项正确。

9. [正确答案] C

   [考点剖析] 查看题目所在句的上下文。采访人说："在家里的时候谁使用电脑呢？"受访人说："在家里，孩子总是使用电脑。"C项"当然，他们没完没了地给朋友发邮件"，这里的they指代孩子们，与上下文内容一致，根据语境并结合各选项的意思可知C项正确。

10. [正确答案] B

    [考点剖析] 查看题目所在句的下文。下文说："15分钟'游览'整个超市！这感觉真的很不错！"内容开始涉及网络购物，刚好和B项"我现在经常在网上购物"相对应，所以B项正确。

Part Ⅱ Vocabulary

11. [正确答案] D

    [考点类型] 形容词

    [考点剖析] 题干中的optimum意为"最佳的"。most acceptable"最容易接受的"；most expressive"最具表现力的"；most favorite"最喜欢的"；most desirable"最令人满意的"。

12. [正确答案] C

    [考点类型] 动词短语

    [考点剖析] 题干中的consists in意为"在于"。is proportionate to"成比例"；is composed of"由……构成"；lies in"在于"；relies on"依靠"。

13. [正确答案] D

    [考点类型] 介词短语

    [考点剖析] 题干中的at the mercy of意为"受……摆布"。for the sake of"为了……"；at the cost of"以……为代价"；in the interest of"为了……的利益"；under the control of"在……控制之下"。

14. [正确答案] A

    [考点类型] 副词

[考点剖析] 题干中的 aggressively 意为"大力地"。vigorously"有力地";rigorously"严厉地";efficiently"高效地";effectively"有效地"。

15. [正确答案] B
    [考点类型] 介词短语
    [考点剖析] 题干中的 lest 意为"唯恐"。in order that"以便";for fear that"唯恐";in case that"如果";in spite that"尽管"。

16. [正确答案] C
    [考点类型] 名词
    [考点剖析] 题干中的 representation 意为"表现,表达"。impression"印象";imagination"想象";expression"表达";presentation"陈述"。

17. [正确答案] B
    [考点类型] 名词
    [考点剖析] 题干中的 scrutiny 意为"审查"。reflection"反映";examination"检查";attack"攻击";pressure"压力"。

18. [正确答案] D
    [考点类型] 形容词
    [考点剖析] 题干中的 handsome 意为"相当大的"。plenty"丰富的";sufficient"足够的";moderate"适度的";considerable"大量的"。

19. [正确答案] B
    [考点类型] 动词短语
    [考点剖析] 题干中的 attributed to 意为"归因于"。focused on"集中于";caused by"由……导致";viewed as"被看作……";taken for"被认为"。

20. [正确答案] B
    [考点类型] 动词
    [考点剖析] 题干中的 promote 意为"推动,促进"。obtain"得到,获得";encourage"鼓励,促进";publicize"宣传,推广";advertise"做广告"。

Part Ⅲ Reading Comprehension

Section A

Passage One

上周,我读了关于一个34岁的英国女士极其惧怕金属叉子的故事。她用了17年的塑料叉子,因为金属叉子和盘子摩擦的声音让她感到恐惧。

很奇怪,是吗?但是无独有偶!对蛇和蜘蛛的恐惧症可能得到广泛的关注,然而,有很多并不是那么明显可怕的事物也能使人们感到紧张。

有些恐惧症看起来可能有点傻,但却能引起严重的精神损害。我的同事玛格达非常害怕鸽子,这个恐惧症正困扰着她的生活。她不敢走在城市的某些地方,当其中一只"带着翅膀的老鼠"突然飞上站台的时候,她会尖叫着跑出地铁。另一位朋友是觉得芝士很恶心。我曾经见到她从一片芝士旁边飞奔而去。那么这种对芝士非理性的恐惧从何而来呢?

恐惧症是我们从基因里继承而来的,还是我们随着时间的推移产生了这些不寻常的焦虑呢?

自从我记事起,我就一直毫无原因地对电梯感到害怕。我童年没有什么可怕的经历,我对密闭空间感觉也还好,但是电梯的某些东西会让我感到紧张。所以,去年当我和我男朋友被困在电梯里的时候(这种事情终归是经常发生的),我就预料到最坏的结果。

当他暗示性地扬起眉毛,建议我们"利用好这个机会"时,我开始不受控制地尖叫。面对最可怕的噩梦,我没有一点兴趣。

但是,当恐惧消退后,我意识到我最害怕的事情发生了,然而并不是那么糟糕。也许有紧张和不适,但是恐惧并没有那么多。

把自己从深深的恐惧中解救出来可能是个很漫长且很困难的过程,但是有时候也许就是迎头面对那么简单。

21. [正确答案] A
    [考点类型] 细节题
    [题目翻译] 这个34岁的英国女士极其害怕金属叉子是因为_____。
        A. 她忍受不了它们与盘子摩擦发出的声音
        B. 她担心叉子会伤害到她
        C. 她以前从来没使用过金属叉子
        D. 她曾经被金属叉子伤害过
    [考点剖析] 根据题干内容,我们可以把本题定位到第一段的最后一句…because the sound of a fork rubbing against a plate gives her a panic attack"……因为金属叉子和盘子摩擦的声音让她感到恐惧"。故A项正确。

22. [正确答案] C
    [考点类型] 词汇题
    [题目翻译] 第三段中的"带着翅膀的老鼠"指的是_____。
        A. 魔鬼   B. 奇异的老鼠
        C. 鸽子   D. 奇怪的鸟
    [考点剖析] 解答词汇题要注意理解该词汇或者短语在原文中的语境含义。短语出现在文章第三段关于一个叫玛格达的人害怕鸽子的例子里,当"rats with wings"出现的时候会让玛格达感到恐惧,那么这个东西就应该是"鸽子"。所以C项正确。

23. [正确答案] C
    [考点类型] 细节题
    [题目翻译] 作者对电梯的恐惧是因为_____。
        A. 她不喜欢待在密闭的空间
        B. 她糟糕的经历
        C. 没有缘由的恐惧症
        D. 独自一人时感到紧张
    [考点剖析] 文章第五段中说 Ever since I can… I have been unreasonably frightened of elevators… no terrible childhood experience… I am fine with confined spaces, but something about elevators makes me nervous. 这两句话已经涵盖四个选项,可以帮助我们得出正确答案。A项和B项与原文相反,D项文章未提及,C项与第一句一致,所以答案为

C项。

24. [正确答案] B
    [考点类型] 细节题
    [题目翻译] 在恐惧消退之后,作者意识到_____。
    A.乘坐电梯能令人感到兴奋   B.可能不如她之前想的那么可怕
    C.她男友的帮助很重要   D.她本可以和她男友度过很愉快的时光
    [考点剖析] 根据题干定位到文章倒数第二段…it wasn't all that bad. Nervous and inconvenient maybe, but terrifying? Not so much. 从中可以明显看出作者发现自己心里恐惧的东西没有想象的那么可怕。所以答案为B项。

25. [正确答案] D
    [考点类型] 推理题
    [题目翻译] 作者分享她的经历的目的是_____。
    A.介绍人们拥有的奇怪的恐惧   B.解释为什么人们会有奇怪的恐惧
    C.说明克服恐惧非常困难   D.鼓励人们战胜恐惧
    [考点剖析] 在文章最后两段,作者说那次电梯事件之后,她认识到她恐惧的电梯并没有她心里想的那么可怕,战胜恐惧也许没那么困难,这正是鼓励人们要积极战胜恐惧。所以答案为D项。

Passage Two

　　美国公众对节食的痴迷已经产生了有史以来最为危险的错误健康理念之一。很多电视广告、电影、杂志文章以及节食产品的标签会使得消费者相信碳水化合物对人体有害,摄入碳水化合物的人们会很快超重。他们建议我们避免食用诸如土豆、米饭和白面包这样的食物,并用肉类和蔬菜代替。一些公司推崇这种理念以促使消费者来买他们的"无碳水化合物"产品。但是,实际情况是:人体需要碳水化合物才能正常运转;而且,需要碳水化合物的人体如果缺失这种膳食元素,最终身体也不会处于健康的状态。

　　我们每天所食用的大部分食物,比如土豆和大米,都含有碳水化合物。与大众理念相反的是,碳水化合物对健康有很多益处:有些能抵抗高血压和心脏病等疾病,有些能预防癌症和中风。不吃这类含碳水化合物的食物可能会使得你的身体得不到由其带来的很多好处。

　　碳水化合物最大的益处之一就是它们能帮助维持我们的器官、组织和细胞的健康状态。科学研究表明,一种叫作"纤维物质"的碳水化合物能降低患心脏病的风险。碳水化合物还含有抗氧化剂,它能保护人体细胞免受带有致癌可能的有害物质的伤害。

　　但是,这并不是说人体只需要摄入含有碳水化合物的食物。我们也需要一定量的蛋白质和脂肪来维持人体健康。但不能完全杜绝摄入碳水化合物。实际上,食物金字塔(健康饮食所推荐的标准)表明,一个人的每餐食物中,面包和谷物应该占6~11成,水果和蔬菜应该占3~4成,而这些全是含有碳水化合物的食物。显而易见,拒绝摄入碳水化合物不是个好主意。

　　想知道什么对你自己的身体真正有利的唯一方式就是去咨询营养学家或饮食学家,他们能帮助你选择适合你的食物,还能指导你做适当的运动项目来减肥或增加肌肉。这些专家们永远不会让你完全杜绝碳水化合物。底线就是:听专家的,而不是听广告商的。

26. [正确答案] D

[考点类型] 词汇题

[题目翻译] 第一段中出现的 exhausted 最有可能的意思是_____。
A. 吃惊的　　　　　　　　B. 饿极了的
C. 衍生的；导出的　　　　D. 丧失的；被剥夺的

[考点剖析] 目标词所在句为…the human body needs carbohydrates to function properly, and a body that relies on carbohydrates but is exhausted of this dietary element is not in good shape after all，前半句是说人体需要碳水化合物，然后 but 转折，让我们猜测人体在这种膳食元素处于何种状态的时候会变得不健康。转折之后应该是相反的状态，猜测的单词含义应该是和"没有,不摄入"等含义相关。结合选项，与之最相近的就是 D 项。

27. [正确答案] B

[考点类型] 细节题

[题目翻译] 根据作者所述，销售"无碳水化合物"产品的广告商_____。
A. 重视消费者的健康　　　B. 说的不是事实
C. 提供健康的选择　　　　D. 为肥胖病负责

[考点剖析] 从文章第一段前几句我们可以看出，公众对节食的痴迷引发了错误的健康理念。一些公司推崇这种理念的目的是销售自己的产品，后面一个明显的转折 But the truth is…才是真实的情况，所以前面的内容应该是不符合实际情况的。由此可知这些公司说的并非实情。所以答案是 B 项。

28. [正确答案] C

[考点类型] 细节题

[题目翻译] 下列哪项不是碳水化合物带给人体健康的益处？
A. 预防中风。　　　　　　B. 预防癌症。
C. 预防纤维质减少。　　　D. 预防心脏病。

[考点剖析] 我们需要在文章中找到碳水化合物带给人体健康的益处，没有提到的就是答案，我们可以从 carbohydrates have many health benefits: some fight… high blood pressure and heart disease, and others help to prevent cancer and stroke 中找到 A、B、D 三项，C 项文中没有提到，所以答案为 C 项。

29. [正确答案] D

[考点类型] 推理题

[题目翻译] 我们能从文章推断出，健康的饮食_____。
A. 含有少量的碳水化合物以及大量的蛋白质和脂肪
B. 含有等量的碳水化合物和蛋白质
C. 需要含有足够的蛋白质而不是脂肪来维持人体所需的能量
D. 要保持碳水化合物、蛋白质和脂肪含量的平衡

[考点剖析] 文章倒数第二段的 This does not mean that the human body can survive on a diet composed entirely of carbohydrates. We also need certain percentages of proteins and fats to maintain healthy bodies 表明我们需要的不仅仅是碳水化合物，还要有一定量

的蛋白质和脂肪。而且,后文说的食物金字塔也是要我们摄入各种元素。所以答案是 D 项。

30. [正确答案] D

    [考点类型] 主旨题

    [题目翻译] 文章的主要目的是_____。

    A. 描述碳水化合物的种类
    B. 解释如何过健康的生活
    C. 提倡更多的锻炼
    D. 提倡健康的饮食

    [考点剖析] 解答主旨题要将各段落的主要含义进行整合。本文先介绍目前大众所认为的节食、避免摄入碳水化合物的观念是错误的。后面介绍碳水化合物对人体健康的好处,并说明人体健康需要的不只是碳水化合物,还有其他元素,即要保持平衡的饮食,并提供了一些建议。由此看出,作者写文章的目的应该是提倡健康的饮食。因此 D 项为正确答案。

Passage Three

在金融危机给我们的教训中,和个人最相关的是美国人不太擅长理财。我们贷着我们负担不起的房屋贷款。我们有飙升的信用卡债务。我们甚至没有足够的退休存款。

为此,金融理财教育的支持者们重新满怀热情地行动着。例如新泽西州和伊利诺伊州等一些州的学区增加了理财课程。财政部和教育部向高中发送课程规划,并鼓励学生参加始于 3 月份的国家金融理财水平竞赛。

比赛中成绩优秀的学生将会获得证书,但是取得长期效果的可能性很小。最终证实,几乎没什么证据能证明,这种促进学生掌握金融理财知识的传统的努力能帮助学生在课堂之外做出更好的决定。即便是在过去金融理财教育运动比较兴盛的十年中,在检测预算、信用卡、保险和投资方面的能力测试中,学生的分数一直呈下降的势头。近来一个对大学生组织的私人理财启动联盟的调查发现,那些在高中参加过金融理财课程的学生的成绩并不比没参加过的学生好。

华盛顿大学教授刘易斯·曼德尔说:"我们需要弄清楚怎样正确处理这件事。"她从事金融理财知识项目研究 15 年后得出结论:目前这些办法并不起作用。越来越多的研究者和教育学者认为需要一个更激进的解决途径。他们建议要在比高中更早的时期开始金融教育,把真正的钱和如何花钱的决定权交到孩子手中,并敞开心扉谈论情感和社会影响与我们如何用钱的关联。

其他的一些方法也能用于处理像商业和社会压力方面的现实生活中的问题,这些问题能影响人们购物的决定。为什么你会如此想要那些昂贵的名牌鞋子?公益性项目"阿福童"的创始人杰鲁·比利莫利亚说:"选择一个立场或者换个方式思考需要有一定的信心。"这个项目旨在帮助儿童获得金融方面的协助,已经有 30 多个国家使用它的课程。"这些课程远不止是关于钱财和储蓄。"

31. [正确答案] D

    [考点类型] 细节题

    [题目翻译] 金融理财教育的目的在于_____。

    A. 重燃美国人理财的热情

B. 加强美国人对金融危机的认识
C. 帮助美国人克服金融危机
D. 让美国人能明智地理财

[考点剖析] 文章第二段首句提到"为此,金融理财教育的支持者们满怀热情地行动着",由此可知原因在第一段。第一段提到美国人不太擅长理财,贷着负担不起的房屋贷款,有飙升的信用卡债务,没有足够的退休存款,因此 D 项为正确答案。

32. [正确答案] A

[考点类型] 推理题

[题目翻译] 根据作者所言,国家金融理财水平竞赛将会是_____。
A. 无效的   B. 值得的
C. 代价高的   D. 被广泛接受的

[考点剖析] 根据题干可定位到第三段,第三段第一句提到 but chances for long-term benefits are slim"但是取得长期效果的可能性很小";第二句提到 As it turns out, there is little evidence that traditional efforts… help students make better decisions outside the classroom,可知事实证明这些做法没能帮助学生,包括后面的具体举例,也都说明了 A 项是正确答案。

33. [正确答案] C

[考点类型] 推理题

[题目翻译] 通过在第三段中说 the financial-literacy movement has gained steam,作者想表达这个运动_____。
A. 受到许多批评   B. 被认为是富于想象的
C. 越来越流行   D. 已经经历了金融危机

[考点剖析] 该短句所在句的开头部分有个很关键的 Even as,句意为"即便是在过去金融理财教育运动……的十年中"。根据语境,前面一直在说支持者们怀有热情地做这件事,但是实际收效并不是很明显,那么这里应该是说,当这个活动处于比较鼎盛或者盛行的时候效果也不明显。所以答案为 C 项。

34. [正确答案] B

[考点类型] 细节题

[题目翻译] 刘易斯·曼德尔认为我们应该先弄清楚如何_____。
A. 更有效地理财   B. 恰当地实行金融理财教育
C. 增强社会的金融教育意识 D. 帮助学生在理财课程中取得好成绩

[考点剖析] 文中第四段开头第一句话就是答案所在句:"We need to figure out how to do this the right way," says Lewis Mandell,…has come to the conclusion that current methods don't work. 在这句话中,如果理解代词 this 指代的内容,就会知晓答案。代词 this 指代前文出现的内容,即金融理财教育。所以答案为 B 项。

35. [正确答案] D

[考点类型] 推理题

[题目翻译] 杰鲁·比利莫利亚最有可能认为商业和社会压力会使一个人的购买决定变得_____。

A. 可接受的 B. 困难的
C. 可行的 D. 不明智的

[考点剖析] 最后一段提到要采用一些方法处理像商业和社会压力方面的实际问题，还列举买昂贵的名牌鞋子的例子，可见这两种因素会对购买行为产生不太好的影响。所以答案为D项。

Passage Four

作弊已经不是什么新鲜事了。但是如今，教育家和管理者们发现学生学术欺骗的情况比以前更加频繁，而且受到惩罚的可能性比过去更小。似乎好学生和差学生都已经接受了作弊这个行为。

为什么学生作弊的情况在增加？没有人真的清楚。有些人认为应该怪罪于当今年轻人道德普遍降低的趋势。其他人将之归结为，如今年轻人比他们理想主义的前辈们更为现实。然而，在20世纪60年代晚期和70年代早期，学生都有着改变世界的想法，而今天的学生面临着适应社会并获得成功的巨大压力。在与全国高中生和大学生的交谈中，年轻的男女学生们都认为作弊变得容易了。有些人暗示他们这样做是为了对他们不尊敬的老师泄愤。其他人把作弊视作一个游戏。也有些人说，只有当他们被抓住的时候，他们才感到羞愧。"竞争很激烈。"一名来自芝加哥的大二学生安娜这样说道。人们从心底感到恐惧。如果做得不好的话，你的生活就会被毁掉。压力不只来自父母和朋友，还有自己本身。要实现目标！要成功！就好像我们只有超过别人才能达到自己的目标一样。

杂志编辑爱德华·韦恩认为学术欺骗现象增多的原因在于学校。他认为，教育管理者和老师太过犹豫不决而不采取行动。阿马里洛的英语系主任德怀特·胡伯有不同看法，他认为这是由测评学生的方式导致的。他说："如果我觉得我被欺骗了，那么我就会去欺骗别人。"他认为只要老师给学生的测试是简短回答式而不是文章问题式，并且是根据学生能记住多少内容而不是根据学生把各种信息串联起来的能力来评定学生的话，学生就会想法钻空子。"作弊这个概念基于一种错误的假设，即教育测试体系是合理合法的，若有人作弊，一定是作弊的学生自己有问题。"他说，"这个答案太简单了。我们得开始审视一下教育测试体系了。"

36. [正确答案] D

   [考点类型] 细节题

   [题目翻译] 教育家们发现作弊的学生_____。

   A. 学习成绩差　　　　　　B. 比过去更可能受到惩罚
   C. 以后也会不诚实　　　　D. 不只是那些成绩不好的学生

   [考点剖析] 结合文章第一段中的…and are less likely to be punished—than in the past可以得知以前受到惩罚的可能性更大，这和B项描述相反。Cheating appears to have gained acceptance among good and poor students alike说明好学生和差学生一样都会作弊，也就是说，作弊的也有好学生，和A项相反，和D项相符。而C项内容文章并未提到。

37. [正确答案] B

   [考点类型] 推理题

   [题目翻译] 根据文章，下列哪项描述正确？

A. 学生在文章式测试中不会作弊。
B. 学生作弊有很深的社会根源。
C. 惩罚是制止作弊的一个有效的方法。
D. 改革测试体系将会消除作弊现象。

[考点剖析] 文章第二段主要讲述了公众对作弊原因的看法,有人认为是年轻人道德降低造成的,有人认为是现在年轻人的实用主义造成的,还有人提到了社会压力等方面,而这些都属于造成作弊现象的社会原因。故 B 项正确。其他三个选项在文章中没有提到,也不能推断出来。

38. [正确答案] D
    [考点类型] 推理题
    [题目翻译] 胡伯先生会同意以下哪项说法?
        A. 父母必须承担作弊现象增加的责任。
        B. 国家应对作弊者采取严厉的惩罚。
        C. 作弊的学生应该被学校开除。
        D. 通过教育改革,作弊现象会有所减少。

    [考点剖析] 根据题干内容,我们定位在文章最后一段,Dwight Huber… sees the matter differently, blaming the rise in cheating on the way students are evaluated… The concept of… on the false assumption that the system is legitimate and there is something wrong… We've got to start looking at the system 说明胡伯先生认为造成作弊现象增多的原因在于教育测试体系的问题,建议开始审视这个体系。由此我们推断出他认为应该对教育测试体系进行改革,从而减少作弊现象的发生。故 D 项正确。

39. [正确答案] C
    [考点类型] 推理题
    [题目翻译] 最后一段中的 the individuals 是指_____。
        A. 老师   B. 父母
        C. 作弊的学生   D. 学校管理者

    [考点剖析] 由原文 The concept of cheating is based on the false assumption… and there is something wrong with the individuals who are doing it 可知,我们要理解的名词刚好是定语从句的先行词,定语从句的意思是"做这件事的人","这件事"指的是"作弊"。所以答案为 C 项。

40. [正确答案] C
    [考点类型] 主旨题
    [题目翻译] 本文主要讨论了_____。
        A. 人们对学生作弊行为的宽容   B. 当今年轻一代道德水准的下滑
        C. 导致学术欺骗现象的因素   D. 消除学术欺骗的方式

    [考点剖析] 文章主旨一般是各段落大意的综合,文章第一段简要描述作弊的现状,后面第二段描述人们对这个现象增多原因的不同看法,第三段仍然举出不同观点。所以答案为 C 项,描述原因是主要内容。

2014年同等学力人员申请硕士学位英语水平全国统一考试答案及详解

Section B

在美国,抚养孩子的核心原则之一是父母应该积极地参与到孩子的教育中:与老师会面,在学校做志愿活动,协助孩子做家庭作业,以及其他一大堆没几个上班的父母有时间做的事情。这些义务已经深深印进了美国人的价值观,很少有父母或老师质疑这些事是否值得去做。

在今年一月份之前,研究人员也很少去质疑。杜克大学两位名叫基斯·罗宾逊和安琪尔·L.哈里斯的社会学教授,开展了有史以来规模最大的研究,研究父母的参与如何影响孩子的学业成绩。结论是:基本上没影响。研究人员仔细梳理了近30年关于美国父母的有价值的调查,并追踪了有关父母参与孩子学业活动的63种不同形式,从辅导孩子做作业,到和孩子讨论大学计划等。研究人员将孩子包括阅读和数学成绩在内的学业表现和父母参与的活动挂钩,以试图证明:经过一段时间后,父母参与其教育较多的孩子是否会进步。

研究人员的发现让人感到意外。大多可测的父母参与形式似乎并没有对孩子的学业有所帮助,甚至适得其反,不管父母是什么种族、什么阶层,以及受教育程度如何。

你是不是每天晚上都检查女儿的作业?两位社会学教授罗宾逊和哈里斯的数据表明,父母的参与不会帮助孩子提高考试分数。孩子上中学以后,父母的帮助可能还会让成绩下滑。罗宾逊说,这是由于很多家长可能已经忘记或者从来没有真正弄懂孩子们在学校所学习的知识。

尽管罗宾逊和哈里斯非常反对这个假设,但他们确实发现有几个习惯可以起作用,比如在小孩子面前大声朗读(不到一半的家长会每天给孩子读书),还有和青少年讨论大学计划。但是这些介入不会发生在学校或者老师面前,而是在家里——政策制定者能够产生最大影响的地方。

评论1

基本上就是一个人是否想让孩子自然发展的选择。家长持续地参与,以及与孩子有意无意地不停沟通做父母的想要什么,这会使孩子们很快成长为父母的样子,或像父母一样思考。

评论2

这也取决于孩子。情感和社会成熟度也与大学和生活中的成功有莫大的关系。也许有些孩子智商高并且对高中感到厌烦,但是这并不意味着他们已经为大学或者工作做好了准备。

评论3

这篇文章没有明确地指明"协助"的含义,但是我理解的是,帮助孩子做练习(比如帮助他们解决数学问题),以及/或者检查他们的功课是否正确,而不只是确保他们已经完成作业那么简单。我觉得后者比前者更有帮助。当然我还希望没有什么研究会让父母丧失监督孩子们的表现的勇气。

41.[正确答案] C

[考点类型] 推理题

[题目翻译] 第一段中的 they 指的是_____。

  A. 原则   B. 研究

  C. 义务   D. 价值观

[考点剖析] 题目考查词汇所在句:These obligations are so baked into American values that few parents stop to ask whether they're worth the effort "这些义务已经深深印进了美国人的价值观,所以很少有父母或老师质疑这些事是否值得去做"。they 指代的应该是前面已经出现的内容,即本句开头提到的 obligations。所以答案为 C 项。

42. [正确答案] A
    [考点类型] 细节题
    [题目翻译] 罗宾逊和哈里斯的研究得出的主要结论是什么？
        A. 父母的参与不一定会帮助孩子。
        B. 经过一段时间后，家长参与其教育较多的孩子会进步。
        C. 学校应该定期与父母沟通。
        D. 成绩低的学生有父母的参与学习效果更好。
    [考点剖析] 文章中显示他们调查结果的句子为：Most measurable forms... yield few academic dividends for kids, or even to backfire（适得其反）—regardless of a parent's race, class, or level of education "大多可测的父母参与似乎并没有对孩子的学业有所帮助，甚至适得其反，不管父母是什么种族、什么阶层，以及受教育程度如何"。所以 A 项的描述与原文一致。B 项和 D 项与原文相反，C 项文中并未提及。

43. [正确答案] D
    [考点类型] 推理题
    [题目翻译] 评论 1 暗示了_____。
        A. 孩子毕竟应该是孩子的样子   B. 父母应该让孩子们自由发展
        C. 持续的父母参与是必需的   D. 父母可能会影响孩子们的思维
    [考点剖析] 评论 1 结尾部分提到的 ...consciously or unconsciously would help the kids grow up or think like the parents sooner than otherwise 说明家长的参与和沟通会影响孩子们的思维。所以 D 项正确。

44. [正确答案] B
    [考点类型] 推理题
    [题目翻译] 写评论 2 的人很可能会认为_____。
        A. 为上大学做好准备是一个情感方面的过程
        B. 高智商并不一定保证成功
        C. 美国的高中经常让人感到厌烦
        D. 社会成熟度足够让人在生活中取得成功
    [考点剖析] 评论 2 的内容主要描述情感和社会成熟度与一个人取得成功的关系，A 项和 D 项比较片面，而 C 项与文章内容不符。该段评论最后提到 Some kids may have the brains... but that doesn't mean they are ready for college or the work place "也许有些孩子智商高并且对高中感到厌烦，但是这并不意味着他们已经为大学或者工作做好了准备"，由此可知 B 项内容与之相符。

45. [正确答案] B
    [考点类型] 推理题
    [题目翻译] 评论 3 的作者会认为下列父母对孩子的协助中哪个比较恰当？
        A. 监督孩子在班级的表现。
        B. 检查孩子的作业是否正确。
        C. 确保孩子做完作业。
        D. 协助孩子做练习。

[考点剖析] 文章最后一段中有第三个评论人的观点 I think the latter is more helpful than the former,所以我们要找到他所同意的后者的做法,从 assisting children in the exercises... rather than simply making sure they've completed their work 可知 B 项为正确选项。

Part Ⅳ Cloze

具有讽刺意味的是,一项研究表明我们是糟糕的送礼者,而这正是因为我们为了能考虑周到,总是花费很长时间。我们想象着朋友打开的是一个让他印象深刻的、昂贵的、带有感情的礼物。我们想象朋友脸上幸福和惊喜的表情,反过来自己也会感到温暖。但是,有件事情是最用心的送礼者也不会过多考虑的:礼物首先是否实用。

在很多情况下,实用性似乎是最佳礼物的敌人。漂亮的珠宝、可爱的手表、完美的毛毯、做工精美的厨房用具,这些东西更容易被人们当作很好的礼品,因为他们除了传达出实用性之外,还传达出了送礼者的关爱。

但是收到礼物的人在乎吗? 通常情况下,回答是否定的。研究者写道,收礼物的人会感到更开心,如果送礼物的人能送给他们恰好需要的东西,而不是通过买给他们那些他们根本不想要的礼物以带给他们惊喜,来试图表现出"体贴周到"。问卷要求送礼物的人和收礼物的人从两个角度来衡量礼物:吸引力(咖啡壶的价钱)和实用性(咖啡壶的质量)。经过多次实验,他们发现:送礼物的人始终基于前者送礼物,而收礼物的人一直喜欢后者。

46. [正确答案] C
    [解析过程] 空格前面的 imagine 后跟动词时,动词须用动名词的形式。

47. [正确答案] A
    [解析过程] 根据语境,前半句是说收礼物朋友的感觉,后半句是说我们自己,也就是送礼物人的感觉。A 项"反过来,作为回报"正确。

48. [正确答案] D
    [解析过程] 此处考查语境含义,送礼物者不会过多考虑的事情是礼物"是否"实用,而不是其他选项的"如何、为什么、何时"实用,所以 D 项最符合语境。

49. [正确答案] A
    [解析过程] 题目所在句的大意为在很多情况下,实用性似乎是最佳礼物的敌人。其他几个选项从意思上说不通。所以应该选 A 项。

50. [正确答案] B
    [解析过程] 前面提到的是通常被人们当作礼物的东西,后文说因为它们传达出了实用性和送礼者的关爱,因此空格处应表示这些东西很容易被当作很好的礼品。make for "有利于,促成",符合语境。

51. [正确答案] D
    [解析过程] 选项中供我们选择的单词有两个含义:吃惊和开心。收到恰好是自己需要的礼物,人们的感觉应该是开心;又因为是在跟收到不是很需要的礼物作比较,所以应该选 D 项。

52. [正确答案] C
    [解析过程] 根据语境,这里将收礼物的人在收到自己恰好需要的礼物和收到不是很需要的礼物的两种不同的情况作比较,中间应该用一个表示转折的词组。所以 C 项正确。

53. [正确答案] A

　　[解析过程] 这句话让我们填一个动词,动词的宾语是 gifts,句子的意思是:让送礼物和收礼物的人从两个角度去_____该选择哪种礼物。所以 A 项"衡量"更符合语境。

54. [正确答案] C

　　[解析过程] 这里是将送礼的人和收礼的人看待礼物的两个角度(desirability"吸引力"和feasibility"实用性")进行对比,并以咖啡壶这一具体礼物为例。对应吸引力的是咖啡壶的价格,那对应实用性的自然是其质量了,所以应该选择 C 项。

55. [正确答案] A

　　[解析过程] 这里是一个平行结构,描述送礼物的人和收礼物的人的不同做法。在结构和语义上应该是类似的,所以答案为 A 项。

Part V　Text Completion

Text One

　　孩子是广告商主要针对的目标,他们这样做也是可以理解的。年轻人的购物和消费比以往任何时候更甚。研究人员指出,那些深深陷进消费主义文化里的孩子更容易患儿童抑郁症和焦虑症,而且与父母的关系也不会太好。他们说:"你不可能让孩子与广告全无接触,因为广告无所不在。所以你可以向你的孩子这样解释,广告商有自己的工作计划,而且雇用他们做广告的公司想要挣钱。他们不会考虑我们的最大利益。"

　　研究者还建议不要看太多电视节目。可以把看电视的时间用其他活动代替,比如读书、一起玩游戏等。

56. [正确答案] A

　　[解析过程] 解答这个题主要是从语义角度来判断,同时可以用另外两个选项来进行排除。

57. [正确答案] C

　　[解析过程] 空格所在句是一个 that 引导的定语从句,定语从句缺少动词和名词作谓语和宾语。C 项符合这个语法结构。

58. [正确答案] B

　　[解析过程] 空格前 spent 一词的常用搭配为 spend some time(in)doing sth.,故 B 项正确。

59. [正确答案] A

　　[解析过程] 这个句子前半句已经是完整的系表结构,如果选择 B 项或 C 项的话,从语义和语法角度来说都不合适。

60. [正确答案] B

　　[解析过程] 从语法角度来说,此处缺少一个并列成分作 explain 的宾语;从语义角度来讲,B 项意为"雇用他们做广告的公司想要挣钱",刚好能和前半句的广告商并列。

61. [正确答案] C

　　[解析过程] 从语法角度来讲,这里可以有个从句作 time 的定语;从语义上看,看电视和前面的 fill the time 相对应。

Text Two

　　加利福尼亚州的一个调查研究组发布了一份《国家高等教育报告》。报告指出,从 1982 年以来,大学的费用已经增长了超过400%。这些费用比其他费用——也包括普通家庭的工资收入——攀升得更快。这个调查组发出警告,这种趋势的持续将会使得高等教育脱离大多数美国人的承受范围,而且这意味着给那些上大学的人带来更多的债务。报告还表示,担心美国正在丧失其在输送年轻人接受大学教育方面的领导地位。

62. [正确答案] C
    [解析过程] 这道题最好用排除法来做,A 项和 C 项都可以放在这里,但是如果先确定出第 63 题的话就比较好选。

63. [正确答案] A
    [解析过程] beyond the reach of sb. 是固定短语,指的是"超出某人的能力范围"。

64. [正确答案] B
    [解析过程] send sb. to some place 是常见的句型,指的是"送某人去某地"。

65. [正确答案] A
    [解析过程] 空格前面是说"比其他费用攀升得更快",A 项"也包括普通家庭的工资收入"与其相照应。

66. [正确答案] B
    [解析过程] put sb./sth. beyond the reach of…"把某人/物置于……能力之外"。

67. [正确答案] C
    [解析过程] the leadership in doing sth."在某方面的领导地位",介词 in 的后面跟动词时,动词须用动名词的形式,只有 C 项符合题意。

Text Three

帝企鹅用它的羽毛来吸入空气。这不仅能帮助它抵御极寒,还能使它的移动速度快上两倍或者三倍。怎么回事呢?海洋生物学家说它是通过从羽毛间释放微小气泡做到的。这些气泡被释放之后,它们就会减少企鹅翅膀表面的摩擦力,从而加快移动速度。

有趣的是,工程师们一直在研究通过使用气泡减少船身摩擦的方式来加快船只航行的速度。但是研究者承认,进一步的调查研究很有挑战性,因为企鹅的翅膀结构复杂,很难被模仿。

68. [正确答案] B
    [解析过程] from between sth."从……之间",这里指的是羽毛之间。其他选项从语法和语义角度来看都不符合题意。

69. [正确答案] A
    [解析过程] 这里应为不定式,需要接动词原形,再根据文中的语境应该选择 A 项"模仿,仿效"。

70. [正确答案] C
    [解析过程] otherwise"否则,不然",文章中该句的意思是,如果不具备这个特点的话,就不能……,其他选项从语法和语义角度来看都不符合题意。

71. [正确答案] D
    [解析过程] enable sb. to do sth."使某人能够做某事"。这里应为不定式,需要接动词原形,再结合语义选择 D 项。

72. [正确答案] C
    [解析过程] 题目所在句的意思是如果帝企鹅的羽毛不能吸入空气的话,它的移动速度就不

能快上两倍或者三倍,由此可知应选 C 项。

73. [正确答案] A

    [解析过程] 根据语义,"释放的气泡"是来自"羽毛间"的,所以选择 A 项。

74. [正确答案] D

    [解析过程] 减少摩擦的目的就是让企鹅加快移动速度,且本句从语法角度来讲已经具备谓语动词 reduce,故用 enabling… 作状语。

75. [正确答案] B

    [解析过程] 前半句的 complexity"复杂性"已经暗示了"很难被模仿",所以答案选择 B 项。

Paper Two 试卷二

Part Ⅵ Translation

1. The social costs of unemployment go far beyond the welfare and unemployment payments made by the government.

   [结构分析] 这是一个简单句。made by the government 作宾语 the welfare and unemployment payments 的后置定语。

   [词义推敲] go far beyond"远远超过"。

   [参考译文] 失业的社会成本远远超出了政府提供的福利和失业补贴。

2. Unemployment increases the chances of divorce, child abuse, and alcoholism, a new federal survey shows.

   [结构分析] 这是一个复合句。a new federal survey shows 是句子的主干,Unemployment… 为 shows 的宾语。

   [词义推敲] the chances of sth."……的可能性";child abuse"虐待儿童";alcoholism"酗酒"。

   [参考译文] 一个新的联邦调查显示,失业增加了离婚、虐待儿童、酗酒的概率。

3. Some experts say the problem is only temporary—that new technology will eventually create as many jobs as it destroys.

   [结构分析] 这是一个复合句。Some experts say 是句子的主干,破折号前面是 say 的宾语。

   [词义推敲] temporary"暂时的"。

   [参考译文] 一些专家认为这个问题是暂时性的,新的技术最终将创造与它毁掉的数量相同的工作岗位。

4. But futurologist Hymen Seymour says the astonishing efficiency of the new technology means there will be a simple net reduction in the amount of human labor that needs to be done.

   [结构分析] 这是一个多重复合句,句式结构比较复杂。futurologist Hymen Seymour says… 是主句;在 says 后省略了 that 的宾语从句里又嵌套了一个宾语从句,宾语从句的主干是 the astonishing efficiency of… means,之后的句子 there will be a simple… 是 means 的宾语;而这个宾语从句里又出现一个 that 引导的定语从句作 labor 的定语。

   [词义推敲] astonishing"惊人的,令人惊讶的";efficiency"效率,效能"。

   [参考译文] 但是未来学家许门·西摩称,新科技的效率惊人,这意味着所需的人类劳动力数量将必然会减少。

5. We should treat this as an opportunity to give people more leisure.

   [结构分析] 这是一个简单句。treat sth. as... "把……视作/当作……"。

   [词义推敲] opportunity "机会"; leisure "闲暇,空闲"。

   [参考译文] 我们应该把这看成一个给人们更多休闲的机会。

6. "It may not be easy, but society will have to reach a new agreement on the division and distribution of labor," Seymour says.

   [结构分析] 引号内是一个含转折关系的并列句。

   [词义推敲] reach an agreement "达成协议"; the division and distribution of labor "劳动力的分工和分配"。

   [参考译文] "这可能并不简单,但社会最终不得不在劳动力的分工和分配方面重新达成一致。"西摩这样说道。

Part VII Writing

这是一道要求写读后感的作文题,给出了作文的题目、故事情境,以及写作的提纲。我们可以根据提纲列出的三点思路去展开:第一段,要对给定的故事情境做简要的描述;第二段,对小刘的成功之道进行简要的评价并发表看法、说明原因,一般写两到三个;第三段,你自己有什么成功经验、有哪些建议。

As is clearly shown in the story, Xiao Liu chose a different way from his classmates after graduation and wrote a different story. Xiao Liu succeeds finally, while most of others live in an ordinary life and lose the encouragement to face huge challenges. Nowadays the way to success has aroused immediate concern and widespread discussion among the general public. From Xiao Liu's experience, we can draw a conclusion that sometimes choosing a road seldom chosen by other people could increase the possibility of success.

On one hand, it can be reasonably argued that there will be more chances if we choose a different way to work or live. If we just do as what others do, there will not be much wealth or resources left for us to make use of. In this case, the chances of success won't be too many. On the other hand, however, there will be risks existing at the same time. The reason why seldom people choose the way may be that it is not a correct way to success, and the people who choose it may face the risk of failure.

I strongly believe that we can do as what Xiao Liu does but need to estimate the risk first. In the process of my growth, I have a lot of successful experience. In my opinion, there are many factors needed for success. The first one that comes to my mind readily is knowledge and skills. They are the basic factors and one can't get success without them. What's more, efforts and the spirit of persisting are key factors to success. No success can come easily and there are many examples that people give up in the half way. We should spare no effort and stick to it then we could achieve the goal.

  这篇范文很巧妙地运用了常见的作文写作模板,并做了灵活替换,所以文章思路和结构都显得比较清晰,自然流畅,给人印象很不错。我们来看一下内容:

  第一段:对给定故事情境做了简要的描述,并做了简要的总结。由于是对给定情境的概述,没有死板地套用过多模板,感觉比较流畅自然。

  第二段:从两个方面阐述"不走寻常路"的成功之道的好处和风险,对故事中小刘的成功之道作出评价,回应作文要求。

  第三段:再次回应作文提纲要求,发表自己对成功的看法,并给出相应的支持理由。

  整篇文章内容丰富,有理有据,思路简单清晰,又合理运用了作文模板,为在作文考试中拿到理想分数提供了有力的保障。

2015 年同等学力人员申请硕士学位
英语水平全国统一考试

Paper One 试卷一（100 minutes）

Part I Oral Communication (15 minutes, 10 points)

Section A

Directions: *In this section there are two incomplete dialogues and each dialogue has three blanks and three choices A, B and C, taken from the dialogue. Fill in each of the blanks with one of the choices to complete the dialogue and mark your answer on the **Answer Sheet**.*

Dialogue One

A. Do you know what a handicapped space is?

B. The signs always tell you how long you can park there and on what days.

C. Then you also need to be aware of the time limits on the street signs.

Student: Can you tell me where I can park?

Clerk: Are you driving a motorcycle or an automobile?

Student: I drive an automobile.

Clerk: Fine. You can either park in the student lot or on the street. __1__

Student: Yes, I have seen those spots.

Clerk: Well, when you see the blue spots with the handicapped sign, do not park there unless you have a special permit. Are you going to be parking in the daytime or evening?

Student: I park in the evenings.

Clerk: __2__ Have you seen those signs?

Student: Yes, I have seen those signs.

Clerk: __3__

Dialogue Two

A. The hours and limitations are printed on the card and this handout.

B. May I have your driver's license, please?

C. Are you familiar with our rules and fines?

Student: Excuse me. I am interested in getting a library card.

Librarian: Sure, let me give you an application. You can fill it out right here at the counter.

Student: Thank you. I'll do it right now.

Librarian: Let me take a look at this for you. __4__

Student: Here it is.

Librarian: You seem to have filled the form out all right. __5__

Student: Yes. I know what to do.

Librarian: __6__

Student: OK. I see.

Librarian: Thank you for joining the library. We look forward to serving you.

Section B

Directions: *In this section there is one incomplete interview which has four blanks and four choices A, B, C and D, taken from the interview. Fill in each of the blanks with one of the choices to complete the interview and mark your answer on the **Answer Sheet**.*

A. And fooled the boys for a while.

B. And I don't think the boys have minded.

C. Well, it's because of my British publisher.

D. All this time I thought you were "J. K.".

Winfrey: So, this is the first time we've met.

Rowling: Yes, it is.

Winfrey: And my producers tell me that your real name is J. O. __7__

Rowling: (laughing) Yeah.

Winfrey: J. K. is...

Rowling: __8__ When the first book came out, they thought "this is a book that will appeal to boys", but they didn't want the boys to know a woman had written it. So they said to me "could we use your initials?" and I said "fine." I only have one initial. I don't have a middle name, so I took my favorite grandmother's name, Kathleen.

Winfrey: __9__

Rowling: Yeah, but not for too long, because I started getting my picture in the press and no one could pretend I was a man anymore.

Winfrey: __10__

Rowling: NO—it hasn't held me back, has it?

Part II Vocabulary (10 minutes, 10 points)

Directions: *In this part there are ten sentences, each with one word or phrase underlined. Choose the one from the four choices marked A, B, C and D that best keeps the meaning of the sentence. Mark your answer on the **Answer Sheet**.*

11. There are several different options for getting Internet access.
    A. choices   B. definitions   C. channels   D. reasons
12. Earth has an atmosphere, which protects the surface from harmful rays.
    A. minerals   B. substances   C. gases   D. beams
13. The manager gave one of the salesgirls an accusing look for her hostile attitude toward customers.
    A. unfriendly   B. optimistic   C. impatient   D. positive
14. Since it is late to change my mind now, I am resolved to carry out the plan.
    A. revise   B. implement   C. review   D. improve
15. Security guards dispersed the crowd that had gathered around the Capitol.
    A. arrested   B. stopped   C. scattered   D. watched
16. To start the program, insert the disk and follow the instructions.
    A. take out   B. turn over   C. track down   D. put in
17. The patient's condition has deteriorated since last night.
    A. improved   B. returned   C. worsened   D. changed
18. I couldn't afford to fly home, and a train ticket was likewise beyond my means.
    A. also   B. nonetheless   C. furthermore   D. otherwise
19. Despite years of searching, scientists have detected no signs of life beyond our own solar system.
    A. within   B. besides   C. outside   D. except
20. I prefer chicken to fish because I am worried about accidentally swallowing a small bone.
    A. intentionally   B. unexpectedly   C. anxiously   D. hurriedly

Part III Reading Comprehension (45 minutes, 25 points)

Section A

Directions: *In this section, there are four passages followed by questions or unfinished statements, each with four suggested answers A, B, C and D. Choose the best answer and mark your answer on the Answer Sheet.*

Passage One

Sometimes a race is not enough. Sometimes a runner just wants to go further. That's what happened to Dennis Martin and Brooke Curran.

Martin, 68, a retired detective from New York City, took up running after his first wife died. Curran, 46, a philanthropist(慈善家) from Alexandria, started running to get out of the house and collect her thoughts. Both she and Martin got good at running but felt the desire to do more. "The more I trained, the better I got," Curran said, "but I would cross the finish line with no sense of accomplishment."

Eventually, they worked up to running marathons(马拉松) (and longer races) in other countries, on other continents. Now both have achieved a notable and increasingly less rate milestone: running the

26.2-mile race on all seven continents.

They are part of a phenomenon that has grown out of the running culture in the past two decades, at the intersection of athleticism and leisure:"runcations," which combine distance running with travel to exotic places. These trips, as expensive as they are physically challenging, are a growing and competitive market in the travel industry.

"In the beginning, running was enough," said Steen Albrechtsen, a press manager. "The classic marathon was the ultimate goal, then came the super marathons, like London and New York. But when 90,000 people a year can take that challenge, it is no longer exciting and adventurous. Hence, the search for new adventures began."

"No one could ever have imagined that running would become the lifestyle activity that it is today," said Thom Gilligan, founder and president of Boston-based Marathon Tours and Travel. Gilligan, who has been in business since 1979, is partly responsible for the seven-continent phenomenon.

It started with a casual talk to an interviewer about his company offering trips to every continent except Antarctica. And then in 1995, Marathon Tours hosted its first Antarctica Marathon on King George Island. Off the tip of the Antarctic Peninsula: 160 runners got to the starting line of a dirt- and ice-trail route via a Russian icebreaker through the Drake Passage.

21. At the beginning, Martin took up running just to _____.

    A. meet requirements of his job

    B. win a running race

    C. join in a philanthropic activity

    D. get away from his sadness

22. Martin and Curran are mentioned as good examples of _____.

    A. winners in the 26.2-mile race on all seven continents

    B. people who enjoy long running as a lifestyle activity

    C. running racers satisfied with their own performance

    D. old people who live an active life after retirement

23. A new trend in the travel industry is the development of _____.

    A. challenging runcations

    B. professional races

    C. Antarctica travel market

    D. expensive tours

24. The classic marathon no longer satisfies some people because _____.

    A. it does not provide enough challenge

    B. it may be tough and dangerous

    C. it involves too fierce a competition

    D. it has attracted too many people

25. The first Antarctica Marathon on King George Island indicates that _____.
   A. international cooperation is a must to such an event
   B. runcations are expensive and physically challenging
   C. Marathon Tours is a leader of the travel industry
   D. adventurous running has become increasingly popular

Passage Two

Before the 1970s, college students were treated as children. So many colleges ran *in loco parentis* system. "*In loco parentis*" is a Latin term meaning "in the place of a parent." It describes when someone else accepts responsibility to act in the interests of a child.

This idea developed long ago in British common law to define the responsibility of teachers toward their students. For years, American courts upheld *in loco parentis* in cases such as Gott versus Berea College in 1913.

Gott owned a restaurant off campus. Berea threatened to expel students who ate at places not owned by the school. The Kentucky high court decided that *in loco parentis* justified that rule.

In loco parentis meant that male and female college students usually had to live in separate buildings. Women had to be back at their dorms by ten or eleven on school nights.

But in the 1960s, students began to protest rules and restrictions like these. At the same time, courts began to support students who were being punished for political and social <u>dissent</u>.

In 1960, Alabama State College expelled six students who took part in a civil rights demonstration. They sued the school and won. After that it became harder and harder to defend *in loco parentis*.

At that time, students were not considered adults until 21. Then, in 1971, the 24th amendment to the Constitution set the voting age at eighteen. So *in loco parentis* no longer really applied.

Slowly, colleges began to treat students not as children, but as adults. Students came to be seen as consumers of educational services.

Gary Dickstein, an assistant vice president at Wright State University in Dayton, Ohio, says *in loco parentis* is not really gone. It just looks different. Today's parents, he says, are often heavily involved in students' lives. They are known as "helicopter parents." They always seem to hover over their children. Gary Dickstein says these parents are likely to question decisions, especially about safety issues and grades. They want to make sure their financial investment is not being wasted.

26. Before the 1970s, many colleges ran *in loco parentis* system because _____.
   A. they could take the place of the students' parents
   B. parents asked them to do it for the interests of their children
   C. this was a tradition established by British colleges
   D. college students were regarded as too young to be treated as adults

27. Who won the case of Gott versus Berea College in 1913?
   A. Berea College.   B. Gott.
   C. It was a win-win case. D. The students.

28. The word "dissent" (Para. 5) probably means "_____".
   A. extreme behaviors   B. violation of laws
   C. strong disagreement   D. wrong doings

29. In 1960, the court ruled that Alabama State College _____.
   A. had no right to expel the students
   B. was justified to have expelled the students
   C. shouldn't interfere with students' daily life
   D. should support civil rights demonstrations

30. According to Gary Dickstein, today's "helicopter parents" _____.
   A. don't set their hearts at rest with college administrators
   B. keep a watchful eye on their children's life and study
   C. care less about their children's education than before
   D. have different opinions on their children's education

Passage Three

We tend to think of plants as the furniture of the natural world. They don't move, they don't make sounds, they don't seem to respond to anything—at least not very quickly. But as is often the case, our human view of the world misses quite a lot. Plants talk to each other all the time. And the language is chemical.

Over the years, scientists have reported that different types of plants, from trees to tomatoes, release compounds into the air to help neighboring plants. These chemical warnings all have the same purpose—to spread information about one plant's disease so other plants can defend themselves. But exactly how plants receive and act on many of these signals is still mysterious.

In this week's *Proceedings of the National Academy of Sciences*, researchers in Japan offer some explanations. They have identified one chemical message and traced it all the way from release to action.

The scientists looked at tomato plants infested(侵害) by common pest, the cutworm caterpillar(毛虫). To start out, they grew plants in two plastic compartments connected by a tube. One plant was infested and placed upwind and the others were uninfested and placed downwind. The downwind plants were later exposed to the cutworm caterpillar. The results showed that plants that had previously been near sick neighbors were able to defend themselves better against the caterpillar.

The researchers also studied leaves from exposed and unexposed plants. They found one compound showed up more often in the exposed plants. The substance is called Hex Vic. When the scientists fed Hex Vic to cutworms, it knocked down their survival rate by 17%. The scientists identified the source of Hex Vic, and sprayed it lightly over healthy plants. Those plants were then able to start producing the caterpillar-killing Hex Vic. Researchers confirmed that uninfested plants have to build their own weapon to fight off bugs and diseases. How do they know when to play defense? They are warned first by their friendly plant neighbors.

It is a complex tale, and it may be happening in more plant species than tomatoes. It may also be happening with more chemical signals that are still unknown to us. For now though, we know that plants not only communicate, they look out for one another.

31. What does the author try to emphasize in Paragraph 1?

   A. How plants communicate is still a mystery.

   B. Enough attention has been paid to plant talk.

   C. Plants are the furniture of the natural world.

   D. Plants can communicate with each other.

32. According to Paragraph 2, what remains unknown is _____.

   A. how plants receive and handle the signals from their neighbors

   B. why plants spread chemical information to their neighbors

   C. how many types of plants release compounds into the air

   D. whether plants send chemical warnings to their neighbors

33. The tomato plants in the experiment were _____.

   A. placed separately but connected through air

   B. exposed to different kinds of pests

   C. exposed to the pest at the same time

   D. placed together in a closed compartment

34. The experiment shows that the infested plant helps its neighbors by _____.

   A. making more Hex Vic to attract the pest

   B. releasing Hex Vic into the air to warn them

   C. letting them know how to produce Hex Vic

   D. producing enough Hex Vic to kill the pest

35. What may be the best title for the passage?

   A. Survival of Plants   B. Plant World

   C. Talking Plants   D. Plant Bug Killer

Passage Four

Vancouver is the best place to live in the Americas, according to a quality-of-life ranking published earlier this month. The city regularly tops such indexes as its clean air, spacious homes and weekend possibilities of sailing and skiing. But its status as a liveable city is threatened by worsening congestion (拥挤). Over the next three decades, another 1 million residents are expected to live in the Greater Vancouver region, adding more cars, bicycles and lorries to roads that are already struggling to serve the existing 2.3 million residents.

A proposal by Vancouver's mayor seeks to prevent the worsening conditions. Upgrades would be made to 2,300 kilometres of road lanes, as well as bus routes and cycle paths. Four hundred new buses would join the fleet of 1,830. There would be more trains and more "seabus" ferry crossings between Vancouver and its wealthy northern suburbs. To get all that, residents must vote to accept an increase in sales tax, from 7% to 7.5%. Polls suggest they will vote no.

Everyone agrees that a more efficient transport system is needed. Confined by mountains to the north, the United States to the south and the Pacific Ocean to the west, Vancouver has spread in the only direction where there is still land, into the Fraser Valley, which just a few decades ago was mostly farmland. The road is often overcrowded.

Yet commuters' suspicion of local bureaucrats may exceed their dislike of congestion. TransLink, which runs public transport in the region, is unloved by taxpayers. Passengers blame it when Skytrain, the light-rail system, comes to a standstill because of mechanical or electrical faults, as happened twice in one week last summer, leaving commuters stuck in carriages with nothing to do but expressing their anger on Twitter. That sort of thing has made voters less willing to pay the C$7.5 billion in capital spending that the ten-year traffic upgrade would involve.

Despite the complaints, Vancouver's transport system is a decent, well-integrated one on which to build, reckons Todd Litman, a transport consultant who has worked for TransLink. "These upgrades are all-important if Vancouver wants to maintain its reputation for being a destination others want to go to," He says.

36. The biggest problem threatening Vancouver as a liveable city is _____.
    A. increasing congestion   B. climate change
    C. shortage of land   D. lack of money

37. The upgrade proposal by Vancouver's mayor may be turned down by residents because _____.
    A. they do not want more people to move in
    B. they are reluctant to move to new places
    C. upgrades would take away their living space
    D. upgrades would add to their financial burdens

38. The only direction for Vancouver to further expand is towards _____.
    A. the east   B. the west   C. the south   D. the north

39. TransLink is mentioned (Para. 4) as an example of _____.
    A. world famous transport companies
    B. local residents' complaints about the bureaucrats
    C. local effort to improve public transport
    D. worsening traffic congestion

40. According to Todd Litman, the upgrade proposal _____.
    A. will solve the traffic problem   B. will benefit local economy
    C. satisfies the transport company   D. deserves public support

Section B

Directions: *In this section, you are required to read one quoted blog and the comments on it. The blog and comments are followed by questions or unfinished statements, each with four suggested answers A, B, C and D. Choose the best answer and mark your answer on the **Answer Sheet**.*

Towards the end of the 1990s, more than a decade and a half after Diet Coke was first introduced, sale of Coca Cola's best-selling low caloric drink appeared to slow down.

However, in the decade that followed, diet sodas grew by more than 30 percent. In 2009, sales pushed above $8.5 billion for the first time. But America's thirst for Diet Coke is running dry again—and this time it could be for good.

The diet soda slowdown isn't merely an American thing—it's also happening worldwide. But the future of diet colas is particularly cloudy in the United States.

Low calorie sodas are fighting a hard battle against not one but two trends among American consumers. The first is that overall soda consumption has been on the decline since before 2000. Diet sodas, though they might come sugar- and calorie-free, are still sodas, something Americans are proving less and less interested in drinking.

The second, and perhaps more significant trend, is a growing mistrust of artificial sweeteners(甜味剂). "Consumers' attitudes towards sweeteners have really changed," said Howard Telford, an industry analyst. "There's a very negative perception about artificial sweeteners. The industry is still trying to get its head around this."

Comment 1

Add me to the number of people addicted to diet colas who quit drinking soda altogether. I honestly think soda is addictive and I'm happy not to be drinking it anymore.

Comment 2

Perhaps the slowdown has something more to do with the skyrocketing cost of soft drinks.

Comment 3

I love diet drinks! Am I unhealthy? Who knows? I guarantee I have a better physique than most 43-year-old men.

Comment 4

This is a silly and shallow piece. The reason for the fall-off is simply the explosion in consumption of bottled waters and energy drinks.

Comment 5

As people learn more about health and wellness, they will consume less sugar, less soda, less artificial sweeteners.

41. What do we know about diet soda sale?

   A. It began to undergo a gradual drop starting from 2000.

   B. It was on the decline since the 1990s but is on the rise now.

   C. It reached its peak in the 2000s but began to drop since then.

   D. It has been decreasing since the 1990s.

42. What does the author think of the prospects of diet soda sale?

   A. It will continue to drop.

   B. It will get better soon.

   C. It is hard to say for sure.

   D. It may have ups and downs.

43. Which comment gives a personal reason for quitting diet colas?

   A. Comment 5.   B. Comment 4.

   C. Comment 3.   D. Comment 1.

44. Which comment supports the author's point of view?
   A. Comment 2.   B. Comment 3.
   C. Comment 4.   D. Comment 5.
45. Which comments disagree with the author on the cause of soda sale slowdown?
   A. Comment 3 and Comment 5.   B. Comment 2 and Comment 4.
   C. Comment 1 and Comment 4.   D. Comment 2 and Comment 3.

Part IV Cloze (10 minutes, 10 points)

Directions: *In this part, there is a passage with ten blanks. For each blank there are four choices marked A, B, C and D. Choose the best answer for each blank and mark your answer on the **Answer Sheet**.*

When asked about the impact of disturbing news on children, one mother said: "My 11-year-old daughter doesn't like watching the news. She has __46__ about what she has seen. One time, she watched a report about a person who killed a family member with a knife. That night she dreamed that she too was being killed." Another interviewee said: "My six-year-old niece saw reports of tornadoes (龙卷风) from elsewhere in the country. For weeks __47__, she was terrified. She __48__ call me on the phone, convinced that a tornado was coming her way and that she was going to die."

Do you think disturbing news reports can frighten children? In one survey, nearly 40 percent of parents said that their children had been __49__ by something they saw in the news and that __50__, the children had feared that a similar event would happen to them or their loved ones. Why? One factor is that children often __51__ the news differently from adults. For example, small children may believe that a __52__ that is broadcast repeatedly is really happening repeatedly.

A second factor is that daily reports of disturbing events can distort a child's __53__ of the world. True, we live in "critical times hard to __54__." But repeated exposure to disturbing news reports can cause children to develop lasting fears. "Children who watch a lot of TV news __55__ to overestimate the occurrence of crime and may perceive the world to be a more dangerous place than it actually is," observes the Kaiser Family Foundation.

46. A. thoughts	B. nightmares	C. ideas	D. pictures
47. A. afterward	B. ago	C. before	D. later
48. A. should	B. might	C. could	D. would
49. A. bored	B. angered	C. upset	D. disappointed
50. A. in no time	B. by all means	C. all the more	D. as a result
51. A. tell	B. interpret	C. narrate	D. treat
52. A. tragedy	B. comedy	C. play	D. drama
53. A. imagination	B. view	C. sight	D. look
54. A. give up	B. stick to	C. deal with	D. set forth
55. A. prefer	B. turn	C. come	D. tend

Part V Text Completion (20 minutes, 20 points)

Directions: *In this part, there are three incomplete texts with 20 questions (ranging from 56 to 75). Above each text there are three or four phrases to be completed. First, use the choices provided in the box to complete the phrases. Second, use the completed phrases to fill in the blanks of the text. Mark your answer on the **Answer Sheet**.*

Text One

A. angrier
B. getting
C. action

Phrases:

    A. which makes you __56__

    B. like __57__ any compensation

    C. to take any __58__

Picture this situation: you have bought a faulty item from a shop and you take it back to complain. You go directly to the shop assistant and tell them your problem. They say they cannot help you, __59__, to the point perhaps where you start insulting the poor shop assistant. This will do you no favours, __60__, or even your money back. If you go directly to the first person you see. You may be wasting your time as they may be powerless __61__. So the important lesson to be learnt is to make sure firstly that you are speaking to the relevant person, the one who has the authority to make decisions.

Text Two

A. the smaller
B. as much as
C. up to a year
D. more likely

Phrases:

    A. 20% __62__ to feel happy

    B. __63__ the physical distance between friends

    C. but not __64__ happiness

    D. lasted for __65__

The new study found that friends of happy people had a greater chance of being happy themselves. And __66__, the larger the effect they had on each other's happiness.

For example, a person was __67__ if a friend living within one and a half kilometers was also happy. Having a happy neighbor who lived next door increased an individual's chance of being happy by 34%. The effects of friends' happiness __68__.

The researchers found that happiness really is contagious(传染的). Sadness also spread among friends, __69__.

Text Three

> A. later regretted
> B. spending
> C. tend to

Phrases:

A. remember past impulse purchases that you __70__
B. you may __71__ purchase on impulse
C. keep __72__ under control

In addition to the external pressure we face from marketing, our own feelings and habits can contribute to excessive spending. Here are some suggestions to help you __73__.

First, resist your impulse buying. Do you enjoy the excitement of shopping and finding a bargain? If so, __74__. To resist, slow down and think realistically about the long-term consequences of buying, owning, and maintaining what you are planning to buy. Stop and __75__. Give yourself a "cool down" period before making your final decision.

Paper Two 试卷二 (50 minutes)

Part Ⅵ Translation (20 minutes, 10 points)

Directions: Translate the following passage into Chinese. Write your answer on the **Answer Sheet**.

Should work be placed among the causes of happiness or be regarded as a burden? Much work is exceedingly tiresome, and an excess of work causes stress and even disease. I think, however, that, provided work is not excessive in amount, even boring work is less harmful than idleness. We sometimes feel a little relief from work; at other times work gives us delight. These feelings arise according to the type of work we are doing and our ability to do that work. Work fills many hours of the day and removes the need to decide what one should do.

Part Ⅶ Writing (30 minutes, 15 points)

Directions: Write a composition in no less than 150 words on the topic: *How Can We Contribute* *to the Environmental Protection*? You should write according to the outline given below. Write your composition on the **Answer Sheet**.

环境保护已成为我们共同的责任。
你认为我们该怎样做才能降低能耗、节省资源、保护地球环境？
请举例说明。

2015年同等学力人员申请硕士学位英语水平全国统一考试

Paper One 试卷一

Part I Oral Communication

Section A

对话一

  A. 你知道哪些是残疾人车位吗？
  B. 这些标志会告诉你，你什么时候能在那儿停车、可以停多久。
  C. 那么你还需要注意街上提示停车时限的标志。

  学生：你能告诉我哪儿可以停车吗？
  员工：你开的是摩托车还是汽车？
  学生：我开的是汽车。
  员工：好的，你可以停在学生停车场或者街上。__1__
  学生：知道，我已经看到那些车位了。
  员工：嗯，当你看到有残疾人标志的蓝色车位时，不要停在那儿，除非你有特别许可证。你打算白天停车还是晚上停车？
  学生：我准备晚上停。
  员工：__2__ 你看见那些标志了吗？
  学生：是的，我看见了。
  员工：__3__

1. [正确答案] A
  [考点剖析] 根据学生的回答"Yes"，可以判断员工的话应该是一个一般疑问句。三个选项中只有 A 项"你知道哪些是残疾人车位吗？"是一般疑问句。

2. [正确答案] C
  [考点剖析] 当员工得知学生是在晚上停车时，便提醒其注意街上标有停车时限的标志。C 项"那么你还需要注意街上提示停车时限的标志"承上启下，符合语境。

3. [正确答案] B
  [考点剖析] 员工在这句话中针对上一句中学生说看到标志进行了回答，应为对标志作出进一步解释。

对话二

A. 时间和限制都印在卡上和这份宣传材料上了。
B. 我可以看一下你的驾驶证吗？
C. 你熟悉我们这儿的规则和惩罚机制吗？

学生：你好，我想办一张图书卡。
图书馆管理员：可以。我给你一张申请表，你可以直接在这儿的柜台上填写它。
学生：谢谢。我马上填。
图书馆管理员：让我看一下这个。__4__
学生：给你。
图书馆管理员：你好像填完表格了。__5__
学生：是的，我知道该怎么做。
图书馆管理员：__6__
学生：好的，我明白了。
图书馆管理员：感谢你加入图书馆，我们期待为你服务。

4. [正确答案] B
   [考点剖析] 本题解题关键在于学生的回答"给你"，说明上句图书馆管理员找学生要了某样东西，B项"我可以看一下你的驾驶证吗？"符合语境。

5. [正确答案] C
   [考点剖析] 本题解题关键同样在于学生的回答，学生回答"是的，我知道该怎么做"，说明上句应该是个一般疑问句，而C项是一般疑问句且符合语境。

6. [正确答案] A
   [考点剖析] 下句学生的回答"好的，我明白了"说明本句是图书馆管理员对某些事项的解释，A项"时间和限制都印在卡上和这份宣传材料上了"符合语境。

Section B

A. 这可骗了男孩们一阵子。
B. 我认为男孩们是不会介意的。
C. 嗯，这是因为我的英国出版商。
D. 我一直以为你叫"J. K."。

温弗里：那么，这是我们第一次见面。
罗琳：是的。
温弗里：我的制片人告诉我，你的真名是J. O.。__7__
罗琳：(笑)是的。
温弗里：J. K.是……
罗琳：__8__当出版第一本书时，他们认为"这是一本可以吸引男孩子的书"，但是又不想让男孩们知道这本书是女人写的，所以他们对我说："可以使用你的姓名首字母吗？"我说"可以"。

但我只有一个姓名首字母,没有中间名,于是我就用了我最爱的祖母的名字——凯瑟琳。

  温弗里:＿＿9＿＿

  罗琳:是的,但是不久,我的照片开始出现在出版物上,没人再能把我当成男人了。

  温弗里:＿＿10＿＿

  罗琳:是的,这对我没有负面影响,不是吗?

7. [正确答案] D

  [考点剖析] 本题解题的关键在于下文提到了"J. K. 是……",说明本句应该提到了 J. K.,而且前面一句正好提及温弗里认为作者的真名叫 J. O.。

8. [正确答案] C

  [考点剖析] 从上句"J. K. 是……"中的省略号可以看出,本句是对其名字的解释,而 because of 正好符合语境。从下文也可以看出,对话是对 J. K. 这一笔名由来的解释。

9. [正确答案] A

  [考点剖析] 本句承接上文,出版商为了吸引男孩子,让作者用了姓名的首字母,骗了男孩们一阵子,而且下文中的"不久"以及句意印证了本句的答案。

10. [正确答案] B

  [考点剖析] 前文说这个名字骗了男孩们一阵子,后文又说作者的照片被刊登在出版物上,没人再能把她当成男人了,那么本句应该是记者对该事的评价:"我认为男孩们是不会介意的"。

Part Ⅱ Vocabulary

11. [正确答案] A

  [考点类型] 名词

  [考点剖析] 题干中的 options 意为"选择,选项"。choices"选择";definitions"定义";channels"频道,海峡";reasons"原因,理由"。

12. [正确答案] D

  [考点类型] 名词

  [考点剖析] 题干中的 rays 意为"光线;射线"。minerals"矿物质,矿产";substances"物质,材料";gases"气体";beams"光线,光束"。分析句意,大气层应该是可以阻挡有害的光线。

13. [正确答案] A

  [考点类型] 形容词

  [考点剖析] 题干中的 hostile 意为"敌对的,怀有敌意的"。unfriendly"不友好的";optimistic"乐观的";impatient"不耐烦的";positive"积极的"。分析句意,因为其中一个女销售员对客户态度不好,所以经理才会责备她。

14. [正确答案] B

  [考点类型] 动词

  [考点剖析] 题干中的 carry out 意为"执行"。revise"修改,修缮";implement"执行,推进";review"复习";improve"改进,提高"。

15. [正确答案] C

[考点类型] 动词

[考点剖析] 题干中的 dispersed 意为"使分散"。arrested"逮捕";stopped"终止,停止";scattered"分散,散落";watched"观看"。分析句意,保安应该是驱散聚集的人群。

16. [正确答案] D

[考点类型] 动词短语

[考点剖析] 题干中的 insert 意为"插入"。take out"取出";turn over"反过来";track down"追踪,追查";put in"放入"。根据常识,电脑的光盘应该是要插入才能被读取。

17. [正确答案] C

[考点类型] 动词

[考点剖析] 题干中的 deteriorated 意为"恶化"。improved"改进,提高";returned"返回";worsened"恶化,变坏";changed"改变"。分析句意,病人的病情应该只能是好转或者恶化了。

18. [正确答案] A

[考点类型] 副词

[考点剖析] 题干中的 likewise 意为"同样"。also"也,同样";nonetheless"然而";furthermore"而且";otherwise"不然"。分析句意,后面应该是说回家的火车票费用我也付不起。

19. [正确答案] C

[考点类型] 介词

[考点剖析] 题干中的 beyond 意为"超出"。within"在……范围内";besides"除了";outside"在……以外";except"除了"。根据常识,目前科学家是在探索太阳系以外有没有生命存在的迹象。

20. [正确答案] B

[考点类型] 副词

[考点剖析] 题干中的 accidentally 意为"意外地,不小心地"。intentionally"有意地";unexpectedly"意外地";anxiously"焦虑地";hurriedly"急匆匆地"。根据常识,吞进鱼刺应该是意外。

Part Ⅲ   Reading Comprehension

Section A

Passage One

有时一场比赛是不够的。有时一个跑步者只是想要跑得更远。丹尼斯·马丁和布鲁克·柯伦就是如此。

68岁的马丁是一位来自纽约的退休侦探,他在第一任妻子去世后开始跑步。46岁的柯伦是一位来自亚历山大的慈善家,她喜欢通过户外跑步的方式整理她的思绪。她和马丁都善于跑步,并且希望可以做得更多。"我训练得越多,进步就越大,"柯伦说道,"但是我在跨过终点线时没什么成就感。"

· 17 ·

最终,他们在其他洲的其他国家跑马拉松赛(和长跑竞赛)。现在这两个人都名声斐然,他们两个人的里程碑事件是在七大洲都参加过26.2英里的赛跑。

在过去的20年中,一种介于运动竞赛和娱乐放松之间的"跑步度假"把远距离长跑和异地旅行结合了起来,它是由跑步文化发展而来的一部分。这种花费昂贵并且对身体素质要求很高的旅行逐渐在旅游业盛行起来。

"一开始,光跑步就足够了,"一位出版经理斯蒂恩•阿尔布雷克特森说道,"经典的马拉松就是人们的终极目标,后来有了超级马拉松,比如伦敦和纽约马拉松赛。但是当每年有9万人可以挑战这项运动时,它就变得不再令人兴奋,也没有什么挑战性了。因此,寻找新的冒险就又开始了。"

"没人能想到跑步在当今会成为一种生活方式。"波士顿马拉松巡回赛和旅行协会会长及创始人汤姆•吉利根说道。吉利根从1979年开始推广这项活动,他从某种程度上促成了这项风靡七大洲的运动。

这起始于他与一位采访者一次偶然的对话,他谈到他的公司提供除前往南极洲以外其他各洲的旅行服务。然后在1995年,马拉松巡回赛协会在乔治王岛举行了第一届南极洲马拉松比赛。在南极半岛的顶端:160名跑步者通过一艘俄国的破冰船穿越了德雷克海峡,到达了一条污迹和冰迹混合的起跑线。

21. [正确答案] D

　　[考点类型] 细节题

　　[题目翻译] 一开始,马丁跑步仅仅是为了_____。

　　　　A. 满足工作的需求

　　　　B. 赢得一场跑步比赛

　　　　C. 参加一项慈善活动

　　　　D. 摆脱悲伤

　　[考点剖析] 第二段第一句 Martin, 68, a retired detective from New York City, took up running after his first wife died 已经交代出他开始跑步是在第一任妻子去世之后。故 D 项"摆脱悲伤"为正确选项。

22. [正确答案] B

　　[考点类型] 细节题

　　[题目翻译] 文中马丁和柯伦是_____的好例子。

　　　　A. 在七大洲举办的26.2英里赛跑中获胜的人

　　　　B. 那些享受长跑并把其当作一种生活方式的人们

　　　　C. 对自己的成绩表示满意的赛跑者

　　　　D. 在退休后过着积极生活的老人们

　　[考点剖析] 从第四段第一句 They are part of a phenomenon... which combine distance running with travel to exotic places 可知他俩很好地把远距离长跑和异地旅行结合了起来。B 项的意思是他们"享受长跑并把其当作一种生活方式",与题意相符。

23. [正确答案] A

　　[考点类型] 细节题

[题目翻译] 旅游业的一个新趋势是_____的发展。

A. 富有挑战性的跑步度假

B. 专业跑步比赛

C. 南极洲旅游市场

D. 昂贵的旅行

[考点剖析] 根据第四段最后一句 These trips, as expensive as they are physically challenging, are a growing and competitive market in the travel industry 可以得知，马拉松跑步已经变成了旅游业的新增长点，故 A 项"富有挑战性的跑步度假"为正确选项。

24. [正确答案] A

[考点类型] 细节题

[题目翻译] 经典的马拉松不再能满足一些人是因为_____。

A. 它不具有足够的挑战性

B. 它可能是艰难和危险的

C. 它是一项过于激烈的竞争

D. 它已经吸引了太多的人

[考点剖析] 根据第五段最后两句 But when 90,000 people a year can take that challenge, it is no longer exciting and adventurous. Hence, the search for new adventures began 得知，当每年有 9 万人可以挑战这项运动以后，它就变得没什么挑战性了。故 A 项"它不具有足够的挑战性"为正确选项。

25. [正确答案] D

[考点类型] 推理题

[题目翻译] 第一次在乔治王岛进行的南极洲马拉松巡回赛表明_____。

A. 国际合作对于这样的一项运动是必需的

B. 跑步度假不仅昂贵而且挑战体力

C. 马拉松巡回赛协会是旅游业的引领者

D. 冒险式的跑步变得越来越受欢迎

[考点剖析] 从最后一段 Off the tip of the Antarctic Peninsula; 160 runners got to the starting line of a dirt- and ice-trail route via a Russian icebreaker through the Drake Passage 可以推断出马拉松比赛难度越来越大、越来越富有挑战性，却仍然吸引着人们参加。故 D 项为正确选项。

Passage Two

20 世纪 70 年代前,大学生都被当作孩子对待。许多大学都有"替代家长制度"。"替代家长"是一个拉丁词汇,意思是"站在家长的角度",即除家长以外的人以孩子的利益为出发点为其负责。

这个想法是很久前由英国普通法衍生而出的,用于界定老师对其学生的责任。许多年来,美国法院支持这个"替代家长制度",如 1913 年戈特对伯利亚学院一案。

戈特在校外有一家餐厅。伯利亚学院威胁学生如果他们不在学校经营的餐厅就餐就会被开除。肯塔基高级法院决定根据"替代家长制度"来裁决。

"替代家长制度"意味着学院里的男女学生须住在不同的楼里。女生在晚上十点或十一点前必须返回宿舍。

但是在20世纪60年代,学生开始抗议类似的规定和限制。同时,法院开始支持那些由于政治或社会异议受到惩罚的学生。

1960年,亚拉巴马州立大学开除了6个参加民权游行的学生。这些学生起诉了学校并且胜诉。在此以后维护"替代家长制度"变得越来越难。

在那时,21岁以下的学生不算成人。此后,在1971年进行第24次宪法修定时,公民的选举权年龄被设置在18岁。因此,"替代家长制度"不再真正适用。

渐渐地,学院开始不再把学生当作孩子,而是当作成年人来对待。学生们开始被视为教育服务的消费者。

加里·迪克斯坦是俄亥俄州代顿市莱特州立大学助理副校长,他说"替代家长制度"并不是真的不存在了。它只是看起来不同了。他说,当今的家长往往会过于介入学生的生活。他们就是所谓的"空降家长"。他们经常管教孩子。加里·迪克斯坦说,这些家长有可能会质疑一些决策,尤其是关于安全问题和学业的决策。他们想要确保他们投入的金钱没有被浪费。

26. [正确答案] D

   [考点类型] 细节题

   [题目翻译] 在20世纪70年代前,许多大学采用"替代家长制度"是因为_____。

   A. 他们可以代替父母

   B. 为了孩子的利益,父母要求他们这么做的

   C. 这是由英国的大学建立的一个传统

   D. 大学生被认为太年轻,不该被当作成人来对待

   [考点剖析] 第一段第一句 Before the 1970s, college students were treated as children 指出那时候大学生还被认为是孩子,故 D 项正确。

27. [正确答案] A

   [考点类型] 细节题

   [题目翻译] 在1913年戈特对伯利亚学院的案件中,谁获胜了?

   A. 伯利亚学院。

   B. 戈特。

   C. 双赢。

   D. 学生们。

   [考点剖析] 第三段第三句 The Kentucky high court decided that *in loco parentis* justified that rule 明确指出法院是根据"替代家长制度"来裁决,因此作为家长方的学院获得了胜利。

28. [正确答案] C

   [考点类型] 词汇题

   [题目翻译] 在第五段中,dissent 的意思是"_____"。

   A. 极端行为

   B. 违反法律

   C. 强烈的异议

   D. 错误的举动

[考点剖析] 根据第五段 But in the 1960s, students began to protest rules and restrictions like these. At the same time, courts began to support students who were being punished for political and social dissent 判断 C 项"强烈的异议"为正确选项。

29. [正确答案] C
    [考点类型] 细节题
    [题目翻译] 在 1960 年,法院判定亚拉巴马州立大学_____。
       A. 没有权利开除学生
       B. 开除学生是合法的
       C. 不应该干涉学生的日常生活
       D. 应该支持民权游行
    [考点剖析] 根据第六段前两句 In 1960, Alabama State College expelled six students who took part in a civil rights demonstration. They sued the school and won 判断 C 项"不应干涉学生的日常生活"符合题意。

30. [正确答案] B
    [考点类型] 细节题
    [题目翻译] 根据加里·迪克斯坦的观点,如今的"空降家长"_____。
       A. 对学校的管理不放心
       B. 监管孩子的生活和学习
       C. 不再像以前那么关心孩子的教育了
       D. 对孩子的教育有着不同的看法
    [考点剖析] 根据最后一段最后三句 They always seem to hover over their children. Gary Dickstein says these parents are likely to question decisions, especially about safety issues and grades. They want to make sure their financial investment is not being wasted 可知"空降家长"经常管教学生,质疑学校关于学生安全和学业的一些决策,因此 B 项"监管孩子的生活和学习"为正确选项。

Passage Three

我们往往把植物当作自然界的家具。他们不会移动、不会发声,看起来似乎不会对任何事情有所反应——至少反应没有那么快。但是通常情况下,我们人类对世界的看法错了很多。植物彼此间一直在交流,它们的语言是化学物质。

多年来,科学家发表报告称,从树到番茄等不同类型的植物通过向空气中释放化合物来帮助邻近的植物。这些化学物质是植物发出的一种警告,目的都是传播一株植物生病的信息以便其他植物可以进行自我防御。但是有关植物如何接收和根据这些信号作出反应仍是个谜。

本周,日本的研究员在《美国科学院院报》中提供了一些解释。他们识别出了一种化学信息,并且追踪了从植物释放这种信息到其起作用的整个过程。

科学家观察了曾遭受过一种常见虫害——毛虫虫害的番茄植株。一开始,他们在两个用管子连接的塑料容器里种上植物。一棵遭受过虫害的植物被放置在上风口,没有遭受过虫害的其他植物被放在下风口。下风口的植物后期被放上毛虫。结果显示那些之前被放在遭受过虫害植物旁边的植物能够更好地抵御虫害。

　　研究人员也研究了遭受过虫害和未遭受过虫害的叶片。他们发现遭受过虫害的叶片含有更多的某种化合物。这种化合物叫作 Hex Vic。当科学家把这种物质喂给毛虫时,毛虫的存活率降低了17%。科学家发现了 Hex Vic 的来源,并且把它喷在健康的植物上。这些植物就可以自己产生杀死毛虫的 Hex Vic 了。研究者确认未遭虫害的植物必须建立起自己的武器以抵御病虫灾害。他们如何知道何时开始防御呢?他们是被友善的植物邻居们提醒了。

　　这是个复杂的故事,并且它可能发生在番茄以外的其他植物上。它可能包含更多不为我们所知的化学信号。现在我们知道植物不仅会互相交流,还会互相照顾。

31. [正确答案] D
　　[考点类型] 细节题
　　[题目翻译] 作者在第一段中想要强调什么?
　　　　A. 植物如何交流还是个谜。
　　　　B. 植物交谈被给予足够的关注。
　　　　C. 植物是自然界的家具。
　　　　D. 植物可以互相交流。
　　[考点剖析] 文章第一段开头说我们认为植物是没有反应、不会动的东西,但本段最后两句否定了这个观点。D 项"植物可以互相交流",符合题意。

32. [正确答案] A
　　[考点类型] 细节题
　　[题目翻译] 根据第二段,我们还不知道的是_____。
　　　　A. 植物是如何接收并处理来自邻居的信号的
　　　　B. 为什么植物把化学信息传递给它们的邻居
　　　　C. 多少种植物在空气中释放化合物
　　　　D. 植物是否向它们的邻居发送化学物质以作为警告信号
　　[考点剖析] 根据第二段最后一句 But exactly how plants receive and act on many of these signals is still mysterious 可知,植物如何接收和处理这些信号仍是个谜,这说明我们对这一问题尚无定论,A 项符合题意。

33. [正确答案] A
　　[考点类型] 细节题
　　[题目翻译] 实验中的番茄植株被_____。
　　　　A. 分开放置,但空气相通
　　　　B. 暴露于不同种类的害虫中
　　　　C. 同时暴露于害虫中
　　　　D. 一起放在一个密闭的分隔间
　　[考点剖析] 从第四段第二句 To start out, they grew plants in two plastic compartments connected by a tube 可知番茄植株被放置在不同的容器里,但是它们通过管子相通。故 A 项符合题意。

34. [正确答案] B
　　[考点类型] 细节题

[题目翻译] 实验显示遭受虫害的植物通过_____来帮助邻居。
A. 产生更多的 Hex Vic 来吸引害虫
B. 在空气中释放 Hex Vic 来提醒它们
C. 让它们知道怎样产生 Hex Vic
D. 产生足够的 Hex Vic 来杀死害虫

[考点剖析] 根据第五段前六句 The researchers also studied leaves from exposed and unexposed plants… Those plants were then able to start producing the caterpillar-killing Hex Vic 可知,植物会释放一种叫 Hex Vic 的物质来提醒别的植物。B 项"在空气中释放 Hex Vic 来提醒它们"符合题意。

35. [正确答案] C
[考点类型] 主旨题
[题目翻译] 文章的最佳标题可能是什么?
A. 植物的生存
B. 植物世界
C. 会说话的植物
D. 植物害虫杀手

[考点剖析] 本文讨论了科学家有关植物信息传递的实验。通过实验,我们发现植物之间不仅会通过发送化学信号进行交流,在遭遇威胁时,它们还会发送化学信号让邻居们警觉起来。文章最后也总结植物不仅会互相交流,还会互相照顾,故 C 项"会说话的植物"为最佳标题。

Passage Four

这个月月初发布的一项生活质量排名显示,温哥华是美洲最适宜居住的地方。这座城市因为其干净的空气、宽敞的住宅以及周末潜在的航海和滑雪时间而经常名列榜首。但是由于变得越来越拥挤,它作为一个宜居城市的地位受到了威胁。在未来 30 年里,预计将会有额外 100 万名居民定居到大温哥华地区。城市的道路已经很难承载已有的 230 万人口了,而新的人口又会带来更多的汽车、自行车和卡车。

温哥华市长提出了一项提议,以防止情况恶化。这项提议包括 2 300 公里的车道、公交线路和自行车车道的升级。公交车数量将在原来 1 830 辆的基础上增加 400 辆。在温哥华和其北部富有的郊区之间,将会有更多的火车和"海上巴士"渡口。为了达成这些目标,居民们必须投票同意将销售税从 7%增加到 7.5%。民意调查显示,人们将投反对票。

每个人都同意这个城市需要更有效率的公共交通系统。温哥华北有大山,南接美国,西邻太平洋,温哥华只能向唯一有土地的方向开发,也就是菲沙河谷,这个地方多年以前大多是农田。那里的道路十分拥挤。

然而上班族对于当地官员的抱怨可能超过他们对交通堵塞的厌恶。经营该地区公共交通的 TransLink 不受纳税人的欢迎。去年夏天,天空列车(轻轨系统)因为机械或电气故障而暂停行驶,这在一个星期内发生了两次。被困在车厢内的通勤者除了通过推特来表达愤怒,什么都做不了。这种事情让选民更加不愿意支付 75 亿加元去支付为期十年的交通升级的成本。

一名在 TransLink 工作的交通顾问托德·利特曼认为,即使人们都在抱怨,温哥华的交通系统仍然是相当不错的、整合良好的工程。"如果温哥华想要维持它那人们最向往之地的名声的话,这种交通系统的升级是极其重要的。"他说。

36. [正确答案] A

    [考点类型] 细节题

    [题目翻译] 对温哥华作为一个宜居城市造成威胁的最大问题是_____。

    A. 越来越拥挤

    B. 气候变化

    C. 缺少土地

    D. 缺少钱

    [考点剖析] 根据第一段第三句 But its status as a liveable city is threatened by worsening congestion 可知,温哥华的宜居地位受到了威胁,是因为城市变得越来越拥挤。

37. [正确答案] D

    [考点类型] 细节题

    [题目翻译] 温哥华市长提出的升级提议可能会被居民拒绝是因为_____。

    A. 他们不想要更多的人搬入

    B. 他们不愿意搬到新地方

    C. 升级将减少他们的生活空间

    D. 升级将增加他们的财务负担

    [考点剖析] 根据第二段最后两句 To get all that, residents must vote to accept an increase in sales tax, from 7% to 7.5%. Polls suggest they will vote no 可知,升级交通系统就意味着要增加销售税,所以人们不愿意。

38. [正确答案] A

    [考点类型] 推理题

    [题目翻译] 温哥华进一步开发的唯一方向是向着_____。

    A. 东部　　　　B. 西部　　　　C. 南部　　　　D. 北部

    [考点剖析] 根据第三段最后两句 Confined by mountains to the north, the United States to the south and the Pacific Ocean to the west, Vancouver has spread in the only direction where there is still land, into the Fraser Valley, which just a few decades ago was mostly farmland. The road is often overcrowded 可知,温哥华的北边有山,南邻美国,西边有太平洋,所以只能往东边扩展。

39. [正确答案] B

    [考点类型] 细节题

    [题目翻译] 在第四段中,TransLink 作为一个_____的例子被提出。

    A. 世界著名的交通公司

    B. 当地居民对官员的抱怨

    C. 当地为提高公共交通能力所做的努力

    D. 加剧的交通拥堵

    [考点剖析] 根据第四段前两句 Yet commuters' suspicion of local bureaucrats may exceed their dislike of congestion. TransLink, which runs public transport in the region, is unloved by taxpayers 可知，人们抱怨当地官员，后面 TransLink 公司是作为论据出现的。

40. [正确答案] D

[考点类型] 推理题

[题目翻译] 根据托德·利特曼所说，升级的提议_____。

A. 将解决交通问题

B. 将对当地的经济有利

C. 满足交通公司的需求

D. 值得公众支持

[考点剖析] 根据最后一段最后一句"These upgrades are all-important if Vancouver wants to maintain its reputation for being a destination others want to go to," He says 可知，如果温哥华想要维持它那人们最向往之地的名声的话，这种交通系统的升级是极其重要的，所以他认为人们应该支持政府升级交通系统。

Section B

到20世纪90年代末，在健怡可口可乐被首次推出15年之后，可口可乐公司最畅销的低卡路里饮料的销量似乎降下来了。

然而，在之后的十年里，无糖汽水的销量增长超过了30%，在2009年，其销售额首次超过了85亿美元。但是，美国人对于健怡可口可乐的热爱又开始枯竭了，并且这一次可能是永久性的。

无糖汽水热度的消退不仅仅发生在美国，还发生在全世界。但是无糖可乐在美国的未来堪忧。

低热量的苏打汽水与在美国消费者中流行的两个趋势作艰难斗争。第一个就是自2000年以来，汽水的总销售量一直在下降。无糖可乐虽然是无糖、无热量的，但它依然是汽水，而事实上美国人越来越不喜欢喝汽水了。

第二点，也可能是相对重要的趋势——人们越来越不相信人工甜味剂了。产业分析家霍华德·泰尔福德说："消费者对于甜味剂的态度确实发生了改变。关于人工甜味剂现在存在着一个非常负面的观点。这个产业仍在尝试解决这个问题。"

评论1

我以前也是很爱喝无糖汽水的，但是现在完全戒掉了。我真的认为喝汽水是上瘾的，我很高兴我再也不想喝它了。

评论2

汽水销售量的降低有可能是因为软饮的价格涨得太快了。

评论3

我爱喝无糖饮料！我不健康吗？谁知道呢？但我保证我比大部分43岁的人都更健康。

评论4

这篇文章太傻、太肤浅了。汽水的销售量减少仅仅是因为瓶装水和能量饮料的消费激增。

评论5

随着人们越来越认识到健康的重要性，人们更趋向于喝低糖、低碳酸、少人工甜味剂的饮料。

41. [正确答案] C
    [考点类型] 细节题
    [题目翻译] 无糖汽水的销售情况怎么样？
              A. 它从2000年起开始逐渐下降。
              B. 它在20世纪90年代下降但现在又在上升。
              C. 它在21世纪初达到顶峰,但是从那以后开始下降。
              D. 它从20世纪90年代起一直在下降。
    [考点剖析] 根据第二段第二句 In 2009, sales pushed above $8.5 billion for the first time. But America's thirst for Diet Coke is running dry again—and this time it could be for good 可知,无糖汽水的销售情况在2009年达到高峰,但之后就再次下降。

42. [正确答案] C
    [考点类型] 细节题
    [题目翻译] 作者认为无糖汽水的销售前景如何？
              A. 将会继续下降。
              B. 不久会转好。
              C. 很难说。
              D. 可能有起有落。
    [考点剖析] 根据第三段第二句 But the future of diet colas is particularly cloudy in the United States 可知,无糖汽水的销售前景是模糊的、不清楚的,即未来是无法确定的。

43. [正确答案] D
    [考点类型] 细节题
    [题目翻译] 哪个评论给出了放弃无糖汽水的个人理由？
              A. 评论5。   B. 评论4。   C. 评论3。   D. 评论1。
    [考点剖析] 评论1说:"我以前也是很爱喝无糖汽水的,但是现在完全戒掉了。我真的认为喝汽水是上瘾的,我很高兴我再也不想喝它了。"该评论以自己为例,给出了戒掉无糖汽水的理由。

44. [正确答案] D
    [考点类型] 细节题
    [题目翻译] 哪个评论支持作者的观点？
              A. 评论2。   B. 评论3。   C. 评论4。   D. 评论5。
    [考点剖析] 根据第四段最后一句 Diet sodas, though they might come sugar- and calorie-free, are still sodas, something Americans are proving less and less interested in drinking 可知,人们因为健康意识不愿意喝含糖、热量高的饮料。这即为作者的观点。评论5 As people learn more about health and wellness, they will consume less sugar, less soda, less artificial sweeteners 表达的是同样的观点。

45. [正确答案] B
    [考点类型] 细节题
    [题目翻译] 哪个评论不赞成作者对于无糖汽水销售量下降的原因分析？
              A. 评论3和5。   B. 评论2和4。   C. 评论1和4。   D. 评论2和3。

[考点剖析] 文中作者认为汽水销售量降低的原因是人们越来越关注健康问题。评论2 Perhaps the slowdown has something more to do with the skyrocketing cost of soft drinks 认为其原因是软饮价格上涨过快。评论4 最后一句 The reason for the fall-off is simply the explosion in consumption of bottled waters and energy drinks 认为其原因是其他饮料的消费激增。这两个评论均与作者的观点不一致。

Part Ⅳ　Cloze

当被问到关于令人不安的新闻对孩子的影响时,一位妈妈表示:"我11岁的女儿不喜欢看这种新闻。看到这种新闻她会做噩梦。有一次,她看到一则关于一个人用刀刺杀亲人的新闻,晚上就梦到自己也被杀死了。"另一位受访者说:"我6岁的侄女看到了关于别的城市刮龙卷风的新闻,之后的几个星期,她都在害怕。她会给我打电话,深信龙卷风要来了,她会死。"

你认为令人不安的新闻会吓到孩子吗?在一项调查中,大约40%的父母说他们的孩子在看到这种新闻时会感到不安。更有甚者,孩子们会害怕有相似的事情发生在他们自己或者他们所爱的人身上。为什么会这样?有一个原因是,孩子与大人解读新闻的方式不同。例如,如果新闻被重复报道,那么小孩子会认为这种悲剧一直在重复发生。

另一个原因是,日常播报这种令人不安的新闻会影响孩子的世界观。的确,我们生活在一个"难以应对的危急时代",但是孩子们不停地接收到这些令人不安的新闻会使得他们长期处于恐惧之中。凯泽家庭基金会观察到,"那些看过太多电视新闻的孩子往往会高估社会犯罪率,并且可能会认为这个世界比实际更危险"。

46. [正确答案] B
　　[解析过程] 根据上下文,空格所在句的大意应为孩子看了不好的新闻后会感到害怕,所以此处应填表示害怕的词,四个选项中只有B项"噩梦"会让人感到害怕。

47. [正确答案] A
　　[解析过程] 此处应表达在看了不好的新闻之后的几个星期中,孩子都会感到害怕。B项、C项表示之前,可排除,而D项表示的是过了几个星期才开始害怕,不符合题意。

48. [正确答案] D
　　[解析过程] 根据上下文,可知此处应为她会给我打电话,would在这里表示意愿。

49. [正确答案] C
　　[解析过程] 根据上下文,前文中提到如 nightmares、frighten 等表现孩子害怕情绪的词汇,所以此处也应该是害怕的情绪,upset"不安的"符合语境。

50. [正确答案] C
　　[解析过程] 此处先说孩子们不安,后说害怕事情发生在自己身上,这两种是递进的情绪,所以这里是说孩子们的恐惧情绪越来越严重。all the more"更加"符合语境。

51. [正确答案] B
　　[解析过程] 根据后文,如果新闻被重复报道,那么孩子会认为这种悲剧也一直在重复发生。所以孩子与大人解读新闻的方式不同,interpret"说明,解释"符合语境。

52. [正确答案] A
　　[解析过程] 根据上下文,文章说的是令人不安的新闻,tragedy"悲剧"最适合文章主题。

53. [正确答案] B
　　[解析过程] view of the world 是固定搭配,意为"世界观"。

54. [正确答案] C

　　[解析过程] 根据上下文,让孩子看令人不安的新闻,会影响他们的世界观。give up"放弃";stick to"坚持";deal with"处理,对付";set forth"启程;详尽地解释",只有 deal with 符合语境。

55. [正确答案] D

　　[解析过程] 此处意为孩子们如果看太多新闻往往会高估社会犯罪率,tend to"倾向于,往往"符合语境。

Part V　Text Completion

Text One

　　想象这种情况:你从商店买了一件有问题的商品,于是你拿着商品回商店投诉。你直接去找了店员,并且告诉他你的问题。他却告诉你他无法帮助你,这使你更加生气了,所以你开始辱骂这个可怜的店员。但这并没有任何用处,例如得不到赔偿,或是得不到退款。如果你只是直接向你遇见的第一个店员抱怨,那也许是在浪费时间,因为他也无力采取任何行动。所以你要学会的重要一课就是,一定要直接去找有权力做决定的相关工作人员。

56. [正确答案] A

　　[解析过程] make sb. + adj."使某人变得怎么样"。这里应填形容词,三个选项中只有 A 项是形容词,并且符合语义。

57. [正确答案] B

　　[解析过程] like"像;如同",后应填入名词性短语,但又因为此处应填与 compensation 搭配的动词,所以此处填入动名词 getting,与 compensation 搭配,意为"得到赔偿"。

58. [正确答案] C

　　[解析过程] 固定搭配。take any action 意为"采取任何行动"。

59. [正确答案] A

　　[解析过程] 本句由后半句对店员态度不好可以推断出前半句为原因,因为生气所以态度不好。

60. [正确答案] B

　　[解析过程] 由前句中提到得不到任何帮助(no favours),再根据上下文可推断出,这里需要的帮助是退款或是得到赔偿。

61. [正确答案] C

　　[解析过程] 此处为动词不定式作定语,意为"他们无力做……",take any action 意为"采取任何行动",符合题意。

Text Two

　　一项新的研究表明有快乐的朋友的人,自己也很有可能变得快乐,而且朋友之间的距离越近,这种快乐的相互影响力就越强。

　　例如,如果距离一个人 1 500 米之内住着一个快乐的朋友,那么这个人感到快乐的可能性增加 20%。而有一个快乐的邻居,一个人感到快乐的可能性会增加 34%。这种朋友间快乐感的影响力可以持续近一年。

研究者发现快乐的确是可以传染的。悲伤也会在朋友之间传播，但没有快乐那么有影响力。

62. [正确答案] D

[解析过程] 此处为 be likely to do sth.，意为"有可能做……"。

63. [正确答案] A

[解析过程] 根据上下文，此处应为对快乐可以互相影响的进一步解释，故可以推断出这里是表述快乐相互影响的范围，此处应为"the + 比较级，the + 比较级"结构，意为"越……越……"。

64. [正确答案] B

[解析过程] as much as 是"和……差不多"的意思，本题可用排除法，其他选项在语法上都不与 happiness 搭配。

65. [正确答案] C

[解析过程] lasted 为"持续"的意思，其后应为持续的时间。

66. [正确答案] B

[解析过程] 此处应和后半句 the larger the effect 放在一起看，为"the + 比较级，the + 比较级"结构，意为"越……越……"。

67. [正确答案] A

[解析过程] 此处为 a person was… 和 likely to do sth. 搭配，意为"人有可能做什么事"。

68. [正确答案] D

[解析过程] 根据上下文可知前面说的是快乐在范围方面的感染力，所以此处应为快乐在时间方面的影响力。

69. [正确答案] C

[解析过程] 根据上下文，这里是对比悲伤和快乐的感染力，意为"悲伤也会在朋友之间传播，但没有快乐那么有影响力"。

Text Three

除了来自市场营销的外部压力，我们自己的情感和习惯也会造成过度消费。以下一些建议可以帮助你控制自己的花销。

首先，抑制冲动消费。你是否很享受逛街、买特价商品带来的兴奋感？如果是这样，你往往会因为冲动而消费。为了抑制这种冲动，你可以让自己平静下来，并且思考一下购买、拥有并且维护你计划买的东西所带来的长期后果。停下来，并且回忆一下上一次令你感到后悔的冲动消费。在你做出最终决定之前，给自己一段"冷静期"。

70. [正确答案] A

[解析过程] 本句可由句意判断出，上一次是怎么样的冲动消费，填入 later regretted 后意为"让你感到后悔的冲动消费"，也可根据 past 判断应填过去式。

71. [正确答案] C

[解析过程] 此处情态动词 may 后应为动词原形。

72. [正确答案] B

[解析过程] keep doing sth. 意为"持续做某事",选现在分词 spending。

73. [正确答案] C

[解析过程] 此处为 help sb. do sth. ,故排除 B 项。根据上下文,C 项符合题意,意为"帮助你控制自己的花销"。

74. [正确答案] B

[解析过程] 根据上下文,此处应为很享受逛街、买特价商品带来的兴奋感,这是冲动消费的一种表现。

75. [正确答案] A

[解析过程] 根据上下文,此处应为对于冲动消费给出的建议,意为"停下来,并且回忆一下上一次令你感到后悔的冲动消费"。

Paper Two 试卷二

Part Ⅵ Translation

1. Should work be placed among the causes of happiness or be regarded as a burden?

   [结构分析] 这是一个一般疑问句,并使用了被动语态。

   [词义推敲] be regarded as 是"被认为……"的意思。

   [参考译文] 我们应该把工作当成快乐的源泉,还是视它为一种负担呢?

2. Much work is exceedingly tiresome, and an excess of work causes stress and even disease.

   [结构分析] 这是一个并列句,以逗号隔开。

   [词义推敲] exceedingly "极度地;极其";tiresome "烦人的;无聊的"。

   [参考译文] 大量的工作让人心情烦闷,超负荷的工作给人造成巨大压力,甚而积劳成疾。

3. I think, however, that, provided work is not excessive in amount, even boring work is less harmful than idleness.

   [结构分析] 这是一个主从复合句,注意此处的 provided 是 if 的意思,引导一个条件状语从句。

   [词义推敲] excessive "过度的,过量的";idleness "懒惰,无聊"。

   [参考译文] 然而,我认为,只要工作不过量,即便没什么乐趣,也比无聊空虚对身体有益。

4. We sometimes feel a little relief from work; at other times work gives us delight.

   [结构分析] 这句话以";"隔开,是并列句。

   [词义推敲] relief "减轻,解除";delight "快乐"。

   [参考译文] 有时我们从工作中获得些许慰藉;有时工作给我们带来快乐。

5. These feelings arise according to the type of work we are doing and our ability to do that work.

   [结构分析] 这是一个主从复合句,定语从句"we are doing"修饰主句的宾语"work","to do that work"作后置定语,修饰"ability"。

   [词义推敲] according to "根据"。

   [参考译文] 这些感觉的产生取决于我们所从事工作的类型以及我们自身的工作能力。

6. Work fills many hours of the day and removes the need to decide what one should do.

[结构分析]在该句中,"to decide what one should do"作后置定语修饰"need",decide 又引导了一个宾语从句"what one should do"。

[词义推敲]fill"填满;填充"。

[参考译文]工作占去了我们一天当中大部分的时间,也不允许我们决定应该做什么。

Part Ⅶ Writing

这是一篇议论文,且给出了提纲。我们可以根据提纲列出的三点思路去展开描述:第一段,提出观点,环境保护是我们共同的责任。第二段,对上段的观点给出具体的措施。第三段,举例说明,并对全篇做一个总结,呼应观点。

Nowadays, more and more people are concerned about the problem of environmental protection, for the pollution has brought us so many bad influences. It is important for us to realize that it is everyone's duty to protect our environment.

To cope with this nation wide problem, our government has started to take a series of effective measures. The most effective way is to save energy and reduce carbon emission. Because every year billions of tons of carbon dioxide are emitted into the air, which in part results in the global warming and climate change.

For me, I am trying to make my own contributions. Firstly, I go to work by bus instead of driving. Secondly, I am getting to form the habit of saving water and electricity. For example, when I brush my teeth and wash my hands, I will never leave the water running all the time. What's more, I even recommend my relatives and friends to do so. By now my ways have been working perfectly and efficiently.

这篇范文围绕提纲,紧扣主题,语言简洁明了,文章思路清晰,没有任何语法和拼写错误,让人印象良好。我们来看一下内容:

第一段:模板例句套用合理,指出越来越多的人正在关注环境保护问题,并在段落最后提出自己的观点——环境保护是我们共同的责任。

第二段:用 to 引导的目的状语,引出具体的措施,并用一个非限制性定语从句说明理由。

第三段:结合自身情况,举例说明。"Firstly, Secondly, What's more",语言简洁,层次分明;"For example"引出自身的例子。

整篇文章有理有据,思路简单清晰,没有什么复杂的单词和华丽的辞藻,可见在考试作文上要想拿到理想的分数,最主要的是切合题意、紧扣提纲、逻辑清楚,同时保证语法和单词正确。

2016年同等学力人员申请硕士学位
英语水平全国统一考试

Paper One 试卷一 (100 minutes)

Part I Oral Communication (15 minutes, 10 points)

Section A

Directions: *In this section there are two incomplete dialogues and each dialogue has three blanks and three choices A, B and C, taken from the dialogue. Fill in each of the blanks with one of the choices to complete the dialogue and mark your answer on the **Answer Sheet**.*

Dialogue One

A. Will you take care of that for me?
B. Does it have anything valuable inside?
C. How do you want to send it?

Clerk: May I help you?
Customer: Yes. I'd like to send this letter to my family in England.
Clerk: Did you write your return address on the envelope?
Customer: Yes, I did.
Clerk: __1__
Customer: I guess I'll send it airmail.
Clerk: __2__
Customer: Yes. I enclosed a check and some photographs.
Clerk: Then you'd better send it by registered mail.
Customer: That's a good idea. __3__
Clerk: I'm sorry, sir. You'll have to take your letter to the next window.

Dialogue Two

A. You can't even stay in the sun for five minutes.
B. I guess so.
C. You want my advice?

Winnie: Oh, man! Nobody can stand this kind of scorching heat.

· 1 ·

Marc: Absolutely! __4__

Winnie: Anyway I guess this afternoon there's nothing we can do but stay home.

Marc: __5__ I don't want to be taken to the hospital for heat exhaustion or something.

Winnie: __6__ Drink a lot of liquids and spare yourself the worst of the heat!

Marc: Yeah, you're right. Got to drink a lot of fluids.

Section B

Directions: *In this section there is one incomplete interview which has four blanks and four choices A, B, C and D, taken from the interview. Fill in each of the blanks with one of the choices to complete the interview and mark your answer on the **Answer Sheet**.*

  A. I literally can't stop.

  B. But now I don't need to worry any more.

  C. You're known as the first billionaire author here.

  D. But that's not just about money.

Interviewer: You have published six popular books. __7__

Interviewee: Yeah.

Interviewer: So how has being the first billionaire author affected your perception of yourself?

Interviewee: I dress better. Well, you can definitely afford better clothes. __8__ I think the single biggest thing that money gave me—and obviously I came from a place where I was a single mother and it really was hand to mouth at one point. It was literally as poor as you can get without being homeless at one point. __9__ Never.

Interviewer: Are you in a place now where you can accept that you will always be rich?

Interviewee: No.

Interviewer: And will you be writing more?

Interviewee: Oh, definitely. I can't, yeah, __10__ Well, I mean, you could tie my hands to my sides, I suppose, but I have to write. For my own mental health, I need to write.

Part II Vocabulary (10 minutes, 10 points)

Directions: *In this part there are ten sentences, each with one word or phrase underlined. Choose the one from the four choices marked A, B, C and D that best keeps the meaning of the sentence. Mark your answer on the **Answer Sheet**.*

11. Such experience helps promote one's <u>alertness</u> to other cultures, as well as a better appreciation of one's own culture.

  A. preference   B. adjustment   C. sensitivity   D. response

12. If you always try to <u>find fault with</u> others, it means that you have gained another shortcoming.

  A. ignore   B. criticize   C. impress   D. follow

13. The election will be <u>brought forward</u> to June as so many people are on holiday in July.

  A. prolonged   B. adapted   C. postponed   D. advanced

14. As to the question of refreshments, I should think orange juice and potato chips will be sufficient.
    A. enough   B. abundant   C. satisfying   D. proper
15. Watching these kids grow brings me satisfaction that is difficult to surpass.
    A. obtain   B. exceed   C. describe   D. forget
16. The journal published a series of articles that reviewed the prospects for a new era of "genetic medicine".
    A. background   B. exploration   C. survey   D. outlook
17. If you don't slow down and take a break, you'll be burned out very quickly.
    A. distressed   B. anxious   C. exhausted   D. upset
18. Following our merging with Smith brothers, the new company will, from now on, be known as Smith and Murphy Inc.
    A. cooperation   B. meeting   C. agreement   D. combination
19. Only native-born citizens are eligible for the U.S. Presidency.
    A. required   B. qualified   C. selected   D. elected
20. It was 38 degrees and the air conditioning barely cooled the room.
    A. simply   B. quickly   C. hardly   D. strongly

Part III Reading Comprehension (45 minutes, 25 points)

Section A

Directions: *In this section, there are four passages followed by questions or unfinished statements, each with four suggested answers A, B, C and D. Choose the best answer and mark your answer on the* ***Answer Sheet***.

Passage One

What did you study at university? If it was something along the lines of law or business, you might want to look away now. That's because according to new research, which has found a link between our university subjects and our personalities, you have selfish, uncooperative tendencies and are not very in touch with your feelings. On the plus side, you're probably the life and soul of a party, the findings suggest.

Researchers analyzed data from more than 13,000 university students who were involved in 12 separate studies. From this, they discovered a correlation between the "Big Five" major personality traits and the subjects they were enrolled on.

For example, those studying law, economics, political science and medicine tended to be much more outgoing than those taking other subjects, the study found. But when it came to "agreeableness"—the tendency towards being helpful, generous and considerate—the lawyers scored particularly low, as did business and economics students.

Arts and humanities students, as well as those studying psychology and politics scored highly for openness, meaning they were curious, imaginative and in touch with their inner feelings, while economists, engineers, lawyers and scientists scored comparatively low. However, the arts and humanities students also tended to be less conscientious and more nervous, typically exhibiting signs of anxiety and moodiness. Psychology students were not far behind arts and humanities students for these traits.

Study author Anna Vedel, from the University of Aarhus in Denmark, said she was surprised by the results. "The effect sizes show that the differences found are not trivial, far from," she said. "On the more humorous side they do confirm our more or less prejudicial stereotypes of the disturbed psychologist, the withdrawn natural scientist, the cynical economist."

And she said that the findings could help those school pupils who currently have no idea what to study at university, as well as helping academics to plan their lectures. "I'm not arguing that these results should play a major role in either guidance or selection, but it might provide some inspiration for students that are in doubt about study choices and want to make a choice based on more than abilities, for example," said Dr Vedel. "Or teachers might better understand their student population."

21. The first paragraph implies that law or business students may _____.
   A. be amused by the research
   B. be interested in the research
   C. dislike the research
   D. enjoy the research

22. According to the research, law students scored particularly low in the trait of _____.
   A. generosity   B. openness   C. anxiety   D. selfishness

23. The word "conscientious" (Para. 4) probably means "_____".
   A. moody   B. sensitive   C. curious   D. careful

24. Anna Vedel stated that the research _____.
   A. confirmed the link between personality and profession
   B. showed that the differences were far from significant
   C. was not reliable because of its prejudicial observation
   D. did not have enough samples to support its findings

25. According to Anna Vedel, the research may help _____.
   A. students make wise choices in finding jobs
   B. teachers understand their students better
   C. students make presentations more academically
   D. school pupils go to better universities

Passage Two

AlphaGo's victory over Go(围棋) champion Lee Se-dol reportedly shocked artificial intelligence experts, who thought such an event was 10 to 15 years away. But if the timing was a surprise, the outcome was not. On the contrary, it was inevitable and entirely foreseeable.

Playing complex games is precisely what computers do supremely well. Just as they beat the world champions at checkers(跳棋) and then chess, they were destined to beat the champion at Go. Yet I don't believe, as some do, that human defeats like this one presage an era of mass unemployment in which awesomely able computers leave most of us with nothing to do. Advancing technology will profoundly change the nature of high-value human skills and that is threatening, but we aren't doomed.

The skills of deep human interaction, the abilities to manage the exchanges that occur only between people, will only become more valuable. Three of these skills stand out. The first, the foundation of the rest, is empathy, which is more than just feeling someone else's pain. It's the ability to perceive what another person is thinking or feeling, and to respond in an appropriate way.

The second is creative problem-solving in groups. Research on group effectiveness shows that the key isn't team cohesion or motivation or even the smartest member's IQ; rather, it's the social sensitivity of the members, their ability to read one another and keep anyone from dominating.

The third critical ability, somewhat surprisingly, is storytelling, which has not traditionally been valued by organizations. Charts, graphs and data analysis will continue to be important, but that's exactly what technology does so well. To change people's minds or inspire them to act, tell them a story.

These skills, though basic to our humanity, are fundamentally different from the skills that have been the basis of economic progress for most of human history, such as logic, knowledge and analysis, which we learned from textbooks and in classrooms. By contrast, the skills of deep human interaction address the often irrational reality of how human beings behave, and we find them not in textbooks but inside ourselves. As computers master ever more complexity, that's where we'll find the source of our continued value.

26. According to the author, AlphaGo's victory _____.
    A. could have happened earlier
    B. came as a pleasant surprise
    C. was an expected result
    D. was more a matter of luck

27. The word "presage" (Para. 2) is closest in meaning to "_____".
    A. survive   B. suffer   C. invent   D. predict

28. What is the author's attitude towards the human future in face of technology?
    A. Unclear.   B. Confused.   C. Worried.   D. Optimistic.

29. Which of the following is the most fundamental to human interaction?
    A. Social sensitivity of group members to understand each other.
    B. Strong ability to share people's feelings and respond.
    C. Team spirit to make sure that everyone is involved.
    D. Inspirational storytelling to motivate people to act.

30. According to the author, the skills of deep human interaction _____.
    A. are the source of true human values in the future
    B. can work with knowledge to make the world better
    C. are similar to the skills of human logic and analysis
    D. can be learned from textbooks and in classrooms

Passage Three

Last year, I went WWOOFing (Willing Workers on Organic Farms) at a beautiful organic farm in

La Reunion. With WWOOFing, volunteers exchange their time and work for food and accommodation. I slept in a cabin in the woods with hedgehogs (刺猬) digging about in the bushes, all different coloured birds singing in the morning and endless rows of palm trees offering shade from the sun.

For me, one of the best ways to get to know a new place is to work with the land, live with the locals and share meals together. This is why I absolutely love WWOOFing. It has got to be one of the best ways to travel. It is a mutually beneficial exchange where everyone involved prioritises people and environment above profit. You get the time and space to deepen a connection with local communities and nature.

There is a lot to learn and each farm has its own unique way of doing things, depending on the environment, climate and soil. At the farm in La Reunion we planted palm trees to harvest the core of the trunk which can be eaten in salads. Before staying with the farm I had only eaten heart of palm from cans which were nothing in comparison to the real thing, fresh from the ground. When potting up the very beginnings of the palm trees, I felt grateful to be a part of the start of the trees' cycle. I was filled with awe that something so small could grow into something so big and strong.

We also did lots of weeding, which helped me to get to know all kinds of different plants, to be able to identify which ones we could use as herbs/medicine/in salads and which were seen as uneatable. I also got to harvest pineapples and guava fruit (番石榴) to make jams which will be sold at the local market.

Of course, not everyone is able to travel far away into the field. The great thing about the skill-share philosophy behind WWOOFing is that it's something we can all do from our own backyard. The focus shifts from money to how we can best support each other in our communities. A fair exchange can make a big difference in the world.

31. WWOOFing enables volunteers to _____.
    A. get food and shelter for their work
    B. travel around La Reunion for free
    C. tell the differences between various birds
    D. have close contact with wild animals

32. The author found his farm life in La Reunion quite _____.
    A. awful   B. rewarding   C. comfortable   D. difficult

33. The author did all of the following on the organic farm EXCEPT _____.
    A. removing weeds   B. planting palm trees
    C. harvesting fruits   D. collecting vegetables

34. The philosophy of WWOOFing is to _____.
    A. improve local environment
    B. make locals live better
    C. unite different communities
    D. advocate a fair exchange

35. This passage is mainly about _____.
    A. the development of WWOOFing

B. a local WWOOFing community
C. a charming WWOOFing experience
D. the system of WWOOFing

Passage Four

Experts say distracted walking is a growing problem, as people of all ages become more dependent on electronic devices for personal and professional matters. They also note pedestrian deaths have been rising in recent years. In 2005, 11% of all US deaths involved pedestrians, but that number rose to 15% in 2014.

The rise in deaths coincides with states introducing bills that target pedestrians. Some states, such as Hawaii, Arkansas, Illinois, Nevada and New York, continue to introduce legislation every year.

The measure recently introduced by New Jersey assembly woman Pamela Lampitt would ban walking while texting and prohibit pedestrians on public roads from using electronic communication devices unless they are hands-free. Violators would face fines of up to $50, 15-day imprisonment or both, which is the same penalty as jaywalking (乱穿马路). Half of the fine would be allocated to safety education about the dangers of walking while texting, said Lampitt.

Some see the proposal as an unnecessary government overreach, while others say they understand Lampitt's reasoning. But most agree that people need to be made aware of the issue. "Distracted pedestrians, like distracted drivers, present a potential danger to themselves and drivers on the road," Lampitt said. "An individual crossing the road distracted by their smartphone presents just as much danger to motorists as someone jaywalking and should be held, at minimum, to the same penalty."

The main question raised about the measure, though, is whether it can be enforced consistently by police officers who usually have more pressing matters to deal with. Some feel that rather than imposing a new law, the state should focus on distracted-walking education. Lampitt said the measure was needed to stop and penalize "risky behavior". She cited a National Safety Council report that showed distracted-walking incidents involving cellphones accounted for an estimated 11,101 injuries from 2000 through 2011.

The study found a majority of those injured were female and most were 40 or younger. Talking on the phone was the most prevalent activity at the time of injury, while texting accounted for 12%. Nearly 80% of the injuries occurred as the result of a fall, while 9% occurred from the pedestrian striking a motionless object.

36. This passage is mainly concerned with _____.
    A. the difficulty in enforcing road regulations
    B. rising deaths caused by distracted walking
    C. the dangers of jaywalking on busy streets
    D. distracted walking involving smartphones

37. The states introducing bills that target pedestrians _____.
    A. have benefited from the bills
    B. find it hard to carry them out

C. have been promoting the legislation

D. will have fewer deaths of pedestrians

38. According to the measure proposed by Lampitt, walking while texting would _____.

    A. become illegal

    B. involve safety education

    C. be blamed publicly

    D. incur a fine of over $50

39. Lampitt reasons that distracted pedestrians are as dangerous as _____.

    A. motorists   B. speeding drivers

    C. jaywalkers   D. drunk drivers

40. Which of the following would the author of the passage most probably agree with?

    A. Males are more vulnerable to distracted-walking injuries.

    B. Police officers are unhappy with the proposed law.

    C. Safety education is more important than penalty.

    D. Rising distracted-walking incidents call for real attention.

Section B

Directions: *In this section, you are required to read one quoted blog and the comments on it. The blog and comments are followed by questions or unfinished statements, each with four suggested answers A, B, C and D. Choose the best answer and mark your answer on the **Answer Sheet**.*

The saying "Clothes Make the Man" dates back some 400 years and it refers to the fact that when people see a well-dressed person, they assume that person is a professional, capable, and (especially in the old days) rich. Therefore, you had to dress like how you wanted to be perceived, what you wanted to eventually achieve. Fast forward 400 years, lots of folks still think the same way. But does it really make a difference?

I happen to be one of those who do not put faith in the old saying. I suppose I might be in the minority but I am a member of an elite club with the likes of Steve Jobs and Bill Gates in my camp.

Perception is not reality; perception is halfway to discovering reality. Perception is drawn from our own impressions, our own belief systems. Is it powerful and influential? Absolutely! Is it all that it seems? Less often than you think. How many times have you cast an initial judgment only to surprise yourself later and learn how you missed out on a great opportunity, person or idea?

Comment 1

In the present era, many associate the well-dressed with being the most successful. It took folks in the business world a long time to overlook the way Steve Jobs wore jeans on the public stage. I did not know Mr. Jobs, though I wish I had. I have heard it said that he invented the concept of "business casual." In my mind that is as much a matter of self-confidence as it is a matter of taste in clothing.

Comment 2

You are wrong about Steve Jobs. He certainly did care about how he was perceived and his appearance was very much calculated to achieve his desired effect. From his early formal business clothing down to the aggressive casualness of his eventual black turtle neck and jeans uniform, his clothes and the impact they made were clearly foremost in his mind.

Comment 3

It reminds me of the story about the philosopher who goes to a formal dinner party in jeans. When asked if he felt out of place because of his clothes, he looked around and said he hadn't noticed.

41. Which of the following might the writer of the passage agree with?

   A. Steve Jobs and Bill Gates dress formally.

   B. We should not judge a person by his clothing.

   C. It is clothes that make the man.

   D. The well-dressed are most likely to succeed.

42. According to the writer of the passage, perception _____.

   A. might prove wrong

   B. is powerful and reliable

   C. is half reality

   D. might be worthless to us

43. The writer of **Comment 1** seems to _____.

   A. dislike the way Steve Jobs dressed for business occasions

   B. suggest that business people have no taste in clothing

   C. believe that the well-dressed are the most successful

   D. think that Steve Jobs' casualness reflected his self-confidence

44. Speaking of Steve Jobs, the writer of **Comment 2** _____.

   A. points out that Steve Jobs was a very aggressive person

   B. suggests that he and Steve Jobs used to be in the same club

   C. holds the same view as the writer of the passage

   D. thinks Steve Jobs' casualness was carefully thought out

45. When he went to the dinner party in jeans (**Comment 3**), the philosopher _____.

   A. thought that people liked his clothes

   B. was not aware of how his clothes looked

   C. felt quite embarrassed

   D. considered himself out of place

Part IV Cloze (10 minutes, 10 points)

Directions: *In this part, there is a passage with ten blanks. For each blank there are four choices marked A, B, C and D. Choose the best answer for each blank and mark your answer on the **Answer Sheet**.*

The history of transportation is very long and full of changes and inventions. It starts __46__ walking, which is not any invention; it just takes energy. People used to walk to get to other places. If you wanted to get somewhere quickly, the __47__ way to do that was to run. Actually, the first invention for transportation __48__ was the shoe. Centuries ago there were no shoes, and people walked barefoot.

　　Then people invented __49__ to transport themselves and materials from one place to another. In some cultures, people invented sledges(雪橇), __50__ are a kind of board that you drag along the ground. You can tie things on the sledge to help carry them, but it's a challenging invention __51__ if you hit a rock with the sledge as you pull it, the contents can __52__. In other cultures, people invented the wheel, which they used to make it easier to move things—and people. That was the beginning of many innovations in transportation.

　　__53__ people had wheels they could invent other ways to travel. They could put the wheel on a board and make it a wagon, and then they could __54__ that wagon to an ox or a horse and ride as well as carry materials. That wheel led to __55__ we have today: trucks, automobiles, and even boats and planes. For example, there were steamboats that used giant wheels that turned with blades, pushing the water and pushing the boat forward.

46. A. on	B. at	C. for	D. with
47. A. possible	B. only	C. one	D. just
48. A. probably	B. luckily	C. really	D. formerly
49. A. methods	B. channels	C. ways	D. measures
50. A. what	B. when	C. where	D. which
51. A. unless	B. but	C. even	D. since
52. A. pull out	B. slip off	C. hold down	D. put down
53. A. Once	B. Then	C. However	D. Yet
54. A. stick	B. make	C. fasten	D. change
55. A. what	B. that	C. which	D. how

Part V Text Completion (20 minutes, 20 points)

　　*Directions: In this part, there are three incomplete texts with 20 questions (ranging from 56 to 75). Above each text there are three or four phrases to be completed. First, use the choices provided in the box to complete the phrases. Second, use the completed phrases to fill in the blanks of the text. Mark your answer on the **Answer Sheet**.*

Text One

```
A. many
B. choose
C. think of
D. way of
```

Phrases:

　　A. __56__ only one language

　　B. __57__ any reason not to

C. in __58__ different ways

D. the most boring __59__ seeing the world

I think every language has a certain way of seeing the world. Each is a whole different world—a whole different mindsets. I couldn't possibly __60__ because it would mean really giving up the possibility to be able to see the world __61__. So the monolingual lifestyle, for me, is the saddest, the loneliest, __62__. There are so many advantages of learning a language; I really can't __63__.

Text Two

A. known
B. idea
C. feel

Phrases:

A. but it may __64__ like forever

B. a person may have no __65__ what is wrong

C. what is __66__ as panic disorder

A panic attack is a sudden feeling of terror. Usually it does not last long, __67__. The cause can be something as normally uneventful as driving over a bridge or flying in an airplane. And it can happen even if the person has driven over many bridges or flown many times before. A fast heartbeat. Sweaty hands. Difficulty breathing. A lightheaded feeling. At first __68__. But these can all be signs of __69__. The first appearance usually is between the ages of eighteen and twenty-four. In some cases it develops after a tragedy, like the death of a loved one, or some other difficult situation.

Text Three

A. lights
B. protect
C. in the dark

Phrases:

A. sit at home __70__

B. turn off all non-essential __71__

C. passed a law to __72__ the sea

I'm a big fan of trying to save the environment, and this month is the WWF(World Wide Fund for Nature) annual Earth Hour. Earth Hour is an event where you __73__ and power between 8-9 pm, things like your TV and computer. However, you don't just __74__ for an hour. Instead, people gather in groups and have fun without using power. Things like dancing, fireworks and musical performances are popular and it's very fun to take part. Earth Hour isn't just about saving energy; people involved in Earth Hour have also planted a forest in Uganda, built solar panels in India and __75__ in Argentina.

Paper Two 试卷二 (50 minutes)

Part VI Translation (20 minutes, 10 points)

Directions: *Translate the following passage into Chinese. Write your answer on the* **Answer Sheet**.

Books are steadily increasing in size: the average number of pages has grown by 25% over the last 15 years. A study of more than 2,500 books appearing on *New York Times* bestseller reveals that the average length has increased from 320 pages in 1999 to 400 pages in 2014. James Finlayson, who carried out the study, believed "there's a relatively consistent pattern of growth year on year." For Finlayson, much of this shift can be explained by the industry's shift towards digital. "When you pick up a large book in a shop," he says, "you can sometimes be intimidated. But if you have a big book on a Kindle(e-book), that's not a consideration."

Part VII Writing (30 minutes, 15 points)

Directions: *Write a composition in no less than 150 words on the topic*: **What do You Think of Advanced Artificial Intelligence**? *You should write according to the outline given below. Write your composition on the* **Answer Sheet**.

Recently, Google's AlphaGo defeated a human Go champion in a series of matches. There has arisen a fear that artificial intelligence will become better than us, and will come to dominate humanity.

List and discuss the reasons why we should or should not fear.

2016年同等学力人员申请硕士学位英语水平全国统一考试

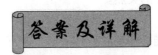

Paper One 试卷一

Part I Oral Communication

Section A

对话一
 A. 你能帮我处理吗?
 B. 里面有什么贵重物品吗?
 C. 你想通过什么方式寄呢?

 职员:有什么需要帮助的吗?
 顾客:是的,我想把这封信寄给我在英国的家人。
 职员:你在信封上写回信地址了吗?
 顾客:写了。
 职员:__1__
 顾客:我想用航空邮件寄。
 职员:__2__
 顾客:有。我附了一张支票和一些照片。
 职员:那你最好寄挂号信。
 顾客:好主意。__3__
 职员:抱歉,先生。你得带着你的信到下一个窗口。

1. [正确答案] C
   [考点剖析] 根据第1题空格下面一行,顾客说"我想用航空邮件寄",可以推断店员在问邮寄方式。

2. [正确答案] B
   [考点剖析] 根据第2题下方顾客回答"有。我附了一张支票和一些照片"可以推断店员询问的是信内物品,只有B项符合语境。

3. [正确答案] A
   [考点剖析] 根据最后店员回答"抱歉,先生。你得带着你的信到下一个窗口"可知顾客在询问原窗口职员能否帮忙处理这件事情。

对话二

　　A.你甚至在太阳底下待不了五分钟。
　　B.我想也是。
　　C.你想要听听我的建议吗?

　　温妮:天哪!没人能忍受这样的炎热。
　　马克:绝对如此! __4__
　　温妮:我想这个下午我们只能待在家里了。
　　马克:__5__ 我不想因为中暑或其他什么事被送进医院。
　　温妮:__6__ 多喝水可以让你免受炎热之苦!
　　马克:对,你说得对。必须喝大量的水。

4. [正确答案] A
　　[考点剖析] 根据温妮说的"没人能够忍受这样的炎热"和马克回答的"绝对如此"可知马克对天气炎热这一事实表示赞同。

5. [正确答案] B
　　[考点剖析] 本题解题的关键在于上文温妮提到的 guess,且 guess 后的内容与马克所述的内容逻辑一致。

6. [正确答案] C
　　[考点剖析] 根据最后马克的回答"对,你说得对。必须喝大量的水"可知温妮在上面的对话中给出了建议。

Section B

　　A.我简直停不下来。
　　B.但是现在我再也不用担心了。
　　C.你是这儿首位身价亿万元的作家。
　　D.但不只是关于金钱。

　　采访人:你已经出版了六本受欢迎的书。__7__
　　受访人:是的。
　　采访人:成为首位身价亿万元的作家如何影响你对自己的看法?
　　受访人:我穿得更好了。嗯,肯定是能买得起更好的衣服了。__8__ 我想金钱给我带来的最大的变化是,我那时候是个单身妈妈,一度真的是只能勉强糊口。除了没有无家可归之外,我一贫如洗。__9__ 而且永远不用担心。
　　采访人:你现在能接受自己永远是富有的这种状态吗?
　　受访人:不。
　　采访人:你还会再写书吗?
　　受访人:绝对会。我不能,是的,__10__ 我的意思是,我想,你可以不让我写,但我不得不写。为了我自己的心理健康,我必须写。

7. [正确答案] C
   [考点剖析] 根据对话第三行采访者的话"成为首位身价亿万元的作家如何影响你对自己的看法?"可知C项为正确答案,四个选项中只有C项提到the first billionaire author。

8. [正确答案] D
   [考点剖析] 第8题空格后的描述讲到金钱以及受访者的家庭状况(单身妈妈,勉强糊口),表明与金钱有关,但不只是钱的事。

9. [正确答案] B
   [考点剖析] 根据第9题空格前的"除了没有无家可归之外,我一贫如洗"和空格后的Never可知,这里应该是一个转折,选项中只有B项"但是现在我再也不用担心了"符合语境。

10. [正确答案] A
    [考点剖析] 根据采访人的最后一个问题"你还会再写书吗?"可知这里是回答是否会继续写作以及原因,并且第10题空格前出现I can't…。A项符合语境。

Part II Vocabulary

11. [正确答案] C
    [考点类型] 名词
    [考点剖析] 题干中的alertness意为"机敏"。preference"倾向,偏爱";adjustment"调整,调节";sensitivity"敏感,灵敏度";response"反应"。

12. [正确答案] B
    [考点类型] 动词
    [考点剖析] 题干中的find fault with意为"批评,挑剔"。ignore"忽视";criticize"批评";impress"给……留下深刻印象";follow"跟随"。

13. [正确答案] D
    [考点类型] 动词
    [考点剖析] 题干中的brought forward意为"提前"。prolonged"拖延";adapted"适应";postponed"使……延期";advanced"将……提前"。

14. [正确答案] A
    [考点类型] 形容词
    [考点剖析] 题干中的sufficient意为"足够的"。enough"足够的";abundant"丰富的";satisfying"令人满意的";proper"适当的"。

15. [正确答案] B
    [考点类型] 动词
    [考点剖析] 题干中的surpass意为"超过"。obtain"获得";exceed"超过";describe"描述";forget"忘记"。

16. [正确答案] D
    [考点类型] 名词
    [考点剖析] 题干中的prospects意为"前景,展望"。background"背景";exploration"探索";survey"调查";outlook"前景"。

17. [正确答案] C

[考点类型] 形容词

[考点剖析] 题干中的 burned out 意为"精疲力竭的"。distressed"痛苦的,忧虑的";anxious"焦虑的";exhausted"疲惫的";upset"难过的"。

18. [正确答案] D

[考点类型] 名词

[考点剖析] 题干中的 merging 意为"合并,结合"。cooperation"合作,协作";meeting"会见";agreement"同意";combination"结合"。

19. [正确答案] B

[考点类型] 形容词

[考点剖析] 题干中的 eligible 意为"具备条件的"。required"必需的";qualified"有资格的";selected"挑选出来的";elected"选举出来的"。

20. [正确答案] C

[考点类型] 副词

[考点剖析] 题干中的 barely 意为"几乎不"。simply"简单地,仅仅";quickly"迅速地";hardly"几乎不";strongly"强有力地"。

Part Ⅲ   Reading Comprehension

Section A

Passage One

你在大学学什么?如果是法律、商科之类的东西,那么你可能现在想把视线移开。因为根据最新研究,大学所学的学科和性格存在关系。如果你学的是法律或商科的话,你可能有自私、不愿与人合作的倾向,且不忠实于自己的情感。此外,研究结果也显示,你可能是一群人中的灵魂人物。

研究者分析了13 000多位大学生所参与的12项独立研究的数据,发现五大人格特质和他们所学的学科存在关系。

例如,研究发现,那些学法学、经济学、政治学和医学的学生比学其他学科的学生更为外向。而当涉及"宜人性"——倾向于乐于助人、慷慨大方和考虑周全这些特质时,律师的得分尤其低,同样低的还有学商科和经济学的学生。

艺术人文学科的学生以及那些学心理学和政治学的学生在开放性方面得分比较高,这意味着他们具有好奇心、想象力,并且能忠实于自己的内心。而经济学家、工程师、律师和科学家在此特质上的得分相对比较低。然而,艺术人文学科的学生不那么认真,且更容易紧张,典型的表现是焦虑和情绪化。学心理学的学生在这些特质上的得分并不低于艺术人文学科的学生。

该研究的作者是来自丹麦奥胡斯大学的安娜·韦德尔,她对研究的结果感到十分惊讶。她说:"效应大小显示研究所发现的差异非常显著,更为有趣的是,结果证实了我们对焦虑不安的心理学家、与世隔绝的自然科学家及愤世嫉俗的经济学家有着刻板印象,这些刻板印象多多少少带有偏见色彩。"

她说,研究结果不仅能帮助那些现在还不知道在大学里该学什么的学生,还能帮助大学教师规划他们的讲座。"我不认为这些结果在指导或选择上会起很大的作用,但可能会给那些在学业选择方面感到迷茫,想要不仅靠能力做出选择的学生一些启发,"韦德尔博士说道,"或者也能帮助老师们更好地了解他们的学生群体。"

21. [正确答案] C
    [考点类型] 推理题
    [题目翻译] 第一段暗示学法律和商科的学生可能_____。
        A. 被这项研究逗笑
        B. 对这项研究感兴趣
        C. 不喜欢这项研究
        D. 喜欢这项研究
    [考点剖析] 第一段第一、二句提到 What did you study at university? If it was something along the lines of law or business, you might want to look away now,关键词 look away 意为"将视线从……移开,不再看……",由此推断,学法律和商科的学生可能不喜欢这项调查研究。

22. [正确答案] A
    [考点类型] 细节题
    [题目翻译] 根据调查,学法学的学生在_____特质上得分明显很低。
        A. 慷慨
        B. 开放
        C. 焦虑
        D. 自私
    [考点剖析] 关键词 particularly low 出现在第三段 But when it came to "agreeableness"—the tendency towards being helpful, generous and considerate—the lawyers scored particularly low…中。A 项 generosity 对应原文中的 generous,意为"慷慨,大方",为正确选项。B 项 openness 是一个迷惑选项,出现在第四段…for openness, meaning they were curious, imaginative and in touch with their inner feelings, while economists, engineers, lawyers and scientists scored comparatively low 中。这里需要注意的是,学法学的学生在 openness 这方面得分相对较低,即 comparatively low,而题干问的是 particularly low,故 B 项不正确。C 项 anxiety 说的是艺术和人文学科的学生,出现在第四段…the arts and humanities students also tended to be less conscientious and more nervous, typically exhibiting signs of anxiety and moodiness 中。D 项 selfishness 在文中第一段 you have selfish, uncooperative tendencies 中就提到,这是学法学学生的特质,所以得分应该是很高的。

23. [正确答案] D
    [考点类型] 词汇题
    [题目翻译] 在第四段中,单词 conscientious 的意思可能是"_____"。
        A. 情绪化的
        B. 敏感的
        C. 好奇的
        D. 仔细的

[考点剖析] conscientious 是"认真的"意思,根据选项中对单词的解析,D 项 careful 与其意思最为相近。

24. [正确答案] A

[考点类型] 细节题

[题目翻译] 安娜·韦德尔声明这项研究_____。

A. 证实了性格与专业之间的联系

B. 显示了差别非常不重要

C. 由于观察具有偏见性,因而不可信

D. 没有足够的例子支持此发现

[考点剖析] 根据 Anna Vedel 定位于第五、六段。第五段 The effect sizes show that the differences found are not trivial, far from 中的 trivial 意为"微不足道的,不重要的",not trivial 则是"重要的,值得注意的",而 B 项中 significant 意为"重要的",但其前面有 far from"远离",那么 far from significant 则意为"不重要的",和原文意思相反。从第六段中 help those school pupils who currently have no idea what to study at university… but it might provide some inspiration for students that are in doubt about study choices…可以知道这个调查能够给那些在选择专业时比较迷惑的学生提供一些帮助,可以根据前文所提到的按不同性格来选择专业,也就是 A 项"证实了性格与专业之间的联系"。C、D 项安娜·韦德尔并没有提及。

25. [正确答案] B

[考点类型] 细节题

[题目翻译] 根据安娜·韦德尔所言,这项研究可能帮助_____。

A. 学生在找工作时做出明智的选择

B. 老师更好地了解学生

C. 学生做出的报告更有学术性

D. 学生上更好的大学

[考点剖析] 根据题干定位至文章第六段,A 项"学生在找工作时做出明智的选择",文章讲的是为学生在选择专业时提供一些帮助。C 项"学生做出的报告更有学术性",而原文中则是 helping academics to plan their lectures,即帮助大学教师规划他们的讲座,academics 指大学教师,所以 C 项和原文不符。D 项"学生上更好的大学",文章第六段中讲的是为学生选择专业提供帮助,而不是上更好的大学。B 项对应文章最后一句话 Or teachers might better understand their student population,也就是帮助老师更好地了解学生。

Passage Two

据报道,AlphaGo 赢了围棋冠军李世石,这令人工智能专家感到震惊。他们认为,这样的事件在 10~15 年后才会发生。但是如果说这个时刻的到来是令人吃惊的,那么这个结果却并不令人意外。相反,这是不可避免的,也是完全可以预见的。

玩复杂的游戏恰恰是计算机特别擅长的。就像计算机先是打败了跳棋冠军,然后是象棋冠

2016年同等学力人员申请硕士学位英语水平全国统一考试答案及详解

军,它们注定也会打败围棋冠军。然而我和有些人一样,认为诸如此类的人类失败并不预示着一个大规模失业时代的到来,在这个时代中,几乎无所不能的计算机让我们中的大多数人无事可做。先进的科技将深刻改变人类技能具有高价值的这一特征,并且会带来威胁,但这并不意味着我们注定会失败。

人类才有的深度人际互动的技能和管理人际交流的能力将变得更有价值。这些技能中有三种脱颖而出。第一种是共鸣,也是其他几种的基础。这不仅是对别人的痛苦感同身受,更是一种理解他人所想、所感,并且能以适当的方式回应的能力。

第二种是在团体中创造性解决问题的能力。关于团队有效性的研究表明,团队凝聚力、动机甚至是最机智成员的IQ水平都不是关键。而成员的社会敏感性、读懂对方并防止任何人独断的能力才是关键所在。

第三种重要的能力是讲故事。这听起来有点让人吃惊,因为讲故事传统上并不被组织所看重。虽然图表和数据分析仍然会很重要,但这也正是技术所能做好的。要想改变人们的思维,激励他们去行动,那么去给他们讲个故事吧。

尽管对我们人类来说这些技能是很基本的,但与那些曾是大部分人类历史中促进经济发展的基础技能截然不同,比如我们从教科书和课堂上所习得的逻辑思维、知识和分析能力。相反,深度人际互动的技能解决了常见的人类非理性行为的问题。我们发现这些技能并不在教科书中,而在我们自身内部。随着计算机掌握了越来越多的复杂技能,我们也将从中发现自身持续价值的源泉。

26. [正确答案] C

  [考点类型] 推理题

  [题目翻译] 作者认为AlphaGo的获胜_____。

  A. 本可以早一点发生

  B. 是一个令人愉快的意外

  C. 是可以预测的结果

  D. 是运气使然

  [考点剖析] 根据第一段最后两句But if the timing was a surprise, the outcome was not. On the contrary, it was inevitable and entirely foreseeable可知作者认为AlphaGo的获胜这一结果并不意外,完全可以预见。

27. [正确答案] D

  [考点类型] 词汇题

  [题目翻译] 与第二段的单词presage词义最接近的是"_____"。

  A. 幸存

  B. 遭受

  C. 发明

  D. 预测

  [考点剖析] 根据题目中的presage定位至文章第二段。era"时代";presage an era of"预示了这样一个时代";presage"预示,预测"。如果不知道词义的话,也可以通过前缀pre-推断。

28. [正确答案] D
    [考点类型] 细节题
    [题目翻译] 面临科技的发展,作者对人类的未来持何种态度?
    A. 不明确的。
    B. 迷惑的。
    C. 担忧的。
    D. 乐观的。
    [考点剖析] 从第二段 Yet I don't believe, as some do, that human defeats like this one presage an era of mass unemployment in which awesomely able computers … and that is threatening, but we aren't doomed 可知作者不赞同计算机将代替人类这一观点,并且认为先进的技术虽然对人类的未来存在着威胁,但人类并非注定会被打败。此外,整篇文章都在表明人类的许多特质和价值是计算机所不能代替的。例如在文章的第三、四、五段,作者分别列举出了三点人类所特有的技能,表明人类在科技发展的时代,仍然具有不可取代的价值,即作者对人类的未来抱有一种积极乐观的态度,故选 D 项。

29. [正确答案] B
    [考点类型] 细节题
    [题目翻译] 以下哪项对人际互动来说是最基本的?
    A. 群体成员相互理解彼此的社会敏感性。
    B. 分担他人的感受并予以回应的强大能力。
    C. 确保每个人都参与的团队精神。
    D. 能激发人们去行动的、鼓舞人心的讲故事技能。
    [考点剖析] 根据题目中的 fundamental 定位至文章第三段对应位置:The first, the foundation of the rest, is empathy, which is more than just feeling someone else's pain. It's the ability to perceive what another person is thinking or feeling, and to respond in an appropriate way"第一种是共鸣,也是其他几种的基础。这不仅是对别人的痛苦感同身受,更是一种理解他人所想、所感,并且能以适当的方式回应的能力"。由此可知 B 项"分担他人的感受并予以回应的强大能力"是人际互动最基本的,故答案选 B 项。A 项在文章第四段中出现,D 项在第五段中出现,但均不是题干中所问的 the most fundamental。C 项文章没有提及。

30. [正确答案] A
    [考点类型] 细节题
    [题目翻译] 在作者看来,深度人际互动的技能_____。
    A. 是未来人类真正价值的源泉
    B. 能与知识一起使世界变得更好
    C. 与人类的逻辑思维和分析能力相似
    D. 可以从书本和课堂中学习到
    [考点剖析] 根据文章最后一句…that's where we'll find the source of our continued value 可知,A 项"是未来人类真正价值的源泉"是正确选项。C、D 项与原文不符,B 项文中没有提及。

Passage Three

去年,我在留尼旺岛一个美丽的有机农场参加了WWOOFing(有机农场志愿工作者组织)。通过WWOOFing,志愿者用时间和工作来换取食物和住宿。我睡在林中小屋,那里的刺猬在灌木丛中挖洞,各种不同颜色的小鸟在清晨唱歌,无尽的棕榈树提供了遮阳处。

对我来说,了解一个新地方的最佳方式之一是在这片土地上工作,与当地人一起吃住。这是我非常喜欢WWOOFing的原因。这也是旅行的最佳方式之一。这里的每个人都把人和环境置于利益之上,形成一种互惠互利的交换。你可以用时间和空间来加深与当地社区和自然的联系。

这儿有很多需要学习的地方,基于环境、气候和土壤的不同,每个农场都有其独特的做事方式。在留尼旺岛的农场,我们种植棕榈树,用收获的树芯拌沙拉吃。在来农场之前,我只吃过罐头里的棕榈芯,与地里新长出来的纯正棕榈芯简直无法相提并论。当栽种棕榈树苗时,我对能参与树木周期的初期阶段满怀感激,对小树苗能够长成参天大树充满着敬畏。

我们也做了很多除草工作,这帮助我了解了各种不同的植物,我能分辨出哪些可以用作草药和药物,哪些可以拌在沙拉里,哪些是不可食用的。我也收获了菠萝和番石榴,以制作可在当地市场出售的果酱。

当然,不是所有人都能大老远地来到这儿。WWOOFing背后折射出的"技能分享"哲学的伟大之处在于这些是我们都可以在自家后院做的事情。其关注点从金钱转换到我们在社区中怎样能最好地支持彼此。一个合理的交换可以使这个世界大为不同。

31. [正确答案] A

    [考点类型] 细节题

    [题目翻译] WWOOFing使志愿者能够_____。

        A. 通过工作来得到食物和住宿

        B. 免费环游留尼旺岛

        C. 找出各种鸟类之间的差异

        D. 与野生动物亲密接触

    [考点剖析] 根据第一段第二句With WWOOFing, volunteers exchange their time and work for food and accommodation"通过WWOOFing,志愿者用时间和工作来换取食物和住宿"可知A项正确。B项"免费环游留尼旺岛"文中没有提及。C项"找出各种鸟类之间的差异"文中没有提及,第一段第三句只讲到all different coloured birds singing in the morning"各种不同颜色的小鸟在清晨唱歌"。D项"与野生动物亲密接触",文中没有提及,第一段第三句只讲到I slept in a cabin in the woods with hedgehogs(刺猬)digging about in the bushes…"我睡在林中小屋,那里的刺猬在灌木丛中挖洞……"。

32. [正确答案] B

    [考点类型] 推理题

    [题目翻译] 作者觉得他在留尼旺岛的农场生活是相当_____。

        A. 糟糕的

        B. 有收获的

        C. 舒适的

        D. 困难的

[考点剖析] 根据题干定位到第三段,第四句提到 I felt grateful to be a part of the start of the trees' cycle"我对能参与树木周期的初期阶段满怀感激"。第五句提到 I was filled with awe that something so small could grow into something so big and strong. "对小树苗能够长成参天大树充满着敬畏"。第四段提到 We also did lots of weeding, which helped me to get to know all kinds of different plants, to be able to identify which ones we could use as herbs/medicine/in salads and which were seen as uneatable"我们也做了很多除草工作,这帮助我了解了各种不同的植物,能分辨出哪些可以用作草药和药物,哪些可以拌在沙拉里,哪些是不可食用的"。综上可以发现作者在留尼旺岛的农场生活是相当有收获的。

33. [正确答案] D
    [考点类型] 细节题
    [题目翻译] 作者在有机农场没做的是_____。
    A. 除草
    B. 种植棕榈树
    C. 收获水果
    D. 收集蔬菜

[考点剖析] 根据题干定位至第三、四段,第三段第二句提到 At the farm in La Reunion we planted palm trees to harvest the core of the trunk which can be eaten in salads"在留尼旺岛的农场,我们种植棕榈树,用收获的树芯拌沙拉吃"。第四段第一句提到 We also did lots of weeding"我们也做了很多除草工作"。第二句提到 I also got to harvest pineapples and guava fruit(番石榴) to make jams which will be sold at the local market"我也收获了菠萝和番石榴,以制作可在当地市场出售的果酱"。故 D 项为正确答案。

34. [正确答案] D
    [考点类型] 细节题
    [题目翻译] WWOOFing 的哲学理念是_____。
    A. 改善当地的环境
    B. 使当地人过得更好
    C. 联合不同的社区
    D. 提倡公平的交换

[考点剖析] 根据题干的 philosophy of WWOOFing 定位到第五段,第二句提到 The great thing about the skill-share philosophy behind WWOOFing is that it's something we can all do from our own backyard"WWOOFing 背后折射出的'技能分享'哲学的伟大之处在于这些是我们都可以在自家后院做的事情"。第三句提到 The focus shifts from money to how we can best support each other in our communities"其关注点从金钱转换到我们在社区中怎样能最好地支持彼此"。第四句提到 A fair exchange can make a big difference in the world"一个合理的交换可以使这个世界大为不同"。故 D 项为正确选项。

35. [正确答案] C
    [考点类型] 主旨题
    [题目翻译] 这篇文章主要是关于_____。
        A. WWOOFing 的发展
        B. 一个本土化的 WWOOFing 社区
        C. 一段丰富的 WWOOFing 经历
        D. WWOOFing 的系统
    [考点剖析] 主旨题要纵观全文来解答。第一段第一句提到 Last year, I went WWOOFing（Willing Workers on Organic Farms）at a beautiful organic farm in La Reunion"去年，我在留尼旺岛一个美丽的有机农场参加了 WWOOFing（有机农场志愿工作者组织）"。第三段和第四段提到作者在此次 WWOOFing 所经历过以及学到的东西，最后一段作者指出 WWOOFing 背后折射出的"技能分享"哲学的伟大之处。综上可知 C 项为正确答案。

Passage Four

专家指出，走路分神是一个日益严重的问题，因为各个年龄段的人都变得越来越依赖电子设备来处理私人及工作事务。他们也指出最近几年行人死亡率正日益升高。在 2005 年，美国死亡人数中有 11% 是行人，而在 2014 年这一数字已上升至 15%。

死亡率上升的同时，一些州引入针对行人的法案。像夏威夷、阿肯色、伊利诺伊、内华达和纽约等一些州每年都持续引入立法。

新泽西女议员帕梅拉·兰皮特最近引入的措施将禁止边走路边发信息，并且禁止走在公共道路上的行人使用电子通信设备，除非他们的手是空闲的。违反者最高将被罚款 50 美元，或者处以 15 天的监禁，或者罚款与监禁一同进行，这与乱穿马路的处罚一样。兰皮特说，一半的罚款将被用于开展关于边走路边发信息所带来的危险的安全教育。

一些人认为，这个提议是政府不必要的过度干涉，而其他人说他们能理解兰皮特的想法。但是大多数人赞成人们需要被唤起对此事的意识。兰皮特说："走路分神的行人就像分神的司机一样，给他们自己以及路上的司机带来了潜在的危险。过马路时，被智能手机分神的个人会和乱穿马路的人一样，给开车的人带来危险，这样的人应该至少被处以相同的罚款。"

然而，这项措施的主要问题是其能否被警察坚持执行，因为警察们通常有更为紧急的事务要处理。有些人认为各州应该关注走路分神教育而不是实施一项新的法律。而兰皮特说，采取措施来阻止和惩罚"危险行为"是非常有必要的。她引用了一份国家安全委员会的报告，报告显示，在 2000—2011 年，行人走路时因手机分神而导致的事故造成大约 11 101 人受伤。

研究发现，大部分受伤者是女性，并且多数年龄在 40 岁以下。在受伤时刻，持手机通话是最为普遍的行为，而发信息占了 12%。近 80% 的人由于摔倒而受伤，而 9% 的行人受伤是因为撞上了静止的物体。

36. [正确答案] B
    [考点类型] 主旨题
    [题目翻译] 此篇文章主要关注_____。
        A. 实施道路管制的困难

B. 走路分神导致死亡率上升

C. 在繁忙街道上乱穿马路的危险

D. 智能手机导致的走路分神

[考点剖析] 从文章第一段 Experts say distracted walking is a growing problem, ... They also note pedestrian deaths have been rising in recent years 中可以得知 B 项 rising deaths caused by distracted walking 为正确选项。A、C、D 项都不是文章讨论的主题。

37. [正确答案] C

[考点类型] 推理题

[题目翻译] 引入针对行人法案的那些州_____。

A. 从法案中获得了利益

B. 发现很难执行这些法案

C. 一直在促进立法

D. 将有更少的行人死亡

[考点剖析] 从第二段的 The rise in deaths coincides with states introducing bills that target pedestrians. Some states, ... continue to introduce legislation every year 中可推断出 C 项 have been promoting the legislation 为正确选项。

38. [正确答案] A

[考点类型] 细节题

[题目翻译] 根据兰皮特提议的措施,边走路边发信息将_____。

A. 违反法律

B. 接受安全教育

C. 被公开责备

D. 被罚款 50 美元以上

[考点剖析] 文章第三段的 Violators would face fines of up to $50, 15-day imprisonment or both 提到违反者最高将被罚款 50 美元,或者处以 15 天监禁,或者罚款与监禁一同进行,由此可知 A 项 become illegal 为正确选项。D 项 incur a fine of over $50,其中 over 意为"超过",是错误选项。

39. [正确答案] C

[考点类型] 细节题

[题目翻译] 兰皮特认为走路分神的行人和_____一样危险。

A. 开车的人

B. 超速的驾驶者

C. 乱穿马路的人

D. 醉驾的司机

[考点剖析] 第四段中兰皮特指出 An individual crossing the road distracted by their smartphone presents just as much danger to motorists as someone jaywalking and should be held, at minimum, to the same penalty "过马路时,被智能手机分神的个人会和乱穿马路的人一样,给开车的人带来危险,这样的人应该至少被处以相同的罚款"。故 C 项为正确选项。

40. [正确答案] D

[考点类型] 细节题

[题目翻译] 下列哪个选项是文章作者最有可能赞同的?

A. 男性更容易因走路分神而受伤。

B. 警察对提议的法案不满。

C. 安全教育比罚款更为重要。

D. 日益增加的走路分神事件需要引起真正的注意。

[考点剖析] 从整篇文章以及第四段前两句 Some see the proposal as an unnecessary government overreach, while others say they understand Lampitt's reasoning. But most agree that people need to be made aware of the issue 可知,D 项 Rising distracted-walking incidents call for real attention 为作者的观点。

Section B

"人靠衣装"这一说法大约起源于 400 年前,指的是,当人们看到穿着好的人时会假定这个人很专业、有能力、很富有(尤其是在过去)。因此,你想要被别人怎样看待,以及你想要达到什么样的效果,就要怎样去穿着。直到今天很多人还是这么想的。但是这真的很重要吗?

我正好是那些不认同这种老说法的人之一。我想我可能是那少部分人,但我是精英俱乐部的一员,和像史蒂夫·乔布斯和比尔·盖茨这类人在同一个阵营。

知觉并不是事实,它是通往发现事实道路的中途。知觉来自我们自己的印象和信念系统。它强大而有影响吗?当然!它是看上去的那样吗?比你想得差远了。有多少次你作出第一判断后,结局让你惊讶,让你认识到你是如何错过了绝佳的机会、重要的人物、奇妙的想法?

评论1

在当下这个时代,很多人把穿着好的人与最成功的人联系在一起。商业人士花了很长时间才能忽视史蒂夫·乔布斯在公开场合穿牛仔裤的穿衣方式。我不认识乔布斯先生,尽管我希望我认识。我曾经听说他发明了"商务便装"的概念。我认为那既与自信相关,也等同程度地与穿衣的品位有关。

评论2

你可能误解了史蒂夫·乔布斯。他确实很在意别人如何看待他,他通过自己的外在来达到想要的效果。从他早期正式的商务装到后来的黑色圆领衫和牛仔制服这一带有攻击性的便装,他的服装以及这些服装的影响非常清晰地印在他的脑海里。

评论3

这使我想起了一位哲学家的故事。有一次,他穿着牛仔裤参加一个正式的晚宴,当被问及是否因为自己的着装而觉得不合时宜时,他看了看四周说,他并没有注意到。

41. [正确答案] B

[考点类型] 推理题

[题目翻译] 下面哪个选项是文章作者可能赞同的?

A. 史蒂夫·乔布斯和比尔·盖茨穿着很正式。

B. 我们不能根据着装来判断一个人。

C. 确实是人靠衣装。

D. 穿着得体的人更可能成功。

[考点剖析] 在文章第一段,作者先引出了整篇博客的讨论主题——一个人的着装反映出他的身份、地位等。作者先说了其他人的观点:大多数人认为好的着装体现出穿衣人的成功、地位等。但是,关键词在于第一段最后一句的 But,作者在此笔锋一转,以一个一般疑问句对大多数人认为的观点提出质疑。在第二、三段,作者表达了自己的观点,他不觉得一个人的着装能够反映他的身份,故 B 项正确。A 项与作者的观点相反,作者在第二段举出这两个人的例子,就是为了证明自己的观点,他认为史蒂夫·乔布斯和比尔·盖茨穿着是随意的,因此 A 项错误。C 项是多数人的观点,并非作者的观点。D 项文中未提及。

42. [正确答案] A

[考点类型] 推理题

[题目翻译] 根据本文作者的观点,知觉_____。

A. 可能是错的

B. 是强大而可靠的

C. 是半现实的

D. 对我们而言可能是没有价值的

[考点剖析] 根据文章第三段 Perception is not reality;perception is halfway to discovering reality…Is it powerful and influential? Absolutely 可知,知觉是通往发现事实道路的中途,故 C 项"(知觉)是半现实的"错误。第三段后面说道:"比你想得差远了。有多少次你作出第一判断后,结局让你惊讶,让你认识到你是如何错过了绝佳的机会、重要的人物、奇妙的想法?"据此可以推测知觉并非都是正确的、可靠的,正是错误的知觉带来了不好的后果,故 A 项正确。B 项"是强大而可靠的"错误,"强大的"文中有提及,是正确的,但是并不是"可靠的"。D 项"对我们而言可能是没有价值的"错误,"知觉"有可能让我们错过好的机会,但并不是说所有的知觉一定是错的、没有价值的。

43. [正确答案] D

[考点类型] 细节题

[题目翻译] 评论1 的作者似乎_____。

A. 不喜欢史蒂夫·乔布斯在商务场合的穿着

B. 暗示商务人士对着装没有品位

C. 认为穿得好的人是最成功的人

D. 认为史蒂夫·乔布斯的随意反映了他的自信

[考点剖析] 评论1 是赞同作者的观点的,根据 In my mind that is as much a matter of self-confidence as it is a matter of taste in clothing"我认为那既与自信相关,也等同程度地与穿衣的品位有关"可知,第一个评论的人认为穿衣反映个人的自信,越是穿着随意,越是自信。

44. [正确答案] D

[考点类型] 细节题

[题目翻译] 说到史蒂夫·乔布斯,评论2 的作者_____。

A. 指出史蒂夫·乔布斯是一个十分有进取心的人
B. 表明他和史蒂夫·乔布斯过去在同一个俱乐部
C. 与这篇博客的作者的观点一样
D. 认为史蒂夫·乔布斯穿着随意是经过认真考虑的

[考点剖析] 第二个评论的第一句You are wrong about Steve Jobs就表明了评论者对于作者的看法持否定的态度，故C项"与这篇博客的作者的观点一样"错误。后面他进一步解释了个人的观点：史蒂夫·乔布斯确实很在意别人如何看待他，他通过自己的外在来达到他想要的效果。从他早期正式的商务装到最后有攻击性的便装，他的服装以及这些服装的影响非常清晰地印在他的脑海里。由此可见，这个评论的作者认为史蒂夫·乔布斯对自己的穿着是经过认真考虑的。A项"指出史蒂夫·乔布斯是一个十分有进取心的人"并不是评论者想要表达的主要内容。B项"表明他和史蒂夫·乔布斯过去在同一个俱乐部"是这个评论没有谈到的。

45. [正确答案] B
    [考点类型] 细节题
    [题目翻译] 在评论3中，当哲学家穿着牛仔裤参加晚宴时，他_____。
    A. 认为人们喜欢他的衣服
    B. 没有意识到自己的穿着
    C. 感到非常尴尬
    D. 觉得自己不合时宜
    [考点剖析] 根据原文可知，当有人问这个哲学家是否感觉自己的穿着不得体时，他环顾了四周，表示自己没有注意到，文中的hadn't noticed 与B项的was not aware of 为同义替换。

Part Ⅳ Cloze

交通发展的历史漫长而又充满了变化和发明。其从步行开始，而步行并不是一种发明，它只消耗能量。人们过去常常走着去其他地方。如果你想快速地去某地，唯一的方式就是跑。事实上，第一项关于交通的发明可能就是鞋了。几个世纪以前，人们是没有鞋的，他们光着脚走路。

随后人们发明了能够把人和货物从一个地方运输到另一地方的方法。在一些文化中，人们发明了雪橇——一种在地面上被拖着走的木板。你可以把货物绑在雪橇上来运输，但同时雪橇也是一项有挑战性的发明，因为如果你拖着雪橇撞上了石头，雪橇上面的货物就会滑落。在其他文化中，人们发明了轮子，便于他们移动人和物体。这就是许多交通发明的开端。

一旦人们发明出轮子，他们就能够发明其他的出行方法。他们可以把轮子放在一块板上，并制成货车。然后人们能够把车固定在牛或者马背上，并且还能装载货物。轮子使我们拥有今天的一切：卡车、汽车甚至船和飞机。比如说轮船就是用巨大的轮子来转动桨叶，推动水流使船前行。

46. [正确答案] D
    [解析过程] 空格所在句的意思为：交通发展的历史从步行开始，步行不是一种发明。start with"从……开始"。

47. [正确答案] B

[解析过程] 空格所在句的意思为:如果你想很快地到达某个地方,唯一的方式就是跑着去。the only way"唯一的方式"。

48. [正确答案] A
    [解析过程] 空格所在句的意思为:事实上,关于交通的第一个发明可能是鞋。probably"可能地";luckily"幸运地";really"事实上";formerly"以前,原来"。从后一句"几个世纪以前,人们是没有鞋的,他们光着脚走路"可知,A项最符合语境。

49. [正确答案] C
    [解析过程] 空格所在句的意思为:随后人们发明了能够把人和货物从一个地方运输到另一地方的方法。methods"方法";channels"通道";ways"方法,方式";measures"措施"。从文章第三段第一句话中 they could invent other ways to travel 可知,C项更符合语境。

50. [正确答案] D
    [解析过程] 空格所在句的意思为:在一些文化中,人们发明了雪橇,雪橇是一种在地面上被拖着走的木板。空格前有逗号,表示后面是非限制性定语从句,而非限制性定语从句一般由 which 引导。

51. [正确答案] D
    [解析过程] 空格所在句的意思为:你可以把货物绑在雪橇上来运输,但同时雪橇也是一项有挑战性的发明,因为如果你拖着雪橇撞上了石头,雪橇上面的货物就会滑落。unless"除非";but"但是";even"甚至";since"因为"。综合选项词义,D项更符合语境。

52. [正确答案] B
    [解析过程] 空格所在句的意思为:如果你拖着雪橇撞上了石头,雪橇上装载的货物就会滑落。slip off"滑落"。

53. [正确答案] A
    [解析过程] 空格所在句的意思为:一旦人们发明出轮子,他们就能够发明其他的出行方法。Once"一旦";Then"然后";However"然而";Yet"但是"。综合选项词义,A项更符合语境。

54. [正确答案] C
    [解析过程] 空格所在句的意思为:然后人们能够把车固定在牛或者马背上,并且还能装载货物。fasten... to..."把……固定在……上"。

55. [正确答案] A
    [解析过程] 空格所在句的意思为:轮子使我们拥有今天的一切,比如说卡车、汽车甚至是船和飞机。此处的 led to 后缺少宾语,have 后也缺少宾语,A项的 what 最符合语境。

Part V Text Completion

Text One

我认为每种语言都有一种看世界的独特方式。每种语言都代表着一种完全不同的思维方式,所呈现的世界也是完全不同的。我不可能只选择一种语言,因为这意味着要放弃能以多种不同的方式去了解这个世界的机会。所以对我来说,单一语言的生活方式是最为悲哀的、最为孤独的、最为无聊的了解世界的方式。学习一门语言有如此多的好处,我真的想不出任何不这么做的理由。

56. [正确答案] B

   [解析过程] choose only one language 为正确搭配,意思是"只选择一种语言"。

57. [正确答案] C

   [解析过程] 本题可采用排除法来做,A 项 many 和 D 项 way of 无法与空格后的 any reason not to 构成搭配,B 项上题已选。

58. [正确答案] A

   [解析过程] in many different ways 为正确搭配,意思是"以多种不同的方式"。

59. [正确答案] D

   [解析过程] 空格前面的 boring 为形容词,空格后面为 seeing,四个选项中只有 way of 符合,即 the most boring way of seeing the world,意为"最为无聊的了解世界的方式"。

60. [正确答案] A

   [解析过程] 空格后面的意思是"因为这意味着要放弃……了解这个世界的机会"。空格后面为一个完整的句子且空格前面只有主语 I,所以空格处所填内容应与主语构成完整的句子,排除 B、C、D 项。

61. [正确答案] C

   [解析过程] 空格前面为一个完整的句子,只有 C 项是介宾短语,能充当状语,修饰整个句子。

62. [正确答案] D

   [解析过程] 从整句来看,这里缺少的是表语,而表语通常由名词和形容词来充当,我们可以看到前面有形容词的最高级,是用来修饰后面的名词的,只有 D 项是带有最高级的名词短语。

63. [正确答案] B

   [解析过程] can 是个情态动词,情态动词后面直接跟动词原形,只有 A 项、B 项是动词原形开头的,但 A 项已经选过,因而只能选 B 项。

Text Two

惊恐发作是一种突如其来的恐惧感受。虽然这种感受通常不会持续很久,但可能感觉很漫长。一些非常平常的事都可能会引起惊恐发作,比如说开车经过一座桥或乘坐飞机。即使这个人之前开车经过很多座桥,或飞行过许多次了,惊恐发作也可能会发生:心跳加快、手心出汗、呼吸困难、头昏眼花。起初人们可能完全不知道是哪里出了问题,但这些都可以看作恐慌症的症状。第一次惊恐发作通常发生在 18~24 岁。在一些情况下,它会在一场悲剧后发生,比如说挚爱的人离世或其他一些困苦的情境。

64. [正确答案] C

   [解析过程] 空格处缺少谓语,且空格前面的 may 为情态动词,因而只能选 C 项。

65. [正确答案] B

   [解析过程] have no idea 为固定搭配,意思是"不知道,不清楚"。

66. [正确答案] A

[解析过程] 空格前面为 be 动词 is,三个选项中只有 known 符合此处的语法结构,be known as 意思是"被认为是"。

67. [正确答案] A

[解析过程] 空格部分独立存在,且空格前面为一个完整的句子,说明后面也需要一个句子,且这两个句子之间必须有连接词,只有 A 项是带有连接词 but 的句子。

68. [正确答案] B

[解析过程] 空格部分应填入一个完整的句子,只有 A 项、B 项符合,但 A 项已被选,故选 B 项。

69. [正确答案] C

[解析过程] 空格前面为介词 of,三个选项中只有 C 项填入后语法正确且符合语境。

Text Three

  我是一个狂热的努力保护环境的人。这个月是世界自然基金会(WWF)一年一度的"地球一小时"月。"地球一小时"是指在晚上八点到九点间,人们关掉所有非必需的电灯和电源,比如说像电视和电脑之类的东西的一项活动。然而,人们不用只是在黑暗中在家坐一个小时,他们可以成群结队地聚在一起,在没有电源的情况下也可以玩得很开心。比如说跳舞、放烟花、音乐表演,这些都非常受欢迎,而且大家也乐于参与其中。"地球一小时"不仅仅节约能源,加入"地球一小时"活动的人们已经在乌干达种下了一片森林,在印度修建了太阳能电池板,在阿根廷通过了一项保护大海的法令。

70. [正确答案] C

[解析过程] sit at home 是一个动词词组,后面应接状语,只有 C 项是介宾短语,能充当状语。

71. [正确答案] A

[解析过程] 该短语意为"关上所有非必需的_____",可见后面缺一个名词,只有 A 项是名词。

72. [正确答案] B

[解析过程] 该短语意为"通过了一项_____大海的法令",说明空格部分缺少的是动词。

73. [正确答案] B

[解析过程] 空格部分缺少的是谓语,且空格前面的时态为一般现在时,排除 C 项。根据句意选 B 项。

74. [正确答案] A

[解析过程] 空格部分缺少谓语动词,且动词应使用原形。

75. [正确答案] C

[解析过程] 空格处缺少谓语部分,且根据 and 前面的时态可知此处为现在完成时。

Paper Two 试卷二

Part Ⅵ Translation

1. Books are steadily increasing in size: the average number of pages has grown by 25% over the last 15 years.

[结构分析] 这句话由两个一般陈述句构成,后一句是对前一句的进一步阐述。

[词义推敲] steadily increase"稳步增长"。

[参考译文] 书籍篇幅呈稳步增长的趋势:在过去的15年中,书籍页码平均增长了25%。

2. A study of more than 2,500 books appearing on *New York Times* bestseller reveals that the average length has increased from 320 pages in 1999 to 400 pages in 2014.

[结构分析] 这是一个主从复合句,that引导宾语从句。

[词义推敲] bestseller"畅销书"。

[参考译文] 一项对位列《纽约时报》畅销书榜的2 500多本书籍的调查显示:书本的平均厚度已由1999年的320页增加到2014年的400页。

3. James Finlayson, who carried out the study, believed "there's a relatively consistent pattern of growth year on year."

[结构分析] 这是一个主从复合句。who引导的定语从句修饰前面的人名,believed后面又接了一个宾语从句。

[词义推敲] carry out "进行;执行";consistent"一贯的;一致的;稳定的";year on year"逐年"。

[参考译文] 执行该项调查的詹姆斯·芬兰森认为"书本的厚度呈相对稳定的逐年增长之势"。

4. For Finlayson, much of this shift can be explained by the industry's shift towards digital.

[结构分析] 这是一个被动句,主语为shift。

[词义推敲] digital"数字的"。

[参考译文] 芬兰森认为,这个变化主要是由产业数字化造成的。

5. "When you pick up a large book in a shop," he says, "you can sometimes be intimidated. But if you have a big book on a Kindle(e-book), that's not a consideration."

[结构分析] 这是一个主从复合句,引号内均为宾语从句,句首的句子为When引导的时间状语从句,if引导条件状语从句。

[词义推敲] intimidate"恐吓,威胁,胁迫";e-book"电子书"。

[参考译文] 他说:"当你在书店拿起一本厚重的书时,有时候你可能会被吓到。但是如果你是在Kindle(电子书)上读篇幅很长的书的话,这就没什么问题了。"

Part Ⅶ Writing

这是一篇陈述观点类的议论文,虽然没有给出具体提纲,但从给出的资料中我们可以自己列出提纲,并据此思路从三点去展开。第一段,提出问题,阐述问题的背景。第二段,提出观点,是否应该对人工智能感到害怕,并给出具体的理由加以讨论。第三段,对全篇做一个总结,重申观点,提出建议。

　　Nowadays, with the rapid development of computer technology, in particular, the artificial intelligence (AI), the application of senior AI in the future has aroused a considerable world-wide concern. It is recently reported that in a ground-breaking fight between man and AI the world champion of the game Go was mercilessly defeated by Deep Mind AlphaGo, a product from Google, which gives rise to some people's fear toward advanced AI in future practice. And they take it for granted that human being would probably be totally controlled by machine.

As far as AI is concerned, I am fully convinced that we are supposed to maintain an objective and positive attitude toward the emerging issue of artificial intelligence. It is known to all that AI is nothing but the simulation of information on the process of conscious thinking, or in another words, it's something that subjects to its inventor's design awareness. Consequently, as long as we are fully conscious of its possible disadvantages, certain restrictions can be input into the program to avoid potential disastrous occurrences. Additionally, it is well hoped that AI and intelligent machines can possibly free human labors from virtually all kinds of jobs.

In that case, above-mentioned discussions can safely lead to the conclusion that what we are supposed to do is but to learn to get along with the inevitable development of computer technology and to adapt to the updated social structure changed by AI.

这篇范文紧扣主题,用词丰富,句式多样,文章思路清晰,没有任何语法和拼写错误,给人印象很不错。我们来看一下内容:

第一段:用模板例句引出问题的背景,指出越来越多的人正关注高级人工智能的应用,并用 It is recently reported that...引出背景事件及人们担忧的原因。

第二段:就问题本身提出自己的观点,并给出具体的理由加以讨论。注意:作者的用语丰富多样,用 as far as... is concerned "就……而言"来引出关注的对象,用 I am fully convinced that...引出自己的观点,而非简单的 I think, In my opinion。连接词 Consequently, Additionally 的运用不仅使文章层次鲜明,更显出作者的词汇量之大,以及对词汇的良好掌握和运用。

第三段:对全篇做出总结,并提出建议。注意:作者在总结时的用词,并非简单的 in a word, to sum up, in conclusion,而是用 above-mentioned discussions can safely lead to the conclusion that...,承上启下,引出一个从句,可见作者不仅对词汇掌握得好,对句式的运用也非常在行。

整篇文章观点鲜明,有理有据,思路清晰。文章在保证语法和单词正确的基础上,采用了丰富多样的词汇和句式,写得非常精彩,这也正是这篇作文能得高分的原因所在。

2017年同等学力人员申请硕士学位
英语水平全国统一考试

Paper One 试卷一（100 minutes）

Part I Oral Communication（15 minutes, 10 points）

Section A

Directions: *In this section there are two incomplete dialogues and each dialogue has three blanks and three choices A, B and C, taken from the dialogue. Fill in each of the blanks with one of the choices to complete the dialogue and mark your answer on the* **Answer Sheet**.

Dialogue One

A. When is it taking place?

B. Is Alan attending?

C. That'll be interesting.

Alice: We're having a meeting tomorrow. Can you make it?
Kevin: 1
Alice: We're planning at 10 o'clock. Is that OK?
Kevin: Yes, that'll be fine.
Alice: We're going to go over last quarter's sales figures.
Kevin: Good. I have some input I'd like to make.
Alice: Frank is also going to make some suggestions on improving the bottom line.
Kevin: 2   He's got keen insights.
Alice: Yes, he's going to outline some new sales strategies.
Kevin: 3
Alice: No, he's flying to San Francisco and won't be able to make it.
Kevin: Oh well, maybe he'll phone in.

Dialogue Two

A. I'll drop by there on my way to class today.

B. I thought you liked the apartment.

C. I've decided to look for a new place.

Roger: Hello.

Ann: Hello Roger? This is Ann.

Roger: Oh hi, Ann. How have you been? How's your new apartment working out?

Ann: Well, that's what I'm calling about. You see, __4__

Roger: Oh, what's the problem with your place now? __5__

Ann: Oh, I do, but it's a little far from campus, and the commute is just killing me. Do you think you could help? I thought you might know more about the housing situation near the school.

Roger: Well, I know there's an apartment complex around the corner that seems to have a few vacancies. __6__

Ann: Hey, thanks a lot.

Roger: No problem.

Section B

Directions: *In this section there is one incomplete interview which has four blanks and four choices A, B, C and D, taken from the interview. Fill in each of the blanks with one of the choices to complete the interview and mark your answer on the **Answer Sheet**.*

A. Thanks, Rachel.

B. That's what we did.

C. we were all talking about some TV shows.

D. it's a real honor to have you here.

Maddow: Joining us now for the interview is Hillary Clinton, former secretary of state, former senator, former first lady. Secretary Clinton, __7__ Thank you for being here.

Clinton: It's great to be here with you. __8__

Maddow: What does a person do after 11 hours of testimony? You're the only human being I know of on Earth that has done 11 straight hours. What did you do after that?

Clinton: Well, I had my whole team come over to my house and we sat around eating Indian food and drinking wine and beer. __9__ It was great.

Maddow: And was it like, "Let's just talk about TV, let's not talk about what just happened?"

Clinton: Yes. Yes, __10__ It was great just to have that chance to thank them because they did a terrific job, you know, kind of being there behind me and getting me ready.

Part II Vocabulary (10 minutes, 10 points)

Directions: *In this part there are ten sentences, each with one word or phrase underlined. Choose the one from the four choices marked A, B, C and D that best keeps the meaning of the sentence. Mark your answer on the **Answer Sheet**.*

11. The specially developed skin paint will wear off in 2-4 days, but can be removed instantly with alcohol.
    A. remain   B. dry   C. work   D. disappear

12. She was tired of his constant complaining and didn't want to tolerate him anymore.
    A. catch up to   B. put up with   C. come up with   D. live up to

13. The supporters of either party have rationalized their own opinion in terms of argument.
    A. with regard to B. in contrast to   C. in addition to   D. as opposed to

14. How is it possible that such widespread deception has come to take place right under our noses?
    A. delay   B. damage   C. fraud   D. shock

15. It is not yet clear whether the deletion of data at the troubled bank was accidental or deliberate.
    A. obvious   B. intentional   C. surprising   D. foolish

16. When required to eat vegetables, many children only do so reluctantly.
    A. automatically   B. anxiously   C. obediently   D. unwillingly

17. Recently, the Internet has given rise to a new type of marketplace.
    A. created   B. conceived   C. increased   D. improved

18. Another 1,000 workers were dismissed when the machinery plant was in difficulties.
    A. taken off   B. driven off   C. put off   D. laid off

19. Credit creates the false idea that you can own things without paying for them.
    A. image   B. illusion   C. imagination   D. impression

20. For the audience to better understand the new concept, the professor elaborated it with many examples.
    A. summarized   B. concluded   C. classified   D. explained

Part III Reading Comprehension (45 minutes, 25 points)

Section A

Directions: *In this section, there are four passages followed by questions or unfinished statements, each with four suggested answers A, B, C and D. Choose the best answer and mark your answer on the* **Answer Sheet**.

Passage One

Under the right circumstances, choosing to spend time alone can be a huge psychological blessing. In the 1980s, the Italian journalist and author Tiziano Terzani, after many years of reporting across Asia, holed himself up in a cabin in Ibaraki Prefecture, Japan. "For a month I had no one to talk to except my dog Baoli," he wrote in his book *A Fortune Teller Told Me*. Terzani passed the time with books, observing nature, "listening to the winds in the trees, watching butterflies, enjoying silence." For the first time in a long while he felt free from the unending anxieties of daily life: "At last I had time to have time."

Terzani's embrace of isolation was relatively unusual: Humans have long considered solitude an inconvenience, something to avoid, a punishment, a realm of loners. Science has often associated it with negative outcomes. Freud, who linked solitude with anxiety, noted that, "in children the first fears relating to situations are those of darkness and solitude." John Cacioppo, a modern social neuro-scientist who has extensively studied loneliness—what he calls "chronic perceived isolation"—contends that, beyond damaging our thinking powers, isolation can even harm our physical health. But increasingly scientists are approaching solitude as something that, when pursued by choice, can prove a therapy.

This is especially true in times of personal disorder, when the instinct is often for people to reach outside of themselves for support. "When people are experiencing crisis it's not always just about you: It's about how you are in society," explains Jack Fong, a sociologist at California State Polytechnic University who has studied solitude.

In other words, when people remove themselves from the social context of their lives, they are better able to see how they're shaped by that context. Thomas Merton, a monk and writer who spent years alone, held a similar notion. "We cannot see things in perspective until we cease to hug them to our breast," he writes in *Thoughts in Solitude*. "People can go for a walk or listen to music and feel that they are deeply in touch with themselves."

21. Tiziano Terzani spent a month alone to _____.
    A. embrace isolation
    B. study butterflies
    C. write a book
    D. look after his dog

22. The word "solitude" (Para. 2) is closest in meaning to "_____".
    A. growing anxious
    B. feeling empty
    C. being helpless
    D. staying alone

23. The opinions of Freud and Cacioppo are cited to show that _____.
    A. children tend to fear darkness and solitude
    B. solitude pursued by choice can be a therapy
    C. chronic isolation can harm interpersonal relations
    D. solitude has long been linked with negative outcomes

24. According to Jack Fong, the sense of personal crisis may be influenced by _____.
    A. an isolated lifestyle
    B. mental disorder
    C. low self-esteem
    D. social context

25. The main idea of the passage is that _____.
    A. solitude should be avoided at all costs
    B. anxieties of daily life may cause personal crisis
    C. choosing to spend time alone can be a blessing
    D. seeking support is useless for tackling personal crisis

Passage Two

Science is finally beginning to embrace animals who were, for a long time, considered second-class citizens.

As Annie Potts of Canterbury University has noted, chickens distinguish among one hundred chicken faces and recognize familiar individuals even after months of separation. When given problems to solve, they reason: hens trained to pick colored buttons sometimes choose to give up an immediate (lesser) food reward for a slightly later (and better) one. Healthy hens may aid friends, and mourn when those friends die.

Pigs respond meaningfully to human symbols. When a research team led by Candace Croney at Penn State University carried wooden blocks marked with X and O symbols around pigs, only the O carriers offered food to the animals. The pigs soon ignored the X carriers in favor of the O's. Then the team switched from real-life objects to T-shirts printed with X or O symbols. Still, the pigs ventured only toward the O-shirted people: they had transferred their knowledge to a two-dimensional format, a not-inconsiderable feat of reasoning.

Fairly soon, I came to see that along with our closest living relatives, cetaceans (鲸目动物) too are masters of cultural learning, and elephants express profound joy and mourning with their social companions. Long-term studies in the wild on these mammals helped to fuel a perspective shift in our society: the public no longer so easily accepts monkeys made to undergo painful procedures in laboratories, elephants forced to perform in circuses, and dolphins kept in small tanks at theme parks.

Over time, though, as I began to broaden out even further and explore the inner lives of fish, chicken, pigs, goats, and cows, I started to wonder: Will the new science of "food animals" bring an ethical revolution in terms of who we eat? In other words, will the breadth of our ethics start to catch up with the breadth of our science?

Animal activists are already there, of course, committed to not eating these animals. But what about the rest of us? Can paying attention to the thinking and feeling of these animals lead us to make changes in who we eat?

26. According to Annie Potts, hens' choice of a later and better reward indicates their ability of _____.
   A. social interaction   B. facial recognition
   C. logical reasoning   D. mutual learning

27. The expression "not-inconsiderable feat" (Para. 3) shows what pigs can do is _____.
   A. extraordinary   B. weird   C. unique   D. understandable

28. What is Paragraph 4 mainly about?
   A. The similarities between mammals and humans.
   B. The necessity of long-term studies on mammals.
   C. A change of public attitude to the treatment of mammals.
   D. A new discovery of how mammals think and feel.

29. What is the author's view on eating "food animals"?
   A. He regrets eating them before.   B. He considers eating them justifiable.
   C. He is not concerned about the issue.   D. He calls for a change in what we eat.

30. What is the best title for the passage?
    A. In Praise of Food Animals　　　　　　B. Food Animals in Science Reports
    C. The Inner Lives of Food Animals　　　D. Food Animals: Past, Present and Future

Passage Three

　　Almost eight decades ago, the American educator Abraham Flexner published an article entitled *The Usefulness of Useless Knowledge*. In it, he argued that the most powerful intellectual and technological breakthroughs usually emerged from research that initially appeared "useless", without much relevance to real life.

　　As a result, it was vital, Flexner said, that these "useless" efforts should be supported, even if they did not produce an immediate payback, because otherwise the next wave of innovation simply would not occur. "Curiosity, which may or may not produce something useful, is probably the outstanding characteristic of modern thinking," he declared.

　　In 1929, Flexner persuaded a wealthy American family, the Bambergers, to use some of their donations to fund the Institute for Advanced Study (IAS) at Princeton to support exactly this kind of "undirected" research.

　　And it paid off: brilliant Jewish scientists fleeing from Nazi Germany, such as Albert Einstein, gathered at the IAS to explore undirected ideas. And while some of these, such as Einstein's own work developing his earlier theory of relativity, did not initially seem valuable, many eventually produced powerful applications (though after many decades).

　　"Without Einstein's theory, our GPS tracking devices would be inaccurate by about seven miles," writes Robbert Dijkgraaf, the current director of the IAS, in the foreword to a newly released reprint of Flexner's article. Concepts such as quantum mechanics (量子力学) or superconductivity also seemed fairly useless at first—but yielded huge dividends at a later date.

　　The reason why the IAS is re-releasing Flexner's article now is that scientists such as Dijkgraaf fear this core principle is increasingly under threat. The Trump administration has released a projected budget that threatens to reduce funding for the arts, science and educational groups. Many Republicans believe that research is better financed by business or philanthropists (慈善家) than by government. But one striking fact about the past century is how much American innovation originated in federal projects; Silicon Valley would never have boomed were it not for the fact that state funding enabled the development of the World Wide Web, for example.

31. What may be the best title for the passage?
    A. The Value of Creative Ideas　　　　　B. The Importance of Basic Research
    C. Innovation in Silicon Valley　　　　　D. In Praise of "Useless" Endeavors
32. According to Abraham Flexner, what is an important feature of modern thinking?
    A. Curiosity.　　　B. Application.　　　C. Devotion.　　　D. Passion.
33. The "undirected" research (Para. 3) refers to research _____.
    A. not funded by government agencies
    B. without any practical purpose in mind

· 6 ·

C. with indefinite experimental methods

D. supported by non-profit organizations

34. Examples of initially "useless" research include all of the following EXCEPT _____.

   A. quantum mechanics   B. theory of relativity

   C. superconductivity   D. GPS tracking devices

35. Flexner's article was reprinted because _____.

   A. businesses in Silicon Valley wish to put pressure on the government

   B. Democrats believe that government funding should go to small businesses

   C. Republicans argue that scientific research should be financed by businesses

   D. some scientists worry that government will cut its funding for basic research

Passage Four

In 1902, Georges Méliès made and released a movie called *A Trip to the Moon*. In this movie, the spaceship was a small capsule, shaped like a bullet, that was loaded into a giant cannon and aimed at the moon.

This movie was based on a book that came out many years earlier by an author named Jules Verne. One of the fans of the book was a Russian man, Konstantin Tsiolkovsky. The book made him think. Could one really shoot people out of a cannon and have them get safely to the moon? He decided one couldn't, but it got him thinking of other ways one could get people to the moon. He spent his life considering this problem and came up with many solutions.

Some of Tsiolkovsky's solutions gave scientists in America and Russia ideas when they began to think about space travel. They also thought about airplanes they and other people had made, and even big bombs that could fly themselves very long distances.

Many scientists spent years working together to solve the problem. They drew and discussed different designs until they agreed on the ones that were the best. Then, they built small models of those designs, and tested and tested them until they felt ready to build even bigger models. They made full-scale rockets, which they launched without any people inside, to test for safety. Often the rockets weren't safe, and they exploded right there on the launch pad, or shot off in crazy directions like a balloon that you blow up and release without tying it first. After many, many tests, they started to send small animals into space. Only after a long time did they ever put a person inside a rocket and shoot him into space.

Even after they began sending people into space, scientists were still trying to improve the shape of the rockets. The design changed many times, and eventually ended up looking like a half-rocket and half-airplane. The machine called space shuttle was used for many years. Now, the government lets private companies try their own designs for spaceships, and they have come up with many different, crazy-looking machines.

36. In the movie *A Trip to the Moon*, the spaceship was sent to the moon _____.
    A. in a capsule   B. in a bullet   C. by a cannon   D. by a gun
37. The movie was based on a book written by _____.
    A. Konstantin Tsiolkovsky   B. an unknown author
    C. Georges Méliès   D. Jules Verne
38. Before the invention of a spaceship, possible solutions of space travel included all of the following EXCEPT _____.
    A. bombs   B. balloons   C. airplanes   D. rockets
39. What is Paragraph 4 mainly about?
    A. It took a long time and hard work to send a person into space.
    B. American scientists worked better than Russian scientists.
    C. Scientists from Russia and America had close cooperation.
    D. The design of the rocket was inspired by the movie *A Trip to the Moon*.
40. The word "shoot" (Para. 4) is closest in meaning to "_____".
    A. send with great force   B. break into many pieces
    C. fix a problem   D. attack with a weapon

Section B

Directions: *In this section, you are required to read one quoted blog and the comments on it. The blog and comments are followed by questions or unfinished statements, each with four suggested answers A, B, C and D. Choose the best answer and mark your answer on the **Answer Sheet**.*

In 2003, I was told by a restaurant owner on a Thai island that local fishermen used to wrap their lunch in banana leaves, which they would then casually toss overboard when done. That was OK, because the leaves decayed and the fish ate them all. But in the past decade, he said, plastic wrap had rapidly replaced banana leaves, so the beach was edged with a crust of plastic.

This is a worldwide problem—we can't point the finger at Thai fishermen. The UK alone produces more than 170m tons of waste every year, much of it food packaging. Now we live in an absurd age where a packet of cookies can have seven layers of wrapping. While it has revolutionised the way we store and consume food, there is now so much of it that landfills (垃圾填埋场) can't cope. Some of it is poisonous, and some of it never degrades. It can take 450 years for some types of plastic bottle to break down. Indeed, as Rachelle Strauss of the UK's Zero Waste Week says, we never actually throw anything "away"—it's really just put somewhere else.

It's easy to despair at the scale of handling the plastic wrap, but it isn't beyond humanity to solve it—look at how the world took action on CFCs (含氯氟烃): there are signs that the hole in the ozone layer is now closing. Food packaging ought to be a doddle.

Comment 1

While as an individual I can do my best to avoid excessive packaging, it is really only government regulation that can force corporations to change their practices.

Comment 2

I never understand why supermarket chains insist on covering products such as bananas and cucumbers in plastic wrap. Why? They have their own packaging—the skin or peel!

Comment 3

I love packaging—if it's well designed of course. It helps us be more hygienic and practical. The solution to these packaging necessities is clearly to encourage the use of bio-degradable packaging.

Comment 4

Before, everything we threw out was bio-degradable and now it's not. Guess it's hard to change that behavior overnight.

41. What is the author's view on the plastic problem in Thailand?

   A. The problem is not unique to Thailand.

   B. There is no point overreacting to the problems.

   C. It is important to raise people's awareness.

   D. The government should be held responsible.

42. "A packet of cookies" is mentioned in Paragraph 2 to _____.

   A. illustrate the problem of excessive packaging

   B. introduce the revolutionary way of packaging

   C. review the gradual development of packaging

   D. emphasize the necessity of food packaging

43. The word "doddle" (Para. 3) probably means "something _____".

   A. no longer useful   B. extremely difficult

   C. beyond imagination   D. easily accomplished

44. Which of the comments is positive about packaging?

   A. Comment 1.   B. Comment 2.   C. Comment 3.   D. Comment 4.

45. Which of the following comments point out ways to solve over-packaging?

   A. Comments 1 and 2.   B. Comments 1 and 3.

   C. Comments 2 and 4.   D. Comments 3 and 4.

Part IV Cloze (10 minutes, 10 points)

Directions: *In this part, there is a passage with ten blanks. For each blank there are four choices marked A, B, C and D. Choose the best answer for each blank and mark your answer on the* **Answer Sheet**.

How many people can live on the face of the earth? No one knows the answer. It depends on how much food people can grow __46__ destroying the environment.

More people now exist than ever before, and the population __47__ growing. Every 15 seconds, about 100 babies are born. Before the end of this century, the earth may __48__ 10 billion people!

To feed everyone, farmers must grow more food. They are trying to do so. World food production has gradually __49__ over the years. In some parts of the world, __50__, the population is growing faster than the food supply. Some experts fear the world will not be able to produce enough food for a __51__ that never stops increasing.

To grow more crops on the same __52__ of land, farmers use fertilizers and pesticides (杀虫剂). Some plant new kinds of grains that produce more food. These things help— __53__ they don't provide perfect solutions. The chemicals in fertilizers and pesticides can pollute water supplies. The new seeds developed by scientists have reached the __54__ of what they can produce.

When hungry people can get no more out of __55__ field, they clear trees from hills and forests for new farmland, and in doing so they expose the soil. Then rain and floods may strip the topsoil from fields. This process is called erosion. Each year erosion steals billions of tons of topsoil from farmers.

46. A. without   B. by   C. against   D. for
47. A. ceases   B. keeps   C. stops   D. stays
48. A. maintain   B. retain   C. hold   D. produce
49. A. exhausted   B. declined   C. raised   D. risen
50. A. however   B. somehow   C. anyway   D. furthermore
51. A. country   B. nation   C. population   D. community
52. A. range   B. amount   C. number   D. level
53. A. hence   B. when   C. but   D. and
54. A. conclusion   B. restriction C. goal   D. limit
55. A. growing   B. surviving   C. remaining   D. existing

Part V Text Completion (20 minutes, 20 points)

Directions: *In this part, there are three incomplete texts with 20 questions (ranging from 56 to 75). Above each text there are three or four phrases to be completed. First, use the choices provided in the box to complete the phrases. Second, use the completed phrases to fill in the blanks of the text. Mark your answer on the **Answer Sheet**.*

Text One

| A. helps |
| B. while |
| C. messages |
| D. closely |

Phrases:

A. you watched __56__ eating it
B. send nerve __57__ to your brain
C. our noses and our brain are very __58__ connected
D. __59__ us remember things

For years, scientists have been studying the special powers of smells. It seems that __60__. When you smell something, the odor goes up your nose to the smelling zones. From here, sense cells __61__ telling it what you smelled.

More than our other four senses, our sense of smell changes our mood and __62__. If you were told to think about popcorn, you'd probably recall its smell. And then you might remember the movie __63__. Our sense of smell also makes us aware of danger—like the smell of smoke.

Text Two

A. give presentations
B. new innovations
C. uploaded

Phrases:

A. how to help poor people with all sorts of __64__
B. all the speeches are __65__ to their website
C. __66__ on a variety of topics

TED is a set of conferences, held in various cities around the world every year. With various speakers—also from various parts of the globe— __67__, for everyone to see.

TED conferences invite speakers to __68__. The different speakers are usually experts in their field and talk about new ideas and recent developments that are important to their work. The speakers are often also well known, with people such as Microsoft giant Bill Gates and world-renowned chimpanzee expert, Jane Goodall, having given talks. There are many talks on environmentalism, for example, and on international development, aid work, and __69__. While the talks cover a wide variety of topics, all speakers have a strict time limit—each presentation must last no longer than 18 minutes.

Text Three

A. to use
B. finding
C. the way

Phrases:

A. good at __70__ information
B. __71__ their brains work
C. __72__ their imagination

The time spent with technology doesn't just give kids new ways of doing things, it changes __73__. For example, an article says that while video games may condition the brain to pay attention to multiple stimuli, they can lead to distraction and decreased memory. Children who always use search engines may become very 74   but not very good at remembering it. In addition, the article said, children who use too much technology may not have enough opportunities 75   or to read and think deeply about the material.

Paper Two 试卷二 (50 minutes)

Part VI Translation (20 minutes, 10 points)

Directions: *Translate the following passage into Chinese. Write your answer on the **Answer Sheet**.*

When it comes to personal finance, we are all looking for ways to save more money. Our household budgets are filled with both big and small expenses that we imagine can be cut out to save us loads of cash or, at the very least, spent better elsewhere. One of the things you have surely considered is using public transportation rather than your own vehicle. It would be easy to assume that public transportation is cheaper, because bus fare is far less expensive than gas, but those are not the only costs to consider. Take a step back to your high school economics class and try to remember the lesson about opportunity costs. These, as you might recall if you were awake for that class, are the things you give up when you choose one option over other options. Although they are not measured in dollars and cents, they still have to be considered whenever you make a financial decision.

Part VII Writing (30 minutes, 15 points)

Directions: *Write a composition in no less than 150 words on the topic: **What Makes Happy Couples Happy**? You should write according to the hints given below. Write your composition on the **Answer Sheet**.*

Happy couples know what is essential to maintain a happy relationship. For instance, daily habits are extremely helpful in making their relationship work.

2017年同等学力人员申请硕士学位英语水平全国统一考试

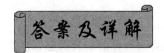

Paper One 试卷一

Part I Oral Communication

Section A

对话一

  A. 什么时候(开会)?

  B. 艾伦会参加吗?

  C. 那会非常有趣。

  爱丽丝:明天我们要开会。你能参加吗?

  凯文:__1__

  爱丽丝:我们计划的时间是10点,你可以吗?

  凯文:好啊,可以。

  爱丽丝:我们要在会上回顾一下上季度的销售情况。

  凯文:好,我很乐意提出一些建议。

  爱丽丝:弗兰克也将针对提高公司盈利方面提出一些建议。

  凯文:__2__ 他有敏锐的洞察力。

  爱丽丝:是的,他会提出一些新的销售策略。

  凯文:__3__

  爱丽丝:不,他飞去圣弗朗西斯科了,赶不回来。

  凯文:哦,他或许可以用电话参加会议。

1. [正确答案] A

  [考点剖析] 根据第1题空格下面一行"我们计划的时间是10点"可以推知此处问的是开会的时间。

2. [正确答案] C

  [考点剖析] 根据空格前后语境可以推知此处为针对弗兰克将提出建议一事给出评论。

3. [正确答案] B

  [考点剖析] 根据空格下面一句"他飞去圣弗朗西斯科了"可以得知,此处涉及另外一个新的人物——艾伦。

对话二

　　A. 今天我去上课时顺便看一下。
　　B. 我本以为你会喜欢这个公寓。
　　C. 我决定找个新的地方。

　　罗杰:哈喽。
　　安:哈喽,是罗杰吗? 我是安。
　　罗杰:哦,安。你好! 最近还好吗? 你的新公寓怎么样?
　　安:这就是我今天打电话的原因。你知道吗, __4__
　　罗杰:哦,你现在的公寓怎么了? __5__
　　安:哦,是的。但是它离学校有点远,每天的通勤简直要了我的命。你能帮帮我吗? 我觉得你可能对校园附近的住房情况比较了解。
　　罗杰:我知道在拐角处有个公寓楼可能还有一些空房。__6__
　　安:非常感谢!
　　罗杰:不客气。

4. [正确答案] C
　　[考点剖析] 根据空格后面的句子"你现在的公寓怎么了"可得知安不想住在现在的公寓。

5. [正确答案] B
　　[考点剖析] 下文的句子最初是一个肯定,后面是一个转折。讲的是关于现在公寓的情况,那肯定的内容应该是说安喜欢目前居住的公寓。

6. [正确答案] A
　　[考点剖析] 根据空格前后的语境内容可知,罗杰了解一些住房情况,安在下文表示感谢,所以推出空格处是罗杰表示愿意提供帮助。

Section B

　　A. 谢谢你,雷切尔。
　　B. 这就是我们所做的事情。
　　C. 我们就是在谈论一些电视节目。
　　D. 您的到来让我们深感荣幸。

　　麦德:现在接受我们采访的是希拉里·克林顿,美国前国务卿、前参议员、前第一夫人。克林顿国务卿, __7__ 感谢您的到来。
　　克林顿:我很高兴来到这里。__8__
　　麦德:一个人在经历 11 个小时的听证会之后会做些什么? 您是我认识的地球上唯一一个参加听证会连续 11 个小时的人。那之后您都做了些什么?
　　克林顿:我让我的整个团队来我家,我们坐在一起吃印度食物,喝葡萄酒和啤酒。__9__ 非常棒!
　　麦德:是不是就像"让我们来谈一谈电视,不要谈发生了什么事"?

克林顿:没错,是的。__10__。我很难有这样的机会去感谢他们,因为他们做得非常棒。你知道的,他们一直在背后支持我,帮我做好准备。

7. [正确答案] D

   [考点剖析] 这个空格在访谈的最开头,介绍并欢迎接受采访的嘉宾,只有D项符合这个语境。

8. [正确答案] A

   [考点剖析] 根据第8题的前一句,主持人对希拉里·克林顿的到来表示欢迎可知,此处应该是希拉里·克林顿对主持人的欢迎表示感谢。

9. [正确答案] B

   [考点剖析] 第9题的前文在讲述听证会后他们做了什么,这个空应该是用一句话做总结,即"这就是我们所做的事情"。

10. [正确答案] C

    [考点剖析] 这个空格是以重复的方式对上文主持人所说的话进行肯定回答。

Part Ⅱ Vocabulary

11. [正确答案] D

    [考点类型] 动词

    [考点剖析] 题干中的 wear off 意为"磨掉;逐渐消失"。remain"保持;依然是;留下";dry"使……变干";work"工作;操作";disappear"消失;不复存在"。

12. [正确答案] B

    [考点类型] 动词短语

    [考点剖析] 题干中的 tolerate 意为"忍受;容忍",catch up to"赶上;逮捕";put up with"忍受;容忍";come up with"赶上;提出";live up to"不辜负;做到"。

13. [正确答案] A

    [考点类型] 介词短语

    [考点剖析] 题干中的 in terms of 意为"就……而言;在……方面"。with regard to"关于;至于";in contrast to"和……对比;与……相反";in addition to"除……之外(还)";as opposed to"与……形成对照"。

14. [正确答案] C

    [考点类型] 名词

    [考点剖析] 题干中的 deception 意为"骗局;诡计"。delay"耽搁;推迟";damage"损害;毁坏";fraud"欺骗;诈欺;骗子";shock"震惊;震动"。

15. [正确答案] B

    [考点类型] 形容词

    [考点剖析] 题干中的 deliberate 意为"故意的"。obvious"明显的;显然的";intentional"有意的;故意的";surprising"令人惊讶的,出人意料的";foolish"愚蠢的;荒谬的"。

16. [正确答案] D

    [考点类型] 副词

    [考点剖析] 题干中的 reluctantly 意为"不情愿地;勉强地"。automatically"自动地;机械地";

anxiously"焦急地;担心地";obediently"顺从地;服从地";unwillingly"勉强地;不情愿地"。

17. [正确答案] A
    [考点类型] 动词
    [考点剖析] 题干中的 given rise to 意为"引起;使发生;导致"。created"造成;创造";conceived"设想;想出";increased"增加;升高";improved"改善;提高"。

18. [正确答案] D
    [考点类型] 动词短语
    [考点剖析] 题干中的 dismissed 意为"开除;解散"。taken off "起飞;脱掉";driven off"驱散;击退";put off"延期;推迟";laid off"解雇;停止"。

19. [正确答案] B
    [考点类型] 名词
    [考点剖析] 题干中的 false idea 意为"假象;错觉"。image"印象;形象";illusion"错觉;幻觉;错误的信仰（或观念）";imagination"想象;想象力";impression"印象;感觉"。

20. [正确答案] D
    [考点类型] 动词
    [考点剖析] 题干中的 elaborated 意为"详细地说明"。summarized"概述;摘要";concluded"结束;总结";classified"分类;归类";explained"说明;解释"。

Part III Reading Comprehension

Section A

Passage One

在适当的情况下,选择独处能让人在心理上获得巨大的幸福感。在20世纪80年代,意大利记者兼作家帝奇亚诺·坦尚尼在从事亚洲报道工作多年之后,隐居在日本茨城县的一个小屋里。他在《算命先生如是说》中写道:"在那一个月里,除了我的狗——宝利,没有一个可以和我聊天的人。"帝奇亚诺·坦尚尼用看书和观察自然来打发时间。"聆听树林里的风声,欣赏着蝴蝶,享受着宁静。"这么久以来,他第一次感到自己远离了日常生活中无休止的焦虑。"我终于真正拥有了时间。"

帝奇亚诺·坦尚尼对孤独的享受是很与众不同的:人类一直认为独处是一种不便,是一种需要避免的事,是一种惩罚,是一种孤独者才有的表现。科学经常把它与消极结果联系起来。弗洛伊德把孤独和焦虑联系在一起,并指出:"在儿童之中,与第一种恐惧相关的情境是黑暗和孤独。"约翰·卡西奥普是一位现代社会神经科学家,他广泛研究孤独,并将其称为"长期感知孤独"。他认为,孤独除了破坏我们的思维能力之外,还会损害我们的身体健康。但是越来越多的科学家认为在人们主动选择独处的时候,它可以成为一种治疗方法。

这一现象在一个人出现问题的时候尤为明显,此时本能往往会让人们寻求外界的帮助。研究过孤独的加州州立理工大学的社会学家杰克·方解释说:"当人们遭遇危机时,它不仅仅关乎个人,还关乎个人与社会之间的关系。"

换句话说,当人们把自己从他们生活的社会环境中解放出来时,他们更能看清自己是如何被这种环境塑造的。托马斯·默顿是一位独居多年的修道士兼作家,他也持有类似的观点。他在《独处中的沉思》一书中写道:"当我们还在与社会环境紧密相连的时候,我们就不能正确地看待事物。人们可以去散步或者听音乐,这样他们会觉得它们与自己是紧密相连的。"

21. [正确答案] A

    [考点类型] 细节题

    [题目翻译] 帝奇亚诺·坦尚尼独自用一个月的时间去_____。

    A. 享受孤独

    B. 研究蝴蝶

    C. 写一本书

    D. 照顾他的狗

    [考点剖析] 根据第一段第二句 holed himself up in a cabin…和第二段第一句 Terzani's embrace of isolation was relatively unusual…这些对帝奇亚诺·坦尚尼在这一个月中所做事情的总体描述,可以得知他是独自享受孤独,而其余选项都是他独处过程中做的具体事情,不能只选其一。

22. [正确答案] D

    [考点类型] 词汇题

    [题目翻译] 第二段中的单词 solitude 与"_____"的意思最接近。

    A. 越来越焦虑

    B. 感觉空虚

    C. 无助

    D. 独自一个人

    [考点剖析] 根据这个词的前一句"帝奇亚诺·坦尚尼对孤独的享受是很与众不同的"以及后文中科学家们对这个词的看法,我们可以得知这个词也是在讲与孤独相关的内容。再结合选项的意思,可知 D 项与其意思最为接近。

23. [正确答案] D

    [考点类型] 细节题

    [题目翻译] 引用弗洛伊德和约翰·卡西奥普的观点是为了说明_____。

    A. 孩子们往往害怕黑暗和孤独

    B. 主动选择的孤独可以成为一种治疗方法

    C. 长期的孤独会损害人际关系

    D. 孤独长期以来与消极结果联系在一起

    [考点剖析] 这两个人都是在说孤独的危害,即 Science has often associated it with negative outcomes,D 项刚好是原文的同义替换。

24. [正确答案] D

    [考点类型] 推理题

    [题目翻译] 根据杰克·方的观点,个人危机可能被_____所影响。

    A. 独处的生活方式

B. 精神失常

C. 自尊心低

D. 社会环境

[考点剖析] 根据题干人物名称以及 personal crisis 定位到文章第三段,杰克·方主要是说个人不是孤立的存在,而是在社会中与他人紧密联系的。所以 D 项"社会环境"为正确选项。

25. [正确答案] C

[考点类型] 主旨题

[题目翻译] 本文的大意是_____。

A. 应该不惜一切代价避免孤独

B. 日常生活的焦虑可能导致个人危机

C. 选择花时间独处可能是一种幸福

D. 寻求支持对解决个人危机无益

[考点剖析] 文章内容一直在围绕"孤独,独处"展开,故排除 B 项和 D 项;文章第一句话 Under the right circumstances, choosing to spend time alone can be a huge psychological blessing"在适当的情况下,选择独处能让人在心理上获得巨大的幸福感"就已经奠定了文章的感情基调并且阐明了文章主题。在文章的后半部分,作者用一些正面的例子说明"选择花时间独处可能是一种幸福"。

Passage Two

科学终于开始接纳长期以来被认为是二等公民的动物。

正如坎特伯雷大学的安妮·波茨所指出的那样,鸡能够在一百只鸡中识别出自己的同伴,甚至在经过几个月的分离之后,仍能识别出熟悉的个体。当需要解决问题时,它们会做出思考:训练母鸡选择有颜色的按钮时,母鸡有时候会选择放弃能立即得到的(较少的)食物奖励,转而选择稍后的(较好的)奖励。健康的母鸡可以给朋友提供帮助,而且当朋友死去时,它们会感到悲伤。

猪对人类符号能做出有意义的反应。由宾夕法尼亚州立大学的坎迪斯·科尼所带领的研究小组带着标有 X 和 O 符号的木块站在猪的附近,而只有带着标有 O 符号的木块的人才给这些猪提供食物。猪很快忽略带有 X 标记木块的人员而青睐有 O 标记的人员。然后,小组人员将木块改为印有 X 或 O 符号的 T 恤衫。猪仍然只是倾向于穿印有 O 符号 T 恤衫的人:它们把自己的知识转化成一个二维的模式,这是一种了不起的推理能力。

很快,我发现除了我们的近亲,鲸目动物也是文化学习的能手,而且大象也能对它们的伙伴表达深深的喜悦和悲哀。对这些哺乳动物的长期野外研究促使我们开始转变视角:公众不再那么容易接受让猴子在实验室经受那些痛苦的研究过程,让大象被迫在马戏团表演以及把那些海豚放在主题公园的一个小水箱中。

然而,随着时间的推移,当我开始更广泛、更深入地探索鱼、鸡、猪、羊和牛的内在生命时,我开始想:"食用动物"这一新的科学是否会给我们吃这些动物的人带来伦理革命?换言之,我们伦理的广度是否会赶上我们科学的广度?

当然,动物保护主义者已经承诺不吃这些动物。但是我们其他人呢?对这些动物的思维和感受的注意会引导我们改变我们所吃的食物吗?

26. [正确答案] C

   [考点类型] 推理题

   [题目翻译] 根据安妮·波茨的观点,母鸡选择后面稍微好些的奖励表明母鸡具备_____的能力。

   A. 社交

   B. 面部识别

   C. 逻辑推理

   D. 相互学习

   [考点剖析] 根据题干定位到文章第二段第二句 When given problems to solve, they reason… "当需要解决问题时,它们会做出思考……",后文叙述母鸡选择后面稍好的奖励是对母鸡具有思考能力这一观点的举例说明,故 C 项正确。

27. [正确答案] A

   [考点类型] 词汇题

   [题目翻译] 第三段中的 not-inconsiderable feat 这一表达是为了说明猪的能力是_____。

   A. 非凡的

   B. 离奇的

   C. 独特的

   D. 不可理解的

   [考点剖析] inconsiderable 本身的意思是"无足轻重的",而前面还有一个否定词"not",因此这里是要表达"非常重要,伟大"的意思。而且根据文章语境,这里是通过举例来说明猪是有逻辑推理能力的,这种能力无疑是了不起的,A 项的意思与此相符。迷惑选项是 C 项,但是文章并未说明猪的这种能力是独特的,所以不能选择 C 项。

28. [正确答案] C

   [考点类型] 细节题

   [题目翻译] 第四段主要是讲_____。

   A. 哺乳动物和人类的相似之处

   B. 对哺乳动物长期研究的必要性

   C. 公众对待哺乳动物的态度的改变

   D. 关于哺乳动物如何思考和感觉的新发现

   [考点剖析] 这一段介绍了对更多哺乳动物进行的研究,然后说这种研究带来公众视角的改变,冒号之后说的是改变的具体内容。Long-term studies in the wild on these mammals helped to fuel a perspective shift in our society…是本段的重点句,也是文章的感情所向。

29. [正确答案] D

   [考点类型] 推理题

[题目翻译] 作者对吃"食用动物"持有的观点是_____。
A. 他后悔之前吃过
B. 他认为吃这些食物是合理的
C. 他不关心这件事
D. 他提倡改变我们所吃的东西

[考点剖析] 文章最后两段内容表明了作者对这个问题的观点。倒数第二段作者给出对这个问题的思考,最后一段说动物保护主义者已承诺不吃这些动物,那其他人会吗?对动物的思维和感受的注意会引导我们改变我们所吃的食物吗?所以可以推测出作者呼吁人们做出改变,不再食用动物。

30. [正确答案] C
[考点类型] 主旨题
[题目翻译] 这篇文章的最佳标题是_____。
A. 赞美食用动物
B. 科学报告中的食用动物
C. 食用动物的内在生命
D. 食用动物:过去、现在和未来

[考点剖析] 纵观全文,作者通过介绍对多种动物的研究,指出很多动物像人一样,也具有逻辑思考能力和内在生命"inner lives"。文章最后,作者呼吁公众改变饮食结构,保护动物。C项"食用动物的内在生命"很好地概括了文章的主题。

Passage Three

大约在80年前,美国教育家亚伯拉罕·弗莱克斯纳发表了一篇题为"无用知识的有用性"的文章。他认为,最强大的知识和技术突破通常来自最初看来"无用"、与现实生活没太大关系的研究。

因此,弗莱克斯纳说,最重要的是,这些看似"无用的"努力应该得到支持,即使没有立刻带来回报。这是因为,若非如此,下一波创新根本不会发生。"好奇心最终不一定能够带来有用之物,但很可能是现代思维的突出特点。"他宣称。

1929年,弗莱克斯纳说服富裕的美国班伯格家族,把他们慷慨捐款中的一部分捐给了普林斯顿高等研究院(IAS),用来支持这种"没有导向的"研究。

此举获得了回报:诸如阿尔伯特·爱因斯坦等逃离纳粹德国的才华横溢的犹太科学家,聚集在IAS探索没有导向的想法。虽然其中一些研究——例如爱因斯坦早期相对论的研究——最初看来并无价值,但许多研究最终产生了强大的应用价值(尽管是在几十年之后)。

"如果没有爱因斯坦的理论,我们的全球定位系统(GPS)跟踪设备的精准度将降低大约7英里。"IAS的现任院长罗伯特·戴德拉在最新出版的弗莱克斯纳的文章重印版的前言中写道。量子力学或超导性等概念起初也看似相当无用——但在日后产生了巨大的利益。

眼下IAS重新出版弗莱克斯纳这篇文章的原因是,戴德拉等科学家担心这条核心原则会越来越受到威胁。特朗普政府已公布了一份预算计划,该计划可能会大幅削减对艺术、科学和教育团体的拨款。许多共和党人认为,研究最好由企业或慈善家出资,而不是由政府来资助。但是,过去一个世纪的一个惊人事实是,美国的创新在很大程度上源于联邦项目;例如,若不是国家资助使万维网(World Wide Web)的研发成为可能,硅谷永远不会兴旺发达。

31. [正确答案] D
    [考点类型] 主旨题
    [题目翻译] 这篇文章的最佳标题可能是_____。
        A. 创造性思维的价值
        B. 基础研究的重要性
        C. 硅谷的创新
        D. 赞扬"无用的"努力
    [考点剖析] 文章第一段就指出,看起来"无用的"知识实际上可以带来很多益处,并且后文多次用例子来支持这一观点。

32. [正确答案] A
    [考点类型] 细节题
    [题目翻译] 亚伯拉罕·弗莱克斯纳认为,现代思维的一个重要特征是_____。
        A. 好奇心
        B. 勤勉
        C. 奉献
        D. 热情
    [考点剖析] 根据题干定位到文章第二段最后一句话 Curiosity, which may or may not produce something useful, is probably the outstanding characteristic of modern thinking"好奇心最终不一定能够带来有用之物,但很可能是现代思维的突出特点"。

33. [正确答案] B
    [考点类型] 细节题
    [题目翻译] 第三段中,"没有导向的"研究指的是_____的研究。
        A. 不由政府机构资助
        B. 没有任何实际目的
        C. 没有明确的实验方法
        D. 由非营利性组织支持
    [考点剖析] 第三段 this kind of undirected research 指的是前文提到的最初看起来"无用",与现实生活没太大关系的研究,而最强大的知识和技术突破通常来自这样的研究,前两段都在围绕这个话题展开。作者在后文继续举例,诸如爱因斯坦等人做的最初看起来没有价值的研究在几十年后产生了强大的应用价值。因此,"undirected" research 应该是那些没有研究目的、最初看起来没什么用的研究。

34. [正确答案] D
    [考点类型] 细节题
    [题目翻译] 最初看起来"无用的"研究不包括_____。
        A. 量子力学

B. 相对论

C. 超导性

D. GPS 跟踪设备

[考点剖析] 文章第四、五段对"无用的"研究进行了具体说明,其中第五段最后一句 Concepts such as quantum mechanics(量子力学) or superconductivity...对应 A 项和 C 项;第四段第二句 And while some of these, such as Einstein's... theory of relativity,...对应 B 项。而第五段第一句 Without Einstein's theory, our GPS... miles 是说如果没有在初期看似"无用的"相对论,GPS 跟踪设备的精准度会降低,这不是说 GPS 跟踪设备是最初看起来"无用的"研究。

35. [正确答案] D

[考点类型] 细节题

[题目翻译] 弗莱克斯纳的文章被再次出版,原因是_____。

A. 硅谷的企业希望给政府施加压力

B. 民主党人认为政府的资金应该流向小企业

C. 共和党人认为科学研究应该由企业来资助

D. 一些科学家担心政府将削减基础研究经费

[考点剖析] 根据题干定位到最后一段前两句...fear this core principle is increasingly under threat. The Trump administration has released a projected budget that threatens to reduce funding for the arts, science and educational groups"……担心这条核心原则会越来越受到威胁。特朗普政府已公布了一份预算计划,该计划可能会大幅削减对于艺术、科学和教育团体的拨款"。D 项刚好和原文对应。

Passage Four

1902 年,乔治·梅里爱制作并发行了一部名为《月球旅行记》的电影。在这部电影中,宇宙飞船是一个形似子弹的小型太空舱,它被装进一个巨大的大炮中瞄准月球。

这部电影是根据一位名叫朱尔斯·维尼的作家多年前出版的一本书创作的。这本书的书迷中有一个名叫康斯坦丁·齐奥尔科夫斯基的俄罗斯人。这本书引发了他的思考。真的能用大炮把人发射出去,让他们安全地登上月球吗?他认为不能,但这让他思考其他能让人们登上月球的方法。他一生都在考虑这个问题,并提出了许多解决办法。

当美国和俄罗斯的科学家们开始思考太空旅行时,齐奥尔科夫斯基的一些解决办法为他们提供了思路。他们也考虑过他们和其他人共同制造的飞机,甚至还有能远距离飞行的大炸弹。

许多科学家花了很多年的时间来共同努力解决这个问题。他们绘制并讨论了不同的设计,直到得到他们认为是最好的方案。然后,他们建造了这些设计的小模型,并进行反复的测试,直到他们觉得已经为建造更大的模型做好了准备。他们制造了一枚全尺寸的火箭,在内部没有任何人员的情况下发射了它,以测试其安全性。通常火箭是不安全的,它们会在发射台上爆炸,或者就像一个被吹气却没有扎好的气球在放气的时候向各个方向胡乱飞一样发射出去。经过许多次的测试后,他们开始把小动物送入太空。在很长一段时间之后,他们才把一个人放进火箭,把他送入太空。

即使在他们开始把人送入太空之后,科学家们仍在努力改进火箭的外形。设计改变了很多次,最终使其看起来既像是火箭又像是飞机。这个叫作航天飞机的机器已经被使用很多年了。现在,政府允许私人公司尝试自己设计宇宙飞船,因此他们发明了许多不同的、看起来很疯狂的飞船。

36. [正确答案] C

    [考点类型] 细节题

    [题目翻译] 在电影《月球旅行记》中,宇宙飞船是_____ 发射到月球的。

        A. 在太空舱里

        B. 在子弹里

        C. 用大炮

        D. 用枪

    [考点剖析] 根据题干定位到文章第一段第二句的…the spaceship was a small capsule, shaped like a bullet, that was loaded into a giant cannon and aimed at the moon。A 项中提到的 capsule 在原文的意思是"……是一个太空舱"而不是 A 项表达的"在太空舱里";"飞船是一个形似子弹"的物体而不是 B 项所说的"在子弹里";D 项文中没有提到过;由文中"装进一个巨大的大炮中瞄准月球"可看出宇宙飞船是用大炮发射的。

37. [正确答案] D

    [考点类型] 细节题

    [题目翻译] 这部电影是根据_____ 写的书创作的。

        A. 康斯坦丁·齐奥尔科夫斯基

        B. 不知名的作家

        C. 乔治·梅里爱

        D. 朱尔斯·维尼

    [考点剖析] 在文章第二段第一句话中很容易找到问题的答案,由 This movie was based on a book that came out many years earlier by an author named Jules Verne 可知 D 项正确。

38. [正确答案] B

    [考点类型] 细节题

    [题目翻译] 在宇宙飞船发明前,可行的太空旅行的方法不包括_____ 。

        A. 炸弹

        B. 气球

        C. 飞机

        D. 火箭

    [考点剖析] 在文章的第三段中,根据 They also thought about airplanes they and other people had made, and even big bombs that could fly themselves very long distances 可知,人们考虑的方法有炸弹和飞机。在第四段中,根据 They made full-scale rockets, which they launched without any people inside, to test for safety 可知,可行的方法还包括火箭。只有 B 项不是太空旅行的方法。

39. [正确答案] A

　　[考点类型] 主旨题

　　[题目翻译] 第四段的大意是_____。

　　　A. 把一个人送入太空需要很长的时间和艰苦的工作

　　　B. 美国科学家比俄罗斯科学家做得更好

　　　C. 来自俄罗斯和美国的科学家密切合作

　　　D. 火箭的设计灵感来源于电影《月球旅行记》

　　[考点剖析] 第四段描述了很多科学家经过很多次的实验和测试才最终把人送入了太空。其实这段的第一句话和最后一句话很明显地概括了第四段的大意。

40. [正确答案] A

　　[考点类型] 推理题

　　[题目翻译] 第四段中 shoot 一词与"_____"的含义最为接近。

　　　A. 以强力发射

　　　B. 成为很多碎片

　　　C. 解决一个问题

　　　D. 用武器攻击

　　[考点剖析] 根据文章语境,前面叙述的是经过多次的测试,科学家能用火箭把动物送到太空,最后也能把人发送到太空,四个选项中只有 A 项与这个含义最为接近。

Section B

　　2003 年,在泰国的一个岛屿上,一家餐馆老板告诉我,当地渔民过去常常用香蕉叶包午餐,然后在吃完午餐后会将这些香蕉叶随意地扔到海里。这种做法是没有问题的,因为叶子腐烂后,鱼会把它们都吃光。但他继续说道,在过去的十年里,塑料包装很快取代了香蕉叶子,所以海滩被一层塑料包裹着。

　　这是一个世界性的问题,我们不能把矛头指向泰国渔民。仅英国每年就会产生超过 1.7 亿吨的垃圾,其中大部分是食品包装。现在我们生活在一个荒谬的时代,一包饼干可以有七层包装。虽然塑料彻底改变了我们存储和食用食物的方式,但是现在它的数量是如此之多,以至于垃圾填埋场已经无法处理。其中有些塑料制品是有毒的,有些甚至不能降解。有些塑料瓶要经过450 年才会分解。正如英国"零废弃物周"的雷切尔·斯特劳斯所说,我们从来没有真正"扔掉"任何东西——实际上只是放在了其他地方。

　　人们很容易对需要处理如此大规模的塑料包装感到绝望,但是人类是有能力解决这个问题的——看一下人类对氯氟烃所采取的措施吧:有迹象表明,臭氧层的空洞正在合拢。食品包装问题应该是个小问题。

评论1

　　虽然作为个人,我可以尽量避免过度使用包装,但是实际上只有政府管制才能迫使企业改变他们的做法。

评论2

　　我一直都不明白为什么超市连锁店坚持用塑料包装香蕉和黄瓜之类的产品。为什么?他们有自己的包装——果壳或果皮!

评论3

我喜欢包装——当然是精心设计的包装。它使我们所食用或使用的物品更加卫生和实用。解决这些包装必需品的方案显然是鼓励使用生物降解包装。

评论4

以前,我们扔掉的东西都是可生物降解的,但现在不是了。我想很难一夜之间改变这种行为。

41. [正确答案] A

　　[考点类型] 细节题

　　[题目翻译] 作者对泰国塑料包装问题的态度是什么?

　　　　　　　A. 这个问题并非泰国独有。

　　　　　　　B. 对问题反应过度没有意义。

　　　　　　　C. 提高人们的意识是很重要的。

　　　　　　　D. 政府应该负责。

　　[考点剖析] 文章第二段第一句明确说明了作者对这个问题的态度;This is a worldwide problem—we can't point the finger at Thai fishermen"这是一个世界性的问题,我们不能把矛头指向泰国渔民"。其他选项文中并未涉及。

42. [正确答案] A

　　[考点类型] 推理题

　　[题目翻译] 第二段提到的"一包饼干"是为了_____。

　　　　　　　A. 说明过度包装的问题

　　　　　　　B. 介绍革命性的包装方式

　　　　　　　C. 回顾包装的逐步发展

　　　　　　　D. 强调食品包装的必要性

　　[考点剖析] 举例是为了支持论点,第二段作者主要是在讲人类制造出数量庞大的垃圾,其中大部分都是食品包装垃圾。而用一包饼干就有七层包装这个例子是为了说明过度包装会制造出过多的垃圾,故 A 项为正确选项。

43. [正确答案] D

　　[考点类型] 推理题

　　[题目翻译] 第三段中,doddle 一词的意思可能是"一些_____事"。

　　　　　　　A. 不再有用的

　　　　　　　B. 极其困难的

　　　　　　　C. 无法想象的

　　　　　　　D. 轻松完成的

　　[考点剖析] 可以从文章的前后语境来推断相关词汇的含义。在这一段,转折之后作者说人类是有能力解决这个问题的,然后举例用臭氧层的空洞正在合拢来进行支持,同理推出食品问题是人类容易解决的问题。所以 D 项最为接近这个意思。

44. [正确答案] C

　　[考点类型] 细节题

[题目翻译] 哪个评论对包装是肯定的？

    A. 评论1。

    B. 评论2。

    C. 评论3。

    D. 评论4。

[考点剖析] 评论3的前两句直接地说明发表评论的人对包装持有肯定态度：I love packaging… It helps us be more hygienic and practical"我喜欢包装……它使我们所食用或使用的物品更加卫生和实用"。

45. [正确答案] B

[考点类型] 细节题

[题目翻译] 下面哪个评论指出了如何解决过度包装问题？

    A. 评论1和2。

    B. 评论1和3。

    C. 评论2和4。

    D. 评论3和4。

[考点剖析] 评论1中提到 it is really only government regulation that can force corporations to change their practices"但是实际上只有政府管制才能迫使企业改变他们的做法"。评论3中提到 The solution to these packaging necessities is clearly to encourage the use of bio-degradable packaging"解决这些包装必需品的方案显然是鼓励使用生物降解包装"。而其他评论都没有提到如何解决这个问题。

Part Ⅳ Cloze

有多少人能在地球上生存？没有人知道答案。这取决于人们在不破坏环境的情况下能种植多少食物。

现在的人口比以往任何时候都多，并且还在持续增长。每15秒就有大约100个婴儿出生。在21世纪末之前，地球可能拥有100亿人口！

为了养活每一个人，农民必须种植更多的粮食，他们也正在尝试这样做。多年来世界粮食产量逐步上升。然而，在世界上一些地区，人口增长的速度超过了粮食供应的速度。一些专家担心，世界将无法为不停增长的人口提供足够的粮食。

为了在同样范围的土地上种植更多的作物，农民们使用化肥和杀虫剂。有些农民种植能生产更多粮食的新品种。这些东西虽然有帮助，但并不能提供完美的解决方案。化肥和杀虫剂中所含有的化学物质会污染水源。科学家研制出的新种子已经达到了它们所能生产粮食的极限。

当饥饿的人无法从现有的田地中获得更多粮食时，他们就会砍伐山上和森林里的树木来获得新的耕地，这样做就会使土壤暴露出来。然后雨水和洪水可能会冲走田地的地表土壤，这个过程叫作侵蚀。每年由洪水所造成的侵蚀都会从农民手中夺走数十亿吨的表层土壤。

46. [正确答案] A

    [解析过程] 空格所在句的意思是：这取决于人们在不破坏环境的情况下能种植多少食物。

    根据语境，这里所表达的意思应该是"在不破坏环境的情况下"，without"没有"，符合文章所要表达的意思。

47. [正确答案] B

[解析过程] 空格所在句的意思是：现在的人口比以往任何时候都多，并且还在持续增长。根据语境，人口数量庞大并且还在持续增加。A项和C项表示"停止"，意思不符，故排除。keeps"保持"，符合语境，且keep doing也是惯用搭配。

48. [正确答案] C

[解析过程] 空格所在句的意思是：在21世纪末之前，地球可能拥有100亿人口！hold"容纳，拥有"。maintain和retain的意思是"保持，维持"，produce的意思是"生产"，它们都不符合文章语境。

49. [正确答案] D

[解析过程] 空格所在句的意思是：多年来世界粮食产量逐步上升。根据语境，粮食生产是呈上升的趋势，正确答案应该在C项和D项之间。而raise是及物动词，后面须跟宾语，故排除。

50. [正确答案] A

[解析过程] 空格所在句的意思是：在世界上一些地区，人口增长的速度超过了粮食供应的速度。前一句的意思是粮食产量呈上升趋势。这两句之间构成转折关系，故选however。

51. [正确答案] C

[解析过程] 空格所在句的意思是：世界将无法为不断增长的人口提供足够的粮食。前文主要是在讲粮食产量和人口上升的问题。所以population"人口"最符合文章所要表达的意思。

52. [正确答案] A

[解析过程] 空格所在句的意思是：为了在同样范围的土地上种植更多的作物……文章的语境表明人口增多，但土地面积却不增加，所以农民需要想办法在同样范围的土地上提高粮食产量。range"范围；类别"，符合文章所要表达的意思。

53. [正确答案] C

[解析过程] 空格所在句的意思是：这些东西虽然有帮助，但并不能提供完美的解决方案。这两句话前后是转折关系，所以C项正确。

54. [正确答案] D

[解析过程] 空格所在句的意思是：科学家研制出的新种子已经达到了它们所能生产粮食的极限。科学家已经让种子的产量达到了最大值，达到了一定的界限范围。limit"限度，限制；界限"，符合文章所要表达的意思。干扰项restriction的意思是"限制；约束"，这个词带有"束缚，约束"的意思，不符合语境。

55. [正确答案] D

[解析过程] 空格所在句的意思是：当饥饿的人无法从现有的田地中获得更多粮食时，他们会……根据语境，人们在现有的土地上无法获取更多粮食的时候，就会想办法开垦新的田地。existing"现存的，现有的"，符合文章所要表达的意思。surviving"未死的，依然健在的"，remaining"剩余的"，都不符合文章的语境。

Part V Text Completion

Text One

多年来,科学家一直在研究嗅觉的特殊能力。我们的鼻子和大脑似乎是紧密相连的。当你闻到某样东西时,气味会从鼻子进入嗅觉区。从这里,感觉细胞向你的大脑发送神经信息,告诉它你闻到了什么。

比起其他四种感觉,我们的嗅觉更能改变我们的情绪,并帮助我们记住事情。如果有人让你想一下爆米花,你可能会想起它的气味。然后你可能会想起你在吃它时看的电影。我们的嗅觉也会使我们意识到危险,比如闻到烟味的时候。

56. [正确答案] B
    [解析过程] 从语境含义来讲,空格处应该填写一个表示"当……的时候"的选项,意思是"边看……边吃……";如果实在不确定,也可以先完成另外3个题目,把此题作为最后一个空来完成。

57. [正确答案] C
    [解析过程] send sb./sth. to some place"把某人或某物送到某地"为习惯用法,所以空格要填写一个名词,nerve message"神经信息"符合语境。

58. [正确答案] D
    [解析过程] 选项已经具备基本句子成分,空格处可以再填一个副词,用来修饰后面的 connected,其他选项的词性在此处均不合理。

59. [正确答案] A
    [解析过程] help sb. do sth. 为固定搭配,意为"帮助某人做某事",且空格后面的单词 us 是宾格,备选项中只有 A 项 helps 才能放在此处。

60. [正确答案] C
    [解析过程] 从语法结构上看,此空缺少从句部分,能构成从句的有 A 项和 C 项,而 A 项的意思不符合这里的语境。

61. [正确答案] B
    [解析过程] 从语法结构上看,这里缺少句子的谓语,符合条件的有 B 项和 D 项。但是 D 项的动词用的是第三人称单数形式。

62. [正确答案] D
    [解析过程] 空格前面的 and 表明要填写一个和前面并列的结构,剩下 A 项和 D 项两个选项;再根据语境含义,可以推测出 D 项最符合语境。

63. [正确答案] A
    [解析过程] 空格处要填写一个成分来修饰空格前面的名词 movie,根据文章语境可以判断出 A 项正确。

Text Two

TED 是一系列会议的名称,每年在世界的多个城市举行。会议上有来自世界各地的各种演讲者,所有的演讲都会上传到 TED 的网站上,供大家观看。

TED 会议邀请演讲者就各种主题进行演讲。不同的演讲者——通常是他们所在领域的专家——谈论他们工作中重要的新观点和最近的发展。演讲者通常也是众所周知的公众人物,比如微软巨人比尔·盖茨和世界著名的黑猩猩专家简·古多尔就曾做过演讲。例如,有许多关于环境保护的讨论,还有关于国际发展、援助工作以及如何使用各种新方法来帮助贫困人口的讨论。虽然会涉及广泛的议题,但所有演讲者都有严格的时间限制,每次演讲不得超过 18 分钟。

64. [正确答案] B

   [解析过程] 此空前面有个介词 of,后面需要接名词词性的单词,选项中只有 B 项符合。

65. [正确答案] C

   [解析过程] 空格前面有系动词 are,后面不能接动词原形,所以只能选择 C 项用以表示被动。意思是"演讲被上传"。

66. [正确答案] A

   [解析过程] 此题用排除法来做,根据前两题的选项,排除过后可选择 A 项。或者根据意思,空格后的意思是"……关于各种主题",根据选项意思只有 A 项"发表演讲"符合语境。

67. [正确答案] B

   [解析过程] 空格前面是一个介词结构,整个句子缺少主干部分,所以空格处应该是完整的主谓宾结构;再根据语境,B 项"所有的演讲都会上传到 TED 的网站上"为正确选项。

68. [正确答案] C

   [解析过程] 空格前面有 to,所以空格处应该填写动词原形形式的单词。

69. [正确答案] A

   [解析过程] 空格处跟 and 前面的内容是并列关系,前面是会议话题的内容;结合各选项可知只有 A 项比较符合主题。

Text Three

在科技上花时间不仅带给孩子们新的做事方式,也改变了他们大脑的运行方式。例如,一篇文章说道,虽然电子游戏可能会使大脑注意到多种刺激,但它们会导致注意力分散和记忆力减退。总是使用搜索引擎的孩子可能会变得非常善于发现信息,但不擅长记住它们。此外,文章还说,使用过多科技的孩子可能没有足够的机会运用他们的想象力去深入地阅读或思考这些材料。

70. [正确答案] B

   [解析过程] be good at doing sth. "擅长做某事",为固定用法,由此推断此空后面应该是 B 项 finding。

71. [正确答案] C

   [解析过程] 这个空后面是个主谓结构的句子,所以可以作修饰前面内容的定语成分。A 项从结构和用法上都不符合,没有 use sth. do 的结构。

72. [正确答案] A

   [解析过程] 空格后面是个名词结构,前面可以用动词构成动宾结构,A 项从意思上也符合。

73. [正确答案] B

   [解析过程] 空格的前面有动词 changes,后面需要接名词作宾语,所以 B 项的核心名词 the way 刚好符合题意。

74. [正确答案] A

   [解析过程] 根据空格后面的 be good at doing sth. 可知,前面刚好可以填入 A 项与之构成并列结构,且从语义上说,but 前后也是转折的意思。

75. [正确答案] C

   [解析过程] have opportunity to do sth. "有机会做某事"为固定搭配,可以推断 C 项的 to use…符合语境。另外,空格后面也有"or"表示并列,所以空格处应该选择和 to read 类似的 to do 结构。

Paper Two　试卷二

Part Ⅵ　Translation

1. When it comes to personal finance, we are all looking for ways to save more money.

   [结构分析]这是一个主从复合句,前面是由 when 引导的时间状语从句。

   [词义推敲]When it comes to…"当说到/谈到……;当涉及……"。

   [参考译文]说到个人理财,我们总是想方设法去节省更多的钱。

2. Our household budgets are filled with both big and small expenses that we imagine can be cut out to save us loads of cash or, at the very least, spent better elsewhere.

   [结构分析]这是一个主从复合句,前面是主句,后面是 that 引导的定语从句修饰先行词 expenses。

   [词义推敲]expenses "费用,开支";loads of cash "大量的现金"。

   [参考译文]我们的家庭预算中充满了我们认为可以节省一大笔钱的大大小小的开支,或者至少觉得这些钱花在别处会更好。

3. One of the things you have surely considered is using public transportation rather than your own vehicle.

   [结构分析]从句 you have surely considered 省略了关系词 that,用以修饰作为主干主语的 One of the things;后面还有一个 rather than 连接的并列结构。

   [词义推敲]rather than "宁可……也不愿;与其……不如……";vehicle "车辆,交通工具"。

   [参考译文]你肯定考虑过其中一项,就是使用公共交通工具而不是你自己的车。

4. It would be easy to assume that public transportation is cheaper, because bus fare is far less expensive than gas, but those are not the only costs to consider.

   [结构分析]这个句子比较长,是一个由 but 引导的并列结构;且在前一个并列分句中还存在一个由 because 引导的原因状语从句,其主句是用形式主语 it 代替真正的主语,真正的主语为 that public transportation is cheaper。

   [词义推敲]assume "假定,设想,认为";far less than "远少于"。

   [参考译文]人们很容易认为公共交通更便宜,因为公交车的票价远低于油价,但这并不是唯

一需要考虑的成本。

5. Take a step back to your high school economics class and try to remember the lesson about opportunity costs.

   [结构分析]这是一个并列句,前后并列的是两个祈使句。

   [词义推敲]take a step back"退后一步"。

   [参考译文]回到你高中的经济学课堂,试着想想有关机会成本的那堂课。

6. These, as you might recall if you were awake for that class, are the things you give up when you choose one option over other options.

   [结构分析]这是一个主从复合句。主句是These are the things…。

   [词义推敲]option"选择"。

   [参考译文]如果那堂课你是清醒着的话,你可能会想起,这些正是当你在诸多选项中做出一个选择时所放弃的东西。

7. Although they are not measured in dollars and cents, they still have to be considered whenever you make a financial decision.

   [结构分析]这是一个主从复合句,主句是they still have to be considered…；Although 和 whenever分别引导让步状语从句和时间状语从句。

   [词义推敲]financial decision"财务决策"。

   [参考译文]尽管它们并不是用金钱来衡量的,但它们是你在做财务决定时仍然不得不考虑的事情。

Part Ⅶ　Writing

这是一篇议论文,题目要求给出了主题——"幸福夫妻的秘诀是什么?",并且在下面给出了相应的例子引导考生的思路。也就是说,文章要围绕夫妻相处之道这个中心来展开。

我们可以整理出写作思路并列出提纲:第一段,提出问题,阐述问题的背景;第二段,阐述夫妻家庭幸福的方法,可适当举例或展开论述;第三段,对全篇做一个总结,重申观点或说明意义。

Nowadays more and more people are paying attention to what makes happy couples happy. This has aroused widespread discussion among the general public. From my perspective, happy family has far-reaching significance to our society and life and there are many ways to make the couples happy.

As a matter of fact, ways that make happy couples happy can be illustrated below. The first one that comes to my mind readily is that those happy couples cultivate common interest. One strength that solid couples have is the trait of sharing hobbies or common interest, as well as joint projects. This is a good way to keep their love longer and longer. What's more, they focus more on what their partners do right than what they do wrong. If you concentrate on finding positive qualities and virtues, I assure you that you will find those as well. Besides, they trust and forgive each other. Forgiveness is a great tool of healing and repair. It provides tremendous relief and prevents relationships from deteriorating. If we add trust to forgiveness, we drive away the resentment that may follow from unresolved issues or unhappy conversations.

There is no easy solution to the problem of keeping a happy family relationship. It is time to raise people's awareness of it. I strongly believe that it benefits not only the couples themselves, but also their relatives and even the society. Only in this way can we hope to make our society more stable and harmonious.

范文点评

　　这篇范文紧扣主题，用词丰富，句式多样，文章思路清晰，详略得当，没有语法和拼写错误，给人印象很不错。我们来看一下内容：

　　第一段：用模板例句引出问题的背景，指出越来越多的人正关注幸福夫妻相处之道，并阐明自己的观点，认为这个话题意义重大，从而引出下段主要内容。

　　第二段：开头就指出本段主要内容，并给出具体的方法和例子。作者用词、用语丰富多样，比如在写具体方法时的句型，第一点"One strength that solid couples have is…"；第二点"What's more, they focus more on + 从句"；第三点用简单句"Besides, they trust and forgive each other"。此外，"the first…""what's more…"等词的运用，也使得文章层次鲜明、富有逻辑。

　　第三段：对全篇做出总结，并提出建议。作者在总结时，用了"There is no easy solution to the problem of…""It is time to…""not only…but also…"等经典佳句表达，且还有最后一句的倒装句等，它们都提升了文章的层次。

　　整篇文章观点鲜明，有理有据。文章在保证语法和单词正确的情况下，采用了丰富多样的词汇和句式，写得非常精彩，这也正是这篇作文能得高分的原因所在。

2018年同等学力人员申请硕士学位
英语水平全国统一考试

Paper One 试卷一（100 minutes）

Part I Oral Communication（15 minutes, 10 points）

Section A

Directions: *In this section there are two incomplete dialogues and each dialogue has three blanks and three choices A, B and C, taken from the dialogue. Fill in each of the blanks with one of the choices to complete the dialogue and mark your answer on the **Answer sheet**.*

Dialogue One

A. How about you?
B. Wanna join us?
C. It's a long weekend.

Tina: I'm so glad the weekend's finally here.
Lewis: Me too. Imagine! __1__ We've got three days in a row.
Tina: So, where're you going?
Lewis: I don't have any plan yet. I'll just play it by ear. __2__
Tina: We're going to go hiking and camping in the mountains.
Lewis: That sounds exciting!
Tina: __3__
Lewis: Hm, let me think about it. I'll let you know later.

Dialogue Two

A. And I'd like the cheapest flight available.
B. What is your destination?
C. And when will you be returning?

Travel Agent: Freedom Travel. How can I help you?
Caller: Yes, I'd like to make a flight reservation for the twenty-third of this month.
Travel Agent: Okay. __4__

Caller: Well. I'm flying to Helsinki, Finland.

Travel Agent: Okay. Let me check what flights are available. __5__

Caller: Uh, well, I'd like to catch a return flight on the twenty-ninth. __6__

Travel Agent: Okay. Let me see. Um, that's flight 1070 from Salt Lake City to New York, Kennedy Airport, transferring to flight 90 from Kennedy to Helsinki. It's only $980.

Caller: Alright, let's go with that.

Section B

Directions: *In this section there is one incomplete interview which has four blanks and four choices A, B, C and D, taken from the interview. Fill in each of the blanks with one of the choices to complete the interview and mark your answer on the **Answer sheet**.*

A. I think the big difference is,

B. What have you done to make this yours?

C. how they look in the Oval Office.

D. you don't need so much heart.

On Donald Trump's 100th day as U.S. president, he spoke with "Face the Nation" host and Chief Washington Correspondent John Dickerson.

Dickerson: What's the difference between negotiating in Washington versus negotiating in business?

Trump: Well, __7__ for what we're doing here, Washington, you really need heart, because you're talking about a lot of people. Whereas business, __8__ You want to make a good deal.

Dickerson: Every president makes the Oval Office theirs. __9__

Trump: Well, a lot of things. We had these incredible flags including the American flags, the Coast Guard flag over here. And I said, "Well, let's see __10__ " So the flags were up. The picture of Thomas Jefferson I put up. The picture of Andrew Jackson I put up because they said his campaign and my campaign tended to mirror each other. So we did a lot of—actually we did a lot of work. It has a much different look than it was previously.

Part II Vocabulary (10 minutes, 10 points)

Directions: *In this part there are ten sentences, each with one word or phrase underlined. Choose the one from the four choices marked A, B, C and D that best keeps the meaning of the sentence. Mark your answer on the **Answer Sheet**.*

11. According to the minister, measures are being taken to introduce more <u>diversity</u> into the education system.

    A. difference B. adversity C. unity D. variety

12. He would <u>once in a while</u> lose his temper when he found himself involved in an argument.

A. rarely   B. often   C. occasionally   D. seldom
13. Intuition is something that cannot be proven, but many people believe in it and use it for decision making.
   A. Instinct   B. Intelligence C. Rationality   D. Experience
14. A global company must be sensitive to the cultures and customs of the countries where it operates.
   A. patient   B. generous   C. emotional   D. responsive
15. At last John Smith stepped down as the company's CEO and returned to his roots in software research.
   A. retired   B. resigned   C. revived   D. reacted
16. Immersed in their experiment, they had no idea what happened just outside their lab.
   A. Concentrated B. Addicted   C. Absorbed   D. Committed
17. Last month the government initiated a public debate on the future direction of the sport policy.
   A. transmitted   B. followed   C. promoted   D. launched
18. My beard started to grow, and I unwillingly complied with the order to shave it off.
   A. considered   B. questioned   C. supported   D. observed
19. As the fighting intensified, the chances of any peace deal diminished.
   A. decreased   B. changed   C. disappeared   D. expanded
20. However superficially appealing such an idea might appear, it was irrational and reckless.
   A. possibly   B. seemingly   C. apparently   D. practically

Part III Reading Comprehension (45 minutes, 25 points)

Section A

Directions: *In this section, there are four passages followed by questions or unfinished statements, each with four suggested answers A, B, C and D. Choose the best answer and mark your answer on the **Answer Sheet**.*

Passage One

Alice Paul Tapper was on a fourth-grade field trip last year when she noticed something that bothered her. The girls were standing in the back of the room, listening politely as the guide spoke. The boys crowded together in the front. They raised their hands to respond to questions, even if they didn't know the answer.

Alice, 10, often doesn't raise her hand in class, even if she's pretty sure she knows the answer. She's nervous she'll get it wrong and feel embarrassed. On that field trip, she figured a lot of other girls were probably keeping quiet, too.

Alice told her mom what she saw. They talked about how girls are often told to be quiet and polite, while boys are encouraged to be bold and assertive. Alice and her mom talk about that kind of thing a lot. She wants boys and girls to have the same opportunities. "Girls are important, and their ideas are important," Alice says. "They should be heard."

Alice's mom is the leader of Alice's Girl Scout troop, in Washington, D. C. She and Alice brought the issue up at their next Girl Scout meeting. Alice found she was right. The other girls said they, too, sometimes hesitated to raise their hands, and they worried that this could hold them back in life. Alice wanted to change that. "If a girl raises her hand, it's one step toward becoming a great leader," she says.

Alice's troop decided to ask the Girl Scouts organization to create a new patch. The new patch was introduced in October 2017. It is called the Raise Your Hand patch. To earn it, a girl has to do three things. She must pledge to raise her hand in class when she thinks she knows the answer—even if she's not 100% sure. She must recruit three girls to make the same pledge. And she must talk about how raising her hand makes her feel.

So far, more than 5,400 girls have earned the Raise Your Hand patch. They live in every state in the U. S., plus Canada, the United Kingdom, Australia, and Ireland. "Girls are powerful," Alice says. "They should raise their hands so they can release the power inside them."

21. What bothered Alice on her field trip last year?

   A. The guide was impolite to the girls.

   B. There were more boys than girls.

   C. The boys made trouble as the guide spoke.

   D. The girls were less responsive than the boys.

22. Girls often don't raise their hands in class because they _____.

   A. don't know the answer pretty well

   B. don't want to get too much attention

   C. are taught to be quiet and polite

   D. are given fewer chances than boys

23. The Raise Your Hand patch was created to _____.

   A. encourage girls to speak up

   B. improve girls' talent for organization

   C. call for more support from girls

   D. highlight the importance of girls

24. The Raise Your Hand patch _____.

   A. has helped girls become leaders

   B. is popular in some states in the U. S.

   C. is spreading all over the world

   D. has attracted thousands of girls

25. Which of the following can be the best title of the passage?

   A. A Show of Hands

   B. A Campaign for Equality

   C. The Girl Scouts Organization

   D. The Story of a New Patch

Passage Two

Stephen Hawking was born on 8 January, 1942 and grew up in St Albans, the eldest of four brothers and sisters. His father was a research biologist and his mother a medical research secretary, so it was not surprising that he was interested in science. As a student he was drawn to physics and maths as he believed they offered the most fundamental insights into the world. But nothing marked him out as special from his classmates at Oxford University.

Stephen got first in Physics from Oxford, and started a PhD at Cambridge. His own private universe expanded when he proposed to his future wife. Jane was also from St Albans, and was a modern languages undergraduate. She had met Hawking at a New Year's party, before his diagnosis. The couple decided to marry quickly, because they did not know how long Stephen had to live. As Stephen's health deteriorated, he took to walking with stick.

Hawking escaped the limits of his disability by training his mind to work in a new way. As he started to lose the use of his limbs, he developed a way of visualizing problems in his mind to reach a solution instead of by writing equations. Some of his colleagues have suggested that this way of thinking has led to his greatest discoveries. Hawking was now working on one of science's most bizarre ideas—black holes, an extreme prediction of Einstein's general theory of relativity.

Hawking's work on black boles helped prove the idea of a "Big Bang" at the birth of the Universe. Developed in the 1940s, Big Bang theory was still not accepted by all scientists. Working with mathematician Roger Penrose, Hawking realized that black holes were like the Big Bang in reverse—and that meant the maths he'd used to describe black boles also described the Big Bang. It was a key moment in showing the Big Bang really happened. As his body deteriorated, Hawking's career was taking off.

26. Hawking developed an early interest in science because _____.

    A. his brothers and sisters loved it

    B. he took related lessons as a kid

    C. he excelled in maths and physics

    D. his parents influenced him

27. What can be learned about Hawking's wife Jane?

    A. She and Hawking came from the same place.

    B. She and Hawking went to the same school.

    C. She married Hawking on New Year's Day.

    D. She didn't know of his disease before their marriage.

28. Hawking's self-trained way of working _____.

    A. helped the recovery of his health

    B. required a lot of equation writing

    C. relied heavily on mental images

    D. was copied by his colleagues

29. The following statements about the Big Bang theory are true EXCEPT _____.

   A. Hawking was its founder

   B. it was connected with black holes

   C. Hawking's research supported it

   D. not all scientists agreed with it

30. As a leading figure in science, Hawking _____.

   A. lived for fifty-five years

   B. wrote many best-selling novels

   C. led some organizations for the disabled

   D. fought against his disease most of his life

Passage Three

Imagine that you're a fly. You're just looking for a place to rest, when you see a nice pink leaf. That looks like a nice place to land. As you rest your feet on the leaf, you notice something strange. This leaf is hairy. You begin to make your move, but you trigger the plant's reaction. Snap! In one-tenth of a second, you are caught in the Venus flytrap. You will be digested in five to twelve days.

Out of about 391,000 plant species in the world, only 600 or so are carnivorous. We call them this because they attract, trap, and eat bugs. Like other plants, they get energy from the sun. But unlike other plants, they get their nutrients from their prey(猎物). Carnivorous plants live in places where the soil lacks nutrients. Most plants get nutrients from the soil. Carnivorous plants have turned to other sources.

Pitcher plants trick their prey into landing on them. They offer nectar(花蜜) bribes to the foolish insects that would take them. True to their name, pitcher plants have deep chambers. Their landing surface is slippery. They have inward pointing hairs, making it hard to escape. The fly lands on the pitcher plant to eat but slips into a pit filled with digestive fluids.

Corkscrew plants have inviting stems. Curved hairs line the inside of these stems. These hairs allow insects to go up the stems, but not back. Going forward leads to the plant's stomach. Bugs who wander into the corkscrew plant find that they are unable to escape. They must march to their own death.

And then there are the bladderworts. They live in water and float near the surface. Their traps are like small bladders(囊状物) hidden beneath the water. Only their flowers are visible from the surface. When bugs swim into the trigger hairs, the plant reacts. The bladder sucks up the prey and the water surrounding it. The prey will be digested within hours.

31. The word "carnivorous" (Para. 2) is closest in meaning to "_____".

   A. nutritious   B. bug-eating   C. plant-eating   D. attractive

32. Which statement would the author most likely agree with?

   A. There are too many species of carnivorous plants.

   B. There are too few plant species in the world.

C. Only a small number of plant species are carnivorous.

D. The majority of plants are carnivorous.

33. Carnivorous plants get their nutrients mainly from _____.

    A. other plants   B. the soil   C. the sun   D. their prey

34. Which of the following best expresses the main idea of the third paragraph?

    A. There are many studies of carnivorous plants.

    B. The pitcher plant tricks bugs into its stomach.

    C. The pitcher plant kills its prey in various ways.

    D. Some plants attract bugs by offering them nectar.

35. As can be inferred, the corkscrew's chamber for digestion is located _____.

    A. somewhere towards its root   B. somewhere towards its top

    C. inside its flowers   D. inside its leaves

Passage Four

Serenity (宁静) is difficult to find in today's fast-paced world. A moment of complete calm seems to be a rare and wonderful find. For me, those precious moments occur on a boat. As legendary sailor Vito Dumas once said: "It's out there at sea that you are really yourself." On deck, enjoying awe-inspiring views, the cares of everyday life blown away on the sea breeze, you can appreciate his point.

Flying is a misery. From airport chaos to the confined space of an aircraft, nothing about commercial aviation appeals to my sense of adventure—or comfort. Favoring boat travel isn't just about managing flight fear, though. Whether I'm on a short ferry crossing or a cruise, the sea provides a true sense of travel, from the impressive physical shift of a ship leaving port to its navigation of the open water. "We are tied to the ocean," John F. Kennedy said. As my ship steers towards an exciting new destination, I feel that <u>affinity</u>.

And I'm not alone. "The journey is part of the holiday," says travel writer Helen Ochyra. "I'll stand out on deck, whatever the weather, and watch the ropes being untied, the boat slipping away from the dock and the landscape drifting farther and farther away."

Tom Bourlet, founder of the Spaghetti Traveler blog, agrees: "On a plane, it's difficult to make out much more than grassland; on the ferry, there is something exciting about seeing land slowly getting closer."

For Cathy Winston, travel editor, it's about the sense of adventure. "Even on a fairly simple journey from A to B," she says, "wide and open sea makes it feel like you could be off to discover new lands. There's a certain romance you don't get on a plane or on a motorway." Winston also values the family-friendly aspects of sea travel. "There's something so relaxing about being on the water, especially with kids," she says.

Whether it's for kid-happy convenience or sheer romance, boats will always be the preferred mode of transport for many travelers. A boat gets me where I want to go, avoiding the rush—and terror—of air travel. And out on the waves, as reality melts away, I always rediscover my own passion for the sea.

36. Which aspect of sea travel is emphasized in the first paragraph?

   A. Extraordinary view.　　　　　　　　B. Complete freedom.

   C. Peace of mind.　　　　　　　　　　D. Sense of adventure.

37. The word "affinity" (Para. 2) is closest in meaning to "_____".

   A. strong emotion　　　　　　　　　　B. close connection

   C. sheer excitement　　　　　　　　　D. impressive moment

38. Who is deeply impressed while watching the boat leaving the dock?

   A. Helen Ochyra.　　　　　　　　　　B. Vito Dumas.

   C. Cathy Winston.　　　　　　　　　　D. John F. Kennedy.

39. According to Tom Bourlet, sea travel is better than air travel in that it _____.

   A. enables people to engage in deeper thought

   B. gives passengers a better chance to relax

   C. provides a more comfortable environment

   D. offers a clearer view of the landscape

40. According to the last two paragraphs, sea travel has all the following benefits EXCEPT _____.

   A. being family-friendly　　　　　　　B. satisfying an adventurous heart

   C. promoting a healthy lifestyle　　　　D. providing relaxation

Section B

Directions: *In this section, you are required to read one quoted blog and the comments on it. The blog and comments are followed by questions or unfinished statements, each with four suggested answers A, B, C and D. Choose the best answer and mark your answer on the **Answer Sheet**.*

At SXSW, the tech and culture conference in Austin, London Mayor Sadiq Khan criticized big tech companies and regulators for failing to stem the spread of hate, misinformation and radical viewpoints online.

The mayor said that governments have been in "<u>dereliction</u> of duty" when it comes to passing regulations to combat the ways technology has negatively affected society. "One of the biggest problems over the last few years is that politicians and governments have just been passive—sitting on their hands—while the tech revolution has happened around them," Khan said in his remarks.

Ultimately, he said, it's up to governments to work with technology businesses and leaders to make sure that technological advancement has the proper checks.

Social media firms are already under new regulatory pressure in Europe, thanks to German laws enacted in January that will fine companies that don't take down problematic content within 24 hours of it being reported.

Khan did not call for this type of regulation but warned that even stricter regulation could be on its way if companies don't respond to government concerns. "Ultimately—there must be greater responsibility taken by some tech companies for the impact they're having on the world."

Comment 1

Looking at this from the point of view of "industry regulation" is simply flawed. At the core of this, it is individuals who are making choices to "post" each and every time. What our society seems to have lost is a sense of personal responsibility.

Comment 2

It's not exactly easy to implement laws that targets content online. The bigger issue is that law enforcement simply doesn't have the resources to act on all these crimes happening on the Internet.

Comment 3

I agree that technology has failed us in at least one very important way: Twitter, Facebook, etc., published and continues to publish untruths and fake "news", that some people assume are accurate. They must do something.

Comment 4

The companies at issue promote the content being objected to. That is the content that drives their revenues and profits. So self-regulation just never works without the threat of harsh regulation.

Comment 5

Information and Communications Technology (ICT), through its evolution, has generally been perceived as beneficial, furthering progress and the common good. But, ICT has not had the foresight to see how the evolving industry can produce unintended consequences. It's time for ICT to step up.

41. The word "dereliction" (Para. 2) probably means "_____".
    A. deliberate neglect   B. potential abuse
    C. constant misjudgment   D. apparent misunderstanding

42. What does Khan emphasize with his remarks in the last paragraph?
    A. Strict British regulation.   B. German-style regulatory laws.
    C. Government-industry cooperation. D. Self-regulation of the industry.

43. According to **Comment 1**, who is to blame for the spread of misinformation?
    A. Businesses.   B. Individuals.
    C. Government officials.   D. Industry leaders.

44. Which of the comments favors strict government regulation?
    A. Comment 2.   B. Comment 3.   C. Comment 4.   D. Comment 5.

45. Which comments agree with Khan on the role of tech companies?
    A. Comments 1 and 4.   B. Comments 2 and 3.
    C. Comments 4 and 5.   D. Comments 3 and 5.

Part IV Cloze (10 minutes, 10 points)

Directions: *In this part, there is a passage with ten blanks. For each blank there are four choices marked A, B, C and D. Choose the best answer for each blank and mark your answer on the **Answer Sheet**.*

Every day, they slowly accumulate. Plates covered in sauces and bread pieces. Bowls with a fine layer of who-knows-what. Forks, knives, and spoons all stuck with bits of this and that. At the end of a long day of work, cooking, cleaning, and, for many, negotiating with small children, a couple has to __46__ the big question: Who is going to do the __47__?

A recent report on family dynamics suggests that the answer to that question can have a significant impact __48__ the health and long lasting of a relationship. The study examined a variety of different household tasks, __49__ shopping, laundry and housecleaning, and found that, for women in families, it's more important to __50__ the responsibility of doing the dishes than any other task. Women who wash the vast majority of the dishes themselves report __51__ relationship conflict and less relationship satisfaction than women with husbands __52__ help. Women are happier about sharing dishwashing __53__ than they are about sharing any other household task.

What is it about dishes? Dan Carlson, assistant professor of family and consumer studies at the University of Utah, and the lead author of the study, offers his own observations: "Doing dishes is gross. __54__, unlike some other household tasks such as cooking or gardening, doing dishes well does not __55__ praises."

46. A. make	B. ask	C. face	D. deal
47. A. cooking	B. laundry	C. homework	D. dishes
48. A. on	B. for	C. to	D. at
49. A. requiring	B. including	C. undertaking	D. organizing
50. A. exchange	B. shoulder	C. take	D. share
51. A. less	B. fewer	C. further	D. more
52. A. which	B. who	C. what	D. whom
53. A. duties	B. problems	C. questions	D. troubles
54. A. Seemingly	B. However	C. Besides	D. Finally
55. A. demand	B. generate	C. mention	D. provide

Part V Text Completion (20 minutes, 20 points)

Directions: *In this part, there are three incomplete texts with 20 questions (ranging from 56 to 75). Above each text there are three or four phrases to be completed. First, use the choices provided in the box to complete the phrases. Second, use the completed phrases to fill in the blanks of the text. Mark your answer on the* **Answer Sheet**.

Text One

> A. so plentiful
> B. showered with
> C. exchange rings

Phrases:

　　A. the bride and groom often __56__
　　B. where the food is __57__
　　C. the couple is often __58__ handfuls of uncooked rice

· 10 ·

Wedding ceremonies in the United States vary as much as the people do. But many weddings, no matter where or how they are performed, include certain traditional customs. For instance, __59__ at the ceremony. The rings are usually worn on the fourth finger of the left hand, and are exchanged in the middle of the ceremony.

After the ceremony, __60__ by friends and family. Rice, as we know, shows productivity and harvest. And then, there is often a party, __61__ that it almost takes the attention away from the people.

Text Two

A. who
B. only
C. the way

Phrases:

A. That number __62__ increases
B. they change __63__ their brains work
C. children __64__ use too much technology

More than a third of children under the age of two use mobile media. __65__ as children age, with 95% of teens 12-17 spending time online.

The time spent with technology doesn't just give kids novel ways of doing things; it can lead to distraction and decreased memory. For example, while video games may condition the brain to pay attention to multiple stimuli, __66__.

Children who always use search engines may become very good at finding information—but not very good at remembering it. In addition, __67__ may not have enough opportunities to use their imagination or to read and think deeply about the material.

Text Three

A. temperature
B. special
C. think
D. other

Phrases:

A. have created a __68__ technique
B. __69__ of eating the peel
C. at a freezing cold __70__
D. similar to __71__ countries

It almost seems too hard to believe, but there is now a banana that has an eatable peel. Most people would never __72__ of a banana. However, banana farmers in Japan __73__ for growing bananas with a peel we can eat. Farmers in Okayama, in the west of Japan, keep their banana trees __74__ of -60℃. The farmers then replant the trees in 27℃ temperatures. The huge change in temperature makes the tree suddenly grow too quickly for the peel to fully mature. This makes the skin thin, soft and sweet enough to eat. Bananas are the most popular fruit in Japan. __75__, Japan imports most of its bananas. About 99% of bananas in Japanese stores are imported. The new technique could mean Japanese people eat more home-grown bananas.

Paper Two 试卷二 (50 minutes)

Part VI Translation (20 minutes, 10 points)

Directions: *Translate the following passage into Chinese. Write your answer on the **Answer Sheet**.*

It's harder and harder to find peace and, especially, quiet. Even in the most remote parts of Alaska the sound of a jet crossing overhead is all too common. Scientists set off across the U.S. to study the audio ecology. They recorded more than a million hours of sound from various sources.

They found that noise pollution is not good for people and it's even worse for animals with more sensitive ears. And the problem is not confined to land but echoes across the seas as well, where human-produced noise interferes with the live of various ocean dwellers. These days on Earth it's rare to hear "silence".

Part VII Writing (30 minutes, 15 points)

Directions: *Write a composition in no less than 150 words on the topic:* ***The Ideal Public Library***. *You could write according to the clues given below. Write your composition on the **Answer Sheet**.*

A library is a place in which reading materials, such as books, periodicals, and newspapers, and often other materials such as musical and video recordings, are kept for use or lending. Describe the public library you would like to have in your neighborhood.

2018年同等学力人员申请硕士学位英语水平全国统一考试

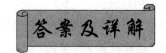

Paper One 试卷一

Part I Oral Communication

Section A

对话一

    A. 你们呢？

    B. 想加入我们吗？

    C. 这是个很长的周末。

蒂娜：我很高兴周末终于来了。

路易斯：我也是。想象一下吧！__1__ 我们有连续三天的时间。

蒂娜：那你要去哪里？

路易斯：我还没有计划。我看情况，__2__

蒂娜：我们打算去爬山，在山里露营。

路易斯：听起来很令人兴奋。

蒂娜：__3__

路易斯：嗯，让我想想吧。我稍后会告诉你。

1. [正确答案] C

    [考点剖析] 通过第1题后面的句子"我们有连续三天的时间"，可以倒推此题表达的意思是这个周末很长。

2. [正确答案] A

    [考点剖析] 从下面蒂娜对本题的回答，可以推知此处是路易斯向蒂娜询问她的安排。

3. [正确答案] B

    [考点剖析] 从第3题前面路易斯对蒂娜周末安排发出的感叹"听起来很令人兴奋"可以看出，他对此很感兴趣，逻辑上蒂娜很可能在此处向路易斯发出邀请。B项也可以从路易斯的回答"嗯，让我想想吧"得到印证。

对话二

    A. 我想订最便宜的机票。

    B. 您的目的地是哪里？

    C. 您什么时候回来？

旅行社代理人:这里是自由旅行社,您有什么需要吗?
打电话者:是的,我想预订本月23号的机票。
旅行社代理人:好的。__4__
打电话者:我要飞往芬兰的赫尔辛基。
旅行社代理人:好的。让我查一下有哪些航班。__5__
打电话者:嗯,我想乘坐29号的回程班机。__6__
旅行社代理人:好的。让我看看。从盐湖城到纽约肯尼迪机场的1070次航班,然后从肯尼迪机场转乘90次航班到赫尔辛基,这样只需980美元。
打电话者:好的,就这样吧。

4.［正确答案］B

　［考点剖析］根据第4题后面打电话者的回答"我要飞往芬兰的赫尔辛基",不难看出此处是旅行社代理人在问打电话者此行的目的地。

5.［正确答案］C

　［考点剖析］根据本题后面打电话者的回答"我想乘坐29号的回程班机",可以推知此处旅行社代理人问的是返程日期。

6.［正确答案］A

　［考点剖析］在本题后面的回答中,旅行社代理人提供了转机的出行方式,并提示"只需980美元",可以倒推出打电话者在询问廉价的航班。

Section B

A. 我认为一个大的区别是,
B. 为了让它属于你,你都做了些什么?
C. 它们在椭圆形办公室里的样子。
D. 你不需要花这么多的心思。

在唐纳德·特朗普成为美国总统的第100天,他跟《面对国家》节目主持人兼华盛顿首席记者约翰·迪克森进行了谈话。
迪克森:在华盛顿谈判和在公司谈判有什么区别?
特朗普:嗯,__7__ 在华盛顿这里做的事情,你真的需要花费心思,因为你的谈话会牵涉很多人。然而在公司谈判中,__8__ 你只想做成一笔好交易。
迪克森:每位总统都把椭圆形办公室变成他们自己的。__9__
特朗普:嗯,很多事情。我们插了很棒的旗帜,有美国国旗,有海岸警卫队的旗帜。我说:"好吧,让我们看看__10__"所以这些旗帜就这样插上了。我挂上了托马斯·杰斐逊的画像,我还挂上了安德鲁·杰克逊的画像,因为人们说我俩的竞选活动异曲同工。我们实际上做了很多工作。它(椭圆办公室)和以前相比有很大的不同。

7.［正确答案］A

　［考点剖析］本题前面迪克森问特朗普在华盛顿谈判和在公司谈判的不同,所以,特朗普对此进行回答,A项"我认为一个大的区别是"在此处起到了很好的承上启下的作用。

8. [正确答案] D

[考点剖析] 在回答中,特朗普先指出了在华盛顿谈判需要花费心思,接着用转折语气强调在公司谈判与此不同,所以 D 项符合上下文语境。

9. [正确答案] B

[考点剖析] 本题前面迪克森提到"每位总统都把椭圆形办公室变成他们自己的",而在之后的访谈中,特朗普讲述了自己在椭圆形办公室的装饰上做的改进,所以 B 项"为了让它属于你,你都做了些什么?"符合上下文语境。

10. [正确答案] C

[考点剖析] 在特朗普的回答中,他首先列出了各种不同的旗帜,在本题前面又说"让我们看看……",只有 C 项"它们在椭圆形办公室里的样子"符合语境。

Part II Vocabulary

11. [正确答案] D

[考点类型] 名词

[考点剖析] 题干中的 diversity 意为"多样性"。difference "不同";adversity "逆境";unity "一致";variety "变化,多样化"。

12. [正确答案] C

[考点类型] 副词

[考点剖析] 题干中的 once in a while 意为"偶尔"。rarely "很少";often "经常";occasionally "偶尔";seldom "很少"。

13. [正确答案] A

[考点类型] 名词

[考点剖析] 题干中的 Intuition 意为"直觉"。Instinct "本能,直觉";Intelligence "智力";Rationality "合理性";Experience "经验"。

14. [正确答案] D

[考点类型] 形容词

[考点剖析] 题干中的 sensitive 意为"敏感的"。patient "耐心的";generous "慷慨的";emotional "情绪的";responsive "反应敏捷的"。

15. [正确答案] B

[考点类型] 动词

[考点剖析] 题干中的 stepped down 意为"让位,退化"。retired "退休";resigned "辞职";revived "使复活";reacted "反应"。

16. [正确答案] C

[考点类型] 形容词

[考点剖析] 题干中的 Immersed 意为"专注的;浸入的"。Concentrated "集中的";Addicted "上瘾的";Absorbed "全神贯注的";Committed "约好的;坚信的"。

17. [正确答案] D

[考点类型] 动词

[考点剖析] 题干中的 initiated 意为"发起;开始"。transmitted "传送";followed "跟随";promoted "提升";launched "发起;开始从事"。

18. [正确答案] D

    [考点类型] 动词

    [考点剖析] 题干中的 complied with 意为"遵守,照做"。considered"考虑";questioned"质疑";supported"支持";observed"遵守"。

19. [正确答案] A

    [考点类型] 动词

    [考点剖析] 题干中的 diminished 意为"减少"。decreased"减少";changed"改变";disappeared"消失";expanded"扩大"。

20. [正确答案] B

    [考点类型] 副词

    [考点剖析] 题干中的 superficially 意为"表面上"。possibly"可能";seemingly"表面上";apparently"显然地";practically"实际地;差不多地"。

Part Ⅲ Reading Comprehension

Section A

Passage One

　　爱丽丝·保罗·塔柏去年四年级的时候参加了一次实地考察,行程中她观察到的一些事使她感到烦恼。她发现,女生都站在房间的后面,礼貌地听着导游讲话,然而男生却簇拥在房间前面,即使不知道答案,他们也举手回答问题。

　　十岁的爱丽丝即使十分确定自己知道答案,她在课堂上也不经常举手。因为她感到紧张,担心出错,并为此感到尴尬。就在那次实地考察中,她发现,许多别的女孩子也都显得过于安静。

　　爱丽丝告诉了妈妈她看到的情况。她们聊到女生常常被告知要保持安静和礼貌,然而男生却被鼓励要保持大胆和自信。爱丽丝和她妈妈就这件事聊了很多。她希望男孩和女孩拥有同样的机会。"女孩很重要,她们的想法也很重要,"爱丽丝说,"女孩们的心声应该被人们听到。"

　　爱丽丝的妈妈是华盛顿特区爱丽丝所在的女童子军队的领队。她和爱丽丝在接下来的一次女童子军会议上提出了这个问题。爱丽丝发现她的想法是对的,其他女孩说她们有时也犹豫要不要举手,她们担心这种情况会在生活中给她们拖后腿。爱丽丝想改变这一点。"如果一个女孩举起了她的手,那么她就在成为伟大领导者的道路上迈进了一步。"她说。

　　爱丽丝的团队决定要求女童子军组织设立一条补充条款。被称为"举起你的手来"的条款于2017年10月推出。为了完成它,女孩必须做三件事。第一,当觉得自己知道答案时,她必须保证在课堂上举手,即使她不是100%确定。第二,她必须使得三名女孩做出同样的承诺。第三,她必须谈论举手后的感觉。

　　到目前为止,已有超过5 400名女孩参与了"举起你的手来"的活动。她们分布在美国的各个州,还有加拿大、英国、澳大利亚和爱尔兰等国家。"女孩很强大,"爱丽丝说,"她们应该举起手来,释放出内心的力量。"

21. [正确答案] D

    [考点类型] 细节题

    [题目翻译] 是什么让爱丽丝在去年的实地考察中感到烦恼?

A. 导游对女孩不礼貌。
B. 男孩比女孩多。
C. 男孩们在导游说话时捣乱。
D. 女孩的积极性不如男孩。

[考点剖析] 根据题目中含有的定位词 bothered Alice 和 on her field trip last year，以及题文同序的一般规律，判断本题的答案主要存在于第一段中的相关描述中，从 The girls were standing in the back… listening politely… The boys crowded together in the front. They raised their hands to respond…, even if they didn't know the answer 可以看出令爱丽丝感到烦恼的是女孩的积极性不如男孩。

22. [正确答案] C

[考点类型] 细节题

[题目翻译] 女孩在课堂上经常不举手，因为她们_____。
A. 不太清楚答案
B. 不想引起太多的关注
C. 被教导要保持安静和礼貌
D. 被给予的机会比男孩少

[考点剖析] 本题问的是女孩不愿举手的原因。本文第二段的主要内容是爱丽丝罗列自己以及别人的情况，并未涉及原因。而从文中第三段第二句 They talked about how girls are often told to be quiet and polite, while boys… 不难看出是因为人们教导女孩要保持安静和礼貌，C 项的意思和此一致。

23. [正确答案] A

[考点类型] 细节题

[题目翻译] 设立"举起你的手来"补充条款的目的是_____。
A. 鼓励女孩大声说出（答案）
B. 提高女孩的组织能力
C. 呼吁女孩给予更多支持
D. 强调女孩的重要性

[考点剖析] 本题考查不定式短语，考点是设立此项补充条款的目的。根据定位词 Raise Your Hand patch 发现第五段第三句出现了该短语，通过仔细阅读后面的句子 She must pledge to raise her hand in class… she must talk about how raising her hand makes her feel 发现这些要求都跟 A 项的 encourage girls to speak up 有关，再参考本篇文章的主题，可知 A 项正确。

24. [正确答案] D

[考点类型] 细节题

[题目翻译] "举起你的手来"补充条款_____。
A. 帮助了女孩成为领导者
B. 在美国的一些州很流行
C. 正在全世界传播
D. 已经吸引了成千上万的女孩

[考点剖析] 根据题目中的 Raise Your Hand patch 及题文同序的一般规律，从第 23 题的出题区域往后在文中寻找。由 more than 5,400 girls have earned the Raise Your Hand patch. They live in every state in the U. S. , plus Canada, the United Kingdom, Australia, and Ireland 中可以看出 D 项跟原文表述相符。A 项在文中没有提及;B 项中的"some states"跟原文中的"every state"矛盾;C 项的传播范围"all over the world"跟原文中提到的传播范围不一致。

25. [正确答案] B

　　[考点类型] 主旨题

　　[题目翻译] 下面哪个选项是本文的最佳标题?

　　　　A. 手秀

　　　　B. 争取平等的运动

　　　　C. 女童子军组织

　　　　D. 一个新的补充条款的故事

　　[考点剖析] 本题具有一定的难度,故建议使用排除法,全文未提到手秀一事,故排除 A 项;本文并非主要在介绍"Girl Scouts Organization"这个童子军组织,故排除 C 项;从 D 项在全文所占的篇幅上来看,该项并未涵盖全文主要内容。另外,该项也未能突出本文的中心,故排除 D 项。本文是通过对该组织发起的"Raise Your Hand"活动的前因后果的介绍,强调爱丽丝为使女孩获得跟男孩一样的发言机会所做出的努力及其最后的效果。

Passage Two

　　史蒂芬·霍金出生于 1942 年 1 月 8 日,在圣奥尔本斯长大,他是家中四个兄弟姐妹中的老大。他的父亲是一名生物学家,母亲是一名医学研究秘书,因此史蒂芬·霍金对科学非常感兴趣也不足为奇。在学生时代,霍金就非常喜欢物理和数学,因为他认为这两门学科提供了对世界最基础的见解。但是在就读牛津大学时,他并没有从他的同学中脱颖而出。

　　史蒂芬在牛津大学获得物理第一名,然后开始在剑桥大学攻读博士。当他向未来的妻子求婚时,他的小宇宙开始膨胀。简也来自圣奥尔本斯,是一名现代语言专业的大学生。她和霍金相识于新年晚会上,当时,霍金还没有被确诊。很快,这对情侣决定结婚,因为他们不知道霍金还能活多久。随着史蒂芬的健康每况愈下,他开始用拐杖走路。

　　霍金训练他的大脑以一种全新的方式工作,以此摆脱身体残疾给他带来的种种限制。随着他逐渐丧失对四肢的控制,他锻炼出一种在脑海中对问题进行想象的方式,而非通过手写公式的方式来解决问题。霍金的一些同事认为,正是这种思维方式帮助他实现了最伟大的发现。霍金当时正在研究科学中最神奇的理论之一——黑洞,这是爱因斯坦的广义相对论的极端预测。

　　霍金对于黑洞的研究有助于证明宇宙诞生时的大爆炸理论。发展于 20 世纪 40 年代的大爆炸理论当时还没有被所有科学家所接受。通过跟数学家罗杰·彭罗斯合作,霍金意识到黑洞就像逆向进行的大爆炸,这就意味着他描述黑洞的数学方式同样也适用于对大爆炸理论的描述。这是证明大爆炸真实发生的一个关键时刻。当霍金的身体开始恶化时,他的事业却开始腾飞。

26. [正确答案] D

　　[考点类型] 细节题

　　[题目翻译] 霍金在早年对科学产生了兴趣,因为_____。

　　　　A. 他的兄弟姐妹都喜欢科学

　　　　B. 他小时候学过相关的课程

C. 他擅长数学和物理
D. 他的父母影响了他

[考点剖析] 根据题目所含的定位词 Hawking 和 early interest in science 及题文同序的一般规律，本题答案可以在文章首段的 His father was a research biologist and his mother a medical research secretary, so it was not surprising that he was interested in science 中找到。因为他的父母都从事与科学相关的职业，所以霍金对科学感兴趣就不足为奇了。

27. [正确答案] A

[考点类型] 细节题

[题目翻译] 对于霍金的妻子简，我们可以从文中得到关于她的什么信息？
A. 她和霍金来自同一个地方。
B. 她和霍金去了同一所学校。
C. 她在新年那天嫁给了霍金。
D. 在结婚之前，她对他的病情一无所知。

[考点剖析] 根据本题的定位词 Hawking's wife Jane 和题文同序的一般规律，可以定位在第二段 His own private universe expanded when he proposed to his future wife 中。并且后面的一句话 Jane was also from St Albans, and… 呼应首段首句 Stephen Hawking was… and grew up in St Albans，所以霍金的妻子简和霍金本人均来自名叫圣奥尔本斯的地方。

28. [正确答案] C

[考点类型] 细节题

[题目翻译] 霍金通过自学掌握的工作方式_____。
A. 帮助他恢复了健康
B. 需要写很多方程式
C. 在很大程度上依赖心理想象
D. 被他的同事模仿

[考点剖析] 根据本题的定位词 self-trained way of working 定位到本文第三段中的首句 Hawking escaped the limits of his disability by training his mind to work in a new way。后面的句子中提到 he developed a way of visualizing problems in his mind to reach a solution instead of…，此句中的 visualizing problems 的意思是对问题进行想象，C 项 relied heavily on mental images 跟这一表述相吻合。

29. [正确答案] A

[考点类型] 细节题

[题目翻译] 以下关于大爆炸理论的陈述均是正确的，除了_____。
A. 霍金是它的创始人
B. 它与黑洞有关
C. 霍金的研究证实了这一理论
D. 不是所有的科学家都同意这个观点

[考点剖析] 本题是一道细节题，需要排除三个正确选项后才能得出本题的答案。根据题目所含有的定位词 the Big Bang theory 很快定位到本文最后一段。从该段中不难

发现Hawking's work on black holes helped prove the idea of a "Big Bang"、Big Bang theory was still not accepted by all scientists,以及and that meant the math he'd used to describe black holes also described the Big Bang分别对应C项、D项、B项,而A项没有对应的陈述。

30. [正确答案] D
    [考点类型] 推理题
    [题目翻译] 作为科学界的领军人物,霍金_____。
        A. 活了55年
        B. 写了许多部畅销小说
        C. 领导过一些残疾人组织
        D. 他一生中大部分时间都在与疾病作斗争
    [考点剖析] 本题可以使用排除法,A项给出了霍金的寿命,根据文中首段首句提到的出生年月"January 1942",考虑到2018年他刚刚逝世不久的新闻背景,通过简单的运算就可排除该项;B、C两项分别提到他写过很多部畅销小说及领导过一些残疾人组织,但本文并未提及,故属无中生有;而D项说他生命中的大多数时间都是在与疾病作斗争,这一事实可以在文中关于他疾病的描述中得到印证。

Passage Three

想象你是一只苍蝇,你正在寻找一个地方休息,这时你看到一片可爱的粉色树叶,这片叶子看起来是个不错的落脚点。当你在这片树叶上休息时,你发现了一些奇怪的事情,这片树叶是毛茸茸的。于是你开始挪动,但是你触发了这个植物的反应机制。突然,在十分之一秒的瞬间,你落入了捕虫草的陷阱,你将在五到十二天内被消化掉。

在世界上大约391 000种植物中,只有600种左右是肉食性植物。我们之所以这么称呼它们,是因为它们可以吸引、捕捉并吃掉虫子。跟其他植物一样,它们需要从太阳中摄取能量。但是不同于其他植物,肉食性植物从它们的猎物中摄取营养。肉食性植物一般生活在土壤贫瘠的地方,大多数植物从土壤中获取营养,但肉食性植物从其他来源中获取营养。

捕虫草诱骗它们的猎物落在它们身上。它们提供花蜜来贿赂愚蠢的昆虫。正如名字所示,捕虫草有深深的体腔,有光滑的着陆面,有着向内生长的刚毛,从而使猎物难以逃脱。苍蝇落到捕虫草上进食,但是却滑入了捕虫草充满消化液的体腔。

螺旋植物有诱人的茎,在茎的内部有着弯曲的绒毛,这些绒毛使昆虫能沿着茎往上爬,而无法回头。如果径直向上爬,昆虫就到达了植物的胃。徘徊在螺旋植物上的虫子发现它们无法逃脱,它们必须走向死亡。

还有一种植物叫狸藻,它们生活在水里并漂浮在水面。它们的陷阱就像藏在水下面的小的囊状物。从表面上看,只能看到它们的花朵。当虫子游向它并触发它的绒毛时,狸藻开始行动。它会吮干猎物和猎物周围的水,猎物会在几个小时内被消化掉。

31. [正确答案] B
    [考点类型] 词汇题
    [题目翻译] carnivorous(第二段)这个词跟"_____"在意思上最接近。
        A. 有营养的   B. 吃虫子的   C. 吃植物的   D. 有吸引力的
    [考点剖析] 根据题目的定位词carnivorous及Para. 2可定位于文中第二段的Out of about

391,000 plant species in the world, only 600 or so are carnivorous. We call them this because they attract, trap, and eat bugs 中。有下划线单词后面的文字对该词进行了解释,因为它们可以吸引、捕捉并吃掉虫子,由此可知 B 项最合适。

32. [正确答案] C
    [考点类型] 推理题
    [题目翻译] 作者最可能同意哪一种说法?
        A. 肉食性植物的种类太多了。
        B. 世界上植物种类太少了。
        C. 只有少数植物是肉食性的。
        D. 大多数植物是肉食性的。
    [考点剖析] 通过对全部选项的观察,发现均在讨论作者关于肉食性植物的种类和数量的说法,文中没有提到种类多少的问题,而原文中提到数量多少的句子只有第二段的第一句,从 Out of about 391,000 plant species in the world, only 600 or so are carnivorous 中"only"一词的感情色彩,不难看出作者认为只有少数植物是肉食性的。

33. [正确答案] D
    [考点类型] 细节题
    [题目翻译] 肉食性植物主要从_____中获取营养。
        A.其他植物   B.土壤   C.太阳   D.它们的猎物
    [考点剖析] 根据本题的定位词…get their nutrients mainly from 锁定答案在第二段第四句的 they get their nutrients from their prey(猎物)中,所以 D 项"their prey"与本句信息吻合。

34. [正确答案] B
    [考点类型] 细节题
    [题目翻译] 下列哪一项最能概括本文第三段的大意?
        A. 有很多关于肉食性植物的研究。
        B. 捕虫草把虫子骗进胃里。
        C. 捕虫草以多种方式杀死猎物。
        D. 有些植物通过提供花蜜来吸引虫子。
    [考点剖析] 第三段指出捕虫草使用引诱的方式让猎物上身,然后利用自身结构的种种特点,最终使猎物滑入其充满消化液的体腔中,而该段最后一句中的 pit filled with digestive fluids 正是该植物的胃"stomach"。

35. [正确答案] B
    [考点类型] 推理题
    [题目翻译] 可以推断,螺旋植物的消化腔位于_____。
        A.靠近根部的地方
        B.靠近顶部的地方
        C.花里面
        D.叶子里面
    [考点剖析] 根据题干中的定位词 the corkscrew's chamber for digestion… 锁定答案在文中倒数第二段的 Corkscrew plants have inviting stems. Curved hairs line the inside of these

stems. These hairs allow insects to go up the stems, but not back. Going forward leads to the plant's stomach 中。因为题目中的 chamber for digestion 就等于文中的 stomach(属于同义替换)，所以昆虫沿着茎往上爬就会来到 chamber for digestion。

Passage Four

　　在如今快节奏的生活里，很难找到宁静。片刻的彻底沉静似乎非常稀有，(一旦找到)便是极佳的发现。对于我来说，这些珍贵的时刻能在船上找到。就像传奇水手维托·杜马斯曾经说道："只有在海上，你才是真正的自己。"在甲板上，欣赏着令人沉醉的美景，让海风吹走你日常的烦恼，这时你对他的话会感同身受。

　　坐飞机旅行是痛苦的。从机场的嘈杂到飞机密闭的空间，商业航空完全不能满足我的探险精神，也不能给我带来舒适感。然而喜欢乘船旅行不仅仅是为了避免飞行的恐惧。无论我是在短途的渡轮上还是在游船上，大海都带来了真正的旅行感受，无论是轮船离开时发生的令人印象深刻的物理位移，还是轮船驶入宽阔的水域。"我们和海洋休戚相关。"约翰·F.肯尼迪如是说。当我的船只驶向令人兴奋的新目的地时，我能感觉到与大海的紧密联系。

　　同时我并不孤独。"旅行是假期的一部分，"旅行作家海伦·欧次亚拉这样说，"无论天气怎样，我都会站在甲板上，看着绳索被解开，船只驶离港口，风景渐行渐远。"

　　汤姆·布莱尔是 Spaghetti Traveler 博客的创始人，他认同我的观点："在飞机上，很难看到除草地之外的地方；但在轮船上，看着陆地越来越近是令人兴奋的。"

　　对于旅行编辑凯西·温斯顿而言，坐船旅行给人带来冒险的感觉。她说："即使是在从 A 到 B 相对简单的旅程中，宽广开阔的大海也能让你感觉到你正动身去发现新大陆，而这种浪漫的感觉，是你在飞机或者高速路上无法体会到的。"温斯顿也非常珍惜海上旅行给人带来的家庭般的温暖。"在海上旅行，尤其是和孩子在一起时，心情是如此的放松。"她说。

　　无论是为了便于给孩子带来快乐还是为了纯粹的浪漫，对于很多旅行者来说，坐船旅行是首选的交通方式。船只可以带着我去想去的地方，避免飞行旅行中的匆忙与惊恐。在乘风破浪中，随着现实的远离，我总能再次找到我对海洋的热爱。

36. [正确答案] C
　　[考点类型] 细节题
　　[题目翻译] 第一段强调了海上旅行的哪一方面？
　　　　　　　A. 非凡的景观。　　　　　　　B. 完全的自由。
　　　　　　　C. 内心的平静。　　　　　　　D. 冒险的感受。
　　[考点剖析] 根据本题的定位词 aspect of sea travel is emphasized 及 the first paragraph 锁定答案在原文第一段。该段首句 Serenity（宁静）is difficult to find in today's fast-paced world 是本段的主题句，后文围绕该主题展开，A moment of complete calm seems to be a rare and wonderful find 及…those precious moments occur on a boat 均围绕主题词 serenity 展开，C 项"Peace of mind"为正确选项。

37. [正确答案] B
　　[考点类型] 词汇题
　　[题目翻译] 第二段中的 affinity 这个词跟"_____"在意思上最接近。
　　　　　　　A. 强烈的情感　　　　　　　B. 紧密的联系
　　　　　　　C. 极度的激动　　　　　　　D. 令人难忘的时刻

2018年同等学力人员申请硕士学位英语水平全国统一考试答案及详解

[考点剖析] affinity 出现在本文第二段的尾句 I feel that affinity 中,本段中呼应本句意思的句子应该是 affinity 前面的句子 We are tied to the ocean"我们和海洋休戚相关",所以作者使用了替换的写作技巧,用 affinity 表达前文提到的人与海洋的关系。

38. [正确答案] A
   [考点类型] 细节题
   [题目翻译] 谁对船离开码头的一幕印象最深刻?
      A. 海伦·欧次亚拉。   B. 维托·杜马斯。
      C. 凯西·温斯顿。   D. 约翰·F. 肯尼迪。
   [考点剖析] 根据本题的定位词 deeply impressed 及 watching the boat leaving the dock 定位答案在第三段中的句子 I'll… the boat slipping away from the dock and the landscape… away 中。题目中的 boat leaving the dock 对应本句 boat slipping away from the dock,本句正是由第三段开头提到的人物海伦·欧次亚拉提出的。

39. [正确答案] D
   [考点类型] 细节题
   [题目翻译] 根据汤姆·布莱尔的说法,海上旅行比乘飞机旅行好是因为前者_____。
      A. 使人们能进行更深入的思考
      B. 给乘客更好的机会放松
      C. 提供一个更加舒适的环境
      D. 提供更清晰的景观视野
   [考点剖析] 根据题目提供的定位词 Tom Bourlet 及 sea travel is better than air travel 可以定位到文章第四段的 On a plane, it's difficult to make out much more than grassland; on the ferry, there is something exciting about seeing land slowly getting closer 中。汤姆认为坐飞机旅行看不到草地以外的地方,而乘船旅行时,当看到陆地越来越清晰的景象时,人就会感到激动,D 项跟本句的意思吻合。

40. [正确答案] C
   [考点类型] 细节题
   [题目翻译] 根据最后两段,海上旅行有以下好处,除了_____。
      A. 适宜家庭出游   B. 满足冒险的愿望
      C. 促进健康的生活方式   D. 使人放松
   [考点剖析] 根据题目中的定位词 last two paragraphs、sea travel 以及 benefits,可将答案锁定到文中最后两段作者总结出的 sea travel 的优点,而题目考的是文中没有提到的优点,所以首先需要明确并排除三个优点,才能找出答案,这正是并列信息题的特点。文中我们发现以下信息"For Cathy Winston, travel editor, it's about the sense of adventure""Winston also values the family-friendly aspects of sea travel""There's something so relaxing about being on the water, especially with kids"分别对应上述的 B 项、A 项、D 项,唯独没有提到 C 项。

Section B

在 SXSW(奥斯汀技术文化大会)上,伦敦市长萨迪克·汗因为大型技术公司和监管机构未能阻止憎恨、虚假和激进的观点在网上的传播,对它们进行了批评。

· 23 ·

市长说,政府在通过制定规章法规来消除技术对社会所产生的负面影响方面,一直处于"玩忽职守"的状态。汗在发言中提到:"在过去几年里,政客和政府最大的问题是:当技术革命在他们周围发生时,他们态度消极被动,无所作为。"

最后,汗说,政府有责任跟技术企业和公司领导合作,以确保技术进步得到恰当的监管。

在欧洲,社交媒体已经感受到了监管的压力。因为根据一月份在德国颁布的新法律,在被报道后24小时内如未撤下有问题的内容,公司将会被罚款。

汗并未呼吁采取这种监管制度,但是他警告说,如果有公司对政府的关注不予回应,政府就将出台更为严厉的规章制度。他指出:"最终,一些技术公司必须为他们对世界产生的影响承担更大的责任。"

评论1

从"行业监管"的角度来看待这个问题是完全错误的。这个问题的核心在于,做出随时发布任何消息的选择的行为方是个体。我们的社会似乎缺少的是个人责任感。

评论2

实施针对网上内容的法律并不容易,更大的问题是,执法部门并没有足够的资源去针对网上发生的所有犯罪行为采取行动。

评论3

我认为,技术至少在一个重要的方面让我们束手无措,如推特、脸书等,过去发布的和即将发布的谎言和虚假新闻,使某些人认为这些新闻是真实的。他们(技术公司)必须为此做些什么。

评论4

这些公司乐于发布遭到人们反对的内容,正是这些内容提高了他们的收益和利润。因此没有严厉的监管,自我监管永远不会奏效。

评论5

信息和通信技术(ICT)的更新向来被广泛地认为是有益的,是可促进进步并产生共同利益的。但是ICT无法预见不断创新的行业会如何带来人们意想不到的后果。现在是ICT发挥作用的时候了。

41. [正确答案] A

  [考点类型] 词汇题

  [题目翻译] 第二段中的 dereliction 这个词最有可能的意思是"_____"。

    A. 故意忽视   B. 潜在的虐待   C. 经常误判   D. 明显的误解

  [考点剖析] 根据题目所含的定位词,可以定位于第二段第一句,再结合该词所在的语境发现,文章首段指出监管者(政府)未能阻止不良信息在网上传播…regulators for failing to stem the spread of hate, misinformation and radical viewpoints online,然后在第二段中提到过去几年里最大的问题是政客和政府的态度消极、无所作为,所以 A 项正确。

42. [正确答案] D

  [考点类型] 推理题

  [题目翻译] 汗在最后一段话中通过他的发言强调了什么?

    A. 英国严格的监管。   B. 德国式的监管法律。

    C. 政府与行业的合作。   D. 行业自律。

  [考点剖析] 最后一段首句提到,汗并不提倡上文介绍的严格的监管,而是警告相关公司如

果不对政府关注的事宜采取行动,监管者(政府)就会采取更为严厉的措施(did not call for this type of regulation but warned that even stricter regulation could be on its way if companies don't respond to government concerns),所以汗强调的仍然是行业自律,而非自律失败后的监管。因为只有在行业自律无效的情况下,监管者才会采取严厉的监管。D项与此相符。

43. [正确答案] B
    [考点类型] 细节题
    [题目翻译] 根据评论1,虚假信息传播的罪魁祸首是谁?
        A. 企业。 B. 个人。 C. 政府官员。 D. 行业领导。
    [考点剖析] 第一个评论认为 At the core of this, it is individuals who are making choices to "post" each and every time. What our society seems to have lost is a sense of personal responsibility,即做出发布消息的选择的是个体,所以应该是个人对传播的信息负责,社会缺少的是个人责任感,所以答案为B项。

44. [正确答案] C
    [考点类型] 细节题
    [题目翻译] 哪一条评论赞成政府的严格监管?
        A. 评论2。 B. 评论3。 C. 评论4。 D. 评论5。
    [考点剖析] 评论4提出 So self-regulation just never works without the threat of harsh regulation "因此没有严厉的外部监管,自我监管永远不会奏效"。所以本评论赞成政府的严格监管。

45. [正确答案] D
    [考点类型] 细节题
    [题目翻译] 哪条评论同意汗关于技术公司的角色的观点?
        A. 评论1和4。 B. 评论2和3。
        C. 评论4和5。 D. 评论3和5。
    [考点剖析] 评论3提到 agree that technology has failed us in at least one very important way …,所以本评论是赞同汗关于技术公司是虚假信息传播的责任方这一观点的。评论5提到 But, ICT has not had the foresight to see how the evolving industry can produce unintended consequences,即ICT未能预见行业发展导致出现意料之外的后果(即虚假信息的传播),故应该对此负责,所以评论5表达的观点跟汗的观点也是基本一致的。

Part IV Cloze

每一天,需要清洗的东西越积越多。盘子上覆盖果酱和面包片,碗里覆盖了一层薄薄的不知道是什么东西的物质。叉子、小刀和汤匙上牢牢地粘上种种杂物。结束了一整天的工作,还要做饭、打扫,以及跟小家伙们谈判,夫妻不得不面对这样的问题:谁来洗碗?

最近一篇关于家庭活力的报道显示,上述问题的答案,对夫妻婚姻关系的健康持久产生着重大的影响。该研究考察了各种各样的家务活,包括购物、洗衣及清扫房屋等,发现对家庭妇女而言,分担洗碗的责任比分担其他家务更重要。调查显示,承担了绝大部分洗碗家务活的妇女与有丈夫帮忙洗碗的妇女相比较而言,前者婚姻关系的矛盾更多,婚姻满意度更差。与其他家务活相比,主妇们对家人能分担其洗碗工作更感欣慰。

关于洗碗还有什么值得讨论呢？犹他大学家庭和消费者研究助理教授丹·卡尔森，也是本项研究的首席作者，给出了他自己的论述："洗碗让人不胜其烦。除此之外，不像其他的家务活，诸如做饭或者园艺，洗碗洗得好并不能带来（别人）更多的赞赏。"

46. [正确答案] C
    [解析过程] 空格所在句的意思是：夫妻面对这个问题。而非反复问自己这个问题。根据搭配，question 与 ask、face 均能搭配，但从语境上（在繁忙的一天过后，这对夫妇必须面对的问题：谁来做……？而不是反复提出这个问题）考虑，可以排除 ask。

47. [正确答案] D
    [解析过程] 空格所在句的意思是：谁来洗碗（do the dishes）。从后文中反复出现的 dishes 可知，本文谈论的是洗碗的问题，且本题与 50 题后面的 doing the dishes 对应。

48. [正确答案] A
    [解析过程] 空格所在句的意思是：对夫妻婚姻关系的健康持久产生重大影响。本句所含短语 have... impact 跟介词 on 是固定搭配，意为"对……产生影响"。

49. [正确答案] B
    [解析过程] 空格所在句的意思是：该项研究考察了各种各样的家务活。本处用单词 including（包括）引出了具体的类别。

50. [正确答案] D
    [解析过程] 本题的 shoulder/take/share 均能跟 responsibility 搭配，其中 shoulder responsibility 跟 take responsibility 意思相近，都有承担责任的意思，但根据前后文语境来看，此处表达的是与配偶分担责任。

51. [正确答案] D
    [解析过程] and 一词表明，空格所在句与后面的 less relationship satisfaction（婚姻满意度更差）是并列的关系，所以只有选 more，构成 more relationship conflict（婚姻关系的矛盾更多）这一搭配，这种并列关系才会存在。

52. [正确答案] B
    [解析过程] 从句子语法结构来看，本处缺少指人的关系代词，在 husbands 后的定语从句中作主语。

53. [正确答案] A
    [解析过程] share 跟 duties 搭配，表示分担责任，跟本句后面的动宾搭配 sharing... task 形成并列和呼应的关系。

54. [正确答案] C
    [解析过程] 前后两句话存在递进关系，A 项意为"表面上"，与本句上下文的逻辑关系无关，B 项表转折，D 项表时间上的最后，只有 C 项能表明上下句的递进关系。

55. [正确答案] B
    [解析过程] 根据语境，洗碗洗得好并不能像前面列出的家务活一样，带来（别人）更多的赞赏。B 项 generate"产生，引起"为正确选项。

Part V Text Completion

Text One

美国的婚礼仪式跟结婚的人群一样具有多样化的特点。尽管举办婚礼的地点和方式有所不同，但是多数婚礼都具有某些传统习俗。例如，新郎新娘在婚礼上交换戒指；戒指通常戴在左手的无名指上；交换戒指通常在仪式中间进行。

仪式结束后，这对夫妇的朋友和家人通常会把生米一捧接一捧地洒在他们身上。正如我们所知，大米的寓意是生产率和收成。然后，婚礼后通常会有一个聚会，聚会上的食物非常丰盛，很快就转移了人们对新婚夫妇的注意。

56. [正确答案] C

[解析过程] the bride and groom often _____，因为 often 是副词，主要跟现在时搭配，所以本处需要填入一个表示现在时的动词。

57. [正确答案] A

[解析过程] where the food is _____，本题空格前面是 be 动词，结合选项来看应该是系表结构，即需要填入一个形容词作表语。

58. [正确答案] B

[解析过程] the couple is often _____ handfuls of uncooked rice，从本题的句子结构来看，存在被动语态（be + 动词过去分词）。

59. [正确答案] A

[解析过程] 从本题紧接的句子 The rings are usually…可以看出 rings 在此处是第二次提到，空白处填入 A 项（……经常交换戒指）后，上下文的逻辑关系就合理了。

60. [正确答案] C

[解析过程] 本题有两条线索。首先是空白处后面的 by friends and family 暗示选项是被动语态；其次是紧接的下一句的主语 Rice，与选项中的 rice 呼应。

61. [正确答案] B

[解析过程] 从本句的结构来看，空白处前面是逗号，满足非限制性定语从句的要求；空白处后面是 that 引导的结果状语从句，跟选项中的单词 so 呼应，B 项能同时满足这两个条件。

Text Two

超过三分之一的两岁以下儿童都在使用移动媒体。这一数字只会随着孩子年龄的增长而增加，在 12～17 岁的青少年中，有95%的人会上网。

花在电子科技上的时间并不只能赋予孩子们新颖的做事方式，它也会导致孩子们的注意力分散和记忆力减退。例如，虽然视频游戏可能会让大脑注意到多种刺激，但它们改变了大脑的运行方式。

总是使用搜索引擎的孩子可能善于发现信息，却不太善于记住这些信息。此外，使用过多电子科技的儿童可能没有足够的机会使用他们的想象力，或深入地阅读和思考学习材料。

62. [正确答案] B

[解析过程] That number _____ increases，空白处需要填入一个副词修饰动词 increases。A 项是指人的关系代词，C 项表示方式，均不能满足本题的语法要求。

63. [正确答案] C

[解析过程] 空白处填入"方式（the way）"后本句意义才成立，意思是：他们改变了大脑运行的方式。

64. [正确答案] A

[解析过程] 本空前面是先行词 children，后面的定语从句缺少指人的关系代词。

65. [正确答案] A
    [解析过程] 从本题所在的语境来看,空白处前面的一句指出使用移动媒体的两岁以下的儿童数量超过三分之一,而空白处后面的句子表明用户则随着年龄的增加而增加到95%,A项(这一数字只会增加)符合这一趋势。

66. [正确答案] B
    [解析过程] 本题所在的句子前面提到视频游戏使大脑注意到多种刺激,而这势必改变大脑的运行方式,B项填入此处符合上下文语境。

67. [正确答案] C
    [解析过程] 空格前面提到,总使用搜索引擎的儿童的问题是不太善于记住搜索到的信息。空白处前面的 In addition 说明接下来的内容跟前面的问题性质是一致的,空白处后面的内容指出,这样的孩子无法运用想象力或进行深度阅读和思考,填入 C 项后,上下文并列的逻辑关系就一目了然了。

Text Three

现在有一种香蕉,它的皮是可以食用的,这似乎让人难以置信,因为大多数人绝不会想去吃香蕉皮。然而,日本的蕉农已经研发出一种特殊的技术来种植皮可食用的香蕉。日本西部冈山的农民,先在零下60℃的寒冷温度下种植香蕉树,然后将树移植到温度为27℃的环境中。温度的巨大变化使得香蕉树突然快速生长,使其果皮无法完全成熟。这使得香蕉皮变得又薄又软又甜,可以食用。香蕉是日本最受欢迎的水果。和其他国家一样,日本的香蕉大部分都是进口的。日本商店里大约99%的香蕉是进口的。这种新技术可能意味着日本人会吃更多本土种植的香蕉。

68. [正确答案] B
    [解析过程] 空白处前面是冠词 a,后面是名词 technique,所以需要填入一个以辅音开头的形容词。

69. [正确答案] C
    [解析过程] 空白处后面是介词短语 of doing sth.,可能填入名词或动词短语,故考虑 A 项和 C 项两个选项,在完成下一题(第 70 题)后可排除 A 项。

70. [正确答案] A
    [解析过程] 从空白处前面的修饰语 freezing cold 的意思来看,需要填入对应的名词 temperature。

71. [正确答案] D
    [解析过程] 空白处跟后面的 countries 构成修饰关系,所以需要填入形容词,D 项是形容词,其填入后的意思是"跟其他国家相似",符合语境。

72. [正确答案] B
    [解析过程] 根据语法,空白处前面是助动词 would never,后面应该跟动词原形,故选 think of eating the peel,而且,空白处前面一句指出,香蕉皮可以食用这件事让人难以置信,B 项填入后,前后两句能构成合理的逻辑关系。

73. [正确答案] A
    [解析过程] 从空白处所在句的结构来看,需要填入的是句子的谓语动词,填入 A 项后,该句意思是蕉农们已经研发出特别的技术,能种植出皮可食用的香蕉。

74. [正确答案] C

[解析过程] 从空白处后面表示温度的介词短语的修饰关系可以看出,需要填入的选项跟温度有关,C项中的 freezing cold 正好跟零下60℃的低温吻合。

75. [正确答案] D

[解析过程] 空白处前面一句提到香蕉是日本最受欢迎的水果,空白处后面的内容表明日本的香蕉大多数靠进口,此处填入剩下的D项,能很好地起到承上启下的作用。

Paper Two 试卷二

Part VI Translation

1. It's harder and harder to find peace and, especially, quiet.

   [结构分析] 这是一个简单句,it 是形式主语,真正的主语是 to find... quiet。

   [词义推敲] peace 多指内心的平静,而 quiet 多指没有声音的、安静的,根据本段语境对这两个词进行区分。

   [参考译文] 寻找平静越来越难,寻求安静尤其如此。

2. Even in the most remote parts of Alaska the sound of a jet crossing overhead is all too common.

   [结构分析] 这是一个简单句,Even in... of Alaska 是本句的状语,the sound of a jet... common 是句子的主干。

   [词义推敲] remote"遥远的,偏远的";jet"喷气式飞机"。

   [参考译文] 即使在阿拉斯加最偏远的地区,从头上传来的喷气式飞机的声音也很常见。

3. Scientists set off across the U.S. to study the audio ecology.

   [结构分析] 本句是简单句,to study the audio ecology 是不定式短语作目的状语。

   [词义推敲] set off 是"动身出发"的意思;audio ecology 可以按字面翻译为"音频/声音生态"。

   [参考译文] 于是,科学家们纷纷动身前往美国各地研究"音频生态"。

4. They recorded more than a million hours of sound from various sources.

   [结构分析] 本句是简单句,句子主干是 They recorded... hours of sound, hours 前面的 a million 是定语,from various sources 是介词短语作地点状语。

   [词义推敲] various"各种各样的",在本次考试中的第11题出现过它的名词形式。

   [参考译文] 他们从不同地方记录的声音时长(总共)超过了一百万小时。

5. They found that noise pollution is not good for people and it's even worse for animals with more sensitive ears.

   [结构分析] 这是一个主从复合句,主句主语是 They,然后由 that 引出一个并列的宾语从句,一个宾语从句是 noise pollution is... people,另一个是 it's even... ears。

   [词义推敲] noise pollution 可以翻译为"噪声污染";sensitive"敏感的",在本次考试中的词汇题部分也出现过。

   [参考译文] 科学家们发现,噪声污染对人类有害,对于那些听觉灵敏的动物们危害尤甚。

6. And the problem is not confined to land but echoes across the seas as well, where human-produced noise interferes with the live of various ocean dwellers.

   [结构分析] 本句是主从复合句,主句是 the problem is... as well,后面是由 where 引导的一个非限制性定语从句。主句中有一个 not... but...结构需要注意。

[词义推敲] confined 是 confine 的过去分词,此处翻译为"受……的限制或限制于";interfere with"干涉,妨碍"。

[参考译文] 另外,噪声污染并不仅仅局限于陆地,其影响甚至波及海洋,人类制造的噪声同样干扰了居住在海洋里的生物。

7. These days on Earth it's rare to hear "silence".

[结构分析] 本句是简单句,it 是形式主语,真正主语是不定式短语 to hear"silence",rare 是表语。

[词义推敲] silence 指寂静或消除了噪声的状态。

[参考译文] 现在要在地球上聆听寂静之声太难了。

Part Ⅶ   Writing

这是一篇说明文,题目即本文的主题:理想的公共图书馆。在给出了本文的题目后,本题明确要求考生描写在自己生活的社区中一个理想的公共图书馆的情况,并且给出了图书馆的定义:图书馆是将各种阅读材料和其他视频、音频材料提供给读者使用或供其借阅的地方。

我们可以根据题目提供的信息整理思路并列出提纲:

第一段,利用考前熟记的背景导入法的经典模板句型开篇:with the development of…。依据图书馆得到政府和全社会重视的大背景,导出本文的话题:理想的公共图书馆。第二段,从不同角度提出理想的社区图书馆的标准和状态,本段是全文的重点。第三段,呼应主题,总结和概述理想的公共图书馆给读者带来的利益。

Nowadays, with the development of social civilization and economy, the government and the society have achieved a common sense that a library should play a far-reaching role in cross-cultural communication and civilization inheritance. Consequently, an ideal public library established in the neighborhood is supposed to be such a place where people feel free to use and borrow various reading materials and even musical and video recordings. As far as I am concerned, an ideal public library serves to meet certain requirements as follows.

To begin with, the library should be in a splendid and spacious building designed with many different floors distinguished by specific functions, such as science fiction section, education and culture section, so as to attract targeted readers for their specific knowledge expansion. Apart from that, it will surely be a gorgeous place as long as the library is decorated by some modern urban sculptures or statues of historical figures representing wisdom and knowledge. Last but not least, an ideal public library should also possess some state-of-the-art computer managerial system providing convenience to common readers while reducing their waiting time and some warm-hearted librarians offering exceptional service.

All in all, when it comes to an ideal public library, what occurs to my mind is the one that comforts our soul with its wits and meets our physical requirements with its facility.

范文点评

本范文在内容、结构和语言三个方面满足了高分作文的标准和要求，具体表现如下：

从内容上来看，本文紧扣主题 the ideal public library，明确提出作者心目中理想的公共图书馆的不同方面的特点，并且在文末对以上标准进行了高度的概括。

从结构上来看，开篇使用了目前最热门的背景导入法，并把经典模板句型有机融入自身书面语言表达系统中。然后在本文的正文部分（body）提供了不同维度的图书馆特点和要求，并在文末呼应开头，使得全文结构紧凑，没有拖泥带水的冗余文字。

从语言表达来看，作者在短短的两百字左右的文字中成功挑战了大纲要求掌握的多个语言难点，本文最大的亮点莫过于此。下面来具体分析：

第一段用"Nowadays, with the development of social civilization and economy…"句型引出了本文写作的时代背景，提出了政府和社会达成的对图书馆高度重视的共识，本句用 that a library should play a far-reaching role in cross-cultural communication and civilization inheritance 成功挑战了同位语从句这一语法难点。然后，Consequently 一词表达了前后内容逻辑上的因果关系，并利用题目给出的信息，强调了图书馆的主要功能，从而导出了理想图书馆的标准。并在本段末句使用经典句型"as far as I am concerned…"引出全文重点段。

第二段是全篇的重点，内容上，作者分别从建筑特色（building）、装饰特色（decorated）和管理系统特色（managerial system）三个方面提出理想图书馆的特点：华丽的（splendid）和宽敞的（spacious）建筑具备多功能分区（specific functions）、现代雕像点缀（decorated by some modern urban sculptures or statures）、先进的图书管理系统（state-of-the-art computer managerial system）。结构上，作者使用了 To begin with…, Apart from that…, Last but not least… 等逻辑联系词，层层铺垫，展开论述。语言上，作者使用的语法结构包括动词的现在分词和过去分词、表目的的不定式短语等非谓语动词形式；在书面词汇的使用上，一系列精准的词汇，如 splendid and spacious building, targeted readers, knowledge expansion, modern urban sculptures or statures, state-of-the-art computer managerial system, warm-hearted librarians, exceptional service 等拉开了与绝大多数考生语言表达能力的距离。

第三段虽然只有 All in all, when it comes to an ideal public library, what occurs to my mind is the one that comforts our soul with its wits and meets our physical requirements with its facility 这句话，但是作者在这短短的34个单词中使用了 when 引导的时间状语从句和 what 引导的主语从句，并使用了 comforts our soul with its wits and meets our physical requirements with its facility 等高度精练的表达，总结了 an ideal public library 应该具有的服务功能。至此，作者的英文书面语言表达能力想必给读者留下了深刻印象。

2019年同等学力人员申请硕士学位
英语水平全国统一考试

Paper One 试卷一 (100 minutes)

Part I Oral Communication (15 minutes, 10 points)

Section A

Directions: *In this section there are two incomplete dialogues and each dialogue has three blanks and three choices A, B and C, taken from the dialogue. Fill in each of the blanks with one of the choices to complete the dialogue and mark your answer on the **Answer Sheet**.*

Dialogue One

A. They are due today.
B. That sounds like a good idea!
C. Got any plans after the class?

Juliane: Hi, Jenny! __1__
Jenny: Not really. What about you?
Juliane: I've got a course paper to write. So I plan to look for some books and study at the library. Do you want to join me?
Jenny: Sure. I need to return some books. __2__ Besides, I can also read some magazines and newspapers there.
Juliane: Fantastic! We can go swimming in the gym after that.
Jenny: __3__ We can chill out a little in such a hot summer.

Dialogue Two

A. You've been saying that forever!
B. There must be ten here.
C. Let's read this book.

Girl: Dad, will you read to me?
Dad: Uh, let me finish the newspaper first?
Girl: __4__
Dad: Well, how about reading the business section of the newspaper together?

Girl: That's boring. __5__ It's about a bear and a cat that become friends. And these books too.

Dad: Whoa, I thought you said one book. __6__

Girl: My teacher, Mrs Green, says you have to read to me every night, and the newspaper doesn't count.

Section B

Directions: *In this section there is one incomplete interview which has four blanks and four choices A, B, C and D, taken from the interview. Fill in each of the blanks with one of the choices to complete the interview and mark your answer on the **Answer Sheet**.*

    A. What is your name?

    B. but that class is already full.

    C. but the computer won't let me.

    D. You're a Comp Lit major?

Stuart: Hello. Can I help you?

Karen: Yes, I hope so. I would like to register for Comp Lit 287.

Stuart: I'm sorry, __7__ And also, students are supposed to register through the touch-tone registration system.

Karen: I know. I already tried to register for it by phone. __8__

Stuart: That's because it's full.

Karen: But I'm a new student here. I thought maybe there was some way I could get into the class. I thought I should come and talk to you in the department office.

Stuart: Well. I could put you on a waiting list. But that doesn't guarantee you will get into the class, __9__

Karen: My name is Karen Huang. That's spelled H-U-A-N-G.

Stuart: Alright. And what is your major?

Karen: I'm a comparative literature major.

Stuart: Wait a minute. __10__

Karen: Yes, that's right. And Professor Cohen told me I need to take Comp Lit 287.

Stuart: The university computer system saves extra places, in class 287 for Comp Lit students.

Karen: Even if the class is full?

Stuart: That's right.

Part II Vocabulary (10 minutes, 10 points)

Directions: *In this part there are ten sentences, each with one word or phrase underlined. Choose the one from the four choices marked A, B, C and D that best keeps the meaning of the sentence. Mark your answer on the **Answer Sheet**.*

11. Once a bed is completed in the factory, it undergoes a <u>rigorous</u> quality control process.

    A. long   B. complex   C. strict   D. complete

12. It saved them an hour during a procedure that would normally take three hours.
    A. merely   B. possibly   C. usually   D. rarely

13. The universe is presumed to contain many other planets with some form of life.
    A. destined   B. intended   C. expected   D. supposed

14. The scene has shocked me because it is something alien to me.
    A. unfair   B. unfamiliar   C. unnecessary   D. uncomfortable

15. The new situation in this area calls for a change in our financial policies.
    A. suggests   B. requires   C. demonstrates   D. identifies

16. He claimed that he had a wonderful job and was well paid, but his mother knew that he had made it all up.
    A. invented   B. invested   C. corrected   D. collected

17. Though many people witnessed the accident, they were not sure about the exact consequences.
    A. orders   B. processes   C. results   D. causes

18. Supported by sufficient evidence, his argument seems to have a great deal of validity.
    A. challenge   B. value   C. truth   D. utility

19. The supply of silver in the mine had diminished, causing great concern among the people of the town.
    A. disappeared   B. erupted   C. expired   D. declined

20. A deficiency of soil nutrients can cause the crop to be of low quality.
    A. lack   B. supply   C. number   D. source

Part III Reading Comprehension (45 minutes, 25 points)

Section A

Directions: *In this section, there are four passages followed by questions or unfinished statements, each with four suggested answers A, B, C and D. Choose the best answer and mark your answer on the Answer Sheet.*

Passage One

As 170 people sat down to dinner, I breathed a sigh of relief: the conference was going well. Running was a part of my job as a university program manager working on a project to boost biotech collaborations between academia and industry. When I started in the role a few years earlier, I thought maybe, after years of career exploration, I had finally found the right job for me. But at the conference, I found myself wondering whether that was really what I wanted from my career. I'm a scientist, not an event planner—but I had been too busy organizing the conference to appreciate the research being discussed. Was it time for yet another change?

I started off as a lab scientist, but then discovered that the highly focused nature of lab work wasn't for me. My next job was at a pharmaceutical company—conducting literature searches. I enjoyed the work, which allowed me to stay close to research and interact with a variety of people. But I was only offered a short-term contract, so after a year I had to move on. I then became a scientific journal editor. I loved the breath of science that I was exposed to, but the job required a lengthy commute. So, I made another dramatic change and moved back to the ivory tower for my current job.

It had become a pattern: I spent a few years in each role only to find that it wasn't quite the right fit. I also realized that maybe I was searching for something that didn't exist.

I began to think about the creative ways to add the scientific stimulation I sought to my work life. With my previous knowledge and my experience as an editor, I realized I had the skill set to do that through freelance and science writing, such as news articles for journals and blogs.

With my former colleagues' positive responses, I finally decided I could do my university job on a less than full-time schedule. Fortunately, my manager agreed.

For the last year, I have been a university program manager/freelance writer, and I have never been happier. Wearing the two roles together has been a bit tricky at times. But I really feel I have a career that is tailored to my needs. I have realized that a career doesn't need to be "off the shelf." Jobs can be mixed and matched to get to one that fits.

21. What did the author think of his conference organizing job in Paragraph 1?

   A. It gave him a sense of achievement.

   B. It proved that he was making progress in his career.

   C. It was not as meaningful as scientific research.

   D. It was too challenging for him.

22. The author left the job as a scientific journal editor because _____.

   A. it demanded high work intensity   B. he was offered only a short contract

   C. he was not satisfied with the pay   D. it was too far from home

23. What does "something" (Para. 3) possibly mean?

   A. A suitable role.   B. An ideal job.

   C. A balanced life.   D. A fixed pattern.

24. What is the author's present job?

   A. He works in a university and also writes on the side.

   B. He is an event planner and also a program manager.

   C. He teaches in a university and also writes books.

   D. He is a full-time manager and also a freelance writer.

25. What is this passage mainly about?

   A. The author's clear career plan.

   B. The author's changing perception of career.

   C. The author's persistence in the face of obstacles.

   D. The author's failure in securing a work contract.

Passage Two

You've probably heard a lot more about "eSports" lately. Major television networks are broadcasting competitions, and even more mainstream media coverage is planned for the new future. What are eSports and why are they so popular?

Loosely defined, eSports are video game competitions. These can be anything from a local tournament (锦标赛) in a video game store to those staged in 25,000-seat arenas, watched live by millions of people around the world. In practical terms, "eSports" refers to the competitions engineered by global organizations that culminate in big-money championship tournaments—dollar figures that can exceed $1,000,000 for winners.

That second question—"Why are they getting so popular?"—is more nuanced. The biggest reason is that fans of games enjoy watching them played at the highest level. It's fun seeing the top players in the world do what they do best. There are plenty of other reasons the eSports community is growing. All of the controversies, drama and compelling individuals from the mainstream sports world exist in eSports as well. Top players move from team to team like free agents, retire and return to competition unexpectedly, and experience unlikely come-from-behind victories and crushing defeats. New challengers consistently emerge on the scene, ready to take down championship teams and generate compelling rivalries. The parallels with traditional sports and eSports are more numerous that many realize.

Perhaps the biggest difference between traditional sports and eSports is the viewers. Unlike mainstream athletic competition, the consumers of eSports are overwhelmingly young and male. For example, over 70 percent of League of Legends' viewers are males, and the vast majority of them under 26. This means a couple of things, both of them appealing to advertisers looking to reach this young and profitable market—the audience will grow as more youngers are introduced, and as they get older, their purchasing power increases.

26. It is stated in Paragraph 1 that eSports have _____.
    A. caused competition among media
    B. drawn an increasing number of youths
    C. created many broadcasting companies
    D. attracted major television networks

27. According to Paragraph 2, eSports _____.
    A. can be staged only in local stadiums   B. can lead to a huge sum of award
    C. may be hard to define precisely   D. maybe loosely linked to video games

28. The word "nuanced" (Para. 3) most probably means _____.
    A. strange   B. outstanding   C. specific   D. complicated

29. Which of the following is NOT a reason for the growth of the eSports community?
    A. The stories about the top players.
    B. The fun of watching top-level performance.
    C. The investment from governments.
    D. The parallels with the mainstream sports.

30. Traditional sports and eSports are different mainly in _____.
   A. their rules   B. their importance   C. their profits   D. their audiences

Passage Three

Senator Kamala Harris was half right in her speech launching her 2020 presidential campaign, when she said we need to address climate change based on "science fact, not science fiction." The truth is, we need both. Science fiction has an important role to play in rescuing the future from the huge challenges we are facing—and the responses to Harris' statement illustrate this perfectly.

When Harris' statement about climate change went out on social media, a number of people pointed out the truth: Science fiction has been helping us to prepare for a world of potentially disastrous climate upheaval for years. But an equal number of loud voices took issue with Harris' warnings about climate change, because in our post-truth era, the scientific consensus about what humans are doing to our planet is still somehow a matter of opinion.

And that's why science fiction is more important than Harris gives it credit for. No amount of scientific evidence will convince deniers—or the vast number of people who merely live in a state of denial. We live in a post-truth era in which facts and fiction are blurring into an indistinguishable mess and power belongs to whoever can tell the best story, true or not. What matters is just how something makes us feel—which is why we need better stories, that, in the words of author Neil Gaiman, "lie in order to tell the truth."

Stories about climate change might be fiction, but they can help to sway people's hearts and minds in a different way than a recitation of the undeniable facts. Science fictions creators have been looking for ways to restore people's faith in the future. Authors such as Alexandra Rowland have started a conversation about creating a new type of stories called "Hope punk" that show people reasons to believe we really can do the hard work of fixing our problems. Some other authors are creating a new genre called "Solar punk" that aims to tell stories about using technological and scientific innovation to help the environment.

When the truth becomes near-impossible to distinguish through the fog of disinformation and "alternative facts," people tend to feel powerless to change the world. Activist L. A. Kauffman says people need to be reminded that "they have more collective power than they realize." Adds Kauffman, "There are truths we can get to through the imagination that are hard to get to through purely factual accounts."

31. How does the author comment on Senator Harris' statement about climate change?
   A. Really confusing.   B. Partially true.
   C. Quite convincing.   D. Totally wrong.

32. The deniers in Paragraph 3 refer to those who deny that _____.
   A. science fiction is important   B. we are in a post-truth era
   C. climate change is a serious issue   D. our opinions actually matter

33. The author cites Neil Caiman in order to emphasize that _____.
   A. fiction may better convey the truth
   B. it is difficult to tell fact from fiction
   C. the power of fiction is overestimated
   D. fiction makes us feel better about ourselves

34. What do "Hope punk" and "Solar punk" have in common?
   A. A focus on technological innovation.
   B. A vivid description of the harsh reality.
   C. An intention to broaden our horizons.
   D. An optimistic outlook for the future.

35. What might be Kauffman's attitude toward science fiction?
   A. Appreciative.　　B. Concerned.　　C. Negative.　　D. Unclear.

Passage Four

Many people have looked to the stars and wondered what it would be like to take a trip into outer space. Ever since the space program began, travelling beyond Earth has been a privilege for a select few, namely, astronauts. The rest of us have had to imagine what it would be like, but that may soon change.

Those who favor expanding space exploration feel that it is time to go beyond the government-funded National Aeronautics and Space Administration (NASA) program and to create opportunities for individuals and businesses to explore outer space. Imagine privately financed research outposts in space, missions to Mars, and mining operations on the Moon. The space frontier could indeed be the next gold rush!

Imagine what it would be like to travel in space. Those who have been lucky enough to visit space have all called it an amazing experience. The view of Earth and the stars must be spectacular, and the experience of living in "zero gravity" would be fascinating. The first American woman to visit space, Sally Ride, said that it was the greatest fun of her life. Imagine the thrill of booking a flight for a weekend stay (or longer) at a space hotel. It turns out that a space hotel would be much easier to design and build than the International Space Station; early estimates of the cost to build the hotels indicate that they would be less expensive if the orbiting hotels were built to accommodate large numbers of space travelers.

The space hotel and the other projects businesses might think up allow people to see what is happening in space with their own eyes. That may lead to more support of NASA and its space research and great appreciation of the funding that the space program now receives.

Those who oppose expanding space exploration argue that the costs are overwhelming and unrealistic. They point to the billions of dollars that would have to be raised through consumers or corporate sponsorship. In addition, civilian space travel is potentially dangerous, and there are many unknown risks involved.

Who would determine the safety of commercial orbiting vehicles, and how would they be insured? Issues like this require time for discussion among groups from many different businesses. Companies that specialize in manufacturing, travel, marketing, insurance, law, and finance would all have to be involved.

Others believe there are simply too many answers and solutions to put civilians in space any time soon. There are also those who question investing in space exploration when there are widespread problems like poverty and disease that need to be addressed on Earth. For these people, commercial space travel will remain science fiction, at least for many years to come.

36. The expression "the next gold rush" (Para. 2) probably means that _____.
    A. gold might be discovered on remote planets
    B. space exploration could be the next investment hotspot
    C. investors are enthusiastic about gold mining in space
    D. private businesses are more interested in space travel

37. It can be learned from Paragraph 3 that _____.
    A. space visitors regret what they have done
    B. space hotels would be very uncomfortable
    C. Sally Ride enjoyed her visit to outer space
    D. the view of the Earth and the stars is boring

38. All of the following are objections to commercial space travel EXCEPT _____.
    A. overwhelming costs   B. potential dangers
    C. unknown risks   D. government opposition

39. The author's attitude towards commercial space travel is _____.
    A. supportive   B. opposing   C. objective   D. indifferent

40. Which of the following might be the best title of the passage?
    A. Civilians in Space   B. Future of Private Space Businesses
    C. Exploration of Outer Space   D. Hotels in Space

Section B

Directions: *In this section, you are required to read one quoted blog and the comments on it. The blog and comments are followed by questions or unfinished statements, each with four suggested answers A, B, C and D. Choose the best answer and mark your answer on the **Answer Sheet**.*

If you try to contact Indy Cube (a provider of workspaces) after 5pm, you receive an automatic message that would make a good demonstration for the fast-growing four-day week movement. "We'll get back to you pretty quickly during working hours," it says. "If you're messaging us outside of these, we're probably busy with other things, like horse-riding, dancing, or good sleep."

The firm is one of a growing number of employers giving their workers an extra day off for the same pay as a five-day week. There is emerging evidence that it can boost productivity for bosses and happiness for workers.

And it is not just small businesses that might be spotting a chance to save a little money by turning the lights off one day a week. One of the biggest organizations to make the switch is Perpetual Guardian whose shift has generated huge global interest, with 406 organizations from around the world asking it for advice.

"This week we have had people contact us from Japan, Canada, the UK, France, Switzerland," said its founder Andrew Barnes. The day off that each worker takes varies, depending on the team's needs at the time, but there has been a change in culture with "less time surfing on social media and fewer unnecessary meetings." said Barnes.

However, Kate Cooper, policy director at the Institute of Leadership and Management argues the reasons behind increases in productivity are not yet clear. Cooper said that "the Hawthorne effect" may be in play, that is, people change their behaviour simply because they feel they are being observed—in this case they feel that by being granted a four-day week they believe their bosses are interested in their work. "How sustainable is that?" Cooper doubts.

Comment 1

I don't exactly disagree with a 4-day week as long as I still have the option to work 5 days and get more money for it.

Comment 2

Middle class conception of work-life balance. It's an interesting idea, but so much need to happen in the UK before this becomes an option for the majority.

Comment 3

True for all these reasons, and I feel there is actually a greater reason: the environment. We need to start producing less stuff in order to reduce the stress on our planet.

Comment 4

I thought this was supposed to be here 20 years ago with the advances in technology.

Comment 5

3 days off a week? Preparing for 7 days off a week.

41. What can we learn about Indy Cube?
    A. It is one of the biggest providers of workspaces.
    B. It is the first company to start the four-day week
    C. Its boss should be happy with a higher productivity.
    D. Its employees are worried about their future income.

42. Barnes thinks the four-day week schedule _____.
    A. will soon be adopted by other companies in the world
    B. has made a positive impact on his company's culture
    C. benefits big companies more than smaller ones
    D. has greatly enhanced his workers' sense of wellbeing

43. By "the Hawthorne effect," Cooper suggests that the effect of a four-day week is _____.
    A. obvious   B. lasting   C. beneficial   D. uncertain

44. Which of the following suggests that the four-day week is currently enjoyed by only a small part of the workforce?
    A. Comment 1.   B. Comment 2.   C. Comment 3.   D. Comment 5.

45. Which of the following expresses that greatest concern about the four-day week?
    A. Comment 1.   B. Comment 2.   C. Comment 4.   D. Comment 5.

Part IV Cloze (10 minutes, 10 points)

Directions: *In this part, there is a passage with ten blanks. For each blank there are four choices marked A, B, C and D. Choose the best answer for each blank and mark your answer on the* **Answer Sheet**.

Cloud computing(云计算) means storing and accessing data and programs over the Internet instead of your computer's hard drive. It __46__ computing over a network, where a program or application may run on many connected computers at the same time.

For some, cloud computing is a metaphor(隐喻) for the Internet. It __47__ uses connected hardware machines called servers. Individual users can use the server's processing power to run an application, store data, or __48__ any other computing task. For businesses, cloud computing is an ideal way to reduce __49__. For example, companies may buy services in the cloud. That is to say, instead of __50__ applications on every single computer in the company, cloud computing would allow workers to log into a Web-based service(a cloud) which hosts all the __51__ individual users would need for their job.

While cloud computing could change the entire computer industry, there are still some __52__ about the security of the data stored on the remote machines. It is true that it promises to save a lot of work. However, this technology __53__ a fundamental question. Is it safe to store one's data on someone else's computer? The cloud service provider needs to establish relevant policies that describe __54__ the data of each user will be accessed and used. Cloud service users should also be able to encrypt(加密) __55__ that is processed or stored within the cloud to prevent unauthorized access.

46. A. predicts   B. involves   C. replaces   D. affects
47. A. necessarily   B. possibly   C. typically   D. really
48. A. get   B. perform   C. show   D. assign
49. A. expenses   B. money   C. income   D. profits
50. A. writing   B. developing   C. fitting   D. installing
51. A. schedules   B. programs   C. projects   D. documents
52. A. concerns   B. cases   C. advantages   D. effects
53. A. proposes   B. collects   C. manages   D. raises
54. A. whether   B. why   C. what   D. how
55. A. system   B. data   C. storage   D. knowledge

Part V   Text Completion (20 minutes, 20 points)

Directions: *In this part, there are three incomplete texts with 20 questions (Ranging from 56 to 75). Above each text there are three or four phrases to be completed. First, use the choices provided in the box to complete the phrases. Second, use the completed phrases to fill in the blanks of the text. Mark your answer on the **Answer Sheet**.*

Text One

A. recover
B. suggested
C. tips

Phrases:

    A. __56__ the balance back to "yes"

    B. help people __57__ from depression and stress disorder

    C. __58__ they could

For decades, scientists have debates whether the cells was possibly in an area of the brain that is responsible for learning, memory and mood regulation. A growing body of research __59__, but then a *Nature* paper last year raised doubts. Now, a new study __60__.

If the memory center of the human brain can grow new cells, it might __61__ and offer new insights into memory and learning. If not, well then, it's just one other way people are different from rats and birds.

Text Two

A. require
B. started
C. petition

Phrases:

    A. __62__ female worker to wear high heels

    B. __63__ a movement to end the requirement

    C. launched an online __64__

Woman across Japan are fed up with having to wear high-heeled shoes to work. One woman is so fed up that she __65__ for female employees to wear the shoes. The movement was called Kutoo. This is a combination of the Japanese words "Kutsu" (Which means shoes) and "Kutsuu" (which is the Japanese word for pain). The movement was started by Japanese actress Yumi Ishikawa. She tweeted about her belief that employers in Japan should not __66__. Ms. Ishikawa also __67__. It asks Japan's Ministry of Health, Labor and Welfare to forbid employers from requiring women to wear certain types of shoes.

Text Three

A. coupled
B. perceptions
C. beverages
D. optimal

Phrases:

    A. important to support __68__ growth

    B. plant-based juices and other __69__

C. __70__ with a unique nutrient package
D. information on consumer's __71__ and understanding

In July 2018, the debate over how to define milk in the future was brought to the forefront when the FDA beg an examining __72__ of plant-based foods and beverages. With the exception of certain soy beverages, __73__ are not appropriate to replace milk as a main beverage choice, particularly for young children. Drinks made from almonds or other nuts, oats or coconuts often contain little or no protein and lack of other key nutrient __74__. Dairy milk has the most balanced distribution of energy from carbohydrates, protein and fat, __75__ that can be difficult to replace in healthy dietary patterns.

Paper Two 试卷二 (50 minutes)

Part VI Translation (20 minutes, 10 points)

Directions: Translate the following passage into Chinese. Write your answer on the **Answer Sheet**.

In life, once on a path, we tend to follow it, for better or worse. What's sad is that even if it's the latter, we often accept it anyway because we are so accustomed to the way things are that we don't even recognize that they could be different.

Here are some techniques that could help broaden the way you think. First, look as if you've never seen. "Beginner's mind" allows you to remain open to new experiences despite any expertise you may have. Then, shift into positive. Take a few moments to think about the things in your life that are going well. This will brighten your mood and free your brain.

Part VII Writing (30 minutes, 15 points)

Directions: Write a composition in no less than 150 words on the topic: **Ways to Live a Simpler Life in Modern World**. You could write according to the clues given below. Write your composition on the **Answer Sheet**.

说明:现代生活过于繁复,各种琐事耗费精力和时间,人们疲于应对。列举几个你认为可以从简生活、重塑人生的几种方式。

2019年同等学力人员申请硕士学位英语水平全国统一考试

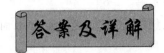

Paper One 试卷一

Part I Oral Communication

Section A

对话一

　　A. 它们今天到期。
　　B. 好主意!
　　C. 课后有什么安排吗?

　　朱莉安:嗨,珍妮! __1__
　　珍妮:没什么事。你呢?
　　朱莉安:我有一份课程论文要写。所以我打算找些书在图书馆学习。你要一起来吗?
　　珍妮:好啊! 我需要还一些书。__2__ 另外,我还可以在那里看一些杂志和报纸。
　　朱莉安:太棒了! 之后我们可以去健身房游泳。
　　珍妮:__3__ 我们可以在炎炎夏日中稍微消消暑。

1. [正确答案] C
　　[考点剖析] 备选选项中只有一个问句,根据珍妮的回答,可以推知此空需要填写问句,而文字内容也回答了问句"是否有安排"的问题,故选择C项。
2. [正确答案] A
　　[考点剖析] 空格前一句的内容是"还书",所以空格的内容选择"书到期",两者构成逻辑关系。故选择A项。
3. [正确答案] B
　　[考点剖析] 根据上句朱莉安"去游泳"的提议可知,空格的内容应是对这个提议的回答,B项符合语境。

对话二

　　A. 你一直都这么说!
　　B. 这都有十本了。
　　C. 我们读这本书吧。

女孩:爸爸,您能给我读故事吗?
爸爸:嗯,先让我看完报纸可以吗?
女孩: __4__
爸爸:那么,一起看报纸的商业板块怎么样?
女孩:太无聊了。__5__ 这是关于一只熊和一只猫成为朋友的故事。还有这些书也是。
爸爸:哇,我以为你说的是一本书。__6__
女孩:我的老师格林太太说,您每天晚上都要给我读书,而且读报纸不算数。

4. [正确答案] A

    [考点剖析] 此空前一句是个问句,所以女儿应该对此进行回答,只有 A 项与问句有关联。

5. [正确答案] C

    [考点剖析] 空格后面的语境:书的内容介绍,与 C 项中女儿提出的"读这本书"相关。所以选择 C 项。

6. [正确答案] B

    [考点剖析] 空格前面表示爸爸以为女儿说的是"一本书",与 B 项中的"十本"相呼应。

Section B

A. 你的名字是什么?

B. 但那门课已经满了。

C. 但是计算机不允许。

D. 你的专业是比较文学?

斯图尔特:你好。我能帮忙吗?

凯伦:是的,我希望如此。我想注册比较文学 287 这门课。

斯图亚特:我很抱歉,__7__ 而且,学生应该使用电话按键系统来注册。

凯伦:我知道。我已经试着用电话注册了。__8__

斯图尔特:那是因为那门课已经满了。

凯伦:但我是这里的新生。我想也许有某种办法让我可以上这堂课,所以我想我应该来办公室和你谈谈。

斯图尔特:嗯。我可以把你列入候补名单,但这不能保证你能上这堂课。__9__

凯伦:我叫黄凯伦。"黄"的拼写是 H-U-A-N-G。

斯图尔特:好的。你的专业是什么?

凯伦:我是比较文学专业的。

斯图尔特:等一下。__10__

凯伦:是的,没错。科恩教授说我要上比较文学 287 这门课。

斯图尔特:学校计算机系统为比较文学专业的学生保留了比较文学 287 这门课的额外名额。

凯伦:即使那堂课已经满了?

斯图尔特:没错。

7. [正确答案] B

　　[考点剖析] 根据上句凯伦表达想注册这门课的意愿可以推知,本句应该是对此进行回答,前面半句表示抱歉,所以空格处选择B项,意思是说课程已满,不能注册,符合语境。

8. [正确答案] C

　　[考点剖析] 根据空格前一句"凯伦试着注册",以及下一句"因为已经满了"可以推知,空格处应该是表达凯伦无法注册的意思,所以C项符合。

9. [正确答案] A

　　[考点剖析] 根据凯伦的回答内容可知空格处应该是针对姓名进行的问话,显然选A项。

10. [正确答案] D

　　[考点剖析] 空格后一句是对一般疑问句的回答;从语境上看,问句是在问凯伦是否是比较文学专业,下面凯伦做了肯定回答。所以答案选择D项。

Part Ⅱ Vocabulary

11. [正确答案] C

　　[考点类型] 形容词

　　[考点剖析] 题干中的 rigorous 意为"严格的,严厉的"。long"长的,长时间的";complex"复杂的;难懂的";strict"严格的,严厉的"; complete"全部的;完整的"。

12. [正确答案] C

　　[考点类型] 副词

　　[考点剖析] 题干中的 normally 意为"通常地,平常地"。merely"仅仅;只不过"; possibly"可能;或许"; usually"通常地;一般地";rarely"很少,不常"。

13. [正确答案] D

　　[考点类型] 动词

　　[考点剖析] 题干中 presumed 意为"假设;假定;推定"。destined"注定;命定"; intended"打算;计划";expected"预料;预计";supposed"认为,推断,假设"。

14. [正确答案] B

　　[考点类型] 形容词

　　[考点剖析] 题干中的 alien 意为"陌生的;不熟悉的"。unfair"不公正的;不公平的";unfamiliar"陌生的;不熟悉的"; unnecessary"不需要的;不必要的"; uncomfortable"使人不舒服的;令人不舒适的"。

15. [正确答案] B

　　[考点类型] 动词

　　[考点剖析] 题干中的 calls for 意为"需要;要求"。suggests"建议;提议";requires"需要;要求";demonstrates"证明;示范,演示"; identifies"认出;鉴定;识别"。

16. [正确答案] A

　　[考点类型] 动词

　　[考点剖析] 题干中的 made it all up 意为"制造,编造"。invented"发明;创造";invested"投资;(把资金)投入";corrected"纠正;改正";collected"收集;收藏"。

17. [正确答案] C

[考点类型] 名词

[考点剖析] 题干中的 consequences 意为"结果；后果"。orders"顺序；次序"；processes"过程；进程"；results"后果；结果"；causes"原因；起因；理由"。

18. [正确答案] D

[考点类型] 名词

[考点剖析] 题干中的 validity 意为"有效性；正确；正确性"。challenge"挑战；质疑"；value"价值；价格"；truth"真理；事实；实质"；utility"实用；效用"。

19. [正确答案] D

[考点类型] 动词

[考点剖析] 题干中的 diminished 意为"减少；降低"。disappeared"消失；不见"；erupted"爆发；突然发出"；expired"失效，终止；到期"；declined"减少，下降，衰落"。

20. [正确答案] A

[考点类型] 名词

[考点剖析] 题干中的 deficiency 意为"缺乏；缺少；不足"。lack"缺乏；短缺"；supply"供应，供给，提供"；number"数字；数量；编号"；source"起源；根源；原因"。

Part Ⅲ Reading Comprehension

Section A

Passage One

当170个人坐下来吃饭时，我松了一口气：会议进行得很顺利。作为一名大学项目经理，我的工作之一就是管理一个促进学术界和工业界之间生物技术合作的项目。几年前，当我开始担任这个职务时，我想也许经过多年的职业探索，我终于找到了适合我的工作。但在会议上，我发现自己在想，这是否真的是我所想要的职业生涯。我是一名科学家，不是一名策划者，但我一直忙于组织会议而无法去理解正在探讨的研究。是时候再做改变了吗？

我一开始是一名实验室科学家，但后来发现，实验室高度集中的工作性质并不适合我。接着我又在一家制药公司工作——进行文献检索。我很喜欢这份工作，这使我可以继续从事研究工作，并且可以和各种各样的人相互交流。但我只得到了一份短期合同，所以一年后我不得不离开。然后我成了一名科学杂志的编辑。我喜欢我所接触到的科学氛围，但这份工作需要很长的通勤时间。所以，我又做了一个巨大的改变，搬回了象牙塔去做我现在的工作。

这已经变成了一种模式：我在每个职位上都花了几年时间，结果却发现这个职位不太适合我。我也意识到也许我在寻找不存在的东西。

我开始思考一些富有创造性的方法来把我所寻求的科学刺激添入我的工作生活中。凭借我以前的知识和作为编辑的经验，我意识到我有能力通过自由撰稿和科学写作来做到这一点，譬如为期刊和博客撰写新闻稿件。

有了我以前的同事的积极回应，我最终决定我可以用少于全职工作的时间来完成我的大学项目工作。幸运的是,我的经理同意了。

在过去的一年里,我一直是一名大学项目经理,同时也是一名自由撰稿人,而且我从未如此快乐过。虽然同时扮演这两个角色有时有点棘手,但我真的觉得我找到了一个能满足我需求的职业。我意识到,一份职业不需要是"现成的"。为了得到一份合适的工作,我们可以把多份工作混合,也可以进行匹配。

21. [正确答案] C

[考点类型] 推理题

[题目翻译] 在第一段中,作者对会议组织工作有何看法?

A. 这让他有成就感。

B. 这证明他在事业上取得了进步。

C. 它没有科学研究那么有意义。

D. 这对他来说太具有挑战性了。

[考点剖析] 本段中间部分转折词 But 之后,作者对这个工作是否是自己想要的产生了疑问和思考,后面 I'm a scientist,... but I had been too busy organizing the conference to appreciate the research being discussed 更是表达了自己因忙于组织会议工作而无暇从事科研。由此,我们可以推断出作者对科研的重视,与目前的工作相比,他认为科研更有意义,故选择 C 项,其他选项无法从文中推出。

22. [正确答案] D

[考点类型] 细节题

[题目翻译] 作者辞去科学杂志编辑的工作是因为_____。

A. 工作强度高

B. 他只得到一份短期合同

C. 他对工资不满意

D. 离家太远

[考点剖析] 根据题干定位到文章第二段倒数第二句话...but the job required a lengthy commute. So, I made another dramatic change...,由于通勤时间长,所以作者做出改变,找了另外一个工作,故选择 D 项。

23. [正确答案] A

[考点类型] 词汇题

[题目翻译] "something"(第三段)可能是什么意思?

A. 合适的职位。

B. 理想的工作。

C. 平衡的生活。

D. 固定的模式。

[考点剖析] 词汇题要注意理解该词汇在语境中的含义。根据本段这几句话的含义可知,作者在每个职位上都花了几年时间,结果却发现这个职位不太适合他。他意识到也许自己在寻找不存在的东西。所以"something"和前面的"role"相互对应,选择 A 项合理。

24. [正确答案] D

[考点类型] 细节题

[题目翻译] 作者目前的工作是什么?

　　A. 他在一所大学工作,同时也在写作。

　　B. 他是一名活动策划人,也是一名项目经理。

　　C. 他在一所大学任教,还写书。

　　D. 他是一名全职经理,也是一名自由撰稿人。

[考点剖析] 根据题干要求,我们定位在文章最后一段 For the last year, I have been a university program manager/freelance writer, … Wearing the two roles together has been a bit tricky at times,由此可以得知作者去年一直是一名大学项目经理,同时也是一名自由撰稿人,他同时在做"university program manager"和"freelance writer"这两个工作。本题重点在于理解"university program manager",该短语的意思是"大学项目经理",理解了这个,就能跳出 A、B、C 三个迷惑选项的陷阱。

25. [正确答案] B

[考点类型] 主旨题

[题目翻译] 这篇文章主要讲的是什么?

　　A. 作者明确的职业规划。

　　B. 作者对职业看法的改变。

　　C. 作者面对困难时的坚持。

　　D. 作者未能获得工作合同。

[考点剖析] 前文内容主要是说,作者一直在寻找一个合适的职位,在每个职位上都会花费几年时间,现在的工作是两个职位的结合。而在文章结尾部分 I have realized that a career… Jobs can be mixed and matched to get to one that fits,作者说他意识到一份职业不需要是"现成的";我们可以把多份工作混合,也可以进行匹配。这说明作者对职业的看法发生了改变。根据选项对比,B 项符合。

Passage Two

　　你最近可能听过很多关于"电子竞技"的报道。主要的电视网络都在播放比赛,甚至更多主流的媒体报道计划在未来也这样做。什么是电子竞技? 为什么它们如此受欢迎?

　　从广义上来说,电子竞技就是电子游戏比赛。可以是一个电子游戏应用商店的地方锦标赛,也可以是那些在拥有 25 000 个座位的竞技场举行的,且有数百万人现场观看的比赛。实际上,"电子竞技"指的是由全球组织策划,并且最终以巨额奖金而告终的冠军锦标赛——获胜者的奖金可超过 1 000 000 美元。

　　第二个问题——"他们为什么变得如此受欢迎?"——就更加复杂了。最重要的原因是,游戏迷喜欢观看最高水平的比赛。看到世界上顶尖的玩家做他们最擅长的事情是很有趣的。还有很多造成电子竞技群体扩张的其他原因。来自主流体育界的所有争议、戏剧性事件和引人注目的人也存在于电子竞技中。顶级玩家像自由玩家一样从一个队转移到另一个队,出人意料地退役并重返比赛,经历一些不太可能的、后来居上的胜利和毁灭性的失败。新的挑战者不断出现在现场,准备击败冠军队并进行引人注目的较量。传统体育运动与电子竞技间的相似点比许多人想象得要多。

也许传统体育运动和电子竞技最大的区别在于观众。与主流体育竞赛不同,电子竞技的消费者大多是年轻男性。例如,超过70%的传奇联盟的观众是男性,其中绝大多数都是26岁以下。这意味着,随着越来越多的年轻人的加入,观众将会增加,并且随着年龄的增长,他们的购买力也会增加——这些都吸引着想要进入这个年轻且营利市场的广告商。

26. [正确答案] D

   [考点类型] 细节题

   [题目翻译] 第一段表明电子竞技_____。

       A.引起了媒体间的竞争

       B.吸引了越来越多的年轻人

       C.创建了许多广播公司

       D.吸引了主要的电视网络

   [考点剖析] 根据本段第二句话 Major television networks are broadcasting competitions, and even more mainstream media coverage is planned for the new future"主要的电视网络都在播放比赛,甚至更多主流的媒体报道计划在未来也这样做"可知,电子竞技吸引了很多主要的电视网络,故选D项。

27. [正确答案] B

   [考点类型] 细节题

   [题目翻译] 根据第二段,电子竞技_____。

       A.只能在当地体育场进行

       B.能获得巨额奖金

       C.可能难以精确定义

       D.可能与电子游戏有着不太紧密的联系

   [考点剖析] 根据第二段最后一句话…that culminate in big-money championship tournaments—dollar figures that can exceed \$1,000,000 for winners"最终以巨额奖金而告终的冠军锦标赛——获胜者奖金可能超过 1 000 000 美元"可知,电子竞技可能获得巨额奖金。而从文中 These can be anything from a local tournament(锦标赛)in a video game store… 可以看出,电子竞技并非只能在体育场进行,与 A 项表述相反。第二段最后一句话的开头 in practical terms 就已经表明,电子竞技是可以被精确定义的,故 C 项错误。D 项在第二段中未提及,故排除。

28. [正确答案] D

   [考点类型] 词汇题

   [题目翻译] 单词"nuanced"(第三段)最可能的意思是_____。

       A.奇怪的   B.杰出的   C.特定的   D.复杂的

   [考点剖析] 词汇题要结合单词本身含义,理解它在句子语境中的含义。本题中 nuanced 的意为"微妙的,复杂的",含义和 D 项相近;从语境上看,本段在讲电子竞技为何如此流行,并且列举了具体的原因,原因确实比较多而且复杂;单词 nuanced 一

词用来概括这些原因的特点,所以它的意思也与"复杂的"接近。

29. [正确答案] C
    [考点类型] 细节题
    [题目翻译] 以下哪项不是电子竞技群体扩张的原因?
    A. 顶级玩家的故事。
    B. 观看顶级表演的乐趣。
    C. 政府的投资。
    D. 与主流体育运动的相似之处。
    [考点剖析] 根据题干要求,我们需要在文章中找到作者提到的原因,没有提到的就是正确答案。我们定位到第三段,The biggest reason is… played at the highest level. It's… the top players… All of the controversies,… from the mainstream sports world exist in eSports as well. Top players move from team to team like free agents,… 从这几句话中可以很容易找到 A、B、D 三项,唯独 C 项"政府的投资"在文中未被提及。

30. [正确答案] D
    [考点类型] 细节题
    [题目翻译] 传统体育运动与电子竞技的主要区别在于_____。
    A. 它们的规则   B. 它们的重要性
    C. 它们的利润   D. 它们的观众
    [考点剖析] 根据题干要求找两者的区别,我们可以定位在最后一段的第一句话 Perhaps the biggest difference between traditional sports and eSports is the viewers,viewers 的意思是观众,找到选项中与它同义或者近义的词就是正确答案,所以选择 D 项。

Passage Three

参议员卡玛拉·哈里斯在她发表的 2020 年总统竞选的演讲中说,我们需要以"科学事实,而不是科幻小说"为基础来解决气候变化问题,她说的有一半是对的。事实上,我们两者都需要。科幻小说在帮助未来摆脱我们所面临的巨大挑战方面扮演着重要的角色,而人们对哈里斯这一说法的回应也完美地说明了这一点。

当哈里斯关于气候变化的声明在社交媒体上发表时,许多人指出了真相:多年来,科幻小说一直在帮助我们为一个潜在灾难性气候剧变的世界做准备。但是,也有同样多的呼声反对哈里斯关于气候变化的警告,因为在我们的后真相时代,关于人类对地球所做的一切的科学共识在某种程度上仍然是一个观点问题。

这就是为什么科幻小说比哈里斯所说的更重要。再多的科学证据都无法说服否认者——或是那些仅仅生活在否认状态中的人。我们生活在一个后真相时代,在这个时代里,事实和小说正在模糊成一个无法区分的整体,权力属于任何能讲出最好故事的人,不管故事是真是假。重要的是,这件事让我们感觉如何——这就是为什么我们需要更好的故事,用作家尼尔·盖曼的话来说就是"为了说真话而说谎"。

关于气候变化的故事可能是虚构的,但比起背诵不可否认的事实,它们可以以不同的方式动摇人们的心灵。科幻小说的创作者一直在寻找恢复人们对未来的信心的方法。像亚历山德拉·

罗兰这样的作者已经开始了一个关于创造一种叫作"希望朋克"的新型故事的对话,它向人们表明人类真的有理由相信自己可以通过努力来解决问题。其他一些作者正在创作一种新的流派,叫作"太阳朋克",它旨在讲述利用技术和科学创新来帮助解决环境问题的故事。

当真相变得几乎不可能透过虚假信息和"替代事实"的迷雾来区分时,人们往往感到无力改变世界。活动家考夫曼说,需要提醒人们"他们拥有的力量比他们意识到的更大"。考夫曼补充道:"我们可以通过想象得到一些事实,这些事实很难通过纯粹的事实叙述得到。"

31. [正确答案] B
   [考点类型] 细节题
   [题目翻译] 作者对哈里斯参议员关于气候变化的声明是如何评论的?
      A. 令人困惑的。   B. 部分正确的。
      C. 相当有说服力的。   D. 完全错误的。
   [考点剖析] 根据题干人名 Senator Harris 定位到文章第一段第一句...was half right...,从中可以看出作者认为哈里斯的说法有一部分是正确的,所以 B 项正确。

32. [正确答案] A
   [考点类型] 细节题
   [题目翻译] 第三段中的否认者是指那些否认_____的人。
      A. 科幻小说很重要
      B. 我们正处于后真相时代
      C. 气候变化是一个严重的问题
      D. 我们的意见实际上很重要
   [考点剖析] 根据题干要求,我们定位到这段的 No amount of scientific evidence will convince deniers—or the vast number of people who merely live in a state of denial,其意思是"再多的科学证据都无法说服否认者——或是那些仅仅生活在否认状态中的人";再根据前一句 And that's why science fiction is more important than Harris gives it credit for 这句是对前一段的总结句,题干所说的否认者否认的观点正是这一句的观点。作者说完这句话之后,接着说"再多的科学证据都无法说服否认者……",所以否认者否认的就是科幻小说很重要这个观点。

33. [正确答案] A
   [考点类型] 推理题
   [题目翻译] 作者引用尼尔·盖曼的话来强调_____。
      A. 小说可以更好地传达真相
      B. 很难从小说中辨别事实
      C. 小说的力量被高估了
      D. 小说让我们对自己感觉更好
   [考点剖析] 根据题干我们发现他说的话出现在第三段最后一句,要理解这句话需要看之前的内容,我们定位到 We live in a post-truth era in which... and power belongs to whoever can tell the best story, true or not. What matters is just how something makes us feel—which is why we need better stories,…"我们生活在一个后真相时代,……

权力属于任何能讲出最好故事的人,不管故事是真是假。重要的是,这件事让我们感觉如何——这就是为什么我们需要更好的故事……"。不管事情是真是假,重要的是谁的故事讲得好,所以在这样的情形下,尼尔说这句话的意思与A项一致。

34. [正确答案] D

   [考点类型] 细节题

   [题目翻译] "希望朋克"和"太阳朋克"有什么共同点?

   A. 注重技术创新。

   B. 对残酷现实的生动描述。

   C. 扩展视野的目的。

   D. 对未来的乐观展望。

   [考点剖析] 根据细节为主题服务的原则,我们定位到这两个例子的前面来找是否有共同的观点。…but they can help to sway people's hearts and minds in a different way… looking for ways to restore people's faith in the future… "Hope punk" that show people reasons to believe we really can do the hard work of fixing our problems。从这几句话我们可以看出,科幻小说的创作者一直在寻找恢复人们对未来的信心的方法。"希望朋克"向人们表明人类真的有理由相信自己可以通过努力来解决问题。"Solar punk" that aims to… help the environment 意为"帮助解决环境问题",所以,他们的共同点是让人们对未来有信心。

35. [正确答案] A

   [考点类型] 细节题

   [题目翻译] 考夫曼对科幻小说的态度是什么?

   A. 欣赏的。   B. 担心的。

   C. 反对的。   D. 不确定的。

   [考点剖析] 作者在第一段就肯定了科幻小说的作用,然后阐述了为什么科幻小说重要,而它的创作者也一直在寻找恢复人们对未来的信心的方法。所以说,作者对科幻小说持有的态度是积极肯定的。

Passage Four

许多人都曾仰望星空,想知道到外太空旅行会是什么样子。自从太空计划开始以来,到地球以外旅行一直是少数人,即宇航员的特权。我们其他人只能想象它会是什么样子,但这很快就会改变。

那些赞同扩大太空探索的人认为,是时候越过政府资助的国家航空航天局(NASA)计划,为个人和企业探索外太空创造机会了。想象一下私人资助的太空研究前哨、火星任务和月球采矿作业。太空前沿可能真的是"下一个淘金热"!

想象一下在太空旅行会是什么样子。那些有幸造访太空的人都称其为一次奇妙的经历。地球和星空的景色一定是壮观的,生活在"零重力"中的经历将是迷人的。第一位访问太空的美国妇女萨莉·赖德说,这是她一生中最大的乐趣。想象一下预订航班在太空旅馆住上一个周末(或更长时间)的激动心情。事实证明,太空旅馆的设计和建造要比国际空间站容易得多;建造这些旅馆的早期估算成本表明,如果建造轨道旅馆来容纳大量的太空旅行者,那么它们的价格就会更低。

太空旅馆和其他商业项目可能会让人们亲眼看到太空中正在发生的事情。这可能会使得美国宇航局及其空间研究得到更多的支持,以及对空间计划目前获得的资金的极大理解。

那些反对扩大太空探索的人认为,太空探索成本巨大而且不切实际。他们指出,数十亿美元将不得不通过消费者或企业赞助筹集。此外,民用太空旅行具有潜在的危险性,而且还涉及许多未知的风险。

谁来决定商用轨道飞行器的安全性,如何保证?像这样的问题需要来自许多不同行业的人进行讨论。专门从事制造、旅游、营销、保险、法律和金融的公司都必须参与其中。

其他人认为,有太多的方法和解决方案可以让平民大众很快进入太空。但当地球上还存在诸如贫穷和疾病等普遍问题有待解决的时候,还有一些人对投资太空探索的做法感到质疑。对这些人来说,商业太空旅行至少在未来几年仍将是科学幻想。

36. [正确答案] B

[考点类型] 词汇题

[题目翻译] "下一个淘金热"(第二段)可能意为_____。

A. 在遥远的行星上可能发现黄金

B. 太空探索可能是下一个投资热点

C. 投资者热衷于在太空中开采黄金

D. 私营企业对太空旅行更感兴趣

[考点剖析] 词汇题需要理解词汇在语境中的含义。文中提到...and to create opportunities for individuals and businesses to explore outer space. Imagine privately financed research outposts in space, missions to Mars, and mining operations on the Moon,"该为个人和企业探索外太空创造机会了。想象一下私人资助的太空研究前哨、火星任务和月球采矿作业",这表示太空中有很多可以进行投资的机会,所以说这个"淘金热"就是在太空中进行投资。

37. [正确答案] C

[考点类型] 推理题

[题目翻译] 从第三段可以看出_____。

A. 太空访客对他们所做的事感到后悔

B. 太空旅馆会很不舒适

C. 萨莉·赖德很享受她的太空之旅

D. 地球和星空的景色很单调

[考点剖析] 本段第二句和第三句在说太空旅行会很奇妙,景色也一定很壮观,而D项的描述跟这个描述是相反的;而后,举了萨莉的例子,用以说明太空之旅的美好,萨莉对此描述为...it was the greatest fun of her life,足见她很喜欢那次太空旅行,所以选择C项。

38. [正确答案] D

[考点类型] 细节题

[题目翻译] 以下所有内容均为反对商业太空旅行的理由,除了_____。

A. 巨额的成本　　　　　　　B. 潜在的危险

C. 未知的风险　　　　　　　D. 政府的反对

[考点剖析] 根据题干"反对商业太空旅行"定位到文章倒数第三段,根据文章信息Those who oppose expanding space exploration argue that the costs are overwhelming and unrealistic. … potentially dangerous, and there are many unknown risks involved 可以很容易找到A、B、C三项提到的内容,唯独D项无法找到,所以选择D项。

39. [正确答案] C

[考点类型] 细节题

[题目翻译] 作者对商业太空旅行的态度是_____。

A. 支持的　　　　　　　　　B. 反对的

C. 客观的　　　　　　　　　D. 漠不关心的

[考点剖析] 作者在文中客观地陈述了支持以及反对太空旅行者的看法,还陈述了一些其他人的观点,但并未明确地表明自己的观点如何,所以作者是持客观态度的。

40. [正确答案] C

[考点类型] 主旨题

[题目翻译] 以下哪一个可能是文章的最佳标题?

A. 太空中的平民

B. 私人太空企业的未来

C. 太空探索

D. 太空旅馆

[考点剖析] 主旨题要注意总结文章的主要内容,通常是各段落的大意之和,不能只是片面的信息,内容过大或过小都不能算是文章主旨,这也是干扰选项的设置特点。本文描述了对太空进行探索的很多方面,比如为个人和私人企业探索创造机会、建立太空旅馆,还有人们对太空探索的不同态度等。所以综合全文内容,可以用C项来概括,虽然文章提到过其他选项,但是都比较片面。

Section B

印地立方体(Indy Cube)是一家工作空间供应商。如果你试图在下午五点后联系它,你将收到一条自动回复消息,此信息很好地展示了快速扩张的四天工作日运动。"我们会很快在工作时间回复您,"它说,"如果您在工作日以外的时间给我们发信息,我们可能正忙于其他事情,如骑马、跳舞或睡个好觉。"

越来越多的公司每周给他们的员工额外一天假期,而且薪水和每周工作五天的相同,这个公司只是其中之一。有新的证据表明,它可以为老板提高生产力并为员工增加幸福感。

2019年同等学力人员申请硕士学位英语水平全国统一考试答案及详解

而且,不仅仅是小企业发现了通过每周关灯一天来节省钱的机会。做出这种转变的最大组织之一是永久守护者(Perpetual Guardian),它的转变引起了全球的巨大兴趣,全球406个组织都在向其征求建议。

该公司的创始人安德鲁·巴恩斯(Andrew Barnes)说:"本周,有日本、加拿大、英国、法国、瑞士等地的人与我们联系。"每个员工休假的时间各不相同,这取决于当时团队的需要,但是在文化观念上发生了变化——"在社交媒体上花费的时间减少了,不必要的会议也减少了"。巴恩斯说。

然而,领导和管理研究所的政策主管凯特·库珀认为,生产力提高的背后原因尚不清楚。库珀说,"霍桑效应"可能在起作用,也就是说,人们改变自己的行为仅仅是因为他们觉得自己正被别人观察——在这种情况下,他们觉得让他们一周工作四天,是因为他们的老板对他们的工作感兴趣。"这可以持续多久?"库珀怀疑道。

评论1

我并非完全不同意一周工作四天,只要我仍然可以选择工作五天,并因此而获得更多的钱。

评论2

中产阶级的工作生活平衡观。这是一个有趣的想法,但在这成为大多数人的选择之前,英国需要改变很多。

评论3

正是这些原因,但是我觉得事实上还有一个更重要的原因:环境。我们需要开始减少物品的生产,以减少地球上的压力。

评论4

我以为这应该是20年前随着科技的进步就出现的。

评论5

一周休息三天?准备每周休息七天吧。

41. [正确答案] C

   [考点类型] 推理题

   [题目翻译] 关于印地立方体(Indy Cube),我们可以得知什么?

   A. 它是最大的工作空间供应商之一。

   B. 这是第一家开始每周四天工作日的公司。

   C. 它的老板应该对更高的生产力感到满意。

   D. 它的员工担心他们未来的收入。

   [考点剖析] 根据文章第二段…There is emerging evidence that it can boost productivity for bosses and happiness for workers"越来越多的公司为员工提供额外的一天假期,而且与一周五天的工资相同。有新的证据表明,它可以为老板提高生产力并且增强员工的幸福感",由此可知印地立方体也是这样做的公司之一,但是并不是第一家,也没提到过是最大的供应商,所以我们推知C项是正确答案,而其他选项未提到过。

42. [正确答案] B
    [考点类型] 细节题
    [题目翻译] 巴恩斯认为每周四天的日程安排_____。
      A. 将很快被世界上的其他公司采用
      B. 对其公司的文化产生了积极影响
      C. 对大公司的益处比对小公司的更多
      D. 大大增强了员工的幸福感
    [考点剖析] 题干要求我们理解的是巴恩斯这个人物的观点,所以定位到第四段...but there has been a change in culture with "less time surfing on social media and fewer unnecessary meetings",由此可以得知,一周工作四天使得他公司的文化观念发生了变化,因为员工"在社交媒体上花费的时间减少了,不必要的会议也减少了"。这一变化对公司有积极的影响。而其他三项都没有提到过。文中并没有比较不同公司受益多少的问题,故C项排除;D项虽然在前文提到过,但是巴恩斯并未提及。

43. [正确答案] D
    [考点类型] 细节题
    [题目翻译] 根据"霍桑效应",库珀认为一周工作四天的影响是_____。
      A. 明显的   B. 持久的   C. 有益的   D. 不确定的
    [考点剖析] 根据文章中库珀所说的话…"the Hawthorne effect" may be in play, … in this case they feel that by being granted a four-day week they believe their bosses are interested in their work. "How sustainable is that?" Cooper doubts. 可知,"霍桑效应"可能在起作用,但是能持续多久呢? 库珀对此持怀疑态度,所以他认为影响是不确定的,故选D项。

44. [正确答案] B
    [考点类型] 细节题
    [题目翻译] 以下哪一项表明,目前只有一小部分劳动力享受每周四天工作日?
      A. 评论1。   B. 评论2。   C. 评论3。   D. 评论5。
    [考点剖析] 评论2 …It's an interesting idea, but so much needs to happen in the UK before this becomes an option for the majority 认为:这是一个有趣的想法,但在这成为大多数人的选择之前,英国需要改变很多。由此可知,目前并非大多数人在享受四天工作日,所以B项符合题意。

45. [正确答案] D
    [考点类型] 细节题
    [题目翻译] 以下哪一项对每周四天工作日的做法担心最多?
      A. 评论1。   B. 评论2。   C. 评论4。   D. 评论5。
    [考点剖析] 评论5的意思是:一周休息三天?准备每周休息七天吧。我们知道,一周共七天,他说准备休息七天,这是不可能的做法。根据他的话可以看出,他对一周四天工作日的做法表示担心,且不是很认同。

2019年同等学力人员申请硕士学位英语水平全国统一考试答案及详解

Part Ⅳ Cloze

"云计算"指的是通过互联网而非电脑硬盘储存和访问数据以及程序。它需要在网络上进行计算,在网络上,一个程序或应用程序可以同时在多台连接的计算机上运行。

对于某些人来说,云计算是互联网的隐喻。它通常使用被称为服务器的连接硬件机器。个人用户可以使用服务器的处理能力来运行应用程序、存储数据或执行其他任何计算任务。对于企业来说,云计算是减少开支的理想方法。例如,公司可以购买云服务。也就是说,云计算不需要在公司的每台计算机上安装应用程序,它可以允许员工登录到一个基于网络的服务(云),该服务承载个人用户工作所需的所有程序。

尽管云计算可能改变整个计算机行业,但人们对于在远程计算机上存储数据的安全性仍然有一些忧虑。的确,它一定会节省大量的工作。然而,这项技术也引发了一个很重要的问题——在别人的电脑上存储数据安全吗?云服务供应商需要制定相关的政策来描述如何访问和使用每个用户的数据。云服务用户还应能够加密在云中处理或存储的数据,以防止未经授权的访问。

46. [正确答案] B

[解析过程] 这是一个词义区分题,空格所在句的意思是:云计算需要在网络上进行计算。根据语境,只有 B 项符合要求。

47. [正确答案] C

[解析过程] 从用法上来看,四项都可以放在此处,但是从语境上看,这句话的意思是:云计算通常使用被称为服务器的连接硬件机器。其他选项的词义放在空格处均说不通,所以选择 C 项。

48. [正确答案] B

[解析过程] perform 一词除了我们熟悉的"表演"含义之外,还有"做;履行;执行"之意。空格处的动词要能够与 task 搭配,"执行……任务"符合语境。

49. [正确答案] A

[解析过程] 此题需要根据对后文语境的理解进行选择。本题四个选项的意思都与金钱有关,后文的主要意思是:云计算不需要在公司的每台计算机上安装应用程序,员工可以登录使用云服务。这相当于节省了公司的开支,与之有关联的选项是 A 项"开支,费用"。

50. [正确答案] D

[解析过程] 空格处要填写的词应该与后面的 application "应用"一词构成语义搭配,再结合空格所在句的意思:云计算不需要在公司的每台计算机上安装应用程序。install "安装"符合此意。

51. [正确答案] B

[解析过程] 本题为词义区分题,空格所在句的意思是:云服务承载个人用户工作所需的所有程序。根据常识,我们也知道云服务承载很多的程序,我们在工作中也使用电脑程序。其他选项的含义都不符合语境。

52. [正确答案] A

[解析过程] 空格所在句的意思是:人们对于在远程计算机上存储数据的安全性仍然有一些

忧虑。后文语境也是在说数据的安全性问题,所以这里应该是人们对这个问题的担心和忧虑。其他选项不符合语境。

53. [正确答案] D

[解析过程] 空格处需要填写一个动词与句子中的 question 一词构成语义搭配,D 项的 raises "提出"刚好可以与之匹配。

54. [正确答案] D

[解析过程] 空格处要填写一个从句的引导词,这里主要是根据词义来进行区分,这句话的意思是:……如何访问和使用每个用户的数据。所以选择 D 项 how 合理。

55. [正确答案] B

[解析过程] 本题是词义区分题,要根据语境选择含义合适的单词。空格后面的定语从句修饰限定要选择的词,意思是,"在云中处理或存储的数据",而且全文一直在说用云服务来存储和处理数据,所以选择 B 项 data。

Part V Text Completion

Text One

几十年来,科学家们对"细胞是否可能存在于大脑中用来负责学习、记忆和情绪调节的区域"这个问题有争议。越来越多的研究表明它们可能是如此,但去年《自然》杂志上的一篇论文却对此提出质疑。现在,一项新的研究将结果颠覆回到"是"。

如果人类大脑的记忆中枢能够生长出新的细胞,它可能会帮助人们从抑郁和应激障碍中恢复过来,并为记忆和学习提供新的视角。如果不是,那么,这只是人类与老鼠和鸟类不同的另一种方式。

56. [正确答案] C

[解析过程] 本题需要从语义上考虑。tip 意为"翻覆;倾覆",这句话的意思是把平衡点颠覆回到"是",在这里是说去年研究结果遭到质疑,而新的研究又证明结果是肯定的。

57. [正确答案] A

[解析过程] 从结构用法上看,recover from 是固定搭配,意思是"从……恢复,治愈";从语义上来看,"帮助人们从抑郁和应激障碍中恢复过来",A 项符合。

58. [正确答案] B

[解析过程] suggest 在这里是"表明"的意思。这个空需要结合下面的文字来理解,从句意上看,"表明它们可能……",符合语境。

59. [正确答案] C

[解析过程] 空格处缺少一个谓语动词,且从后面的句子结构和语境看,此处的时态应该是过去时;从语义上看,"越来越多的研究表明它们可能是如此"符合逻辑,所以选择 C 项。

60. [正确答案] A

[解析过程] 空格缺少谓语动词,且主语是单数形式,所以 A 项符合。从内容上看,争论的结果发生变化,新的研究结果和去年一篇持怀疑态度的论文相反,使得研究结果又变成肯定的。

61. [正确答案] B

[解析过程] 空格前面的情态动词要求空格处必须是动词原形形式,只有 B 项符合,且从句子语境上来看也合理。

Text Two

日本各地的妇女都厌倦了穿高跟鞋上班。一位女士对此非常厌烦,于是她发起了一场运动来结束对女员工穿高跟鞋的要求,这场运动叫作"Kutoo"。这是日文单词"kutsu"(意思是"鞋子")和"kutsuu"(意思是"疼痛")的组合。这场运动是由日本女演员石川优实发起的。她在推特上说,她认为日本的雇主不应该要求女员工穿高跟鞋。石川女士还发起了网上请愿,要求厚生劳动省(健康、劳工及福利部)禁止雇主要求妇女穿某些类型的鞋。

62. [正确答案] A

[解析过程] require sb. to do sth. 是固定用法,其他两项无此用法;且从语义上考虑,"要求女员工穿高跟鞋"也符合语境。

63. [正确答案] B

[解析过程] 此处需要填写一个动词,B 项从词性和词义上看都合理,本句的意思是"发起了一场运动来结束这个要求"。

64. [正确答案] C

[解析过程] 先从用法方面考虑,此处要求填写的单词须是名词词性,只有 C 项符合;再从语义上看,"发起网上请愿"也符合语境。

65. [正确答案] B

[解析过程] 空格所在句是一个从句,从句缺少谓语动词,而从句主语是第三人称单数,所以答案锁定在 B 项和 C 项;再从语义上看,"发起了一场运动来结束对女员工穿高跟鞋的要求"符合语境。

66. [正确答案] A

[解析过程] 从结构用法上看,空格前面有情态动词,要求后面接动词原形,只有 A 项符合;从语义上看,"不应该要求女员工穿高跟鞋"也符合语境。

67. [正确答案] C

[解析过程] 空格处前面是主语,缺少谓语动词,而主语是第三人称单数,所以 A 项不符合,B 项和 C 项从语义角度区分,结合后一句话,C 项"发起网上请愿"符合语境。

Text Three

2018 年 7 月,当食品和药物管理局要求消费者提供有关对植物果汁和其他饮料的认知和理解的审查信息时,关于未来如何定义牛奶的辩论被推到了最前沿。除某些大豆饮料外,植物果汁和其他饮料不适合替代牛奶作为主要饮料的选择,尤其是对孩子而言。由杏仁或其他坚果、燕麦或椰子制成的饮料通常很少含有或根本不含蛋白质,而且缺乏其他关键营养素,而这些营养素对维持最佳生长非常重要。乳制品是碳水化合物、蛋白质和脂肪中能量分布最均衡的,再加上独特的营养组合,使得其在健康的饮食模式中很难被替代。

68. [正确答案] D
　　[解析过程] 从语法角度结合备选项考虑,这里需要填写一个形容词来修饰growth,再结合语境,只有D项符合。

69. [正确答案] C
　　[解析过程] 空格前面有并列连词and,说明这个空跟前面的juices并列,意思是植物果汁和其他饮料。从结构和语义上只有C项符合。

70. [正确答案] A
　　[解析过程] couple with "与……结合"是固定搭配,且从语义角度来看也符合。

71. [正确答案] B
　　[解析过程] 空格后面有并列连词and,这要求空格内容要与understanding并列;从语义上来看,"关于消费者的认知和理解的信息"符合语境。

72. [正确答案] D
　　[解析过程] 从结构上看,介词of前面需要加名词类的内容,答案锁定在B项和D项之中;而从语义上区分,"消费者对……的认知和理解的信息",D项符合语境。

73. [正确答案] B
　　[解析过程] 空格所在句缺少主语成分,所以答案也应该在B项和D项中选择;根据语义,B项"植物果汁和其他饮料"符合语境。

74. [正确答案] A
　　[解析过程] 从语义上看,A项"对维持最佳生长非常重要"符合此处语境。

75. [正确答案] C
　　[解析过程] 空格后面的从句是用来限定空格里的名词,从语义上看,"再加上独特的营养组合"符合语境。

Paper Two　试卷二

Part Ⅵ　Translation

1. In life, once on a path, we tend to follow it, for better or worse.
　　[结构分析] 这是一个简单句,we tend to follow it 是本句的主干。
　　[词义推敲] once "一旦,曾经";tend to "倾向于;有助于"。
　　[参考译文] 在生活中,一旦走上了一条道路,不论好坏,我们往往会在这条路上走下去。

2. What's sad is that even if it's the latter, we often accept it anyway because we are so accustomed to the way things are that we don't even recognize that they could be different.
　　[结构分析] 这个句子结构比较复杂,为主从复合句。句子的主干为 What's sad is that…,为主系表结构。what引导的从句充当句子的主语,that引导的从句充当句子的表语,即 even if it's the latter, we often accept it anyway because we are so accustomed to the way things are that we don't even recognize that they could be different。在表语从句中镶嵌了一个由even if引导的让步状语从句,其主干中又包含了一个由because引导的原因状语从句。在原因状语从句中包含了一个由so…that…引导的结果状语从句,things are 为省略了that 的定语从句修饰 the way,recognize 后还有一个由that 引导的宾语从句。

[词义推敲] the latter "后者"; accustomed to "习惯于;适应于"。

[参考译文] 令人难过的是,即使这条路是不好的那条路,我们也经常会接受它,因为我们如此习惯事物存在的方式,以至于我们甚至没有意识到可能有不同的路可以走。

3. Here are some techniques that could help broaden the way you think.

[结构分析] 这是一个主从复合句。that 引导的定语从句修饰名词 techniques。

[词义推敲] broaden "拓宽,拓展"。

[参考译文] 这里有一些方法可以帮你拓展思路。

4. First, look as if you've never seen.

[结构分析] 这是一个主从复合句。as if 引导的从句作表语。

[词义推敲] as if "好像,仿佛"。

[参考译文] 首先,当作你从来没遇到过这样的情况。

5. "Beginner's mind" allows you to remain open to new experiences despite any expertise you may have.

[结构分析] allows you to remain 是句子主干的谓语部分;you may have 是省略了引导词 that 的定语从句,来修饰名词 expertise。

[词义推敲] allows sb. to do "允许某人做某事"; despite "尽管"; expertise "专业知识"。

[参考译文] 尽管之前你可能有专业的知识,但是"初学者思维"可以让你对新的阅历持开放态度。

6. Then, shift into positive.

[结构分析] 这是一个简单句,省略了主语 you。

[词义推敲] positive "积极的"。

[参考译文] 然后,保持积极乐观。

7. Take a few moments to think about the things in your life that are going well.

[结构分析] 本句是一个主从复合句。主句的谓语动词是 take, 后面 that are going well 是定语从句修饰 the things。

[词义推敲] going well "进展顺利"。

[参考译文] 花点时间想想生活中进展顺利的事情。

8. This will brighten your mood and free your brain.

[结构分析] 本句是一个简单句,and 连接了两个并列谓宾结构。

[词义推敲] brighten "(使)更明亮;(使)快活起来"; free "释放;使自由;解放;使摆脱"。

[参考译文] 这会让你的心情变得愉快,让你的大脑得到解放。

Part Ⅶ　Writing

这是一篇说明文,题目就是本文的主题:从简生活的几种方式。给出题目后,本题给出了中文提示,便于考生更准确地理解题目要求,把握主题方向。

我们可以根据题目提供的信息,整理思路并列出提纲:

第一段,利用考前熟记的背景导入法的经典模板句型开篇:with the development of...。介绍写作主题的大背景:随着经济的发展,我们的生活繁杂紧张,充满压力,这影响着我们的健康。随后导出本文话题:如何简化生活? 第二段,举出简化生活的三种不同方式,并适当展开。这是本文的重点。第三段,总结并呼应主题——简化生活有益。

With the development of national economy, our days are so rushed and filled with distractions that they seem to be bursting. It's a huge source of stress for most people, and stress is perhaps the most important factor determining whether we're healthy or sick. More and more people began to pay attention to how to live a simple life. So how can we simplify our life?

There are various ways to simplify our life and these are the steps I followed, which I've found to work really well. The first one that comes to my mind readily is to know what's important and limit tasks. The simple version of simplifying is "to identify what's important, and eliminate the rest." Limiting tasks helps us focus, and we have to acknowledge that we're not going to get everything done in one day. What's more, we need to slow down. We rush through our days, almost in a single frenetic anxiety-filled non-stop movement. Life won't collapse if we aren't rushing from task to task, email to email. Besides, enjoy the simple pleasures. We can pause, take a moment to reflect, smile and enjoy the current task before moving on.

Simplicity reduces the heaviness in life. It makes life lighter and happier. Everyone may have his own way to simplify his life. Anyway, it's not incredibly hard. I believe that there will be a better life if we can make our life simpler.

本文在内容、结构和语言表达三方面满足了高分作文的标准和要求,具体表现如下:

从内容上看,本文紧扣主题——简化生活的方式,把简化生活的方式作为重点,详略得当。

从结构上看,开篇使用了背景导入法,并把经典模板句型灵活地融入自身书面语言的表达中,而非生搬硬套;然后在本文正文部分,列举了简化生活的不同方式,紧扣主题;并在结尾段呼应开头,使得全文结构紧凑,行文流畅。

从语言表达上看,遣词用句丰富多变,体现出作者的语言功底深厚,对英语语言知识理解透彻、运用灵活。

第一段第一句用 With the development of national economy, …句型引出话题背景,并且使用经典的 so… that… 句型;第二句用现在分词做后置定语,并使用 whether 引导的从句结构,交代简化生活的重要性,说明压力会影响人体健康;第三、四句说越来越多的人开始关注这件事,引出话题。

第二段是全篇的重点段落,开头用总起句,交代本段主要内容;后面从明确重点事件、限定任务,放慢节奏,享受简单快乐三大方面来举例说明简化生活的方式。结构上使用了 The first one that comes to my mind… What's more, … 以及 Besides, …等逻辑连系词,层次清晰,逐步展开;而且在列举方式后适当地展开论述,使得行文内容充实有力。从语言结构上看,定语从句、名词性从句等句型交替使用,运用灵活。

第三段,再次描述简化生活带来的好处,呼应首段。